OCP

Oracle Certified Professional
Java SE 11 Programmer I

Study Guide
Exam 1Z0-815

OCP
Oracle Certified Professional Java SE 11 Programmer I
Study Guide
Exam 1Z0-815

Jeanne Boyarsky

Scott Selikoff

SYBEX®
A Wiley Brand

Acknowledgments

Scott and Jeanne would like to thank numerous individuals for their contribution to this book. Thank you to Kathryn Duggan for guiding us through the process and making the book better in so many ways. Thank you to Janeice DelVecchio for being our technical editor as we wrote this book. Janeice pointed out many subtle errors in addition to the big ones. And thank you to Elena Felder for being our technical proofreader and finding the errors that we managed to sneak by Janeice. This book also wouldn't be possible without many people at Wiley, including Kenyon Brown, Pete Gaughan, Kathleen Wisor, Kim Wimpsett, Nancy Carrasco, and so many others.

Jeanne would personally like to thank Chris Kreussling for knowing almost a decade ago that she would someday write a book. He was a great mentor for many years and definitely shaped her career. Jeanne would also like to thank Cathy Sung for all the support and coaching as Jeanne grew as a tech lead. Nicolai Parlog and Juan Moreno were helpful when looking for module information. Scott was a great co-author improving everything Jeanne wrote while writing his own chapters. A big thank-you to everyone at CodeRanch.com who asked and responded to questions and comments about our Java 8 books. Finally, Jeanne would like to thank all of the new programmers at CodeRanch.com and FIRST robotics teams FRC 694, FTC 310, and FTC 479 for the constant reminders of how new programmers think.

Scott could not have reached this point without his wife Patti and family, whose love and support makes this book possible. He would like to thank his twin daughters, Olivia and Sophia, and youngest daughter, Elysia, for their patience and understanding especially when it was "time for Daddy to work in his office!" Scott would like to extend his gratitude to his wonderfully patient co-author, Jeanne, on this, their fourth book. He doesn't know how she puts up with him, but he's glad she does and thrilled at the quality of books we produce. A big thanks to Matt Dalen, who has been a great friend, sounding board, and caring father to Olivia and Adeline. Joel McNary introduced Scott to CodeRanch.com and encouraged him to post regularly, a step that changed his life. Finally, Scott would like to thank his mother and retired teacher, Barbara Selikoff, for teaching him the value of education, and his father, Mark Selikoff, for instilling in him the benefits of working hard.

Last but not least, both Scott and Jeanne would like to give a big thank-you to the readers of our Java 8 certification books. Hearing from all of you who enjoyed the book and passed the exam is a great feeling. A special thank-you to Campbell Ritchie, who fielded an almost uncountable number of the questions on CodeRanch.com, helping readers understand the material better. We'd also like to thank those who pointed out errors and made suggestions for improvements in our practice exams book. As of August 2019, the top two were Juerg Bauman and Tamas Szekeres. We would also like to thank Noorul Hameed and Nurettin Armucutu for running a tight race for third-place errata reporter.

About the Authors

Jeanne Boyarsky was selected as a Java Champion in 2019. She has worked as a Java developer for more than 17 years at a bank in New York City where she develops, mentors, and conducts training. Besides being a senior moderator at CodeRanch.com in her free time, she works on the forum code base. Jeanne also mentors the programming division of a FIRST robotics team where she works with students just getting started with Java. She also speaks at several conferences each year.

Jeanne got her Bachelor of Arts degree in 2002 and her Master in Computer Information Technology degree in 2005. She enjoyed getting her Master's degree in an online program while working full-time. This was before online education was cool! Jeanne is also a Distinguished Toastmasters and a Scrum Master. You can find out more about Jeanne at www.jeanneboyarsky.com.

Scott Selikoff is a professional software consultant, author, and owner of Selikoff Solutions, LLC, which provides software development solutions to businesses in the tri-state New York City area. Skilled in a plethora of software languages and platforms, Scott specializes in full-stack database-driven systems, cloud-based applications, microservice architectures, and service-oriented architectures.

A native of Toms River, New Jersey, Scott achieved his Bachelor of Arts degree from Cornell University in Mathematics and Computer Science in 2002, after three years of study. In 2003, he received his Master of Engineering degree in Computer Science, also from Cornell University.

As someone with a deep love of education, Scott has always enjoyed teaching others new concepts. He's given lectures at Cornell University and Rutgers University, as well as conferences including Oracle Code One and The Server Side Java Symposium. Scott lives in New Jersey with his loving wife, Patti, three amazing daughters, twins Olivia and Sophia and little Elysia, along with two very playful dogs, Webby and Georgette. You can find out more about Scott at www.linkedin.com/in/selikoff.

Jeanne and Scott are both moderators on the CodeRanch.com forums and can be reached there for question and comments. They also co-author a technical blog called Down Home Country Coding at www.selikoff.net.

In addition to this book, Scott and Jeanne are also authors of the following best-selling Java 8 certification books: *OCA Oracle Certified Associate Java SE 8 Programmer I Study Guide* (Sybex, 2015) and *OCP Oracle Certified Professional Java SE 8 Programmer II Study Guide* (Sybex, 2016). These two books have been combined into the single release: *OCA/OCP Java SE 8 Programmer Certification Kit: Exam 1Z0-808 and Exam 1Z0-809* (Sybex 2016). They have also written a book of practice test questions for the Java 8 certification exams: *OCA/OCP Java SE 8 Programmer Practice Tests* (Sybex, 2017).

Contents at a Glance

Contents

Introduction

This book is for those studying for the IZ0-815 (Java SE Programmer I) or IZ0-811 (Java Foundations) exam along with those looking to learn Java more deeply.

If you've taken the OCA 7 or OCA 8 exam, note that the IZ0-815 exam is a lot tougher. While covering more basic topics, the exam is at the same level of difficulty as the OCP 7 and OCP 8 exams.

In this introduction, we will cover important information about the exam before moving on to information about this book. Finally, this introduction ends with an assessment test so that you can see how much studying lays ahead of you.

Understanding the Exam

At the end of the day, the exam is a list of questions. The more you know about the structure of the exam, the better you are likely to do. For example, knowing how many questions the exam contains allows you to manage your progress and time remaining better. In this section, we discuss the details of the exam, along with some history of previous certification exams.

Choosing Which Exam to Take

Java is about 25 years old, celebrating being "born" in 1995. As with anything 25 years old, there is a good amount of history and variation between different versions of Java. Over the years, the certification exams have changed to cover different topics. The names of the exams have even changed.

Oracle released two exams each for Java 7 and Java 8. The first exam tended to be easier and completing it granted you the title of Oracle Certified Associate (OCA). The second exam was a lot more difficult, with much longer questions, and completing it granted you the title of Oracle Certified Professional (OCP).

Oracle did not release an exam for Java 9 or Java 10, probably because neither of these are Long Term Support (LTS) releases (more on that in Chapter 1, "Welcome to Java"). With Java 11, Oracle decided to discontinue both the OCA certification and its associated exam. You still have to take two exams to earn an OCP title. There's also a basic Java Foundations exam that we will describe shortly.

Figure I.1 shows these past and current Java certifications. This image is helpful if you run into material online that references older exams. It is also helpful if you have an older certification and are trying to determine where it fits in.

FIGURE I.1   Past and current Java certifications

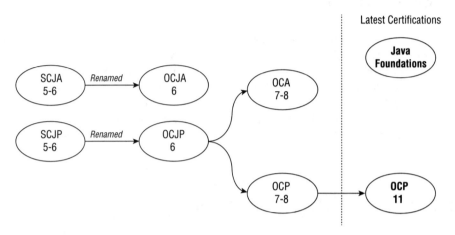

The first exam, and the one this book is designed to prepare you for, is the 1Z0-815 Programmer I exam. It covers a lot of basic Java properties including class structure, methods, inheritance, and modules. It is somewhat similar, but significantly more difficult, than the previous OCA 7/8 exams. If you've taken a previous OCA exam, it might help to think of the 1Z0-815 exam as containing much of the same OCA content, but with the level of difficulty of the original OCP exam. This means questions are longer, answers often have multiple parts, and the level of depth of the material is significantly more difficult.

The second exam is the 1Z0-816 Programmer II exam. It is quite similar to the previous OCP 7/8 exams, with a number of new topics such as annotations, modules, and security added in. We've included notes throughout this book on some topics that aren't in scope for the 1Z0-815 exam but will be when you study for the 1Z0-816 exam.

> Oracle has also released a 1Z0-817 OCP Upgrade Exam for those who hold an existing Sun Certified Programmer 6 (SCJP 6), OCP 6, OCP 7, or OCP 8 title. The objectives for the upgrade exam are quite similar to the 1Z0-816 Programmer II exam.

Oracle also offers a 1Z0-811 Java Foundations exam. This is often for a novice programmer or nonprogrammers. If you are planning to take the Java Foundations exam, this book prepares you as well. You will get to skip some parts of the book, so be sure to read the objectives/chapter mapping later in this introduction. The Java Foundations exam is an easier exam but does not serve as a prerequisite for the OCP certification. If you are considering taking the Java Foundations exam, please see the linked blog post from our book page to weigh the pros and cons of each exam:

`http://www.selikoff.net/ocp11-1`

Figure I.2 reviews the exams you need to take in order to earn the latest Java certifications. This book will prepare you for your choice of the 1Z0-815 and the 1Z0-811 exams.

FIGURE I.2   Latest Java certification exams

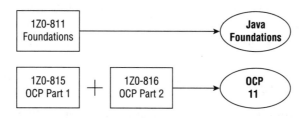

Broad Objectives

In previous certification exams, the list of exam objectives tended to include specific topics, classes, and APIs that you needed to know for the exam. For example, take a look at a previous objective for the 1Z0-808 (OCA 8) exam:

> *Compare and contrast the features and components of Java such as: platform independence, object orientation, encapsulation, etc.*

Now compare it with the equivalent objective for the 1Z0-815 exam:

> *Identify key features of the Java language*

Notice the difference? The older version is more detailed and describes specific topics you will need to understand. The newer version is a lot vaguer. It also gives the exam writers a lot more freedom to, say, insert a new feature without having to update the list of objectives.

So, how do you know what to study? By reading this study guide, of course! We've spent years studying the certification exams, in all of their forms, and have carefully cultivated topics, material, and practice questions that we are confident can lead to successfully passing the exam.

Changes to the Exam

At the time of this book being published, all three OCP 11 certification exams contain 80 questions and have a duration of 3 hours. The 1Z0-815 and 1Z0-816 exams require a passing score of 63%, while the 1Z0-817 exam requires a passing score of 61%. The 1Z0-811 Java Foundation exam is a little different than the OCP exams. It contains 75 questions and has a duration of 2.5 hours, and it requires a score of 65% to pass.

Oracle has a tendency to fiddle with the length of the exam and the passing score once it comes out. Oracle also likes to "tweak" the exam topics over time. It wouldn't be a surprise for Oracle to make minor changes to the exam objectives, the number of questions, or the passing score after this book goes to print.

If there are any changes to the exam after this book is published, we will note them on the book page of our blog:

http://www.selikoff.net/ocp11-1

Exam Questions

The 1Z0-815 exam consists of multiple-choice questions. There are between four and seven possible answers. If a question has more than one answer, the question specifically states exactly how many correct answers there are. This book does not do that. We say "Choose all that apply" to make the questions harder. This means the questions in this book are generally harder than those on the exam. The idea is to give you more practice so you can spot the correct answer more easily on the real exam.

If you read about older versions of the exam online, you might see references to drag-and-drop questions. These questions had you do a puzzle on how to complete a piece of code. Luckily, these are no longer on the exam.

Many of the questions on the exam are code snippets rather than full classes. Saving space by not including imports leaves room for lots of other code. In Chapter 1, we provide advice on reading code in various formats.

Out-of-Scope Material

When you take the exam, you may see some questions that appear to be out of scope. *Don't panic!* Oftentimes, these questions do not require knowing anything about the topic to answer the question. For example, after reading this book you should be able to spot that the following does not compile, even if you have no idea what LocalDate and ChronoUnit are:

```
final LocalDate holiday = LocalDate.now();
holiday = LocalDate.now().plus(5,ChronoUnit.HOURS);
```

While the classes and enums used in this question are not in scope for the exam, the reason it does not compile is. In particular, you should know that you cannot reassign a variable marked final.

See, not so scary is it? Expect to see at least a few structures on the exam that you are not familiar with. If they aren't part of your exam preparation material, then you don't need to understand them to answer the question.

Question Topic Tips

The following list of topics is meant to give you an idea of the types of questions and oddities that you might come across on the exam. Being aware of these categories of such questions will help you get a higher score on the exam.

Questions with Extra Information Provided   Imagine the question includes a statement that `XMLParseException` is a checked exception. It's fine if you don't know what an `XMLParseException` is or what XML is for that matter. (If you are wondering, it is a format for data.) This question is a gift. You know the question is about checked and unchecked exceptions.

Questions with Embedded Questions   To answer some questions on the exam, you may have to actually answer two or three subquestions. For example, the question may contain two blank lines, and the question may ask you to choose the two answers that fill in each blank. In some cases, the two answer choices are not related, which means you're really answering multiple questions, not just one! Another place this is seen is in a question that includes a `print()` statement that outputs multiple variables. Each question has to be tracked independently. These questions are among the most difficult and time-consuming on the exam because they contain multiple, often independent, questions to answer. Unfortunately, the exam does not give partial credit, so take care when answering questions like these.

Questions with Unfamiliar APIs   Suppose a question shows a method with a `Path` parameter. If you see a class or method that wasn't covered in this book, assume it works as you would expect. Some of these APIs you might come across, such as `LocalDate`, were on the Java 8 exam and are not part of the Java 11 exams. Assume that the part of the code using that API is correct and look very hard for other errors.

Questions with Unfamiliar Concepts   You might see some more advanced Java concepts like an enum or inner classes that use aspects not covered in this book. While you need to know more for the 1Z0-816 exam, the 1Z0-815 only tests the basics of these features. Again, you can assume the unfamiliar provided code is correct and the question is testing something else.

Questions with Made Up or Incorrect Concepts   In the context of a word problem, the exam may bring up a term or concept that does not make any sense such as saying an interface inherits from a class, which is not a correct statement. In other case, they may use a keyword that does not exist in Java, like `struct`. For these, you just have to read them carefully and recognize when the exam is using invalid terminology.

Questions That Are Really Out of Scope   When introducing new questions, Oracle includes them as unscored questions at first. This allows them to see how real exam takers do without impacting your score. You will still receive the number of questions as the exam lists. However, a few of them may not count. These unscored questions may contain out-of-scope material or even errors. They will not be marked as unscored, so you still have to do your best to answer them. Follow the previous advice to assume that anything you haven't seen before is correct. That will cover you if the question is being counted!

Reading This Book

It might help to have some idea about how this book has been written. This section contains details about some of the common structures and features you will find in this book, where to go for additional help, and how to obtain bonus material for this book.

Who Should Buy This Book

If you want to become certified as a Java programmer, this book is definitely for you. If you want to acquire a solid foundation in Java and your goal is to prepare for the exam, this book is also for you. You'll find clear explanations of the concepts you need to grasp and plenty of help to achieve the high level of professional competency you need in order to succeed in your chosen field.

This book is intended to be understandable to anyone who has a tiny bit of Java knowledge. If you've never read a Java book before, we recommend starting with a book that teaches programming from the beginning and then returning to this study guide.

This book is for anyone from high school students to those beginning their programming journey to experienced professionals who need a review for the certification.

How This Book Is Organized

This book consists of 11 chapters plus supplementary information: an Appendix, a glossary (online), this introduction, and the bonus exam. You might have noticed that there are more than 11 exam objectives. We organized what you need to know to make it easy to learn and remember. Each chapter begins with a list of the objectives that are covered in that chapter.

The chapters are organized as follows:

Chapter 1: Welcome to Java describes the basics of Java such as how to run a program. It also includes the benefits of Java and key terminology.

Chapter 2: Java Building Blocks focuses on variables such as primitives and object data types and scoping variables. It also discusses garbage collection.

Chapter 3: Operators explains operations with variables. It also talks about casting and the precedence of operators.

Chapter 4: Making Decisions covers on core logical constructs such as conditionals and loops.

Chapter 5: Core Java APIs introduces you to `String`, `StringBuilder`, array, and various types.

Chapter 6: Lambdas and Functional Interfaces shows how use lambdas and four key functional interfaces. The focus is implementing and calling `Predicate`, `Consumer`, `Supplier`, and `Comparator`.

Chapter 7: Methods and Encapsulation explains how to write methods. It also shows the four access modifiers.

Chapter 8: Class Design covers constructors and superclasses. It also includes method overriding.

Chapter 9: Advanced Class Design adds interfaces and abstract classes. It also introduces inner classes.

Chapter 10: Exceptions shows the different types of exception classes and how to use them. It also includes different uses of try statements.

Chapter 11: Modules details the benefits of the new module feature. It shows how to compile and run module programs from the command line.

At the end of each chapter, you'll find a few elements you can use to prepare for the exam.

Summary   This section reviews the most important topics that were covered in the chapter and serves as a good review.

Exam Essentials   This section summarizes highlights that were covered in the chapter. You should be able to convey the information requested.

Review Questions   Each chapter concludes with at least 20 review questions. You should answer these questions and check your answers against the ones provided in the Appendix. If you can't answer at least 80% of these questions correctly, go back and review the chapter, or at least those sections that seem to be giving you difficulty.

> The review questions, assessment test, and other testing elements included in this book are *not* derived from the real exam questions, so don't memorize the answers to these questions and assume that doing so will enable you to pass the exam. You should learn the underlying topic, as described in the text of the book. This will let you answer the questions provided with this book *and* pass the exam. Learning the underlying topic is also the approach that will serve you best in the workplace—the ultimate goal of a certification.

To get the most out of this book, you should read each chapter from start to finish before going to the chapter-end elements. They are most useful for checking and reinforcing your understanding. Even if you're already familiar with a topic, you should skim the chapter. There are a number of subtleties to Java that you could easily not encounter even when working with Java for years.

Conventions Used in This Book

This book uses certain typographic styles to help you quickly identify important information and to avoid confusion over the meaning of words such as on-screen prompts. In particular, look for the following styles:

- *Italicized text* indicates key terms that are described at length for the first time in a chapter. (Italics are also used for emphasis.)

- A monospaced font indicates code or command-line text.
- *Italicized monospaced text* indicates a variable.

In addition to these text conventions, which can apply to individual words or entire paragraphs, a few conventions highlight segments of text.

 A note indicates information that's useful or interesting. It is often something to pay special attention to for the exam.

Sidebars

A sidebar is like a note but longer. The information in a sidebar is useful, but it doesn't fit into the main flow of the text.

 Real World Scenario

Real-World Scenario

A real-world scenario is a type of sidebar that describes a task or an example that's particularly grounded in the real world. This is something that is useful in the real world but is not going to show up on the exam.

Getting Help

Both of the authors are moderators at CodeRanch.com. This site is a quite large and active programming forum that is very friendly toward Java beginners. It has a forum just for this exam called Programmer Certification. It also has a forum called Beginning Java for non-exam-specific questions. As you read the book, feel free to ask your questions in either of those forums. It could be you are having trouble compiling a class or that you are just plain confused about something. You'll get an answer from a knowledgeable Java programmer. It might even be one of us.

Interactive Online Learning Environment and Test Bank

We've put together some really great online tools to help you pass the IZ0-815 exam. The interactive online learning environment that accompanies this study guide provides a test bank and study tools to help you prepare for the exam. By using these tools you can dramatically increase your chances of passing the exam on your first try.

The online test bank includes the following:

Sample Tests   Many sample tests are provided throughout this book and online, including the assessment test, which you'll find at the end of this introduction, and the chapter tests that include the review questions at the end of each chapter. In addition, there are two bonus practice exams. Use these questions to test your knowledge of the study guide material. The online test bank runs on multiple devices.

Flashcards   The online text bank includes two sets of flashcards specifically written to hit you hard, so don't get discouraged if you don't ace your way through them at first! They're there to ensure that you're really ready for the exam. And no worries—armed with the review questions, practice exams, and flashcards, you'll be more than prepared when exam day comes! Questions are provided in digital flashcard format (a question followed by a single correct answer). You can use the flashcards to reinforce your learning and provide last-minute test prep before the exam.

Resources   A glossary of key terms from this book and their definitions is available as a fully searchable PDF.

Go to www.wiley.com/go/Sybextestprep to register and gain access to this interactive online learning environment and test bank with study tools.

Studying for the Exam

This section includes suggestions and recommendations for how you should prepare for the certification exam. If you're an experienced test taker or you've taken a certification test before, most of this should be common knowledge. For those who are taking the exam for the first time, don't worry! We'll present a number of tips and strategies to help you prepare for the exam.

Creating a Study Plan

Rome wasn't built in a day, so you shouldn't attempt to study for the exam in only one day. Even if you have been certified with a previous version of Java, the new test includes features and components unique to the Java 9, 10, and 11 that are covered in this text.

Once you have decided to take the test, you should construct a study plan that fits with your schedule. We recommend that you set aside some amount of time each day, even if it's just a few minutes during lunch, to read or practice for the exam. The idea is to keep your momentum going throughout the exam preparation process. The more consistent you are in how you study, the better prepared you will be for the exam. Try to avoid taking a few days or weeks off from studying or you're likely to spend a lot of time relearning existing material instead of moving on to new material.

Creating and Running the Code

Although some people can learn Java just by reading a textbook, that's not how we recommend that you study for a certification exam. We want you to be writing your own Java sample applications throughout this book so that you don't just learn the material, but that you understand the material as well. For example, it may not be obvious why the following line of code does not compile, but if you try to compile it yourself, the Java compiler will tell you the problem:

```
float value = 102.0; // DOES NOT COMPILE
```

 A lot of people post the question "Why does this code not compile?" on the CodeRanch.com forum. If you're stuck or just curious about a behavior in Java, we encourage you to post to the forum. There are a large number of members of the Java community standing by to help you.

Sample Test Class

Throughout this book, we present numerous code snippets and ask you whether they'll compile or not and what their output will be. You will place these snippets inside a simple Java application that starts, executes the code, and terminates. You can accomplish this by compiling and running a public class containing a public static void main(String[] args) method and adding the necessary import statements, such as the following:

```java
// Add any necessary import statements here
public class TestClass {
    public static void main(String[] args) {
        // Add test code here

        // Add any print statements here
        System.out.println("Hello World!");
    }
}
```

This application isn't particularly interesting—it just outputs "Hello World!" and exits. That said, you could insert many of the code snippets presented in this book in the main() method to determine whether the code compiles, as well as what the code outputs when it does compile.

Real World Scenario

IDE Software

While studying for the exam, you should develop code using a text editor and command-line Java compiler. Some of you may have prior experience with Integrated Development Environments (IDEs), such as Eclipse or IntelliJ. An IDE is a software application that facilitates software development for computer programmers. Although such tools are extremely valuable in developing software, they can interfere with your ability to spot problems readily on the exam.

Identifying Your Weakest Link

The review questions in each chapter are designed to help you hone in on those features of the Java language where you may be weak and that are required knowledge for the exam. For each chapter, you should note which questions you got wrong, understand why you got them wrong, and study those areas even more. After you've reread the chapter and written lots of code, you can do the review questions again. In fact, you can take the review questions over and over to reinforce your learning as long as you explain to yourself why it is correct.

"Overstudying" the Online Practice Exam

Although we recommend reading this book and writing your own sample applications multiple times, redoing the online practice exam over and over can have a negative impact in the long run. For example, some individuals study the practice exam so much that they end up memorizing the answers. In this scenario, they can easily become over-confident; that is, they can achieve perfect scores on the practice exams but may fail the actual exam.

Understanding the Question

The majority of questions on the exam will contain code snippets and ask you to answer questions about them. For those items containing code snippets, the number-one question we recommend that you answer before attempting to solve the question is this:

Does the code compile?

It sounds simple, but many people dive into answering the question without checking whether the code actually compiles. If you can determine whether or not a particular set of code compiles and what line or lines cause it to not compile, answering the question often becomes easy.

Applying the Process of Elimination

Although you might not immediately know the correct answer to a question, if you can reduce the question from five answers to three, your odds of guessing the correct answer will be markedly improved. Moreover, if you can reduce a question from four answers to two, you'll double your chances of guessing the correct answer!

The exam software allows you to eliminate answer choices by right-clicking an answer choice, which causes the text to be struck through, as shown in the following example:

A. ~~123~~

B. Elephant

C. ~~Vulture~~

D. The code does not compile due to line n1.

Even better, the exam software remembers which answer choices you have eliminated anytime you go back to the question. You can undo the crossed-out answer simply by right-clicking the choice again.

Sometimes you can eliminate answer choices quickly without reading the entire question. In some cases, you may even be able to solve the question based solely on the answer choices. If you come across such questions on the exam, consider it a gift. Can you correctly answer the following question in which the application code has been left out?

5. Which line, when inserted independently at line m1, allows the code to compile?

```
- Code Omitted -
```

A. public abstract final int swim();

B. public abstract void swim();

C. public abstract swim();

D. public abstract void swim() {}

E. public void swim() {}

Without reading the code or knowing what line m1 is, we can actually eliminate 3 of the 5 answer choices. Options A, C, and D contain invalid declarations, which you'll learn about in Chapter 9, leaving us with options B and E as the only possible correct answers.

Skipping Difficult Questions

The exam software also includes an option to "mark" a question and review all marked questions at the end of the exam. If you are pressed for time, answer a question as best you can and then mark it to come back to later.

All questions are weighted equally, so spending 10 minutes answering 5 questions correctly is a lot better use of your time than spending 10 minutes on a single question. If you finish the exam early, you have the option of reviewing the marked questions, as well as all of the questions on the exam if you so choose.

Being Suspicious of Strong Words

Many questions on the exam include answer choices with descriptive sentences rather than lines of code. When you see such questions, be wary of any answer choice that includes strong words such as "must," "all," or "cannot." If you think about the complexities of programming languages, it is rare for a rule to have no exceptions or special cases. Therefore, if you are stuck between two answers and one of them uses "must" while the other uses "can" or "may," you are better off picking the one with the weaker word since it is a more ambiguous statement.

Using the Provided Writing Material

Depending on your particular testing center, you will be provided with a sheet of blank paper or a whiteboard to use to help you answer questions. In our experience, a whiteboard with marker and eraser is more commonly handed out. If you sit down and you are not provided with anything, make sure to ask for such materials.

After you have determined that the program does compile, it is time to understand what the program does! One of the most useful applications of writing material is tracking the state of primitive and reference variables. For example, let's say you encountered the following code snippet on a question about garbage collection:

```
Object o = new Turtle();
Mammal m = new Monkey();
Animal a = new Rabbit();
o = m;
```

In a situation like this, it can be helpful to draw a diagram of the current state of the variable references. As each reference variable changes which object it points to, you would erase or cross out the arrow between them and draw a new one to a different object.

Using the writing material to track state is also useful for complex questions that involve a loop, especially questions with embedded loops. For example, the value of a variable might change five or more times during a loop execution. You should make use of the provided writing material to improve your score.

While you cannot bring any outside material into the exam, you can write down material at the start of the exam. For example, if you have trouble remembering which functional interfaces take which generic arguments, then it might be helpful to draw a table at the start of the exam on the provided writing material. You can then use this information to answer multiple questions.

Choosing the Best Answer

Sometimes you read a question and immediately spot a compiler error that tells you exactly what the question is asking. Other times, though, you may stare at a method declaration for a couple of minutes and have no idea what the question is asking. While you might not know for sure which answer is correct in these situations, there are some test-taking tips that can improve the probability that you will pick the correct answer.

Unlike some other standardized tests, there's no penalty for answering a question incorrectly versus leaving it blank. If you're nearly out of time or you just can't decide on an answer, select a random answer and move on. If you've been able to eliminate even one answer, then your guess will be better than blind luck.

Answer All Questions!

You should set a hard stop at five minutes of time remaining on the exam to ensure that you've answered each and every question. Remember, if you fail to answer a question, you'll definitely get it wrong and lose points, but if you guess, there's at least a chance that you'll be correct. There's no harm in guessing!

When in doubt, we generally recommend picking a random answer that includes "Does not compile" if available, although which choice you select is not nearly as important as making sure that you do not leave any questions unanswered on the exam!

Getting a Good Night's Rest

Although a lot of people are inclined to cram as much material as they can in the hours leading up to the exam, most studies have shown that this is a poor test-taking strategy. The best thing we can recommend that you do before the exam is to get a good night's rest!

Given the length of the exam and number of questions, the exam can be quite draining, especially if this is your first time taking a certification exam. You might come in expecting to be done 30 minutes early, only to discover that you are only a quarter of the way through the exam with half the time remaining. At some point, you may begin to panic, and it is in these moments that these test-taking skills are most important. Just remember to take a deep breath, stay calm, eliminate as many wrong answers as you can, and make sure to answer each and every question. It is for stressful moments like these that being well rested with a good night's sleep will be most beneficial!

Taking the Exam

So you've decided to take the exam? We hope so if you've bought this book! In this section, we discuss the process of scheduling and taking the exam, along with various options for each.

Scheduling the Exam

The exam is administered by Pearson VUE and can be taken at any Pearson VUE testing center. To find a testing center or register for the exam, go to:

http://pearsonvue.com

Next, search for *Oracle* as the exam provider. If you haven't been to the test center before, we recommend visiting in advance. Some testing centers are nice and professionally run. Others stick you in a closet with lots of people talking around you. You don't want to be taking the test with people complaining about their broken laptops nearby!

At this time, you can reschedule the exam without penalty until up to 24 hours before. This means you can register for a convenient time slot well in advance knowing that you can delay if you aren't ready by that time. Rescheduling is easy and can be done completely on the Pearson VUE website. This may change, so check the rules before paying.

The At-Home Online Option

Oracle now offers online-proctored exams that can be taken in the comfort of your own home. You choose a specific date and time, like a proctored exam, and take it at your computer.

While this option may be appealing for a lot of people, especially if you live far away from a testing center, there are number of restrictions:

- Your session will be closely monitored by another individual from a remote location.

- You must set up a camera and microphone, and they must be on for the entire exam. At the start, you will also need to turn the camera around the room to show your workspace to prove you are not in reach of exam material.

- You must be alone in a completely isolated space for the duration of the test. If someone comes in during your test, your test will be invalidated.

- You cannot have any papers, material, or items in your immediate vicinity.

- Unlike exam centers that provide writing material, writing down any notes or use of scratch paper is prohibited. You do get to make notes on an digital whiteboard within the exam software.

- Stopping for any reason, including a restroom break, is prohibited.

With so many rules, you want to think carefully before taking the test at home. If you do plan to go this route, please visit Oracle's website for additional restrictions or changes to these requirements.

The Day of the Exam

When you go to take the exam, remember to bring two forms of ID including one that is government issued. See Pearson's list of acceptable IDs here:

http://www.pearsonvue.com/policies/1S.pdf

Try not to bring too much extra with you as it will not be allowed into the exam room. While you will be allowed to check your belongings, it is better to leave extra items at home or in the car.

You will not be allowed to bring paper, your phone, and the like into the exam room with you. Some centers are stricter than others. At one center, tissues were even taken away from us! Most centers allow keeping your ID and money. They watch you taking the exam, though, so don't even think about writing notes on money.

As we mentioned earlier, the exam center will give you writing materials to use during the exam, either scratch paper or a whiteboard. If you aren't given these materials, remember to ask. These items will be collected at the end of the exam.

Finding Out Your Score

In the past, you would find out right after finishing the exam if you passed. Now you have to wait nervously until you can check your score online. Many test takers check their score from a mobile device as they are walking out of the test center.

If you go onto the Pearson VUE website, it will just have a status of "Taken" rather than your result. Oracle uses a separate system for scores. You'll need to go to Oracle's CertView website to find out whether you passed and your score:

http://certview.oracle.com

It usually updates shortly after you finish your exam but can take up to an hour in some cases. In addition to your score, you'll also see objectives for which you got a question wrong.

Reviewing Exam Objectives

This book has been written to cover every objective on the Java SE 11 Programmer I exam along with most of the Java Foundations exam objectives.

Java SE 11 Programmer I (1Z0-815)

The following table provides a breakdown of this book's exam coverage for the Java SE 11 Programmer I (1Z0-815) exam, showing you the chapter where each objective or subobjective is covered:

Exam Objective	Chapter
Understanding Java Technology and environment	
Describe Java Technology and the Java development	1
Identify key features of the Java language	1
Creating a Simple Java Program	
Create an executable Java program with a main class	1
Compile and run a Java program from the command line	1
Create and import packages	1
Working with Java Primitive Data Types and String APIs	
Declare and initialize variables (including casting and promoting primitive data types)	2, 3
Identify the scope of variables	2
Use local variable type inference	2
Create and manipulate Strings	5
Manipulate data using the StringBuilder class and its methods	5
Using Operators and Decision Constructs	
Use Java operators including the use of parentheses to override operator precedence	3
Use Java control statements including if, if/else, switch	4
Create and use do/while, while, for and for each loops, including nested loops, use break and continue statements	4
Working with Java Arrays	
Declare, instantiate, initialize and use a one-dimensional array	5
Declare, instantiate, initialize and use a two-dimensional array	5

Exam Objective	Chapter
Describing and using Objects and Classes	
Declare and instantiate Java objects, and explain objects' lifecycles (including creation, dereferencing by reassignment, and garbage collection)	2
Define the structure of a Java class	1
Read or write to object fields	2
Creating and Using Methods	
Create methods and constructors with arguments and return values	7, 8
Create and invoke overloaded methods	7
Apply the static keyword to methods and fields	7
Applying Encapsulation	
Apply access modifiers	7
Apply encapsulation principles to a class	7
Reusing Implementations Through Inheritance	
Create and use subclasses and superclasses	8
Create and extend abstract classes	9
Enable polymorphism by overriding methods	8
Utilize polymorphism to cast and call methods, differentiating object type versus reference type	8
Distinguish overloading, overriding, and hiding	8
Programming Abstractly Through Interfaces	
Create and implement interfaces	9
Distinguish class inheritance from interface inheritance including abstract classes	9
Declare and use List and ArrayList instances	5, 6
Understanding Lambda Expressions	6

Exam Objective	Chapter
Handling Exceptions	
Describe the advantages of Exception handling and differentiate among checked, unchecked exceptions, and Errors	10
Create try-catch blocks and determine how exceptions alter program flow	10
Create and invoke a method that throws an exception	10
Understanding Modules	
Describe the Modular JDK	11
Declare modules and enable access between modules	11
Describe how a modular project is compiled and run	11

Java Foundations (1Z0-811)

The following table provides a breakdown of this book's exam coverage for the Java Foundations (1Z0-811) exam, showing you the chapter where each objective or sub-objective is covered.

 A few topics are on the Java Foundations exam, but not the 1Z0-815. Those are covered here:

> http://www.selikoff.net/java-foundations

Additionally, the objectives for the Java Foundations exam may be updated when Oracle updates the Java Foundations exam for Java 11. Check our website for those updates as well.

Exam Objective	Chapter
What is Java?	
Describe the features of Java	1
Describe the real-world applications of Java	1 + online

Exam Objective	Chapter
Java Basics	
Describe the Java Development Kit (JDK) and the Java Runtime Environment (JRE)	1
Describe the components of object-oriented programming	1
Describe the components of a basic Java program	1
Compile and execute a Java program	1
Basic Java Elements	
Identify the conventions to be followed in a Java program	1
Use Java reserved words	2
Use single-line and multi-line comments in java programs	2
Import other Java packages to make them accessible in your code	1
Describe the java.lang package	1
Working with Java Data Types	
Declare and initialize variables including a variable using final	2
Cast a value from one data type to another including automatic and manual promotion	2
Declare and initialize a String variable	2
Working with Java Operators	
Use basic arithmetic operators to manipulate data including +, -, *, /, and %	2
Use the increment and decrement operators	2
Use relational operators including ==, !=, >, >=, <, and <=	2
Use arithmetic assignment operators	2
Use conditional operators including &&, ||, and ?	2
Describe the operator precedence and use of parentheses	2

Exam Objective	Chapter
Working with the String Class	
Develop code that uses methods from the String class	5
Format Strings using escape sequences including %d, %n, and %s	Online
Working with Random and Math Classes	
Use the Random class	Online
Use the Math class	5
Using Decision Statements	
Use the decision making statement (if-then and if-then-else)	4
Use the switch statement	4
Compare how == differs between primitives and objects	3
Compare two String objects by using the compareTo and equals methods	5
Using Looping Statements	
Describe looping statements	4
Use a for loop including an enhanced for loop	4
Use a while loop	4
Use a do- while loop	4
Compare and contrast the for, while, and do-while loops	4
Develop code that uses break and continue statements	4
Debugging and Exception Handling	
Identify syntax and logic errors	1, 2, 3, 4, 5
Use exception handling	10
Handle common exceptions thrown	10
Use try and catch blocks	10

Exam Objective	Chapter
Arrays and ArrayLists	
Use a one-dimensional array	5
Create and manipulate an ArrayList	5
Traverse the elements of an ArrayList by using iterators and loops including the enhanced for loop	5 + online
Compare an array and an ArrayList	5
Classes and Constructors	
Create a new class including a main method	1
Use the private modifier	7
Describe the relationship between an object and its members	8
Describe the difference between a class variable, an instance variable, and a local variable	2, 8
Develop code that creates an object's default constructor and modifies the object's fields	8
Use constructors with and without parameters	8
Develop code that overloads constructors	8
Java Methods	
Describe and create a method	7
Create and use accessor and mutator methods	7
Create overloaded methods	7
Describe a static method and demonstrate its use within a program	7

Taking the Assessment Test

Use the following assessment test to gauge your current level of skill in Java. This test is designed to highlight some topics for your strengths and weaknesses so that you know which chapters you might want to read multiple times. Even if you do well on the assessment test, you should still read the book from cover to cover, as the real exam is quite challenging.

The Assessment Test

1. What is the result of the following program?

```
1: public class MathFunctions {
2:     public static void addToInt(int x, int amountToAdd) {
3:         x = x + amountToAdd;
4:     }
5:     public static void main(String[] args) {
6:         var a = 15;
7:         var b = 10;
8:         MathFunctions.addToInt(a, b);
9:         System.out.println(a);    } }
```

   A. 10

   B. 15

   C. 25

   D. Compiler error on line 3

   E. Compiler error on line 8

   F. None of the above

2. What is the output of the following program? (Choose all that apply.)

```
1:  interface HasTail { int getTailLength(); }
2:  abstract class Puma implements HasTail {
3:     protected int getTailLength() { return 4; }
4:  }
5:  public class Cougar implements HasTail {
6:     public static void main(String[] args) {
7:         var puma = new Puma();
8:         System.out.println(puma.getTailLength());
9:     }
10:    public int getTailLength(int length) { return 2; }
11: }
```

A. 2

B. 4

C. The code will not compile because of line 3.

D. The code will not compile because of line 5.

E. The code will not compile because of line 7.

F. The code will not compile because of line 10.

G. The output cannot be determined from the code provided.

3. What is the output of the following code snippet?

```java
int moon = 9, star = 2 + 2 * 3;
float sun = star>10 ? 1 : 3;
double jupiter = (sun + moon) - 1.0f;
int mars = --moon <= 8 ? 2 : 3;
System.out.println(sun+"-"+jupiter+"-"+mars);
```

A. 1-11-2

B. 3.0-11.0-2

C. 1.0-11.0-3

D. 3.0-13.0-3

E. 3.0f-12-2

F. The code does not compile because one of assignments requires an explicit numeric cast.

4. How many times is the word true printed?

```java
var s1 = "Java";
var s2 = "Java";
var s3 = "Ja".concat("va");
var s4 = s3.intern();
var sb1 = new StringBuilder();
sb1.append("Ja").append("va");

System.out.println(s1 == s2);
System.out.println(s1.equals(s2));
System.out.println(s1 == s3);
System.out.println(s1 == s4);
System.out.println(sb1.toString() == s1);
System.out.println(sb1.toString().equals(s1));
```

A. Once

B. Twice

C. Three times

D. Four times

E. Five times

F. Six times

G. The code does not compile.

5. The following code appears in a file named `Flight.java`. What is the result of compiling this source file?

```
1: public class Flight {
2:     private FlightNumber number;
3:
4:     public Flight(FlightNumber number) {
5:         this.number = number;
6:     } }
7: public class FlightNumber {
8:     public int value;
9:     public String code; }
```

A. The code compiles successfully and two bytecode files are generated: `Flight.class` and `FlightNumber.class`.

B. The code compiles successfully and one bytecode file is generated: `Flight.class`.

C. A compiler error occurs on line 2.

D. A compiler error occurs on line 4.

E. A compiler error occurs on line 7.

6. Which of the following will run a modular program?

A. `java -cp modules mod/class`

B. `java -cp modules -m mod/class`

C. `java -cp modules -p mod/class`

D. `java -m modules mod/class`

E. `java -m modules -p mod/class`

F. `java -p modules mod/class`

G. `java -p modules -m mod/class`

7. What is the result of executing the following code snippet?

```
final int score1 = 8, score2 = 3;
char myScore = 7;
switch (myScore) {
    default:
    score1:
    2: 6: System.out.print("great-");
    4: System.out.print("good-"); break;
    score2:
    1: System.out.print("not good-");
}
```

A. great-good-

B. good-

C. not good-

D. great-good-not-good-

E. The code does not compile because default is not a keyword in Java.

F. The code does not compile for a different reason.

8. Which of the following lines can fill in the blank to print true? (Choose all that apply.)

```
10: public static void main(String[] args) {
11:     System.out.println(_____);
12: }
13: private static boolean test(Predicate<Integer> p) {
14:     return p.test(5);
15: }
```

A. test(i -> i == 5)

B. test(i -> {i == 5;})

C. test((i) -> i == 5)

D. test((int i) -> i == 5)

E. test((int i) -> {return i == 5;})

F. test((i) -> {return i == 5;})

9. Which of the following are valid instance members of a class? (Choose all that apply.)

A. var var = 3;

B. Var case = new Var();

C. void var() {}

D. int Var() { var _ = 7; return _;}

E. String new = "var";

F. var var() { return null; }

10. Which of the following types can be inserted into the blank that allows the program to compile successfully? (Choose all that apply.)

```
1:  import java.util.*;
2:  interface CanSwim {}
3:  class Amphibian implements CanSwim {}
4:  abstract class Tadpole extends Amphibian {}
5:  public class FindAllTadPole {
6:      public static void main(String[] args) {
7:          var tadpoles = new ArrayList<Tadpole>();
8:          for (Amphibian amphibian : tadpoles) {
9:              _____ tadpole = amphibian;
10: } } }
```

A. CanSwim

B. Boolean

C. Amphibian

D. Tadpole

E. Object

F. None of the above; the program contains a compilation error.

11. Which of the following expressions compile without error? (Choose all that apply.)

A. `int monday = 3 + 2.0;`

B. `double tuesday = 5_6L;`

C. `boolean wednesday = 1 > 2 ? !true;`

D. `short thursday = (short)Integer.MAX_VALUE;`

E. `long friday = 8.0L;`

F. `var saturday = 2_.0;`

G. None of the above

12. Suppose you have a module named com.vet. Where could you place the following module-info.java file to create a valid module?

```
public module com.vet {
    exports com.vet;
}
```

A. At the same level as the com folder

B. At the same level as the vet folder

C. Inside the vet folder

D. None of the above

13. What is the result of compiling and executing the following program?

```
1:  public class FeedingSchedule {
2:      public static void main(String[] args) {
3:          var x = 5;
4:          var j = 0;
5:          OUTER: for (var i = 0; i < 3;)
6:              INNER: do {
7:                  i++;
8:                  x++;
9:                  if (x > 10) break INNER;
10:                 x += 4;
11:                 j++;
12:             } while (j <= 2);
13:         System.out.println(x);
14: } }
```

A. 10

B. 11

C. 12

D. 17

E. The code will not compile because of line 5.

F. The code will not compile because of line 6.

14. Which statement about the following method is true?

```
5:  public static void main(String... unused) {
6:      System.out.print("a");
7:      try (StringBuilder reader = new StringBuilder()) {
8:          System.out.print("b");
9:          throw new IllegalArgumentException();
10:     } catch (Exception e || RuntimeException e) {
11:         System.out.print("c");
12:         throw new FileNotFoundException();
13:     } finally {
14:         System.out.print("d");
15: } }
```

A. It compiles and prints abc.

B. It compiles and prints abd.

C. It compiles and prints abcd.

D. One line contains a compiler error.

E. Two lines contain a compiler error.

F. Three lines contain a compiler error.

G. It compiles but prints an exception at runtime.

15. Which of the following are true statements? (Choose all that apply.)

A. The JDK contains a compiler.

B. The JVM contains a compiler.

C. The javac command creates a file containing bytecode.

D. The java command creates a file containing bytecode.

E. The JDK is contained in the JVM.

F. The JVM is contained in the JDK.

16. Which lines in Tadpole give a compiler error? (Choose all that apply.)

```
1:  package animal;
2:  public class Frog {
3:      protected void ribbit() { }
```

```
4:     void jump() { }
5:   }
```

```
1:   package other;
2:   import animal.*;
3:   public class Tadpole extends Frog {
4:       public static void main(String[] args) {
5:           Tadpole t = new Tadpole();
6:           t.ribbit();
7:           t.jump();
8:           Frog f = new Tadpole();
9:           f.ribbit();
10:          f.jump();
11:      } }
```

A. 5

B. 6

C. 7

D. 8

E. 9

F. 10

17. What is the output of the following program?

```
1:   class Deer {
2:       public Deer() {System.out.print("Deer");}
3:       public Deer(int age) {System.out.print("DeerAge");}
4:       protected boolean hasHorns() { return false; }
5:   }
6:   public class Reindeer extends Deer {
7:       public Reindeer(int age) {System.out.print("Reindeer");}
8:       public boolean hasHorns() { return true; }
9:       public static void main(String[] args) {
10:          Deer deer = new Reindeer(5);
11:          System.out.println("," + deer.hasHorns());
12:  } }
```

A. ReindeerDeer,false

B. DeerAgeReindeer,true

C. DeerReindeer,true

D. DeerReindeer,false

E. ReindeerDeer,true

F. DeerAgeReindeer,false

G. The code will not compile because of line 4.

H. The code will not compile because of line 12.

18. What is printed by the following code? (Choose all that apply.)

```java
int[] array = {6,9,8};
List<Integer> list = new ArrayList<>();
list.add(array[0]);
list.add(array[2]);
list.set(1, array[1]);
list.remove(0);
System.out.println(list);
System.out.println("C" + Arrays.compare(array,
    new int[] {6, 9, 8}));
System.out.println("M" + Arrays.mismatch(array,
    new int[] {6, 9, 8}));
```

A. [8]

B. [9]

C. [Ljava.lang.String;@160bc7c0

D. C-1

E. C0

F. M-1

G. M0

H. The code does not compile.

19. Which statements about the following program are true? (Choose all that apply.)

```java
1:  public class Grasshopper {
2:      public Grasshopper(String n) {
3:          name = n;
4:      }
5:      public static void main(String[] args) {
6:          Grasshopper one = new Grasshopper("g1");
7:          Grasshopper two = new Grasshopper("g2");
8:          one = two;
9:          two = null;
10:         one = null;
11:     }
12:     private String name;
13: }
```

A. Immediately after line 8, no `Grasshopper` objects are eligible for garbage collection.

B. Immediately after line 9, no `Grasshopper` objects are eligible for garbage collection.

C. Immediately after line 8, only one `Grasshopper` object is eligible for garbage collection.

D. Immediately after line 9, only one `Grasshopper` object is eligible for garbage collection.

E. Immediately after line 10, only one `Grasshopper` object is eligible for garbage collection.

F. The code does not compile.

20. Which of the following statements about error handling in Java are correct? (Choose all that apply.)

A. Checked exceptions are intended to be thrown by the JVM (and not the programmer).

B. Checked exceptions are required to be handled or declared.

C. Errors are intended to be thrown by the JVM (and not the programmer).

D. Errors are required to be caught or declared.

E. Runtime exceptions are intended to be thrown by the JVM (and not the programmer).

F. Runtime exceptions are required to be handled or declared.

21. Which of the following are valid method modifiers that cannot be used together in a method declaration? (Choose all that apply.)

A. `null` and `final`

B. `abstract` and `private`

C. `public` and `private`

D. `nonstatic` and `abstract`

E. `private` and `final`

F. `abstract` and `static`

G. `protected` and `abstract`

22. Which of the following are true to sort the list? (Choose all that apply.)

```
13: int multiplier = 1;
14: multiplier *= -1;
15: List<Integer> list = List.of(99, 66, 77, 88);
16: list.sort(_____);
```

A. Line 14 must be removed for any of the following lambdas to compile.

B. Line 14 may remain for any of the following lambdas to compile.

C. `(x, y) -> multiplier * y.compareTo(x)`

D. `x, y -> multiplier * y.compareTo(x)`

E. `(x, y) -> return multiplier * y.compareTo(x)`

F. `x, y -> return multiplier * y.compareTo(x)`

Answers to Assessment Test

1. B. The code compiles successfully, so options D and E are incorrect. The value of a cannot be changed by the addToInt() method, no matter what the method does, because only a copy of the variable is passed into the parameter x. Therefore, a does not change, and the output on line 9 is 15. For more information, see Chapter 7.

2. C, D, E. The program contains three compiler errors. First, the method getTailLength() in the interface HasTail is implicitly to be public, since it is an abstract interface method. Therefore, line 3 does not compile since it is an invalid override, reducing the visibility of the method, making option C correct. Next, the class Cougar implements an overloaded version of getTailLength() with a different signature than the abstract interface method it inherits. For this reason, the declaration of Cougar is invalid, and option D is correct. Finally, option E is correct, since Puma is marked abstract and cannot be instantiated. For more information, see Chapter 9.

3. B. Initially, moon is assigned a value of 9, while star is assigned a value of 8. The multiplication operator (*) has a higher order of precedence than the addition operator (+), so it gets evaluated first. Since star is not greater than 10, sun is assigned a value of 3, which is promoted to 3.0f as part of the assignment. The value of jupiter is (3.0f + 9) - 1.0, which is 11.0f. This value is implicitly promoted to double when it is assigned. In the last assignment, moon is predecremented from 9 to 8, with the value of the expression returned as 8. Since 8 is less than or equal to 8 is true, mars is set to a value of 2. The final output is 3.0-11.0-2, making option B the correct answer. Note that while Java outputs the decimal for both float and double values, it does not output the f for float values. For more information, see Chapter 3.

4. D. String literals are used from the string pool. This means that s1 and s2 refer to the same object and are equal. Therefore, the first two print statements print true. The concat() method forces a new String to be created making the third print statement print false. The intern() method reverts the String to the one from the string pool. Therefore, the fourth print statement prints true. The fifth statement print statement prints false because toString() uses a method to compute the value, and it is not from the string pool. The final print statement again prints true because equals() looks at the values of String objects. For more information, see Chapter 5.

5. E. The code does not compile because Java allows at most one public class in the same file. Either the FlightNumber class must not be declared public or it should be moved to its own source file named FlightNumber.java. The compiler error occurs on line 7, so the answer is option E. For more information, see Chapter 1.

6. G. This exam requires knowing how to run at the command line. The new -p option specifies the module path. The new -m option precedes the program to be run in the format moduleName/fullyQualifiedClassName. Option G is the only one that matches these requirements. For more information, see Chapter 11.

7. F. The code does not compile because `switch` statements require case statements before the colon (`:`). For example, `case score1:` would compile. For this reason, option F is the correct answer. If the six missing `case` statements were added throughout this snippet, then the `default` branch would be executed as 7 is not matched in any of the `case` statements, resulting in an output of `great-good-` and making option A correct. For more information, see Chapter 4.

8. A, C, F. The `Predicate` interface takes a single parameter and returns a `boolean`. Lambda expressions with one parameter are allowed to omit the parentheses around the parameter list, making options A and C equivalent and both correct. The `return` statement is optional when a single statement is in the body, making option F correct. Option B is incorrect because a `return` statement must be used if braces are included around the body. Options D and E are incorrect because the type is `Integer` in the predicate and `int` in the lambda. Autoboxing works for collections not inferring predicates. If these two were changed to `Integer`, they would be correct. For more information, see Chapter 6.

9. C. Option A is incorrect because `var` is only allowed as a type for local variables, not instance members. Options B and E are incorrect because `new` and `case` are reserved words and cannot be used as identifiers. Option C is correct, as `var` can be used as a method name. Option D is incorrect because a single underscore (`_`) cannot be used as an identifier starting with Java 9. Finally, option F is incorrect because `var` cannot be specified as the return type of a method. For more information, see Chapter 2.

10. A, C, E. The for-each loop implicitly casts each `Tadpole` object to an `Amphibian` reference, which is permitted because `Tadpole` is a subclass of `Amphibian`. From there, any supertype of `Amphibian` is permitted without an explicit cast. This includes `CanSwim`, which `Amphibian` implements, and `Object`, which all classes extend from, making options A and E correct. Option C is also correct since the reference is being cast to the same type. Option B is incorrect, since `Boolean` is not a supertype of `Amphibian`. Option D is also incorrect. Even though the underlying object is a `Tadpole` instance, it requires an explicit cast on line 9 since the reference type is `Amphibian`. Option F is incorrect because there are options that allow the code to compile. For more information, see Chapter 8.

11. B, D. Option A does not compile, as the expression `3 + 2.0` is evaluated as a `double`, and a `double` requires an explicit cast to be assigned to an `int`. Option B compiles without issue, as a `long` value can be implicitly cast to a `double`. Option C does not compile because the ternary operator (`? :`) is missing a colon (`:`), followed by a second expression. Option D is correct. Even though the `int` value is larger than a `short`, it is implicitly cast to a `short`, which means the value will wrap around to fit in a `short`. Option E is incorrect, as you cannot use a decimal (`.`) with the `long` (`L`) postfix. Finally, option F is incorrect, as an underscore cannot be used next to a decimal point. For more information, see Chapter 3.

12. D. If this were a valid `module-info.java` file, it would need to be placed at the root directory of the module, which is option A. However, a module is not allowed to use the `public` access modifier. Option D is correct because the provided file does not compile regardless of placement in the project. For more information, see Chapter 11.

13. C. The code compiles and runs without issue; therefore, options E and F are incorrect. This type of problem is best examined one loop iteration at a time:

- On the first iteration of the outer loop i is 0, so the loop continues.

- On the first iteration of the inner loop, i is updated to 1 and x to 6. The if statement branch is not executed, and x is increased to 10 and j to 1.

- On the second iteration of the inner loop (since j = 1 and 1 <= 2), i is updated to 2 and x to 11. At this point, the if branch will evaluate to true for the remainder of the program run, which causes the flow to break out of the inner loop each time it is reached.

- On the second iteration of the outer loop (since i = 2), i is updated to 3 and x to 12. As before, the inner loop is broken since x is still greater than 10.

- On the third iteration of the outer loop, the outer loop is broken, as i is already not less than 3. The most recent value of x, 12, is output, so the answer is option C.

For more information, see Chapter 4.

14. F. Line 5 does not compile as the FileNotFoundException thrown on line 12 is not handled or declared by the method. Line 7 does not compile because StringBuilder does not implement AutoCloseable and is therefore not compatible with a try-with-resource statement. Finally, line 10 does not compile as RuntimeException is a subclass of Exception in the multi-catch block, making it redundant. Since this method contains three compiler errors, option F is the correct answer. For more information, see Chapter 10.

15. A, C, F. The Java Development Kit (JDK) is used when creating Java programs. It contains a compiler since it is a development tool making option A correct and option B incorrect. The JDK contains a Java Virtual Machine (JVM) making option F correct and option E incorrect. The compiler creates bytecode making option C correct and option D incorrect. For more information, see Chapter 1.

16. C, E, F. The jump() method has default (package-private) access, which means it can be accessed only from the same package. Tadpole is not in the same package as Frog, causing lines 7 and 10 to give a compiler error, making options C and F correct. The ribbit() method has protected access, which means it can only be accessed from a subclass reference or in the same package. Line 6 is fine because Tadpole is a subclass. Line 9 does not compile because the variable reference is to a Frog, making option E correct. This is the trickiest question you can get on this topic on the exam. For more information, see Chapter 7.

17. C. The code compiles and runs without issue, so options G and H are incorrect. First, the Reindeer object is instantiated using the constructor that takes an int value. Since there is no explicit call to the parent constructor, the compiler inserts super() as the first line of the constructor on line 7. The parent constructor is called, and Deer is printed on line 2. The flow returns to the constructor on line 7, which prints Reindeer. Next, the method hasHorns() is called. The reference type is Deer, and the underlying object type is Reindeer. Since Reindeer correctly overrides the hasHorns() method, the version in Reindeer is called, printing true. For these reasons, option C is the correct answer. For more information, see Chapter 8.

18. B, E, F. The array is allowed to use an anonymous initializer because it is in the same line as the declaration. The ArrayList uses the diamond operator. This specifies the type matches the one on the left without having to retype it. After adding the two elements, list contains [6, 8]. We then replace the element at index 1 with 9, resulting in [6, 9]. Finally, we remove the element at index 0, leaving [9] and making option B correct. Option C is incorrect because arrays output something that looks like a reference rather than a nicely printed list of values.

    Option E is correct because the compare() method returns 0 when the arrays are the same length and have the same elements. Option F is correct because the mismatch() method returns a -1 when the arrays are equivalent. For more information, see Chapter 5.

19. C, D. Immediately after line 8, only Grasshopper g1, created on line 6, is eligible for garbage collection since both one and two point to Grasshopper g2, making option C correct and option A incorrect. Immediately after line 9, we still only have Grasshopper g1 eligible for garbage collection, since one points to it. For this reason, option B is incorrect and option D is correct. Reference two now points to null. Immediately after line 10, both Grasshopper objects are eligible for garbage collection since both one and two point to null, making option E incorrect. The code does compile, so option F is incorrect. Although it is traditional to declare instance variables early in the class, you don't have to. For more information, see Chapter 2.

20. B, C. Only checked exceptions are required to be handled or declared, making option B correct and option F incorrect. An Error is intended to be thrown by the JVM and never caught by the programmer, making option C correct and options A, D, and E incorrect. While a programmer could throw or catch an Error, this would be a horrible practice. For more information, see Chapter 10.

21. B, C, F. First, null and nonstatic are not valid method modifiers, making options A and D incorrect. Options B and F are correct, as abstract methods cannot be marked private or static, since they then would not be able to be overridden. Option C is also correct, as you cannot declare two access modifiers on the same method. Finally, options E and G are two sets of valid modifiers that can be used together in a method declaration. Using private with final is allowed, albeit redundant. For more information, see Chapter 9.

22. A. This is a great example to practice the process of elimination. The first thing to notice is that multiplier is not effectively final since it is reassigned. None of the lambdas will compile, making option A correct. The next step is to look at the lambda syntax. Options D and F are invalid because lambdas with more than one parameter must have parentheses. Options E and F are invalid because a return statement may not be used in a lambda without a block present. While option C at least compiles, the code fails at runtime because List.of() creates an immutable list. This is tricky as none of the lambdas will work successfully. Therefore, option A is the only correct answer. For more information, see Chapter 6.

Chapter

1

Welcome to Java

OCP EXAM OBJECTIVES COVERED IN THIS CHAPTER:

✓ **Understanding Java Technology and Environment**

- Describe Java Technology and the Java development environment

- Identify key features of the Java language

✓ **Creating a Simple Java Program**

- Create an executable Java program with a main class

- Compile and run a Java program from the command line

- Create and import packages

✓ **Describing and Using Objects and Classes**

- Define the structure of a Java class

Welcome to the beginning of your journey to achieve a Java 11 certification. We assume this isn't the first Java programming book you've read. Although we do talk about the basics, we do so only because we want to make sure you have all the terminology and detail you'll need for the 1Z0-815 exam. If you've never written a Java program before, we recommend you pick up an introductory book on any version of Java. Examples include *Head First Java, 2nd Edition* (O'Reilly Media, 2009); *Java for Dummies* (For Dummies, 2017), *Murach's Java Programming* (Murach, 2017), or *Thinking in Java, 4th Edition* (Prentice Hall, 2006). It's okay if the book covers an older version of Java—even Java 1.3 is fine. Then come back to this certification study guide.

This chapter covers the fundamentals of Java. You'll better understand the Java environments and benefits of Java. You'll also see how to define and run a Java class and learn about packages.

Learning About the Java Environment

The Java environment consists of understanding a number of technologies. In the following sections, we will go over the key terms and acronyms you need to know for the exam and then discuss what software you need to study for the exam.

Major Components of Java

The *Java Development Kit* (JDK) contains the minimum software you need to do Java development. Key pieces include the compiler (javac), which converts .java files to .class files, and the launcher java, which creates the virtual machine and executes the program. We will use both later in this chapter when running programs at the command line. The JDK also contains other tools including the archiver (jar) command, which can package files together, and the API documentation (javadoc) command for generating documentation.

The javac program generates instructions in a special format that the java command can run called *bytecode*. Then java launches the *Java Virtual Machine* (JVM) before running the code. The JVM knows how to run bytecode on the actual machine it is on. You can think of the JVM as a special magic box on your machine that knows how to run your .class file.

Where Did the JRE Go?

In previous versions of Java, you could download a Java Runtime Environment (JRE) instead of the full JDK. The JRE was a subset of the JDK that was used for running a program but could not compile one. It was literally a subset. In fact, if you looked inside the directory structure of a JDK in older versions of Java, you would see a folder named jre.

In Java 11, the JRE is no longer available as a stand-alone download or a subdirectory of the JDK. People can use the full JDK when running a Java program. Alternatively, developers can supply an executable that contains the required pieces that would have been in the JRE. The jlink command creates this executable.

While the JRE is not in scope for the exam, knowing what changed may help you eliminate wrong answers.

When writing a program, there are common pieces of functionality and algorithms that developers need. Luckily, we do not have to write each of these ourselves. Java comes with a large suite of *application programming interfaces* (APIs) that you can use. For example, there is a StringBuilder class to create a large String and a method in Collections to sort a list. When writing a program, it is helpful to look what pieces of your assignment can be accomplished by existing APIs.

You might have noticed that we said the JDK contains the minimum software you need. Many developers use an *integrated development environment* (IDE) to make writing and running code easier. While we do not recommend using one while studying for the exam, it is still good to know that they exist. Common Java IDEs include Eclipse, IntelliJ IDEA, and NetBeans.

Downloading a JDK

Every six months, the version number of Java gets incremented. Java 11 came out in September 2018. This means that Java 11 will not be the latest version when you download the JDK to study for the exam. However, you should still use Java 11 to study with since this is a Java 11 exam. The rules and behavior can change with later versions of Java. You wouldn't want to get a question wrong because you studied with a different version of Java!

Every three years, Oracle has a *long-term support* (LTS) release. Unlike non-LTS versions that are supported for only six months, LTS releases have patches and upgrades available for at least three years. Even after the next LTS, Java 17, comes out, be sure to use Java 11 to study for the Java 11 certification exam.

 Oracle changed the licensing model for its JDK. While this isn't on the exam, you can read more about the licensing changes and other JDKs from the links on our book's website:

http://www.selikoff.net/ocp11-1/

We recommend using the Oracle distribution of Java 11 to study for this exam. Note that Oracle's JDK is free for personal use as well as other scenarios. Alternatively, you can use OpenJDK, which is based on the same source code.

> The Oracle distribution requires you to register for an Oracle account if you don't already have one. This is the same Oracle account you will use to get your exam scores, so you will have to do this at some point anyway.

Identifying Benefits of Java

Java has some key benefits that you'll need to know for the exam.

Object Oriented   Java is an object-oriented language, which means all code is defined in classes, and most of those classes can be instantiated into objects. We'll discuss this more throughout the book. Many languages before Java were procedural, which meant there were routines or methods but no classes. Another common approach is functional programming. Java allows for functional programming within a class, but object-oriented is still the main organization of code.

Encapsulation   Java supports access modifiers to protect data from unintended access and modification. Most people consider encapsulation to be an aspect of object-oriented languages. Since the exam objectives call attention to it specifically, so do we. In fact, Chapter 7, "Methods and Encapsulation," covers it extensively.

Platform Independent   Java is an interpreted language that gets compiled to bytecode. A key benefit is that Java code gets compiled once rather than needing to be recompiled for different operating systems. This is known as "write once, run everywhere." The portability allows you to easily share pre-compiled pieces of software. When studying for the 1Z0-816 exam, you'll learn that it is possible to write code that throws an exception in some environments, but not others. For example, you might refer to a file in a specific directory. If you get asked about running Java on different operating systems on the 1Z0-815 exam, the answer is that the same class files run everywhere.

Robust   One of the major advantages of Java over C++ is that it prevents memory leaks. Java manages memory on its own and does garbage collection automatically. Bad memory management in C++ is a big source of errors in programs.

Simple   Java was intended to be simpler to understand than C++. In addition to eliminating pointers, it got rid of operator overloading. In C++, you could write a + b and have it mean almost anything.

Secure   Java code runs inside the JVM. This creates a sandbox that makes it hard for Java code to do evil things to the computer it is running on. On the 1Z0-816 exam, there is even an exam objective for security.

Multithreaded   Java is designed to allow multiple pieces of code to run at the same time. There are also many APIs to facilitate this task. You'll learn about some of them when studying for the 1Z0-816 exam.

Backward Compatibility   The Java language architects pay careful attention to making sure old programs will work with later versions of Java. While this doesn't always occur, changes that will break backward compatibility occur slowly and with notice. *Deprecation* is a technique to accomplish this where code is flagged to indicate it shouldn't be used. This lets developers know a different approach is preferred so they can start changing the code.

Understanding the Java Class Structure

In Java programs, classes are the basic building blocks. When defining a *class*, you describe all the parts and characteristics of one of those building blocks. To use most classes, you have to create objects. An *object* is a runtime instance of a class in memory. An object is often referred to as an *instance* since it represents a single representation of the class. All the various objects of all the different classes represent the state of your program. A *reference* is a variable that points to an object.

In the following sections, we'll look at fields, methods, and comments. We'll also explore the relationship between classes and files.

Fields and Methods

Java classes have two primary elements: *methods*, often called functions or procedures in other languages, and *fields*, more generally known as variables. Together these are called the *members* of the class. Variables hold the state of the program, and methods operate on that state. If the change is important to remember, a variable stores that change. That's all classes really do. It's the programmer who creates and arranges these elements in such a way that the resulting code is useful and, ideally, easy for other programmers to understand.

Other building blocks include interfaces, which you'll learn about in Chapter 9, "Advanced Class Design," and enums, which you'll learn about in detail when you study for the 1Z0-816 exam.

The simplest Java class you can write looks like this:

```
1: public class Animal {
2: }
```

Java calls a word with special meaning a *keyword*. Other classes can use this class since there is a public keyword on line 1. The class keyword indicates you're defining a class. Animal gives the name of the class. Granted, this isn't an interesting class, so let's add your first field.

```
1: public class Animal {
2:     String name;
3: }
```

The line numbers aren't part of the program; they're just there to make the code easier to talk about.

On line 2, we define a variable named name. We also define the type of that variable to be a String. A String is a value that we can put text into, such as "this is a string". String is also a class supplied with Java. Next you can add methods.

```java
1: public class Animal {
2:     String name;
3:     public String getName() {
4:         return name;
5:     }
6:     public void setName(String newName) {
7:         name = newName;
8:     }
9: }
```

On lines 3–5, you've defined your first method. A method is an operation that can be called. Again, public is used to signify that this method may be called from other classes. Next comes the return type—in this case, the method returns a String. On lines 6–8 is another method. This one has a special return type called *void*. The void keyword means that no value at all is returned. This method requires information be supplied to it from the calling method; this information is called a *parameter*. The setName() method has one parameter named newName, and it is of type String. This means the caller should pass in one String parameter and expect nothing to be returned.

Two pieces of the method are special. The method name and parameter types are called the *method signature*. In this example, can you identify the method name and parameters?

```java
public int numberVisitors(int month)
```

The method name is numberVisitors. There's one parameter named month, which is of type int, which is a numeric type.

The *method declaration* consists of additional information such as the return type. In this example, the return type is int.

Comments

Another common part of the code is called a *comment*. Because comments aren't executable code, you can place them in many places. Comments can make your code easier to read. You won't see many comments on the exam since the exam creators are trying to make the code harder to read. You will see them in this book as we explain the code. And we hope you use them in your own code. There are three types of comments in Java. The first is called a single-line comment:

```java
// comment until end of line
```

A single-line comment begins with two slashes. The compiler ignores anything you type after that on the same line. Next comes the multiple-line comment:

```
/* Multiple
 * line comment
 */
```

A multiple-line comment (also known as a multiline comment) includes anything starting from the symbol /* until the symbol */. People often type an asterisk (*) at the beginning of each line of a multiline comment to make it easier to read, but you don't have to. Finally, we have a Javadoc comment:

```
/**
 * Javadoc multiple-line comment
 * @author Jeanne and Scott
 */
```

This comment is similar to a multiline comment except it starts with /**. This special syntax tells the Javadoc tool to pay attention to the comment. Javadoc comments have a specific structure that the Javadoc tool knows how to read. You probably won't see a Javadoc comment on the exam. Just remember it exists so you can read up on it online when you start writing programs for others to use.

As a bit of practice, can you identify which type of comment each of the following six words is in? Is it a single-line or a multiline comment?

```
/*
 * // anteater
 */
// bear
// // cat
// /* dog */
/* elephant */
/*
 * /* ferret */
 */
```

Did you look closely? Some of these are tricky. Even though comments technically aren't on the exam, it is good to practice to look at code carefully.

OK, on to the answers. The comment containing anteater is in a multiline comment. Everything between /* and */ is part of a multiline comment—even if it includes a single-line comment within it! The comment containing bear is your basic single-line comment. The comments containing cat and dog are also single-line comments. Everything from // to the end of the line is part of the comment, even if it is another type of comment. The comment containing elephant is your basic multiline comment.

The line with ferret is interesting in that it doesn't compile. Everything from the first /* to the first */ is part of the comment, which means the compiler sees something like this:

```
/* */ */
```

We have a problem. There is an extra */. That's not valid syntax—a fact the compiler is happy to inform you about.

Classes vs. Files

Most of the time, each Java class is defined in its own `.java` file. It is usually `public`, which means any code can call it. Interestingly, Java does not require that the class be `public`. For example, this class is just fine:

```
1: class Animal {
2:    String name;
3: }
```

You can even put two classes in the same file. When you do so, at most one of the classes in the file is allowed to be public. That means a file containing the following is also fine:

```
1: public class Animal {
2:    private String name;
3: }
4: class Animal2 {
5: }
```

If you do have a public class, it needs to match the filename. The declaration `public class Animal2` would not compile in a file named `Animal.java`. In Chapter 7, we will discuss what access options are available other than `public`.

Writing a *main()* Method

A Java program begins execution with its `main()` method. A `main()` method is the gateway between the startup of a Java process, which is managed by the Java Virtual Machine (JVM), and the beginning of the programmer's code. The JVM calls on the underlying system to allocate memory and CPU time, access files, and so on. In this section, you will learn how to create a `main()` method, pass a parameter, and run a program both with and without the `javac` step.

Checking Your Version of Java

Before we go any further, please take this opportunity to ensure you have the right version of Java on your path.

```
javac -version
java -version
```

Both of these commands should include a version number that begins with the number 11.

Creating a *main()* Method

The main() method lets the JVM call our code. The simplest possible class with a main() method looks like this:

```
1: public class Zoo {
2:     public static void main(String[] args) {
3:
4:     }
5: }
```

This code doesn't do anything useful (or harmful). It has no instructions other than to declare the entry point. It does illustrate, in a sense, that what you can put in a main() method is arbitrary. Any legal Java code will do. In fact, the only reason we even need a class structure to start a Java program is because the language requires it. To compile and execute this code, type it into a file called Zoo.java and execute the following:

```
javac Zoo.java
java Zoo
```

If you don't get any error messages, you were successful. If you do get error messages, check that you've installed the Java 11 JDK, that you have added it to the PATH, and that you didn't make any typos in the example. If you have any of these problems and don't know what to do, post a question with the error message you received in the Beginning Java forum at CodeRanch (www.coderanch.com/forums/f-33/java).

To compile Java code, the file must have the extension .java. The name of the file must match the name of the class. The result is a file of bytecode by the same name, but with a .class filename extension. Remember that bytecode consists of instructions that the JVM knows how to execute. Notice that we must omit the .class extension to run Zoo.java.

The rules for what a Java code file contains, and in what order, are more detailed than what we have explained so far (there is more on this topic later in the chapter). To keep things simple for now, we'll follow this subset of the rules:

- Each file can contain only one public class.
- The filename must match the class name, including case, and have a .java extension.

Suppose we replace line 3 in Zoo.java with the following:

```
3: System.out.println("Welcome!");
```

When we compile and run the code again, we'll get the line of output that matches what's between the quotes. In other words, the program will output Welcome!.

Let's first review the words in the main() method's signature, one at a time. The keyword public is what's called an *access modifier*. It declares this method's level of exposure to potential callers in the program. Naturally, public means anyplace in the program. You'll learn more about access modifiers in Chapter 7.

The keyword *static* binds a method to its class so it can be called by just the class name, as in, for example, Zoo.main(). Java doesn't need to create an object to call the main()

method—which is good since you haven't learned about creating objects yet! In fact, the JVM does this, more or less, when loading the class name given to it. If a main() method isn't present in the class we name with the .java executable, the process will throw an error and terminate. Even if a main() method is present, Java will throw an exception if it isn't static. A nonstatic main() method might as well be invisible from the point of view of the JVM. You'll see static again in Chapter 7.

The keyword void represents the *return type*. A method that returns no data returns control to the caller silently. In general, it's good practice to use void for methods that change an object's state. In that sense, the main() method changes the program state from started to finished. We will explore return types in Chapter 7 as well. (Are you excited for Chapter 7 yet?)

Finally, we arrive at the main() method's parameter list, represented as an array of java.lang.String objects. In practice, you can write any of the following:

```
String[] args
String args[]
String... args;
```

The compiler accepts any of these. The variable name args hints that this list contains values that were read in (arguments) when the JVM started. The characters [] are brackets and represent an array. An array is a fixed-size list of items that are all of the same type. The characters ... are called varargs (variable argument lists). You will learn about String in Chapter 2, "Java Building Blocks." Arrays and varargs will follow in Chapter 5, "Core Java APIs."

While the previous example used the common args parameter name, you can use any valid variable name you like. The following three are also allowed:

```
String[] options
String options []
String... options;
```

Passing Parameters to a Java Program

Let's see how to send data to our program's main() method. First we modify the Zoo program to print out the first two arguments passed in:

```java
public class Zoo {
    public static void main(String[] args) {
        System.out.println(args[0]);
        System.out.println(args[1]);
    }
}
```

The code args[0] accesses the first element of the array. That's right: array indexes begin with 0 in Java. To run it, type this:

```
javac Zoo.java
java Zoo Bronx Zoo
```

The output is what you might expect:

```
Bronx
Zoo
```

The program correctly identifies the first two "words" as the arguments. Spaces are used to separate the arguments. If you want spaces inside an argument, you need to use quotes as in this example:

```
javac Zoo.java
java Zoo "San Diego" Zoo
```

Now we have a space in the output:

```
San Diego
Zoo
```

To see if you follow that, what do you think this outputs?

```
javac Zoo.java
java Zoo San Diego Zoo
```

The answer is two lines. The first one is San, and the second is Diego. Since the program doesn't read from args[2], the third element (Zoo) is ignored.

All command-line arguments are treated as String objects, even if they represent another data type like a number:

```
javac Zoo.java
java Zoo Zoo 2
```

No matter. You still get the values output as String values. In Chapter 2, you'll learn how to convert String values to numbers.

```
Zoo
2
```

Finally, what happens if you don't pass in enough arguments?

```
javac Zoo.java
java Zoo Zoo
```

Reading args[0] goes fine, and Zoo is printed out. Then Java panics. There's no second argument! What to do? Java prints out an exception telling you it has no idea what to do with this argument at position 1. (You'll learn about exceptions in Chapter 10, "Exceptions.")

```
Zoo
Exception in thread "main" java.lang.ArrayIndexOutOfBoundsException:
Index 1 out of bounds for length 1
    at Zoo.main(Zoo.java:4)
```

To review, the JDK contains a compiler. Java class files run on the JVM and therefore run on any machine with Java rather than just the machine or operating system they happened to have been compiled on.

Running a Program in One Line

Starting in Java 11, you can run a program without compiling it first—well, without typing the javac command that is. Let's create a new class:

```java
public class SingleFileZoo {
   public static void main(String[] args) {
      System.out.println("Single file: " + args[0]);
   }
}
```

We can run our SingleFileZoo example without actually having to compile it.

```
java SingleFileZoo.java Cleveland
```

Notice how this command passes the name of the Java file. When we compiled earlier, we wrote java Zoo. When running it as a one-liner, we write java SingleFileZoo.java. This is a key difference. After you first compiled with javac, you then passed the java command the name of the class. When running it directly, you pass the java command the name of the file. This feature is called launching *single-file source-code* programs. The name cleverly tells you that it can be used only if your program is one file. This means if your program has two .java files, you still need to use javac. By contrast, you cannot use this new feature for a single-file program with two classes in it. In fact, you can't refer to any .class files that didn't come with the JDK.

Now, suppose you have a class with invalid syntax in it. What do you think happens when we run java Learning.java?

```java
public class Learning {
   public static void main(String[] args) {
      UhOh;   // DOES NOT COMPILE
      System.out.println("This works!");
   }
}
```

Java is still a compiled language, which means the code is being compiled in memory and the java command can give you a compiler error.

```
Learning.java:3: error: not a statement
   UhOh; // DOES NOT COMPILE
   ^
1 error
error: compilation failed
```

Notice how we said "in memory." Even if the code compiles properly, no .class file is created. This faster way of launching single-file source-code programs will save you time as you study for the exam. You'll be writing a lot of tiny programs. Having to write one line to run them instead of two will be a relief! However, compiling your code in advance using javac will result in the program running faster, and you will definitely want to do that for real programs.

Table 1.1 highlights the differences between this new feature and the traditional way of compiling. You'll learn about imports in the next section, but for now, just know they are a way of using code written by others.

TABLE 1.1   Running programs

Full command	Single-file source-code command
javac HelloWorld.java java HelloWorld	java HelloWorld.java
Produces a class file	Fully in memory
For any program	For programs with one class
Can import code in any available Java library	Can only import code that came with the JDK

Understanding Package Declarations and Imports

Java comes with thousands of built-in classes, and there are countless more from developers like you. With all those classes, Java needs a way to organize them. It handles this in a way similar to a file cabinet. You put all your pieces of paper in folders. Java puts classes in *packages*. These are logical groupings for classes.

We wouldn't put you in front of a file cabinet and tell you to find a specific paper. Instead, we'd tell you which folder to look in. Java works the same way. It needs you to tell it which packages to look in to find code.

Suppose you try to compile this code:

```
public class ImportExample {
    public static void main(String[] args) {
        Random r = new Random();   // DOES NOT COMPILE
        System.out.println(r.nextInt(10));
    }
}
```

The Java compiler helpfully gives you an error that looks like this:

```
Random cannot be resolved to a type
```

This error could mean you made a typo in the name of the class. You double-check and discover that you didn't. The other cause of this error is omitting a needed *import* statement. Import statements tell Java which packages to look in for classes. Since you didn't tell Java where to look for Random, it has no clue.

Trying this again with the `import` allows you to compile.

```java
import java.util.Random;  // import tells us where to find Random
public class ImportExample {
    public static void main(String[] args) {
        Random r = new Random();
        System.out.println(r.nextInt(10));  // print a number 0-9
    }
}
```

Now the code runs; it prints out a random number between 0 and 9. Just like arrays, Java likes to begin counting with 0.

As you can see in the previous example, Java classes are grouped into packages. The `import` statement tells the compiler which package to look in to find a class. This is similar to how mailing a letter works. Imagine you are mailing a letter to 123 Main St., Apartment 9. The mail carrier first brings the letter to 123 Main St. Then she looks for the mailbox for apartment number 9. The address is like the package name in Java. The apartment number is like the class name in Java. Just as the mail carrier only looks at apartment numbers in the building, Java only looks for class names in the package.

Package names are hierarchical like the mail as well. The postal service starts with the top level, looking at your country first. You start reading a package name at the beginning too. If it begins with java or javax, this means it came with the JDK. If it starts with something else, it likely shows where it came from using the website name in reverse. For example, `com.amazon.javabook` tells us the code came from Amazon.com. After the website name, you can add whatever you want. For example, `com.amazon.java.my.name` also came from Amazon.com. Java calls more detailed packages *child packages*. The package `com.amazon.javabook` is a child package of `com.amazon`. You can tell because it's longer and thus more specific.

You'll see package names on the exam that don't follow this convention. Don't be surprised to see package names like `a.b.c`. The rule for package names is that they are mostly letters or numbers separated by periods (.). Technically, you're allowed a couple of other characters between the periods (.). The rules are the same as for variable names, which you'll see in Chapter 2. The exam may try to trick you with invalid variable names. Luckily, it doesn't try to trick you by giving invalid package names.

In the following sections, we'll look at imports with wildcards, naming conflicts with imports, how to create a package of your own, and how the exam formats code.

Wildcards

Classes in the same package are often imported together. You can use a shortcut to import all the classes in a package.

```java
import java.util.*;    // imports java.util.Random among other things
public class ImportExample {
   public static void main(String[] args) {
      Random r = new Random();
      System.out.println(r.nextInt(10));
   }
}
```

In this example, we imported java.util.Random and a pile of other classes. The * is a wildcard that matches all classes in the package. Every class in the java.util package is available to this program when Java compiles it. It doesn't import child packages, fields, or methods; it imports only classes. (There is a special type of import called the *static import* that imports other types, which you'll learn more about in Chapter 7.)

You might think that including so many classes slows down your program execution, but it doesn't. The compiler figures out what's actually needed. Which approach you choose is personal preference—or team preference if you are working with others on a team. Listing the classes used makes the code easier to read, especially for new programmers. Using the wildcard can shorten the import list. You'll see both approaches on the exam.

Redundant Imports

Wait a minute! We've been referring to System without an import, and Java found it just fine. There's one special package in the Java world called java.lang. This package is special in that it is automatically imported. You can type this package in an import statement, but you don't have to. In the following code, how many of the imports do you think are redundant?

```java
1:  import java.lang.System;
2:  import java.lang.*;
3:  import java.util.Random;
4:  import java.util.*;
5:  public class ImportExample {
6:     public static void main(String[] args) {
7:        Random r = new Random();
8:        System.out.println(r.nextInt(10));
9:     }
10: }
```

The answer is that three of the imports are redundant. Lines 1 and 2 are redundant because everything in java.lang is automatically considered to be imported. Line 4 is also redundant in this example because Random is already imported from java.util.Random. If line 3 wasn't present, java.util.* wouldn't be redundant, though, since it would cover importing Random.

Another case of redundancy involves importing a class that is in the same package as the class importing it. Java automatically looks in the current package for other classes.

Let's take a look at one more example to make sure you understand the edge cases for imports. For this example, Files and Paths are both in the package java.nio.file. You don't need to memorize this package for the 1Z0-815 exam (but you should know it for the 1Z0-816 exam). When testing your understanding of packages and imports, the 1Z0-815 exam may use packages you may never have seen before. The question will let you know which package the class is in if you need to know that in order to answer the question.

What imports do you think would work to get this code to compile?

```java
public class InputImports {
    public void read(Files files) {
        Paths.get("name");
    }
}
```

There are two possible answers. The shorter one is to use a wildcard to import both at the same time.

```java
import java.nio.file.*;
```

The other answer is to import both classes explicitly.

```java
import java.nio.file.Files;
import java.nio.file.Paths;
```

Now let's consider some imports that don't work.

```java
import java.nio.*;          // NO GOOD - a wildcard only matches
                           // class names, not "file.Files"

import java.nio.*.*;        // NO GOOD - you can only have one wildcard
                           // and it must be at the end

import java.nio.file.Paths.*; // NO GOOD - you cannot import methods
                           // only class names
```

Naming Conflicts

One of the reasons for using packages is so that class names don't have to be unique across all of Java. This means you'll sometimes want to import a class that can be found in multiple places. A common example of this is the Date class. Java provides implementations of java.util.Date and java.sql.Date. This is another example where you don't need to know the package names for the 1Z0-815 exam—they will be provided to you. What import could we use if we want the java.util.Date version?

```
public class Conflicts {
    Date date;
    // some more code
}
```

The answer should be easy by now. You can write either import java.util.*; or import java.util.Date;. The tricky cases come about when other imports are present.

```
import java.util.*;
import java.sql.*; // causes Date declaration to not compile
```

When the class is found in multiple packages, Java gives you a compiler error.

```
error: reference to Date is ambiguous
    Date date;
    ^
    both class java.sql.Date in java.sql and class java.util.Date in java.util match
```

In our example, the solution is easy—remove the import java.sql.Date that we don't need. But what do we do if we need a whole pile of other classes in the java.sql package?

```
import java.util.Date;
import java.sql.*;
```

Ah, now it works. If you explicitly import a class name, it takes precedence over any wildcards present. Java thinks, "The programmer really wants me to assume use of the java.util.Date class."

One more example. What does Java do with "ties" for precedence?

```
import java.util.Date;
import java.sql.Date;
```

Java is smart enough to detect that this code is no good. As a programmer, you've claimed to explicitly want the default to be both the java.util.Date and java.sql.Date implementations. Because there can't be two defaults, the compiler tells you the following:

```
error: reference to Date is ambiguous
    Date date;
    ^
    both class java.util.Date in java.util and class java.sql.Date in java.sql match
```

If You Really Need to Use Two Classes with the Same Name

Sometimes you really do want to use Date from two different packages. When this happens, you can pick one to use in the import and use the other's fully qualified class name [the package name, a period (.), and the class name] to specify that it's special. Here's an example:

```java
import java.util.Date;

public class Conflicts {
   Date date;
   java.sql.Date sqlDate;

}
```

Or you could have neither with an import and always use the fully qualified class name.

```java
public class Conflicts {
   java.util.Date date;
   java.sql.Date sqlDate;

}
```

Creating a New Package

Up to now, all the code we've written in this chapter has been in the *default package*. This is a special unnamed package that you should use only for throwaway code. You can tell the code is in the default package, because there's no package name. On the exam, you'll see the default package used a lot to save space in code listings. In real life, always name your packages to avoid naming conflicts and to allow others to reuse your code.

Now it's time to create a new package. The directory structure on your computer is related to the package name. In this section, just read along. We will cover how to compile and run the code in the next section.

Suppose we have these two classes in the C:\temp directory:

```java
package packagea;
public class ClassA {
}

package packageb;
import packagea.ClassA;
public class ClassB {
   public static void main(String[] args) {
```

```
    ClassA a;
    System.out.println("Got it");
  }
}
```

When you run a Java program, Java knows where to look for those package names. In this case, running from C:\temp works because both packagea and packageb are underneath it.

What do you think happens if you run java packageb/ClassB.java? This does not work. Remember that you can use the java command to run a file directly only when that program is contained within a single file. Here, ClassB.java relies on ClassA.

Compiling and Running Code with Packages

You'll learn Java much more easily by using the command line to compile and test your examples. Once you know the Java syntax well, you can switch to an IDE. But for the exam, your goal is to know details about the language and not have the IDE hide them for you.

Follow this example to make sure you know how to use the command line. If you have any problems following this procedure, post a question in the Beginning Java forum at CodeRanch (www.coderanch.com/forums/f-33/java). Describe what you tried and what the error said.

The first step is to create the two files from the previous section. Table 1.2 shows the expected fully qualified filenames and the command to get into the directory for the next steps.

TABLE 1.2   Setup procedure by operating system

Step	Windows	Mac/Linux
1. Create first class.	C:\temp\packagea\ClassA.java	/tmp/packagea/ClassA.java
2. Create second class.	C:\temp\packageb\ClassB.java	/tmp/packageb/ClassB.java
3. Go to directory.	cd C:\temp	cd /tmp

Now it is time to compile the code. Luckily, this is the same regardless of the operating system. To compile, type the following command:

```
javac packagea/ClassA.java packageb/ClassB.java
```

If this command doesn't work, you'll get an error message. Check your files carefully for typos against the provided files. If the command does work, two new files will be created: packagea/ClassA.class and packageb/ClassB.class.

Compiling with Wildcards

You can use an asterisk to specify that you'd like to include all Java files in a directory. This is convenient when you have a lot of files in a package. We can rewrite the previous javac command like this:

```
javac packagea/*.java packageb/*.java
```

However, you cannot use a wildcard to include subdirectories. If you were to write javac *.java, the code in the packages would not be picked up.

Now that your code has compiled, you can run it by typing the following command:

```
java packageb.ClassB
```

If it works, you'll see Got it printed. You might have noticed that we typed ClassB rather than ClassB.class. As discussed earlier, you don't pass the extension when running a program.

Figure 1.1 shows where the .class files were created in the directory structure.

FIGURE 1.1   Compiling with packages

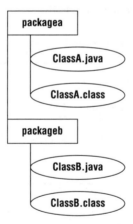

Using an Alternate Directory

By default, the javac command places the compiled classes in the same directory as the source code. It also provides an option to place the class files into a different directory. The -d option specifies this target directory.

Java options are case sensitive. This means you cannot pass -D instead of -d.

If you are following along, delete the ClassA.class and ClassB.class files that were created in the previous section.

Where do you think this command will create the file ClassA.class?

```
javac -d classes packagea/ClassA.java packageb/ClassB.java
```

The correct answer is classes/packagea/ClassA.class. The package structure is preserved under the requested target directory. Figure 1.2 shows this new structure.

FIGURE 1.2   Compiling with packages and directories

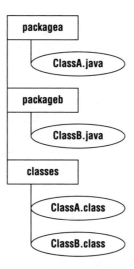

To run the program, you specify the classpath so Java knows where to find the classes. There are three options you can use. All three of these do the same thing:

```
java -cp classes packageb.ClassB
java -classpath classes packageb.ClassB
java --class-path classes packageb.ClassB
```

Notice that the last one requires two dashes (--), while the first two require one dash (-). If you have the wrong number of dashes, the program will not run.

Three Classpath Options

You might wonder why there are three options for the classpath. The -cp option is the short form. Developers frequently choose the short form because we are lazy typists. The -classpath and --class-path versions can be clearer to read but require more typing. The exam can use any of these, so be sure to learn all three.

Table 1.3 and Table 1.4 review the options you need to know for the exam. In Chapter 11, "Modules," you will learn additional options specific to modules.

TABLE 1.3   Options you need to know for the exam: `javac`

Option	Description

`-cp <classpath>`
`-classpath <classpath>`
`--class-path <classpath>`
	Location of classes needed to compile the program

`-d <dir>`	Directory to place generated class files

TABLE 1.4   Options you need to know for the exam: `java`

Option	Description

`-cp <classpath>`
`-classpath <classpath>`
`--class-path <classpath>`
	Location of classes needed to run the program

Compiling with JAR Files

Just like the `classes` directory in the previous example, you can also specify the location of the other files explicitly using a classpath. This technique is useful when the class files are located elsewhere or in special JAR files. A *Java archive* (JAR) file is like a zip file of mainly Java class files.

On Windows, you type the following:

```
java -cp ".;C:\temp\someOtherLocation;c:\temp\myJar.jar" myPackage.MyClass
```

And on macOS/Linux, you type this:

```
java -cp ".:/tmp/someOtherLocation:/tmp/myJar.jar" myPackage.MyClass
```

The period (.) indicates you want to include the current directory in the classpath. The rest of the command says to look for loose class files (or packages) in `someOtherLocation` and within `myJar.jar`. Windows uses semicolons (;) to separate parts of the classpath; other operating systems use colons.

Just like when you're compiling, you can use a wildcard (*) to match all the JARs in a directory. Here's an example:

```
java -cp "C:\temp\directoryWithJars\*" myPackage.MyClass
```

This command will add all the JARs to the classpath that are in directoryWithJars. It won't include any JARs in the classpath that are in a subdirectory of directoryWithJars.

Creating a JAR File

Some JARs are created by others, such as those downloaded from the Internet or created by a teammate. Alternatively, you can create a JAR file yourself. To do so, you use the jar command. The simplest commands create a jar containing the files in the current directory. You can use the short or long form for each option.

```
jar -cvf myNewFile.jar .
jar --create --verbose --file myNewFile.jar .
```

Alternatively, you can specify a directory instead of using the current directory.

```
jar -cvf myNewFile.jar -C dir .
```

There is no long form of the -C option. Table 1.5 lists the options you need to use the jar command to create a jar file. In Chapter 11, you will learn another option specific to modules.

TABLE 1.5   Options you need to know for the exam: jar

Option	Description
-c --create	Creates a new JAR file
-v --verbose	Prints details when working with JAR files
-f \<fileName> --file \<fileName>	JAR filename
-C \<directory>	Directory containing files to be used to create the JAR

Running a Program in One Line with Packages

You can use single-file source-code programs from within a package as long as they rely only on classes supplied by the JDK. This code meets the criteria.

```java
package singleFile;

import java.util.*;

public class Learning {
   private ArrayList list;
   public static void main(String[] args) {
      System.out.println("This works!");
   }
}
```

You can run either of these commands:

```java
java Learning.java           // from within the singleFile directory
java singleFile/Learning.java // from the directory above singleFile
```

Ordering Elements in a Class

Now that you've seen the most common parts of a class, let's take a look at the correct order to type them into a file. Comments can go anywhere in the code. Beyond that, you need to memorize the rules in Table 1.6.

TABLE 1.6   Order for declaring a class

Element	Example	Required?	Where does it go?
Package declaration	package abc;	No	First line in the file
Import statements	import java.util.*;	No	Immediately after the package (if present)
Class declaration	public class C	Yes	Immediately after the import (if any)
Field declarations	int value;	No	Any top-level element in a class
Method declarations	void method()	No	Any top-level element in a class

Let's look at a few examples to help you remember this. The first example contains one of each element:

```
package structure;        // package must be first non-comment
import java.util.*;       // import must come after package
public class Meerkat {  // then comes the class
   double weight;         // fields and methods can go in either order
   public double getWeight() {
      return weight; }
   double height;     // another field - they don't need to be together
}
```

So far, so good. This is a common pattern that you should be familiar with. How about this one?

```
/* header */
package structure;
// class Meerkat
public class Meerkat { }
```

Still good. We can put comments anywhere, and imports are optional. In the next example, we have a problem:

```
import java.util.*;
package structure;       // DOES NOT COMPILE
String name;             // DOES NOT COMPILE
public class Meerkat { } // DOES NOT COMPILE
```

There are two problems here. One is that the package and import statements are reversed. Though both are optional, package must come before import if present. The other issue is that a field attempts a declaration outside a class. This is not allowed. Fields and methods must be within a class.

Got all that? Think of the acronym PIC (picture): package, import, and class. Fields and methods are easier to remember because they merely have to be inside a class.

You need to know one more thing about class structure for the 1Z0-815 exam: multiple classes can be defined in the same file, but only one of them is allowed to be public. The public class matches the name of the file. For example, these two classes must be in a file named Meerkat.java:

```
1: public class Meerkat { }
2: class Paw { }
```

A file is also allowed to have neither class be public. As long as there isn't more than one public class in a file, it is okay.

Now you know how to create and arrange a class. Later chapters will show you how to create classes with more powerful operations.

Code Formatting on the Exam

Not all questions will include package declarations and imports. Don't worry about missing package statements or imports unless you are asked about them. The following are common cases where you don't need to check the imports:

- Code that begins with a class name
- Code that begins with a method declaration
- Code that begins with a code snippet that would normally be inside a class or method
- Code that has line numbers that don't begin with 1

This point is so important that we are going to reinforce it with an example. Does this code compile?

```
public class MissingImports {
    Date date;
    public void today() {}
}
```

Yes! The question was not about imports, so you have to assume that import java.util is present.

On the other hand, a question that asks you about packages, imports, or the correct order of elements in a class is giving you clues that the question is virtually guaranteed to be testing you on these topics! Also note that imports will be not removed to save space if the package statement is present. This is because imports go after the package statement.

You'll see code that doesn't have a main() method. When this happens, assume any necessary plumbing code like the main() method and class definition were written correctly. You're just being asked if the part of the code you're shown compiles when dropped into valid surrounding code.

Another thing the exam does to save space is to merge code on the same line. You should expect to see code like the following and to be asked whether it compiles. (You'll learn about ArrayList in Chapter 5—assume that part is good for now.)

```
6: public void getLetter(ArrayList list) {
7:     if (list.isEmpty()) { System.out.println("e");
8:     } else { System.out.println("n");
9: }  }
```

The answer here is that it does compile because the line break between the if statement and println() is not necessary. Additionally, you still get to assume the necessary class definition and imports are present. Now, what about this one? Does it compile?

```
1: public class LineNumbers {
2:     public void getLetter(ArrayList list) {
3:         if (list.isEmpty()) { System.out.println("e");
4:         } else { System.out.println("n");
5: }  } }
```

For this one, you would answer "Does not compile." Since the code begins with line 1, you don't get to assume that valid imports were provided earlier. The exam will let you know what package classes are in unless they're covered in the objectives. You'll be expected to know that `ArrayList` is in `java.util`—at least you will once you get to Chapter 5 of this book!

> Remember that extra whitespace doesn't matter in Java syntax. The exam may use varying amounts of whitespace to trick you.

Summary

The Java Development Kit (JDK) is used to do software development. It contains the compiler (`javac`), which turns source code into bytecode. It also contains the Java Virtual Machine (JVM) launcher (`java`), which launches the JVM and then calls the code. Application programming interfaces (APIs) are available to call reusable pieces of code.

Java code is object-oriented, meaning all code is defined in classes. Access modifiers allow classes to encapsulate data. Java is platform independent, compiling to bytecode. It is robust and simple by not providing pointers or operator overloading. Java is secure because it runs inside a virtual machine. Finally, the language facilitates multithreaded programming and strives for backward compatibility.

Java classes consist of members called fields and methods. An object is an instance of a Java class. There are three styles of comments: a single-line comment (`//`), a multiline comment (`/* */`), and a Javadoc comment (`/** */`).

Java begins program execution with a `main()` method. The most common signature for this method run from the command line is `public static void main(String[] args)`. Arguments are passed in after the class name, as in `java NameOfClass firstArgument`. Arguments are indexed starting with 0.

Java code is organized into folders called packages. To reference classes in other packages, you use an `import` statement. A wildcard ending an `import` statement means you want to `import` all classes in that package. It does not include packages that are inside that one. The package `java.lang` is special in that it does not need to be imported.

For some class elements, order matters within the file. The package statement comes first if present. Then come the `import` statements if present. Then comes the class declaration. Fields and methods are allowed to be in any order within the class.

Exam Essentials

Identify benefits of Java.   Benefits of Java include object-oriented design, encapsulation, platform independence, robustness, simplicity, security, multithreading, and backward compatibility.

Define common acronyms.   The JDK stands for Java Development Kit and contains the compiler and JVM launcher. The JVM stands for Java Virtual Machine, and it runs byte-code. API is an application programming interface, which is code that you can call.

Be able to write code using a *main()* method.   A main() method is usually written as `public static void main(String[] args)`. Arguments are referenced starting with `args[0]`. Accessing an argument that wasn't passed in will cause the code to throw an exception.

Understand the effect of using packages and imports.   Packages contain Java classes. Classes can be imported by class name or wildcard. Wildcards do not look at subdirectories. In the event of a conflict, class name imports take precedence.

Be able to recognize misplaced statements in a class.   Package and `import` statements are optional. If present, both go before the class declaration in that order. Fields and methods are also optional and are allowed in any order within the class declaration.

Review Questions

1. Which of the following are true statements? (Choose all that apply.)
   - **A.** Java allows operator overloading.
   - **B.** Java code compiled on Windows can run on Linux.
   - **C.** Java has pointers to specific locations in memory.
   - **D.** Java is a procedural language.
   - **E.** Java is an object-oriented language.
   - **F.** Java is a functional programming language.

2. Which of the following are true? (Choose all that apply.)
   - **A.** javac compiles a `.class` file into a `.java` file.
   - **B.** javac compiles a `.java` file into a `.bytecode` file.
   - **C.** javac compiles a `.java` file into a `.class` file.
   - **D.** java accepts the name of the class as a parameter.
   - **E.** java accepts the filename of the `.bytecode` file as a parameter.
   - **F.** java accepts the filename of the `.class` file as a parameter.

3. Which of the following are true if this command completes successfully? (Choose all that apply.)

   ```
   java MyProgram.java
   ```

   - **A.** A `.class` file is created.
   - **B.** MyProgram can reference classes in the package `com.sybex.book`.
   - **C.** MyProgram can reference classes in the package `java.lang`.
   - **D.** MyProgram can reference classes in the package `java.util`.
   - **E.** None of the above. The program needs to be run as `java MyProgram`.

4. Given the following classes, which of the following can independently replace `INSERT IMPORTS HERE` to make the code compile? (Choose all that apply.)

   ```
   package aquarium;
   public class Tank { }

   package aquarium.jellies;
   public class Jelly { }

   package visitor;
   INSERT IMPORTS HERE
   public class AquariumVisitor {
       public void admire(Jelly jelly) { } }
   ```

A. `import aquarium.*;`

B. `import aquarium.*.Jelly;`

C. `import aquarium.jellies.Jelly;`

D. `import aquarium.jellies.*;`

E. `import aquarium.jellies.Jelly.*;`

F. None of these can make the code compile.

5. Which are included in the JDK? (Choose all that apply.)

   A. javac

   B. Eclipse

   C. JVM

   D. javadoc

   E. jar

   F. None of the above

6. Given the following classes, what is the maximum number of imports that can be removed and have the code still compile?

```
package aquarium;
public class Water { }

package aquarium;
import java.lang.*;
import java.lang.System;
import aquarium.Water;
import aquarium.*;
public class Tank {
    public void print(Water water) {
        System.out.println(water); } }
```

   A. 0

   B. 1

   C. 2

   D. 3

   E. 4

   F. Does not compile

7. Given the following classes, which of the following snippets can independently be inserted in place of INSERT IMPORTS HERE and have the code compile? (Choose all that apply.)

```
package aquarium;
public class Water {
    boolean salty = false;
```

```
     }

     package aquarium.jellies;
     public class Water {
        boolean salty = true;
     }

     package employee;
     INSERT IMPORTS HERE
     public class WaterFiller {
        Water water;
     }
```

A. import aquarium.*;

B. import aquarium.Water;

import aquarium.jellies.*;

C. import aquarium.*;

import aquarium.jellies.Water;

D. import aquarium.*;

import aquarium.jellies.*;

E. import aquarium.Water;

import aquarium.jellies.Water;

F. None of these imports can make the code compile.

8. Given the following command, which of the following classes would be included for compilation? (Choose all that apply.)

```
javac *.java
```

A. Hyena.java

B. Warthog.java

C. land/Hyena.java

D. land/Warthog.java

E. Hyena.groovy

F. Warthog.groovy

9. Given the following class, which of the following calls print out Blue Jay? (Choose all that apply.)

```
public class BirdDisplay {
   public static void main(String[] name) {
      System.out.println(name[1]);
} }
```

A. `java BirdDisplay Sparrow Blue Jay`

B. `java BirdDisplay Sparrow "Blue Jay"`

C. `java BirdDisplay Blue Jay Sparrow`

D. `java BirdDisplay "Blue Jay" Sparrow`

E. `java BirdDisplay.class Sparrow "Blue Jay"`

F. `java BirdDisplay.class "Blue Jay" Sparrow`

10. Which of the following are legal entry point methods that can be run from the command line? (Choose all that apply.)

A. `private static void main(String[] args)`

B. `public static final main(String[] args)`

C. `public void main(String[] args)`

D. `public static void test(String[] args)`

E. `public static void main(String[] args)`

F. `public static main(String[] args)`

11. Which of the following are true statements about Java? (Choose all that apply.)

A. Bug-free code is guaranteed.

B. Deprecated features are never removed.

C. Multithreaded code is allowed.

D. Security is a design goal.

E. Sideways compatibility is a design goal.

12. Which options are valid on the `javac` command without considering module options? (Choose all that apply.)

A. `-c`

B. `-C`

C. `-cp`

D. `-CP`

E. `-d`

F. `-f`

G. `-p`

13. Which options are valid on the `java` command without considering module options? (Choose all that apply.)

A. `-c`

B. `-C`

C. `-cp`

D. `-d`

E. `-f`

F. `-p`

14. Which options are valid on the `jar` command without considering module options? (Choose all that apply.)

    A. `-c`

    B. `-C`

    C. `-cp`

    D. `-d`

    E. `-f`

    F. `-p`

15. What does the following code output when run as `java Duck Duck Goose`?

    ```
    public class Duck {
        public void main(String[] args) {
            for (int i = 1; i <= args.length; i++)
                System.out.println(args[i]);
    } }
    ```

    A. `Duck Goose`

    B. `Duck ArrayIndexOutOfBoundsException`

    C. `Goose`

    D. `Goose ArrayIndexOutOfBoundsException`

    E. None of the above

16. Suppose we have the following class in the file `/my/directory/named/A/Bird.java`. Which of the answer options replaces `INSERT CODE HERE` when added independently if we compile from `/my/directory`? (Choose all that apply.)

    ```
    INSERT CODE HERE
    public class Bird { }
    ```

    A. `package my.directory.named.a;`

    B. `package my.directory.named.A;`

    C. `package named.a;`

    D. `package named.A;`

    E. `package a;`

    F. `package A;`

17. Which of the following are true? (Choose all that apply.)

    ```
    public class Bunny {
        public static void main(String[] x) {
            Bunny bun = new Bunny();
    } }
    ```

    A. Bunny is a class.

    B. bun is a class.

    C. main is a class.

    D. Bunny is a reference to an object.

    E. bun is a reference to an object.

    F. main is a reference to an object.

    G. The main() method doesn't run because the parameter name is incorrect.

18. Which answer options represent the order in which the following statements can be assembled into a program that will compile successfully? (Choose all that apply.)

```
X: class Rabbit {}
Y: import java.util.*;
Z: package animals;
```

    A. X, Y, Z

    B. Y, Z, X

    C. Z, Y, X

    D. Y, X

    E. Z, X

    F. X, Z

19. Which are not available for download from Oracle for Java 11? (Choose all that apply.)

    A. JDK

    B. JRE

    C. Eclipse

    D. All of these are available from Oracle.

20. Which are valid ways to specify the classpath when compiling? (Choose all that apply.)

    A. -cp

    B. -classpath

    C. --classpath

    D. -class-path

    E. --class-path

Chapter

2

Java Building Blocks

OCP EXAM OBJECTIVES COVERED IN THIS CHAPTER:

✓ **Working With Java Primitive Data Types and String APIs**

- ▪ Declare and initialize variables (including casting and promoting primitive data types)

- ▪ Identify the scope of variables

- ▪ Use local variable type inference

✓ **Describing and Using Objects and Classes**

- ▪ Declare and instantiate Java objects, and explain objects' lifecycles (including creation, dereferencing by reassignment, and garbage collection)

- ▪ Read or write to object fields

As the old saying goes, you have to learn how to walk before you can run. Likewise, you have to learn the basics of Java before you can build complex programs. In this chapter, we'll be presenting the basic structure of Java classes, variables, and data types, along with the aspects of each that you need to know for the exam. For example, you might use Java every day but be unaware you cannot create a variable called 3dMap or this. The exam expects you to know and understand the rules behind these principles. While most of this chapter should be review, there may be aspects of the Java language that are new to you since they don't come up in practical use often.

Creating Objects

Our programs wouldn't be able to do anything useful if we didn't have the ability to create new objects. Remember from Chapter 1, "Welcome to Java," that an object is an instance of a class. In the following sections, we'll look at constructors, object fields, instance initializers, and the order in which values are initialized.

Calling Constructors

To create an instance of a class, all you have to do is write new before the class name and add parentheses after it. Here's an example:

```
Park p = new Park();
```

First you declare the type that you'll be creating (Park) and give the variable a name (p). This gives Java a place to store a reference to the object. Then you write new Park() to actually create the object.

Park() looks like a method since it is followed by parentheses. It's called a *constructor*, which is a special type of method that creates a new object. Now it's time to define a constructor of your own:

```java
public class Chick {
    public Chick() {
        System.out.println("in constructor");
    }
}
```

There are two key points to note about the constructor: the name of the constructor matches the name of the class, and there's no return type. You'll likely see a method like this on the exam:

```
public class Chick {
   public void Chick() { }  // NOT A CONSTRUCTOR
}
```

When you see a method name beginning with a capital letter and having a return type, pay special attention to it. It is *not* a constructor since there's a return type. It's a regular method that does compile but will not be called when you write new Chick().

The purpose of a constructor is to initialize fields, although you can put any code in there. Another way to initialize fields is to do so directly on the line on which they're declared. This example shows both approaches:

```
public class Chicken {
   int numEggs = 12;  // initialize on line
   String name;
   public Chicken() {
      name = "Duke";  // initialize in constructor
   }
}
```

For most classes, you don't have to code a constructor—the compiler will supply a "do nothing" default constructor for you. There are some scenarios that do require you declare a constructor. You'll learn all about them in Chapter 8, "Class Design."

Some classes provide built-in methods that allow you to create new instances without using a constructor or the new keyword. For example, in Chapter 5, "Core Java APIs," you'll create instances of Integer using the valueOf() method. Methods like this will often use new with a constructor in their method definition. For the exam, remember that anytime a constructor is used, the new keyword is required.

Reading and Writing Member Fields

It's possible to read and write instance variables directly from the caller. In this example, a mother swan lays eggs:

```
public class Swan {
   int numberEggs;                            // instance variable
   public static void main(String[] args) {
      Swan mother = new Swan();
      mother.numberEggs = 1;                  // set variable
```

```
        System.out.println(mother.numberEggs);  // read variable
    }
}
```

The "caller" in this case is the main() method, which could be in the same class or in another class. Reading a variable is known as *getting* it. The class gets numberEggs directly to print it out. Writing to a variable is known as *setting* it. This class sets numberEggs to 1.

In Chapter 7, "Methods and Encapsulation," you'll learn how to use encapsulation to protect the Swan class from having someone set a negative number of eggs.

You can even read values of already initialized fields on a line initializing a new field:

```
1: public class Name {
2:     String first = "Theodore";
3:     String last = "Moose";
4:     String full = first + last;
5: }
```

Lines 2 and 3 both write to fields. Line 4 both reads and writes data. It reads the fields first and last. It then writes the field full.

Executing Instance Initializer Blocks

When you learned about methods, you saw braces ({}). The code between the braces (sometimes called "inside the braces") is called a *code block*. Anywhere you see braces is a code block.

Sometimes code blocks are inside a method. These are run when the method is called. Other times, code blocks appear outside a method. These are called *instance initializers*. In Chapter 7, you'll learn how to use a static initializer.

How many blocks do you see in the following example? How many instance initializers do you see?

```
1: public class Bird {
2:     public static void main(String[] args) {
3:         { System.out.println("Feathers"); }
4:     }
5:     { System.out.println("Snowy"); }
6: }
```

There are four code blocks in this example: a class definition, a method declaration, an inner block, and an instance initializer. Counting code blocks is easy: you just count the number of pairs of braces. If there aren't the same number of open ({) and close (}) braces or they aren't defined in the proper order, the code doesn't compile. For example, you cannot use a closed brace (}) if there's no corresponding open brace ({) that it matches written earlier in the code. In programming, this is referred to as the *balanced parentheses problem*, and it often comes up in job interview questions.

When you're counting instance initializers, keep in mind that they cannot exist inside of a method. Line 5 is an instance initializer, with its braces outside a method. On the other hand, line 3 is not an instance initializer, as only called when the main() method is executed. There is one additional set of braces on lines 1 and 6 that constitute the class declaration.

Following Order of Initialization

When writing code that initializes fields in multiple places, you have to keep track of the order of initialization. This is simply the order in which different methods, constructors, or blocks are called when an instance of the class is created. We'll add some more rules to the order of initialization in Chapter 8. In the meantime, you need to remember:

- Fields and instance initializer blocks are run in the order in which they appear in the file.
- The constructor runs after all fields and instance initializer blocks have run.

Let's look at an example:

```
1:  public class Chick {
2:      private String name = "Fluffy";
3:      { System.out.println("setting field"); }
4:      public Chick() {
5:          name = "Tiny";
6:          System.out.println("setting constructor");
7:      }
8:      public static void main(String[] args) {
9:          Chick chick = new Chick();
10:         System.out.println(chick.name); } }
```

Running this example prints this:

```
setting field
setting constructor
Tiny
```

Let's look at what's happening here. We start with the main() method because that's where Java starts execution. On line 9, we call the constructor of Chick. Java creates a new object. First it initializes name to "Fluffy" on line 2. Next it executes the println() statement in the instance initializer on line 3. Once all the fields and instance initializers have run, Java returns to the constructor. Line 5 changes the value of name to "Tiny", and line 6 prints another statement. At this point, the constructor is done, and then the execution goes back to the println() statement on line 10.

Order matters for the fields and blocks of code. You can't refer to a variable before it has been defined:

```
{ System.out.println(name); }  // DOES NOT COMPILE
private String name = "Fluffy";
```

You should expect to see a question about initialization on the exam. Let's try one more. What do you think this code prints out?

```
public class Egg {
   public Egg() {
      number = 5;
   }
   public static void main(String[] args) {
      Egg egg = new Egg();
      System.out.println(egg.number);
   }
   private int number = 3;
   { number = 4; } }
```

If you answered 5, you got it right. Fields and blocks are run first in order, setting number to 3 and then 4. Then the constructor runs, setting number to 5. You will see a lot more of rules and examples covering order of initialization in Chapter 8.

Understanding Data Types

Java applications contain two types of data: primitive types and reference types. In this section, we'll discuss the differences between a primitive type and a reference type.

Using Primitive Types

Java has eight built-in data types, referred to as the Java *primitive types*. These eight data types represent the building blocks for Java objects, because all Java objects are just a complex collection of these primitive data types. That said, a primitive is not an object in Java nor does it represent an object. A primitive is just a single value in memory, such as a number or character.

The Primitive Types

The exam assumes you are well versed in the eight primitive data types, their relative sizes, and what can be stored in them. Table 2.1 shows the Java primitive types together with their size in bits and the range of values that each holds.

TABLE 2.1   Primitive types

Keyword	Type	Example
boolean	true or false	true
byte	8-bit integral value	123
short	16-bit integral value	123
int	32-bit integral value	123
long	64-bit integral value	123L
float	32-bit floating-point value	123.45f
double	64-bit floating-point value	123.456
char	16-bit Unicode value	'a'

Is String a Primitive?

No, it is not. That said, String is often mistaken for a ninth primitive because Java includes built-in support for String literals and operators. You'll learn more about String in Chapter 5, but for now just remember they are objects, not primitives.

There's a lot of information in Table 2.1. Let's look at some key points:

- The float and double types are used for floating-point (decimal) values.
- A float requires the letter f following the number so Java knows it is a float.
- The byte, short, int, and long types are used for numbers without decimal points. In mathematics, these are all referred to as integral values, but in Java, int and Integer refer to specific types.
- Each numeric type uses twice as many bits as the smaller similar type. For example, short uses twice as many bits as byte does.
- All of the numeric types are signed in Java. This means that they reserve one of their bits to cover a negative range. For example, byte ranges from -128 to 127. You might be surprised that the range is not -128 to 128. Don't forget, 0 needs to be accounted for too in the range.

You won't be asked about the exact sizes of most of these types, although you should know that a byte can hold a value from -128 to 127.

Real World Scenario

Signed and Unsigned: *short* and *char*

For the exam, you should be aware that short and char are closely related, as both are stored as integral types with the same 16-bit length. The primary difference is that short is *signed*, which means it splits its range across the positive and negative integers. Alternatively, char is *unsigned*, which means range is strictly positive including 0. Therefore, char can hold a higher positive numeric value than short, but cannot hold any negative numbers.

The compiler allows them to be used interchangeably in some cases, as shown here:

```
short bird = 'd';
char mammal = (short)83;
```

Printing each variable displays the value associated with their type.

```
System.out.println(bird);   // Prints 100
System.out.println(mammal); // Prints S
```

This usage is not without restriction, though. If you try to set a value outside the range of short or char, the compiler will report an error.

```
short reptile = 65535;  // DOES NOT COMPILE
char fish = (short)-1;  // DOES NOT COMPILE
```

Both of these examples would compile if their data types were swapped because the values would then be within range for their type. You'll learn more about casting in Chapter 3, "Operators."

So you aren't stuck memorizing data type ranges, let's look at how Java derives it from the number of bits. A byte is 8 bits. A bit has two possible values. (These are basic computer science definitions that you should memorize.) 2^8 is $2 \times 2 = 4 \times 2 = 8 \times 2 = 16 \times 2 = 32 \times 2 = 64 \times 2 = 128 \times 2 = 256$. Since 0 needs to be included in the range, Java takes it away from the positive side. Or if you don't like math, you can just memorize it.

Floating-Point Numbers and Scientific Notation

While integer values like short and int are relatively easy to calculate the range for, floating-point values like double and float are decidedly not. In most computer systems, floating-point numbers are stored in scientific notation. This means the numbers are stored as two numbers, a and b, of the form $a \times 10^b$.

This notation allows much larger values to be stored, at the cost of accuracy. For example, you can store a value of 3×10^{200} in a double, which would require a lot more than 8 bytes if every digit were stored without scientific notation (84 bytes in case you were wondering). To accomplish this, you only store the first dozen or so digits of the number. The name *scientific notation* comes from science, where often only the first few significant digits are required for a calculation.

Don't worry, for the exam you are not required to know scientific notation or how floating-point values are stored.

The number of bits is used by Java when it figures out how much memory to reserve for your variable. For example, Java allocates 32 bits if you write this:

```
int num;
```

Writing Literals

There are a few more things you should know about numeric primitives. When a number is present in the code, it is called a *literal*. By default, Java assumes you are defining an int value with a numeric literal. In the following example, the number listed is bigger than what fits in an int. Remember, you aren't expected to memorize the maximum value for an int. The exam will include it in the question if it comes up.

```
long max = 3123456789;  // DOES NOT COMPILE
```

Java complains the number is out of range. And it is—for an int. However, we don't have an int. The solution is to add the character L to the number:

```
long max = 3123456789L;  // now Java knows it is a long
```

Alternatively, you could add a lowercase l to the number. But please use the uppercase L. The lowercase l looks like the number 1.

Another way to specify numbers is to change the "base." When you learned how to count, you studied the digits 0–9. This numbering system is called *base 10* since there are 10 numbers. It is also known as the *decimal number system*. Java allows you to specify digits in several other formats:

- Octal (digits 0–7), which uses the number 0 as a prefix—for example, 017
- Hexadecimal (digits 0–9 and letters A–F/a–f), which uses 0x or 0X as a prefix—for example, 0xFF, 0xff, 0XFf. Hexadecimal is case insensitive so all of these examples mean the same value.
- Binary (digits 0–1), which uses the number 0 followed by b or B as a prefix—for example, 0b10, 0B10

You won't need to convert between number systems on the exam. You'll have to recognize valid literal values that can be assigned to numbers.

Literals and the Underscore Character

The last thing you need to know about numeric literals is that you can have underscores in numbers to make them easier to read:

```
int million1 = 1000000;
int million2 = 1_000_000;
```

We'd rather be reading the latter one because the zeros don't run together. You can add underscores anywhere except at the beginning of a literal, the end of a literal, right before a decimal point, or right after a decimal point. You can even place multiple underscore characters next to each other, although we don't recommend it.

Let's look at a few examples:

```
double notAtStart = _1000.00;           // DOES NOT COMPILE
double notAtEnd = 1000.00_;             // DOES NOT COMPILE
double notByDecimal = 1000_.00;         // DOES NOT COMPILE
double annoyingButLegal = 1_00_0.0_0;   // Ugly, but compiles
double reallyUgly = 1_____2;       // Also compiles
```

Using Reference Types

A *reference type* refers to an object (an instance of a class). Unlike primitive types that hold their values in the memory where the variable is allocated, references do not hold the value of the object they refer to. Instead, a reference "points" to an object by storing the memory address where the object is located, a concept referred to as a *pointer*. Unlike other languages, Java does not allow you to learn what the physical memory address is. You can only use the reference to refer to the object.

Let's take a look at some examples that declare and initialize reference types. Suppose we declare a reference of type java.util.Date and a reference of type String:

```
java.util.Date today;
String greeting;
```

The today variable is a reference of type Date and can only point to a Date object. The greeting variable is a reference that can only point to a String object. A value is assigned to a reference in one of two ways:

- A reference can be assigned to another object of the same or compatible type.
- A reference can be assigned to a new object using the new keyword.

For example, the following statements assign these references to new objects:

```
today = new java.util.Date();
greeting = new String("How are you?");
```

The today reference now points to a new Date object in memory, and today can be used to access the various fields and methods of this Date object. Similarly, the greeting reference points to a new String object, "How are you?". The String and Date objects do not have names and can be accessed only via their corresponding reference. Figure 2.1 shows how the reference types appear in memory.

FIGURE 2.1   An object in memory can be accessed only via a reference.

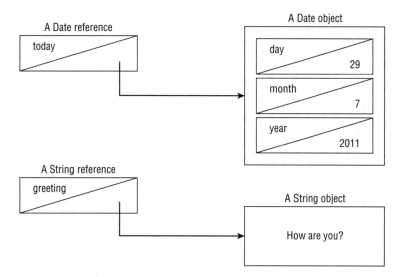

Distinguishing between Primitives and Reference Types

There are a few important differences you should know between primitives and reference types. First, reference types can be assigned null, which means they do not currently refer to an object. Primitive types will give you a compiler error if you attempt to assign them null. In this example, value cannot point to null because it is of type int:

```
int value = null;   // DOES NOT COMPILE
String s = null;
```

But what if you don't know the value of an int and want to assign it to null? In that case, you should use a numeric wrapper class, such as Integer, instead of int. Wrapper classes will be covered in Chapter 5.

Next, reference types can be used to call methods, assuming the reference is not null. Primitives do not have methods declared on them. In this example, we can call a method on reference since it is of a reference type. You can tell length is a method because it has () after it. See if you can understand why the following snippet does not compile:

```
4: String reference = "hello";
5: int len = reference.length();
6: int bad = len.length(); // DOES NOT COMPILE
```

Line 6 is gibberish. No methods exist on len because it is an int primitive. Primitives do not have methods. Remember, a String is not a primitive, so you can call methods like length() on a String reference, as we did on line 5.

Finally, notice that all the primitive types have lowercase type names. All classes that come with Java begin with uppercase. Although not required, it is a standard practice, and you should follow this convention for classes you create as well.

Declaring Variables

You've seen some variables already. A *variable* is a name for a piece of memory that stores data. When you declare a variable, you need to state the variable type along with giving it a name. For example, the following code declares two variables. One is named zooName and is of type String. The other is named numberAnimals and is of type int.

```
String zooName;
int numberAnimals;
```

Now that we've declared a variable, we can give it a value. This is called *initializing* a variable. To initialize a variable, you just type the variable name followed by an equal sign, followed by the desired value:

```
zooName = "The Best Zoo";
numberAnimals = 100;
```

Since you often want to initialize a variable right away, you can do so in the same statement as the declaration. For example, here we merge the previous declarations and initializations into more concise code:

```
String zooName = "The Best Zoo";
int numberAnimals = 100;
```

In the following sections, we'll look at how to properly define variables in one or multiple lines.

Identifying Identifiers

It probably comes as no surprise to you that Java has precise rules about identifier names. An *identifier* is the name of a variable, method, class, interface, or package. Luckily, the rules for identifiers for variables apply to all of the other types that you are free to name.

There are only four rules to remember for legal identifiers:

- Identifiers must begin with a letter, a $ symbol, or a _ symbol.
- Identifiers can include numbers but not start with them.

- Since Java 9, a single underscore _ is not allowed as an identifier.
- You cannot use the same name as a Java reserved word. A *reserved word* is special word that Java has held aside so that you are not allowed to use it. Remember that Java is case sensitive, so you can use versions of the keywords that only differ in case. Please don't, though.

Don't worry—you won't need to memorize the full list of reserved words. The exam will only ask you about ones that are commonly used, such as class and for. Table 2.2 lists all of the reserved words in Java.

TABLE 2.2 Reserved words

abstract	assert	boolean	break	byte
case	catch	char	class	const*
continue	default	do	double	else
enum	extends	false**	final	finally
float	for	goto*	if	implements
import	instanceof	int	interface	long
native	new	null**	package	private
protected	public	return	Short	static
strictfp	super	switch	synchronized	this
throw	throws	transient	true**	try
void	volatile	while	_ (*underscore*)	

* The reserved words const and goto aren't actually used in Java. They are reserved so that people coming from other programming languages don't use them by accident—and in theory, in case Java wants to use them one day.
** true/false/null are not actually reserved words, but literal values. Since they cannot be used as identifier names, we include them in this table.

Prepare to be tested on these rules. The following examples are legal:

```
long okidentifier;
float $OK2Identifier;
boolean _alsoOK1d3ntifi3r;
char __SStillOkbutKnotsonice$;
```

These examples are not legal:

```
int 3DPointClass;      // identifiers cannot begin with a number
byte hollywood@vine;   // @ is not a letter, digit, $ or _
String *$coffee;       // * is not a letter, digit, $ or _
double public;         // public is a reserved word
short _;               // a single underscore is not allowed
```

Style: camelCase

Although you can do crazy things with identifier names, please don't. Java has conventions so that code is readable and consistent. This consistency includes *camel case*, often written as camelCase for emphasis. In camelCase, the first letter of each word is capitalized.

The camelCase format makes identifiers easier to read. Which would you rather read: `Thisismyclass` name or `ThisIsMyClass` name? The exam will mostly use common conventions for identifiers, but not always. When you see a nonstandard identifier, be sure to check if it is legal. If it's not, you get to mark the answer "does not compile" and skip analyzing everything else in the question.

 Real World Scenario

Identifiers in the Real World

Most Java developers follow these conventions for identifier names:

- Method and variable names are written in camelCase with the first letter being lowercase.

- Class and interface names are written in camelCase with the first letter being uppercase. Also, don't start any class name with $, as the compiler uses this symbol for some files.

Also, know that valid letters in Java are not just characters in the English alphabet. Java supports the Unicode character set, so there are thousands of characters that can start a legal Java identifier. Some are non-Arabic numerals that may appear after the first character in a legal identifier. Luckily, you don't have to worry about memorizing those for the exam. If you are in a country that doesn't use the English alphabet, this is useful to know for a job.

Style: snake_case

Another style you might see both on the exam and in the real world or in other languages is called *snake case*, often written as snake_case for emphasis. It simply uses an underscore (_) to separate words, often entirely in lowercase. The previous example would be written as `this_is_my_class` name in snake_case.

While both camelCase and snake_case are perfectly valid syntax in Java, the development community functions better when everyone adopts the same style convention. With that in mind, Oracle (and Sun before it) recommends everyone use camelCase for class and variable names. There are some exceptions, though. Constant `static final` values are often written in snake_case, such as `THIS_IS_A_CONSTANT`. In addition, enum values tend to be written with snake_case, as in `Color.RED`, `Color.DARK_GRAY`, and so on.

Declaring Multiple Variables

You can also declare and initialize multiple variables in the same statement. How many variables do you think are declared and initialized in the following example?

```
void sandFence() {
    String s1, s2;
    String s3 = "yes", s4 = "no";
}
```

Four `String` variables were declared: s1, s2, s3, and s4. You can declare many variables in the same declaration as long as they are all of the same type. You can also initialize any or all of those values inline. In the previous example, we have two initialized variables: s3 and s4. The other two variables remain declared but not yet initialized.

This is where it gets tricky. Pay attention to tricky things! The exam will attempt to trick you. Again, how many variables do you think are declared and initialized in the following code?

```
void paintFence() {
    int i1, i2, i3 = 0;
}
```

As you should expect, three variables were declared: i1, i2, and i3. However, only one of those values was initialized: i3. The other two remain declared but not yet initialized. That's the trick. Each snippet separated by a comma is a little declaration of its own. The initialization of i3 only applies to i3. It doesn't have anything to do with i1 or i2 despite being in the same statement. As you will see in the next section, you can't actually use i1 or i2 until they have been initialized.

Another way the exam could try to trick you is to show you code like this line:

```
int num, String value; // DOES NOT COMPILE
```

This code doesn't compile because it tries to declare multiple variables of *different* types in the same statement. The shortcut to declare multiple variables in the same statement is legal only when they share a type.

Legal, valid, and *compiles* are all synonyms in the Java exam world. We try to use all the terminology you could encounter on the exam.

To make sure you understand this, see if you can figure out which of the following are legal declarations:

```
4: boolean b1, b2;
5: String s1 = "1", s2;
6: double d1, double d2;
7: int i1; int i2;
8: int i3; i4;
```

The first statement on line 4 is legal. It declares two variables without initializing them. The second statement on line 5 is also legal. It declares two variables and initializes only one of them.

The third statement on line 6 is *not* legal. Java does not allow you to declare two different types in the same statement. Wait a minute! Variables d1 and d2 are the same type. They are both of type double. Although that's true, it still isn't allowed. If you want to declare multiple variables in the same statement, they must share the same type declaration and not repeat it. double d1, d2; would have been legal.

The fourth statement on line 7 is legal. Although int does appear twice, each one is in a separate statement. A semicolon (;) separates statements in Java. It just so happens there are two completely different statements on the same line. The fifth statement on line 8 is *not* legal. Again, we have two completely different statements on the same line. The second one on line 8 is not a valid declaration because it omits the type. When you see an oddly placed semicolon on the exam, pretend the code is on separate lines and think about whether the code compiles that way. In this case, the last two lines of code could be rewritten as follows:

```
int i1;
int i2;
int i3;
i4;
```

Looking at the last line on its own, you can easily see that the declaration is invalid. And yes, the exam really does cram multiple statements onto the same line—partly to try to trick you and partly to fit more code on the screen. In the real world, please limit yourself to one declaration per statement and line. Your teammates will thank you for the readable code.

Initializing Variables

Before you can use a variable, it needs a value. Some types of variables get this value set automatically, and others require the programmer to specify it. In the following sections, we'll look at the differences between the defaults for local, instance, and class variables.

Creating Local Variables

A *local variable* is a variable defined within a constructor, method, or initializer block. For simplicity, we will focus primarily on local variables within methods in this section, although the rules for the others are the same.

Local variables do not have a default value and must be initialized before use. Furthermore, the compiler will report an error if you try to read an uninitialized value. For example, the following code generates a compiler error:

```
4: public int notValid() {
5:     int y = 10;
6:     int x;
7:     int reply = x + y; // DOES NOT COMPILE
8:     return reply;
9: }
```

The y variable is initialized to 10. However, because x is not initialized before it is used in the expression on line 7, the compiler generates the following error:

```
Test.java:7: variable x might not have been initialized
    int reply = x + y; // DOES NOT COMPILE
            ^
```

Until x is assigned a value, it cannot appear within an expression, and the compiler will gladly remind you of this rule. The compiler knows your code has control of what happens inside the method and can be expected to initialize values.

The compiler is smart enough to recognize variables that have been initialized after their declaration but before they are used. Here's an example:

```
public int valid() {
    int y = 10;
    int x; // x is declared here
    x = 3; // and initialized here
    int reply = x + y;
    return reply;
}
```

The compiler is also smart enough to recognize initializations that are more complex. In this example, there are two branches of code:

```
public void findAnswer(boolean check) {
    int answer;
    int otherAnswer;
    int onlyOneBranch;
    if (check) {
        onlyOneBranch = 1;
```

```
      answer = 1;
   } else {
      answer = 2;
   }
   System.out.println(answer);
   System.out.println(onlyOneBranch); // DOES NOT COMPILE
}
```

The answer variable is initialized in both branches of the if statement, so the compiler is perfectly happy. It knows that regardless of whether check is true or false, the value answer will be set to something before it is used. The otherAnswer variable is initialized but never used, but the compiler is equally as happy. Remember, the compiler is only concerned if you try to use uninitialized local variables; it doesn't mind the ones you never use.

The onlyOneBranch variable is initialized only if check happens to be true. The compiler knows there is the possibility for check to be false, resulting in uninitialized code, and gives a compiler error. You'll learn more about the if statement in Chapter 4, "Making Decisions."

> On the exam, be wary of any local variable that is declared but not initialized in a single line. This is a common place on the exam that could result in a "Does not compile" answer. As you saw in the previous examples, you are not required to initialize the variable on the same line it is defined, but be sure to check to make sure it's initialized before it's used on the exam.

Passing Constructor and Method Parameters

Variables passed to a constructor or method are called *constructor parameters* or *method parameters*, respectively. These parameters are local variables that have been pre-initialized. In other words, they are local variables that have been initialized before the method is called, by the caller. The rules for initializing constructor and method parameters are the same, so we'll focus primarily on method parameters.

In the previous example, check is a method parameter.

```
public void findAnswer(boolean check) {}
```

Take a look at the following method checkAnswer() in the same class:

```
public void checkAnswer() {
   boolean value;
   findAnswer(value);  // DOES NOT COMPILE
}
```

The call to findAnswer() does not compile because it tries to use a variable that is not initialized. While the caller of a method checkAnswer() needs to be concerned about the variable being initialized, once inside the method findAnswer(), we can assume the local variable has been initialized to some value.

Defining Instance and Class Variables

Variables that are not local variables are defined either as instance variables or as class variables. An *instance variable*, often called a field, is a value defined within a specific instance of an object. Let's say we have a Person class with an instance variable name of type String. Each instance of the class would have its own value for name, such as Elysia or Sarah. Two instances could have the same value for name, but changing the value for one does not modify the other.

On the other hand, a *class variable* is one that is defined on the class level and shared among all instances of the class. It can even be publicly accessible to classes outside the class without requiring an instance to use. In our previous Person example, a shared class variable could be used to represent the list of people at the zoo today. You can tell a variable is a class variable because it has the keyword static before it. You'll learn about this in Chapter 7. For now, just know that a variable is a class variable if it has the static keyword in its declaration.

Instance and class variables do not require you to initialize them. As soon as you declare these variables, they are given a default value. You'll need to memorize everything in Table 2.3 except the default value of char. To make this easier, remember that the compiler doesn't know what value to use and so wants the simplest value it can give the type: null for an object and 0/false for a primitive.

TABLE 2.3   Default initialization values by type

Variable type	Default initialization value
boolean	false
byte, short, int, long	0
float, double	0.0
char	'\u0000' (NUL)
All object references (everything else)	null

Introducing *var*

Starting in Java 10, you have the option of using the keyword var instead of the type for local variables under certain conditions. To use this feature, you just type var instead of the primitive or reference type. Here's an example:

```
public void whatTypeAmI() {
   var name = "Hello";
   var size = 7;
}
```

The formal name of this feature is *local variable type inference*. Let's take that apart. First comes *local variable*. This means just what it sounds like. You can only use this feature for local variables. The exam may try to trick you with code like this:

```
public class VarKeyword {
   var tricky = "Hello"; // DOES NOT COMPILE
}
```

Wait a minute! We just learned the difference between instance and local variables. The variable `tricky` is an instance variable. Local variable type inference works with local variables and not instance variables.

> In Chapter 4, you'll learn that var can be used in for loops, and as you'll see in Chapter 6, "Lambdas and Functional Interfaces," with some lambdas as well. In Chapter 10, "Exceptions," you'll also learn that var can be used with try-with-resources. All of these cases are still internal to a method and therefore consistent with what you learn in this chapter.

Type Inference of *var*

Now that you understand the local variable part, it is time to go on to what *type inference* means. The good news is that this also means what it sounds like. When you type var, you are instructing the compiler to determine the type for you. The compiler looks at the code on the line of the declaration and uses it to infer the type. Take a look at this example:

```
7:   public void reassignment() {
8:      var number = 7;
9:      number = 4;
10:     number = "five";  // DOES NOT COMPILE
11: }
```

On line 8, the compiler determines that we want an `int` variable. On line 9, we have no trouble assigning a different `int` to it. On line 10, Java has a problem. We've asked it to assign a `String` to an `int` variable. This is not allowed. It is equivalent to typing this:

```
int number = "five";
```

> If you know a language like JavaScript, you might be expecting var to mean a variable that can take on any type at runtime. In Java, var is still a specific type defined at compile time. It does not change type at runtime.

So, the type of var can't change at runtime, but what about the value? Take a look at the following code snippet:

```
var apples = (short)10;
apples = (byte)5;
apples = 1_000_000;  // DOES NOT COMPILE
```

The first line creates a var named apples with a type of short. It then assigns a byte of 5 to it, but did that change the data type of apples to byte? Nope! As you will learn in Chapter 3, the byte can be automatically promoted to a short, because a byte is small enough that it can fit inside of short. Therefore, the value stored on the second line is a short. In fact, let's rewrite the example showing what the compiler is really doing when it sees the var:

```
short apples = (short)10;
apples = (byte)5;
apples = 1_000_000;  // DOES NOT COMPILE
```

The last line does not compile, as one million is well beyond the limits of short. The compiler treats the value as an int and reports an error indicating it cannot be assigned to apples.

If you didn't follow that last example, don't worry, we'll be covering numeric promotion and casting in the next chapter. For now, you just need to know that the value for a var can change after it is declared but the type never does.

For simplicity when discussing var in the following sections, we are going to assume a variable declaration statement is completed in a single line. For example, you could insert a line break between the variable name and its initialization value, as in the following example:

```
7:  public void breakingDeclaration() {
8:      var silly
9:          = 1;
10: }
```

This example is valid and does compile, but we consider the declaration and initialization of silly to be happening on the same line.

Examples with *var*

Let's go through some more scenarios so the exam doesn't trick you on this topic! Do you think the following compiles?

```
3:  public void doesThisCompile(boolean check) {
4:      var question;
5:      question = 1;
6:      var answer;
7:      if (check) {
8:          answer = 2;
9:      } else {
10:         answer = 3;
11:     }
12:     System.out.println(answer);
13: }
```

The code does not compile. Remember that for local variable type inference, the compiler looks only at the line with the declaration. Since question and answer are not assigned values on the lines where they are defined, the compiler does not know what to make of them. For this reason, both lines 4 and 6 do not compile.

You might find that strange since both branches of the if/else do assign a value. Alas, it is not on the same line as the declaration, so it does not count for var. Contrast this behavior with what we saw a short while ago when we discussed branching and initializing a local variable in our findAnswer() method.

Now we know the initial value used to determine the type needs to be part of the same statement. Can you figure out why these two statements don't compile?

```
4: public void twoTypes() {
5:     int a, var b = 3;   // DOES NOT COMPILE
6:     var n = null;       // DOES NOT COMPILE
7: }
```

Line 5 wouldn't work even if you replaced var with a real type. All the types declared on a single line must be the same type and share the same declaration. We couldn't write int a, int v = 3; either. Likewise, this is not allowed:

```
5:     var a = 2, b = 3;  // DOES NOT COMPILE
```

In other words, Java does not allow var in multiple variable declarations.

Line 6 is a single line. The compiler is being asked to infer the type of null. This could be any reference type. The only choice the compiler could make is Object. However, that is almost certainly not what the author of the code intended. The designers of Java decided it would be better not to allow var for null than to have to guess at intent.

---

var and *null*

While a var cannot be initialized with a null value without a type, it can be assigned a null value after it is declared, provided that the underlying data type of the var is an object. Take a look at the following code snippet:

```
13: var n = "myData";
14: n = null;
15: var m = 4;
16: m = null;  // DOES NOT COMPILE
```

Line 14 compiles without issue because n is of type String, which is an object. On the other hand, line 16 does not compile since the type of m is a primitive int, which cannot be assigned a null value.

It might surprise you to learn that a var can be initialized to a null value if the type is specified. You'll learn about casting in Chapter 3, but the following does compile:

```
17: var o = (String)null;
```

Since the type is provided, the compiler can apply type inference and set the type of the var to be String.

Let's try another example. Do you see why this does not compile?

```java
public int addition(var a, var b) {  // DOES NOT COMPILE
   return a + b;
}
```

In this example, a and b are method parameters. These are not local variables. Be on the lookout for var used with constructors, method parameters, or instance variables. Using var in one of these places is a good exam trick to see if you are paying attention. Remember that var is only used for local variable type inference!

Time for two more examples. Do you think this is legal?

```java
package var;

public class Var {
   public void var() {
      var var = "var";
   }
   public void Var() {
      Var var = new Var();
   }
}
```

Believe it or not, this code does compile. Java is not case sensitive, so Var doesn't introduce any conflicts as a class name. Naming a local variable var is legal. Please don't write code that looks like this at your job! But understanding why it works will help get you ready for any tricky exam questions Oracle could throw at you!

There's one last rule you should be aware of. While var is not a reserved word and allowed to be used as an identifier, it is considered a reserved type name. A *reserved type name* means it cannot be used to define a type, such as a class, interface, or enum. For example, the following code snippet does not compile because of the class name:

```java
public class var {  // DOES NOT COMPILE
   public var() {
   }
}
```

 We're sure if the writers of Java had a time machine, they would likely go back and make var a reserved word in Java 1.0. They could have made var a reserved word starting in Java 10 or 11, but this would have broken older code where var was used as a variable name. For a large enough project, making var a reserved word could involve checking and recompiling millions of lines of code! On the other hand, since having a class or interface start with a lowercase letter is considered a bad practice prior to Java 11, they felt pretty safe marking it as a reserved type name.

It is often inappropriate to use var as the type for every local variable in your code. That just makes the code difficult to understand. If you are ever unsure of whether it is appropriate to use var, there are numerous style guides out there that can help. We recommend the one titled "Style Guidelines for Local Variable Type Inference in Java," which is available at the following location. This resource includes great style suggestions.

https://openjdk.java.net/projects/amber/LVTIstyle.html

Review of *var* Rules

We complete this section by summarizing all of the various rules for using var in your code. Here's a quick review of the var rules:

1. A var is used as a local variable in a constructor, method, or initializer block.

2. A var cannot be used in constructor parameters, method parameters, instance variables, or class variables.

3. A var is always initialized on the same line (or statement) where it is declared.

4. The value of a var can change, but the type cannot.

5. A var cannot be initialized with a null value without a type.

6. A var is not permitted in a multiple-variable declaration.

7. A var is a reserved type name but not a reserved word, meaning it can be used as an identifier except as a class, interface, or enum name.

That's a lot of rules, but we hope most are pretty straightforward. Since var is new to Java since the last exam, expect to see it used frequently on the exam. You'll also be seeing numerous ways var can be used throughout this book.

 Real World Scenario

var in the Real World

The var keyword is great for exam authors because it makes it easier to write tricky code. When you work on a real project, you want the code to be easy to read.

Once you start having code that looks like the following, it is time to consider using var:

```
PileOfPapersToFileInFilingCabinet pileOfPapersToFile =
   new PileOfPapersToFileInFilingCabinet();
```

You can see how shortening this would be an improvement without losing any information:

```
var pileOfPapersToFile = new PileOfPapersToFileInFilingCabinet();
```

Managing Variable Scope

You've learned that local variables are declared within a method. How many local variables do you see in this example?

```java
public void eat(int piecesOfCheese) {
    int bitesOfCheese = 1;
}
```

There are two local variables in this method. The bitesOfCheese variable is declared inside the method. The piecesOfCheese variable is a method parameter and, as discussed earlier, it is also a local variable. Both of these variables are said to have a *scope* local to the method. This means they cannot be used outside of where they are defined.

Limiting Scope

Local variables can never have a scope larger than the method they are defined in. However, they can have a smaller scope. Consider this example:

```java
3: public void eatIfHungry(boolean hungry) {
4:     if (hungry) {
5:         int bitesOfCheese = 1;
6:     } // bitesOfCheese goes out of scope here
7:     System.out.println(bitesOfCheese);  // DOES NOT COMPILE
8: }
```

The variable hungry has a scope of the entire method, while variable bitesOfCheese has a smaller scope. It is only available for use in the if statement because it is declared inside of it. When you see a set of braces ({}) in the code, it means you have entered a new block of code. Each block of code has its own scope. When there are multiple blocks, you match them from the inside out. In our case, the if statement block begins at line 4 and ends at line 6. The method's block begins at line 3 and ends at line 8.

Since bitesOfCheese is declared in an if statement block, the scope is limited to that block. When the compiler gets to line 7, it complains that it doesn't know anything about this bitesOfCheese thing and gives an error:

```
error: cannot find symbol
    System.out.println(bitesOfCheese);  // DOES NOT COMPILE
                       ^
    symbol:   variable bitesOfCheese
```

Nesting Scope

Remember that blocks can contain other blocks. These smaller contained blocks can reference variables defined in the larger scoped blocks, but not vice versa. Here's an example:

```
16: public void eatIfHungry(boolean hungry) {
17:    if (hungry) {
18:        int bitesOfCheese = 1;
19:        {
20:            var teenyBit = true;
21:            System.out.println(bitesOfCheese);
22:        }
23:    }
24:    System.out.println(teenyBit);  // DOES NOT COMPILE
25: }
```

The variable defined on line 18 is in scope until the block ends on line 23. Using it in the smaller block from lines 19 to 22 is fine. The variable defined on line 20 goes out of scope on line 22. Using it on line 24 is not allowed.

Tracing Scope

The exam will attempt to trick you with various questions on scope. You'll probably see a question that appears to be about something complex and fails to compile because one of the variables is out of scope.

Let's try one. Don't worry if you aren't familiar with if statements or while loops yet. It doesn't matter what the code does since we are talking about scope. See if you can figure out on which line each of the five local variables goes into and out of scope:

```
11: public void eatMore(boolean hungry, int amountOfFood) {
12:    int roomInBelly = 5;
13:    if (hungry) {
14:        var timeToEat = true;
15:        while (amountOfFood > 0) {
16:            int amountEaten = 2;
17:            roomInBelly = roomInBelly - amountEaten;
18:            amountOfFood = amountOfFood - amountEaten;
19:        }
20:    }
21:    System.out.println(amountOfFood);
22: }
```

The first step in figuring out the scope is to identify the blocks of code. In this case, there are three blocks. You can tell this because there are three sets of braces. Starting from the innermost set, we can see where the while loop's block starts and ends. Repeat this as we go out for the `if` statement block and method block. Table 2.4 shows the line numbers that each block starts and ends on.

TABLE 2.4   Tracking scope by block

Line	First line in block	Last line in block
while	15	19
if	13	20
Method	11	22

Now that we know where the blocks are, we can look at the scope of each variable. hungry and amountOfFood are method parameters, so they are available for the entire method. This means their scope is lines 11 to 22. The variable roomInBelly goes into scope on line 12 because that is where it is declared. It stays in scope for the rest of the method and so goes out of scope on line 22. The variable timeToEat goes into scope on line 14 where it is declared. It goes out of scope on line 20 where the `if` block ends. Finally, the variable amountEaten goes into scope on line 16 where it is declared. It goes out of scope on line 19 where the `while` block ends.

You'll want to practice this skill a lot! Identifying blocks and variable scope needs to be second nature for the exam. The good news is that there are lots of code examples to practice on. You can look at any code example on any topic in this book and match up braces.

Applying Scope to Classes

All of that was for local variables. Luckily the rule for instance variables is easier: they are available as soon as they are defined and last for the entire lifetime of the object itself. The rule for class, aka `static`, variables is even easier: they go into scope when declared like the other variable types. However, they stay in scope for the entire life of the program.

Let's do one more example to make sure you have a handle on this. Again, try to figure out the type of the four variables and when they go into and out of scope.

```
1:  public class Mouse {
2:      final static int MAX_LENGTH = 5;
3:      int length;
4:      public void grow(int inches) {
5:          if (length < MAX_LENGTH) {
6:              int newSize = length + inches;
7:              length = newSize;
8:          }
9:      }
10: }
```

In this class, we have one class variable, MAX_LENGTH; one instance variable, length; and two local variables, inches and newSize. The MAX_LENGTH variable is a class variable because it has the static keyword in its declaration. In this case, MAX_LENGTH goes into scope on line 2 where it is declared. It stays in scope until the program ends.

Next, length goes into scope on line 3 where it is declared. It stays in scope as long as this Mouse object exists. inches goes into scope where it is declared on line 4. It goes out of scope at the end of the method on line 9. newSize goes into scope where it is declared on line 6. Since it is defined inside the if statement block, it goes out of scope when that block ends on line 8.

Reviewing Scope

Got all that? Let's review the rules on scope:

- *Local variables*: In scope from declaration to end of block
- *Instance variables*: In scope from declaration until object eligible for garbage collection
- *Class variables*: In scope from declaration until program ends

Not sure what garbage collection is? Relax, that's our next and final section for this chapter.

Destroying Objects

Now that we've played with our objects, it is time to put them away. Luckily, the JVM automatically takes care of that for you. Java provides a garbage collector to automatically look for objects that aren't needed anymore.

Remember from Chapter 1, your code isn't the only process running in your Java program. Java code exists inside of a Java Virtual Machine (JVM), which includes numerous processes independent from your application code. One of the most important of those is a built-in garbage collector.

All Java objects are stored in your program memory's *heap*. The heap, which is also referred to as the *free store*, represents a large pool of unused memory allocated to your Java application. The heap may be quite large, depending on your environment, but there is always a limit to its size. After all, there's no such thing as a computer with infinite memory. If your program keeps instantiating objects and leaving them on the heap, eventually it will run out of memory and crash.

In the following sections, we'll look at garbage collection.

 **Real World Scenario**

Garbage Collection in Other Languages

One of the distinguishing characteristics of Java since its very first version is that it auto-mates performs garbage collection for you. In fact, other than removing references to an object, there's very little you can do to control garbage collection directly in Java.

While garbage collection is pretty standard in most programming languages now, some languages, such as C, do not have automatic garbage collection. When a developer finishes using an object in memory, they have to manually deallocate it so the memory can be reclaimed and reused.

Failure to properly handle garbage collection can lead to catastrophic performance and security problems, the most common of which is for an application to run out of memory. Another similar problem, though, is if secure data like a credit card number stays in memory long after it is used and is able to be read by other programs. Luckily, Java handles a lot of these complex issues for you.

Understanding Garbage Collection

Garbage collection refers to the process of automatically freeing memory on the heap by deleting objects that are no longer reachable in your program. There are many different algorithms for garbage collection, but you don't need to know any of them for the exam. If you are curious, though, one algorithm is to keep a counter on the number of places an object is accessible at any given time and mark it eligible for garbage collection if the counter ever reaches zero.

Eligible for Garbage Collection

As a developer, the most interesting part of garbage collection is determining when the memory belonging to an object can be reclaimed. In Java and other languages, *eligible for garbage collection* refers to an object's state of no longer being accessible in a program and therefore able to be garbage collected.

Does this mean an object that's eligible for garbage collection will be immediately garbage collected? Definitely not. When the object actually is discarded is not under your control, but for the exam, you will need to know at any given moment which objects are eligible for garbage collection.

Think of garbage-collection eligibility like shipping a package. You can take an item, seal it in a labeled box, and put it in your mailbox. This is analogous to making an item eligible for garbage collection. When the mail carrier comes by to pick it up, though, is not in your control. For example, it may be a postal holiday or there could be a severe weather event. You can even call the post office and ask them to come pick it up right away, but there's no way to guarantee when and if this will actually happen. Hopefully, they come by before your mailbox fills with packages!

As a programmer, the most important thing you can do to limit out-of-memory problems is to make sure objects are eligible for garbage collection once they are no longer needed. It is the JVM's responsibility to actually perform the garbage collection.

Calling *System.gc()*

Java includes a built-in method to help support garbage collection that can be called at any time.

```
public static void main(String[] args) {
   System.gc();
}
```

What is the System.gc() command *guaranteed* to do? Nothing, actually. It merely *suggests* that the JVM kick off garbage collection. The JVM may perform garbage collection at that moment, or it might be busy and choose not to. The JVM is free to ignore the request.

When is System.gc() *guaranteed* to be called by the JVM? Never, actually. While the JVM will likely run it over time as available memory decreases, it is not guaranteed to ever actually run. In fact, shortly before a program runs out of memory and throws an OutOfMemoryError, the JVM will *try* to perform garbage collection, but it's not guaranteed to succeed.

For the exam, you need to know that System.gc() is not guaranteed to run or do anything, and you should be able to recognize when objects become eligible for garbage collection.

Tracing Eligibility

How does the JVM know when an object is eligible for garbage collection? The JVM waits patiently and monitors each object until it determines that the code no longer needs that memory. An object will remain on the heap until it is no longer reachable. An object is no longer reachable when one of two situations occurs:

- The object no longer has any references pointing to it.
- All references to the object have gone out of scope.

Objects vs. References

Do not confuse a reference with the object that it refers to; they are two different entities. The reference is a variable that has a name and can be used to access the contents of an object. A reference can be assigned to another reference, passed to a method, or returned from a method. All references are the same size, no matter what their type is.

An object sits on the heap and does not have a name. Therefore, you have no way to access an object except through a reference. Objects come in all different shapes and sizes and consume varying amounts of memory. An object cannot be assigned to another object, and an object cannot be passed to a method or returned from a method. It is the object that gets garbage collected, not its reference.

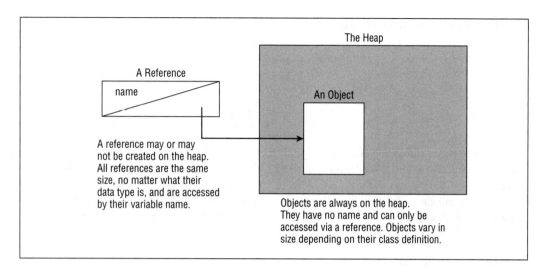

A Reference

name

A reference may or may not be created on the heap. All references are the same size, no matter what their data type is, and are accessed by their variable name.

The Heap

An Object

Objects are always on the heap. They have no name and can only be accessed via a reference. Objects vary in size depending on their class definition.

Realizing the difference between a reference and an object goes a long way toward understanding garbage collection, the new operator, and many other facets of the Java language. Look at this code and see whether you can figure out when each object first becomes eligible for garbage collection:

```
1: public class Scope {
2:    public static void main(String[] args) {
3:       String one, two;
4:       one = new String("a");
5:       two = new String("b");
6:       one = two;
7:       String three = one;
8:       one = null;
9:    } }
```

When you get asked a question about garbage collection on the exam, we recommend you draw what's going on. There's a lot to keep track of in your head, and it's easy to make a silly mistake trying to keep it all in your memory. Let's try it together now. Really. Get a pencil and paper. We'll wait.

Got that paper? Okay, let's get started. On line 3, write **one** and **two** (just the words— no need for boxes or arrows yet since no objects have gone on the heap yet). On line 4, we have our first object. Draw a box with the string **"a"** in it and draw an arrow from the word one to that box. Line 5 is similar. Draw another box with the string **"b"** in it this time and an arrow from the word two. At this point, your work should look like Figure 2.2.

FIGURE 2.2 Your drawing after line 5

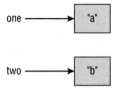

On line 6, the variable one changes to point to "b". Either erase or cross out the arrow from one and draw a new arrow from one to "b". On line 7, we have a new variable, so write the word **three** and draw an arrow from three to "b". Notice that three points to what one is pointing to right now and not what it was pointing to at the beginning. This is why you are drawing pictures. It's easy to forget something like that. At this point, your work should look like Figure 2.3.

FIGURE 2.3 Your drawing after line 7

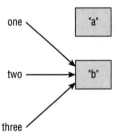

Finally, cross out the line between one and "b" since line 8 sets this variable to null. Now, we were trying to find out when the objects were first eligible for garbage collection. On line 6, we got rid of the only arrow pointing to "a", making that object eligible for garbage collection. "b" has arrows pointing to it until it goes out of scope. This means "b" doesn't go out of scope until the end of the method on line 9.

---

finalize()

Java allows objects to implement a method called finalize(). This feature can be confusing and hard to use properly. In a nutshell, the garbage collector would call the finalize() method once. If the garbage collector didn't run, there was no call to finalize(). If the garbage collector failed to collect the object and tried again later, there was no second call to finalize().

This topic is no longer on the exam. In fact, it is deprecated in Object as of Java 9, with the official documentation stating, "The finalization mechanism is inherently problematic." We mention the finalize() method in case Oracle happens to borrow from an old exam question. Just remember that finalize() can run zero or one times. It cannot run twice.

Summary

In this chapter, we described the building blocks of Java—most important, what a Java object is, how it is referenced and used, and how it is destroyed. This chapter lays the foundation for many topics that we will revisit throughout this book.

For example, we will go into a lot more detail on primitive types and how to use them in Chapter 3. Creating methods will be covered in Chapter 7. And in Chapter 8, we will discuss numerous rules for creating and managing objects. In other words, learn the basics, but don't worry if you didn't follow everything in this chapter. We will go a lot deeper into many of these topics in the rest of the book.

To begin with, constructors create Java objects. A constructor is a method matching the class name and omitting the return type. When an object is instantiated, fields and blocks of code are initialized first. Then the constructor is run.

Next, primitive types are the basic building blocks of Java types. They are assembled into reference types. Reference types can have methods and be assigned to null. Numeric literals are allowed to contain underscores (_) as long as they do not start or end the literal and are not next to a decimal point (.).

Declaring a variable involves stating the data type and giving the variable a name. Variables that represent fields in a class are automatically initialized to their corresponding 0, null, or false values during object instantiation. Local variables must be specifically initialized before they can be used. Identifiers may contain letters, numbers, $, or _. Identifiers may not begin with numbers. Local variables may use the var keyword instead of the actual type. When using var, the type is set once at compile time and does not change.

Moving on, scope refers to that portion of code where a variable can be accessed. There are three kinds of variables in Java, depending on their scope: instance variables, class variables, and local variables. Instance variables are the non-static fields of your class. Class variables are the static fields within a class. Local variables are declared within a constructor, method, or initializer block.

Finally, garbage collection is responsible for removing objects from memory when they can never be used again. An object becomes eligible for garbage collection when there are no more references to it or its references have all gone out of scope.

Exam Essentials

Be able to recognize a constructor.   A constructor has the same name as the class. It looks like a method without a return type.

Be able to identify legal and illegal declarations and initialization.   Multiple variables can be declared and initialized in the same statement when they share a type. Local variables require an explicit initialization; others use the default value for that type. Identifiers may contain letters, numbers, $, or _, although they may not begin with numbers. Also, you cannot define an identifier that is just a single underscore character _. Numeric literals may contain underscores between two digits, such as 1_000, but not in other places, such as _100_.0_. Numeric literals can begin with 1-9, 0, 0x, 0X, 0b, and 0B, with the latter four indicating a change of numeric base.

Be able to use var correctly.   A var is used for a local variable inside a constructor, a method, or an initializer block. It cannot be used for constructor parameters, method parameters, instance variables, or class variables. A var is initialized on the same line where it is declared, and while it can change value, it cannot change type. A var cannot be initialized with a null value without a type, nor can it be used in multiple variable declarations. Finally, var is not a reserved word in Java and can be used as a variable name.

Be able to determine where variables go into and out of scope.   All variables go into scope when they are declared. Local variables go out of scope when the block they are declared in ends. Instance variables go out of scope when the object is eligible for garbage collection. Class variables remain in scope as long as the program is running.

Know how to identify when an object is eligible for garbage collection.   Draw a diagram to keep track of references and objects as you trace the code. When no arrows point to a box (object), it is eligible for garbage collection.

Review Questions

1. Which of the following are valid Java identifiers? (Choose all that apply.)

   A. _

   B. _helloWorld$

   C. true

   D. java.lang

   E. Public

   F. 1980_s

   G. _Q2_

2. What lines are printed by the following program? (Choose all that apply.)

   ```
   1:  public class WaterBottle {
   2:      private String brand;
   3:      private boolean empty;
   4:      public static float code;
   5:      public static void main(String[] args) {
   6:          WaterBottle wb = new WaterBottle();
   7:          System.out.println("Empty = " + wb.empty);
   8:          System.out.println("Brand = " + wb.brand);
   9:          System.out.println("Code = " + code);
   10:    } }
   ```

   A. Line 8 generates a compiler error.

   B. Line 9 generates a compiler error.

   C. Empty =

   D. Empty = false

   E. Brand =

   F. Brand = null

   G. Code = 0.0

   H. Code = 0f

3. Which of the following code snippets about var compile without issue when used in a method? (Choose all that apply.)

   A. var spring = null;

   B. var fall = "leaves";

   C. var evening = 2; evening = null;

   D. var night = new Object();

   E. var day = 1/0;

F. `var winter = 12, cold;`

G. `var fall = 2, autumn = 2;`

H. `var morning = ""; morning = null;`

4. Which of the following statements about the code snippet are true? (Choose all that apply.)

```
4: short numPets = 5L;
5: int numGrains = 2.0;
6: String name = "Scruffy";
7: int d = numPets.length();
8: int e = numGrains.length;
9: int f = name.length();
```

A. Line 4 generates a compiler error.

B. Line 5 generates a compiler error.

C. Line 6 generates a compiler error.

D. Line 7 generates a compiler error.

E. Line 8 generates a compiler error.

F. Line 9 generates a compiler error.

5. Which statements about the following class are true? (Choose all that apply.)

```
1:  public class River {
2:     int Depth = 1;
3:     float temp = 50.0;
4:     public void flow() {
5:        for (int i = 0; i < 1; i++) {
6:           int depth = 2;
7:           depth++;
8:           temp--;
9:        }
10:       System.out.println(depth);
11:       System.out.println(temp); }
12:    public static void main(String... s) {
13:       new River().flow();
14: } }
```

A. Line 3 generates a compiler error.

B. Line 6 generates a compiler error.

C. Line 7 generates a compiler error.

D. Line 10 generates a compiler error.

E. The program prints 3 on line 10.

F. The program prints 4 on line 10.

G. The program prints 50.0 on line 11.

H. The program prints 49.0 on line 11.

6. Which of the following are correct? (Choose all that apply.)

   A. An instance variable of type float defaults to 0.

   B. An instance variable of type char defaults to null.

   C. An instance variable of type double defaults to 0.0.

   D. An instance variable of type int defaults to null.

   E. An instance variable of type String defaults to null.

   F. An instance variable of type String defaults to the empty string "".

   G. None of the above

7. Which of the following are correct? (Choose all that apply.)

   A. A local variable of type boolean defaults to null.

   B. A local variable of type float defaults to 0.0f.

   C. A local variable of type double defaults to 0.

   D. A local variable of type Object defaults to null.

   E. A local variable of type boolean defaults to false.

   F. A local variable of type float defaults to 0.0.

   G. None of the above

8. Which of the following are true? (Choose all that apply.)

   A. A class variable of type boolean defaults to 0.

   B. A class variable of type boolean defaults to false.

   C. A class variable of type boolean defaults to null.

   D. A class variable of type long defaults to null.

   E. A class variable of type long defaults to 0L.

   F. A class variable of type long defaults to 0.

   G. None of the above

9. Which of the following statements about garbage collection are correct? (Choose all that apply.)

   A. Calling System.gc() is guaranteed to free up memory by destroying objects eligible for garbage collection.

   B. Garbage collection runs on a set schedule.

   C. Garbage collection allows the JVM to reclaim memory for other objects.

   D. Garbage collection runs when your program has used up half the available memory.

    E. An object may be eligible for garbage collection but never removed from the heap.

    F. An object is eligible for garbage collection once no references to it are accessible in the program.

    G. Marking a variable final means its associated object will never be garbage collected.

10. Which statements about the following class are correct? (Choose all that apply.)

```
1:   public class PoliceBox {
2:       String color;
3:       long age;
4:       public void PoliceBox() {
5:           color = "blue";
6:           age = 1200;
7:       }
8:       public static void main(String []time) {
9:           var p = new PoliceBox();
10:          var q = new PoliceBox();
11:          p.color = "green";
12:          p.age = 1400;
13:          p = q;
14:          System.out.println("Q1="+q.color);
15:          System.out.println("Q2="+q.age);
16:          System.out.println("P1="+p.color);
17:          System.out.println("P2="+p.age);
18: } }
```

    A. It prints Q1=blue.

    B. It prints Q2=1200.

    C. It prints P1=null.

    D. It prints P2=1400.

    E. Line 4 does not compile.

    F. Line 12 does not compile.

    G. Line 13 does not compile.

    H. None of the above

11. Which of the following legally fill in the blank so you can run the main() method from the command line? (Choose all that apply.)

```
public static void main(_____) {}
```

    A. String... var

    B. String My.Names[]

C. `String[] 123`

D. `String[] _names`

E. `String... $n`

F. `var names`

G. `String myArgs`

12. Which of the following expressions, when inserted independently into the blank line, allow the code to compile? (Choose all that apply.)

```
public void printMagicData() {
    double magic = _____;
    System.out.println(magic);
}
```

A. `3_1`

B. `1_329_.0`

C. `3_13.0_`

D. `5_291._2`

E. `2_234.0_0`

F. `9___6`

G. `_1_3_5_0`

H. None of the above

13. Suppose we have a class named `Rabbit`. Which of the following statements are true? (Choose all that apply.)

```
1:  public class Rabbit {
2:      public static void main(String[] args) {
3:          Rabbit one = new Rabbit();
4:          Rabbit two = new Rabbit();
5:          Rabbit three = one;
6:          one = null;
7:          Rabbit four = one;
8:          three = null;
9:          two = null;
10:         two = new Rabbit();
11:         System.gc();
12: } }
```

A. The `Rabbit` object created on line 3 is first eligible for garbage collection immediately following line 6.

B. The `Rabbit` object created on line 3 is first eligible for garbage collection immediately following line 8.

C. The Rabbit object created on line 3 is first eligible for garbage collection immediately following line 12.

D. The Rabbit object created on line 4 is first eligible for garbage collection immediately following line 9.

E. The Rabbit object created on line 4 is first eligible for garbage collection immediately following line 11.

F. The Rabbit object created on line 4 is first eligible for garbage collection immediately following line 12.

G. The Rabbit object created on line 10 is first eligible for garbage collection immediately following line 11.

H. The Rabbit object created on line 10 is first eligible for garbage collection immediately following line 12.

14. Which of the following statements about var are true? (Choose all that apply.)

A. A var can be used as a constructor parameter.

B. The type of var is known at compile time.

C. A var cannot be used as an instance variable.

D. A var can be used in a multiple variable assignment statement.

E. The value of var cannot change at runtime.

F. The type of var cannot change at runtime.

G. The word var is a reserved word in Java.

15. Given the following class, which of the following lines of code can independently replace INSERT CODE HERE to make the code compile? (Choose all that apply.)

```
public class Price {
    public void admission() {
        INSERT CODE HERE
        System.out.print(amount);
    } }
```

A. int Amount = 0b11;

B. int amount = 9L;

C. int amount = 0xE;

D. int amount = 1_2.0;

E. double amount = 1_0_.0;

F. int amount = 0b101;

G. double amount = 9_2.1_2;

H. double amount = 1_2_.0_0;

16. Which statements about the following class are correct? (Choose all that apply.)

```
1: public class ClownFish {
2:     int gills = 0, double weight=2;
3:     { int fins = gills; }
4:     void print(int length = 3) {
5:         System.out.println(gills);
6:         System.out.println(weight);
7:         System.out.println(fins);
8:         System.out.println(length);
9: } }
```

- **A.** Line 2 contains a compiler error.
- **B.** Line 3 contains a compiler error.
- **C.** Line 4 contains a compiler error.
- **D.** Line 7 contains a compiler error.
- **E.** The code prints 0.
- **F.** The code prints 2.0.
- **G.** The code prints 2.
- **H.** The code prints 3.

17. Which statements about classes and its members are correct? (Choose all that apply.)

- **A.** A variable declared in a loop cannot be referenced outside the loop.
- **B.** A variable cannot be declared in an instance initializer block.
- **C.** A constructor argument is in scope for the life of the instance of the class for which it is defined.
- **D.** An instance method can only access instance variables declared before the instance method declaration.
- **E.** A variable can be declared in an instance initializer block but cannot be referenced outside the block.
- **F.** A constructor can access all instance variables.
- **G.** An instance method can access all instance variables.

18. Which statements about the following code snippet are correct? (Choose all that apply.)

```
3:  var squirrel = new Object();
4:  int capybara = 2, mouse, beaver = -1;
5:  char chipmunk = -1;
6:  squirrel = "";
7:  beaver = capybara;
```

```
8:  System.out.println(capybara);
9:  System.out.println(mouse);
10: System.out.println(beaver);
11: System.out.println(chipmunk);
```

A. The code prints 2.

B. The code prints -1.

C. The code prints the empty String.

D. The code prints: null.

E. Line 4 contains a compiler error.

F. Line 5 contains a compiler error.

G. Line 9 contains a compiler error.

H. Line 10 contains a compiler error.

19. Assuming the following class compiles, how many variables defined in the class or method are in scope on the line marked `// SCOPE` on line 14?

```
1:  public class Camel {
2:      { int hairs = 3_000_0; }
3:      long water, air=2;
4:      boolean twoHumps = true;
5:      public void spit(float distance) {
6:          var path = "";
7:          { double teeth = 32 + distance++; }
8:          while(water > 0) {
9:              int age = twoHumps ? 1 : 2;
10:             short i=-1;
11:             for(i=0; i<10; i++) {
12:                 var Private = 2;
13:             }
14:             // SCOPE
15:         }
16:     }
17: }
```

A. 2

B. 3

C. 4

D. 5

E. 6

F. 7

G. None of the above

20. What is the output of executing the following class?

```
1:  public class Salmon {
2:      int count;
3:      { System.out.print(count+"-"); }
4:      { count++; }
5:      public Salmon() {
6:          count = 4;
7:          System.out.print(2+"-");
8:      }
9:      public static void main(String[] args) {
10:         System.out.print(7+"-");
11:         var s = new Salmon();
12:         System.out.print(s.count+"-"); } }
```

A. 7-0-2-1-

B. 7-0-1-

C. 0-7-2-1-

D. 7-0-2-4-

E. 0-7-1-

F. The class does not compile because of line 3.

G. The class does not compile because of line 4.

H. None of the above.

21. Which statements about the following program are correct? (Choose all that apply.)

```
1:  public class Bear {
2:      private Bear pandaBear;
3:      protected void finalize() {}
4:      private void roar(Bear b) {
5:          System.out.println("Roar!");
6:          pandaBear = b;
7:      }
8:      public static void main(String[] args) {
9:          Bear brownBear = new Bear();
10:         Bear polarBear = new Bear();
11:         brownBear.roar(polarBear);
12:         polarBear = null;
13:         brownBear = null;
14:         System.gc(); } }
```

A. The object created on line 9 is eligible for garbage collection after line 13.

B. The object created on line 9 is eligible for garbage collection after line 14.

    C. The object created on line 10 is eligible for garbage collection after line 12.

    D. The object created on line 10 is eligible for garbage collection after line 13.

    E. Garbage collection is guaranteed to run.

    F. Garbage collection might or might not run.

    G. Garbage collection is guaranteed not to run.

    H. The code does not compile.

22. Which of the following are valid instance variable declarations? (Choose all that apply.)

    A. `var _ = 6000_.0;`

    B. `var null = 6_000;`

    C. `var $_ = 6_000;`

    D. `var $2 = 6_000f;`

    E. `var var = 3_0_00.0;`

    F. `var #CONS = 2_000.0;`

    G. `var %C = 6_000_L;`

    H. None of the above

Chapter

3

Operators

OCP EXAM OBJECTIVES COVERED IN THIS CHAPTER:

✓ **Using Operators and Decision Constructs**

- Use Java operators including the use of parentheses to override operator precedence

✓ **Working With Java Primitive Data Types and String APIs**

- Declare and initialize variables (including casting and promoting primitive data types)

In the previous chapter, we talked a lot about defining variables, but what can you do with a variable once it is created? This chapter introduces operators and shows how you can use them to combine existing values and create new values. We'll show you how to apply operators to various primitive data types, including introducing you to operators that can be applied to objects.

Understanding Java Operators

Before we get into the fun stuff, let's cover a bit of terminology. A Java *operator* is a special symbol that can be applied to a set of variables, values, or literals—referred to as operands—and that returns a result. The term *operand*, which we'll use throughout this chapter, refers to the value or variable the operator is being applied to. The output of the operation is simply referred to as the result. For example, in a + b, the operator is the addition operator (+), and values a and b are the operands. If we then store the result in a variable c, such as c = a + b, then the variable c and the result of a + b become the new operands for our assignment operator (=).

We're sure you have been using the addition (+) and subtraction (-) operators since you were a little kid. Java supports many other operators that you need to know for the exam. While many should be review for you, some (such as the compound assignment operators) may be new to you.

Types of Operators

In general, three flavors of operators are available in Java: unary, binary, and ternary. These types of operators can be applied to one, two, or three operands, respectively. For the exam, you'll need to know a specific subset of Java operators, how to apply them, and the order in which they should be applied.

Java operators are not necessarily evaluated from left-to-right order. For example, the second expression of the following Java code is actually evaluated from right to left given the specific operators involved:

```java
int cookies = 4;
double reward = 3 + 2 * --cookies;
System.out.print("Zoo animal receives: "+reward+" reward points");
```

In this example, you would first decrement cookies to 3, then multiply the resulting value by 2, and finally add 3. The value would then be automatically promoted from 9 to 9.0 and assigned to reward. The final values of cookies and reward would be 9.0 and 3, respectively, with the following printed:

```
Zoo animal receives: 9.0 reward points
```

If you didn't follow that evaluation, don't worry. By the end of this chapter, solving problems like this should be second nature.

Operator Precedence

When reading a book or a newspaper, some written languages are evaluated from left to right, while some are evaluated from right to left. In mathematics, certain operators can override other operators and be evaluated first. Determining which operators are evaluated in what order is referred to as *operator precedence*. In this manner, Java more closely follows the rules for mathematics. Consider the following expression:

```
var perimeter = 2 * height + 2 * length;
```

The multiplication operator (*) has a higher precedence than the addition operator (+), so the *height* and *length* are both multiplied by 2 before being added together. The assignment operator (=) has the lowest order of precedence, so the assignment to the *perimeter* variable is performed last.

Unless overridden with parentheses, Java operators follow *order of operation*, listed in Table 3.1, by decreasing order of operator precedence. If two operators have the same level of precedence, then Java guarantees left-to-right evaluation. For the exam, you only need to know the operators shown in bold in Table 3.1.

TABLE 3.1 Order of operator precedence

Operator	Symbols and examples
Post-unary operators	*expression*++, *expression*--
Pre-unary operators	++*expression*, --*expression*
Other unary operators	-, !, ~, +, (**type**)
Multiplication/division/modulus	*, /, %
Addition/subtraction	+, -
Shift operators	<<, >>, >>>
Relational operators	<, >, <=, >=, instanceof

TABLE 3.1 Order of operator precedence *(continued)*

Operator	Symbols and examples
Equal to/not equal to	**==, !=**
Logical operators	**&, ^, |**
Short-circuit logical operators	**&&, ||**
Ternary operators	*boolean expression* **?** *expression1* **:** *expression2*
Assignment operators	**=, +=, -=, *=, /=,** %=, &=, ^=, |=, <<=, >>=, >>>=

We recommend that you keep Table 3.1 handy throughout this chapter. For the exam, you need to memorize the order of precedence in this table. Note that you won't be tested on some operators, like the shift operators, although we recommend that you be aware of their existence.

Applying Unary Operators

By definition, a *unary* operator is one that requires exactly one operand, or variable, to function. As shown in Table 3.2, they often perform simple tasks, such as increasing a numeric variable by one or negating a `boolean` value.

TABLE 3.2 Unary operators

Operator	Description
!	Inverts a `boolean`'s logical value
+	Indicates a number is positive, although numbers are assumed to be positive in Java unless accompanied by a negative unary operator
-	Indicates a literal number is negative or negates an expression
++	Increments a value by 1
--	Decrements a value by 1
(*type*)	Casts a value to a specific type.

Even though Table 3.2 includes the casting operator, we'll postpone discussing casting until the "Assigning Values" section later in this chapter, since that is where it is commonly used.

Logical Complement and Negation Operators

Since we're going to be working with a lot of numeric operators in this chapter, let's get the `boolean` one out of the way first. The *logical complement operator* (!) flips the value of a `boolean` expression. For example, if the value is `true`, it will be converted to `false`, and vice versa. To illustrate this, compare the outputs of the following statements:

```
boolean isAnimalAsleep = false;
System.out.println(isAnimalAsleep);  // false
isAnimalAsleep = !isAnimalAsleep;
System.out.println(isAnimalAsleep);  // true
```

Likewise, the *negation operator*, -, reverses the sign of a numeric expression, as shown in these statements:

```
double zooTemperature = 1.21;
System.out.println(zooTemperature);  // 1.21
zooTemperature = -zooTemperature;
System.out.println(zooTemperature);  // -1.21
zooTemperature = -(-zooTemperature);
System.out.println(zooTemperature);  // -1.21
```

Notice that in the last example we used parentheses, (), for the negation operator, -, to apply the negation twice. If we had instead written --, then it would have been interpreted as the decrement operator and printed -2.21. You will see more of that decrement operator shortly.

Based on the description, it might be obvious that some operators require the variable or expression they're acting upon to be of a specific type. For example, you cannot apply a negation operator (-) to a `boolean` expression, nor can you apply a logical complement operator (!) to a numeric expression. Be wary of questions on the exam that try to do this, as they'll cause the code to fail to compile. For example, none of the following lines of code will compile:

```
int pelican = !5;         // DOES NOT COMPILE
boolean penguin = -true;  // DOES NOT COMPILE
boolean peacock = !0;     // DOES NOT COMPILE
```

The first statement will not compile because in Java you cannot perform a logical inversion of a numeric value. The second statement does not compile because you cannot numerically negate a `boolean` value; you need to use the logical inverse operator. Finally, the last statement does not compile because you cannot take the logical complement of a numeric value, nor can you assign an integer to a `boolean` variable.

Keep an eye out for questions on the exam that use the logical complement operator or numeric values with boolean expressions or variables. Unlike some other programming languages, in Java, 1 and true are not related in any way, just as 0 and false are not related.

Increment and Decrement Operators

Increment and decrement operators, ++ and --, respectively, can be applied to numeric variables and have a high order of precedence, as compared to binary operators. In other words, they often get applied first in an expression.

Increment and decrement operators require special care because the order in which they are attached to their associated variable can make a difference in how an expression is processed. If the operator is placed before the operand, referred to as the *pre-increment operator* and the *pre-decrement operator*, then the operator is applied first and the value returned is the *new value* of the expression. Alternatively, if the operator is placed after the operand, referred to as the *post-increment operator* and the *post-decrement operator*, then the *original value* of the expression is returned, with operator applied after the value is returned.

The following code snippet illustrates this distinction:

```
int parkAttendance = 0;
System.out.println(parkAttendance);        // 0
System.out.println(++parkAttendance);      // 1
System.out.println(parkAttendance);        // 1
System.out.println(parkAttendance--);      // 1
System.out.println(parkAttendance);        // 0
```

The first pre-increment operator updates the value for parkAttendance and outputs the new value of 1. The next post-decrement operator also updates the value of parkAttendance but outputs the value before the decrement occurs.

For the exam, it is critical that you know the difference between expressions like parkAttendance++ and ++parkAttendance. The increment and decrement operators will be in multiple questions, and confusion about which value is returned could cause you to lose a lot of points on the exam.

One common practice in a certification exam, albeit less common in the real world, is to apply multiple increment or decrement operators to a single variable on the same line:

```
int lion = 3;
int tiger = ++lion * 5 / lion--;
System.out.println("lion is " + lion);
System.out.println("tiger is " + tiger);
```

This one is more complicated than the previous example because lion is modified two times on the same line. Each time it is modified, as the expression moves from left to right, the value of lion changes, with different values being assigned to the variable. As you'll recall from our discussion on operator precedence, order of operation plays an important part in evaluating this example.

So how do you read this code? First, lion is incremented and returned to the expression, which is multiplied by 5. We can simplify this:

```
int tiger = 4 * 5 / lion--;  // lion assigned value of 4
```

Next, lion is decremented, but the original value of 4 is used in the expression, leading to this:

```
int tiger = 4 * 5 / 4;  // lion assigned value of 3
```

Finally, we evaluate multiplication and division from left to right. The product of the first two numbers is 20. The divisor 4 divides 20 evenly, resulting in an assignment of 5 to tiger. The result is then printed:

```
lion is 3
tiger is 5
```

Working with Binary Arithmetic Operators

Next, we move on to operators that take two arguments, called *binary operators*. Binary operators are by far the most common operators in the Java language. They can be used to perform mathematical operations on variables, create logical expressions, and perform basic variable assignments. Binary operators are often combined in complex expressions with other binary operators; therefore, operator precedence is very important in evaluating expressions containing binary operators.

In this section, we'll start with binary arithmetic operators, shown in Table 3.3. In the following sections, we'll expand to other binary operators that you need to know for the exam.

TABLE 3.3   Binary arithmetic operators

Operator	Description
+	Adds two numeric values
-	Subtracts two numeric values
*	Multiplies two numeric values
/	Divides one numeric value by another
%	Modulus operator returns the remainder after division of one numeric value by another

Arithmetic Operators

Arithmetic operators are often encountered in early mathematics and include addition (+), subtraction (-), multiplication (*), division (/), and modulus (%). If you don't know what modulus is, don't worry—we'll cover that shortly. Arithmetic operators also include the unary operators, ++ and --, which we covered already. As you may have noticed in Table 3.1, the *multiplicative* operators (*, /, %) have a higher order of precedence than the *additive* operators (+, -). Take a look at the following expression:

```
int price = 2 * 5 + 3 * 4 - 8;
```

First, you evaluate the 2 * 5 and 3 * 4, which reduces the expression to this:

```
int price = 10 + 12 - 8;
```

Then, you evaluate the remaining terms in left-to-right order, resulting in a value of price of 14. Make sure you understand why the result is 14 because you'll likely see this kind of operator precedence question on the exam.

 All of the arithmetic operators may be applied to any Java primitives, with the exception of boolean. Furthermore, only the addition operators + and += may be applied to String values, which results in String concatenation. You will learn more about these operators and how they apply to String values in Chapter 5, "Core Java APIs."

Adding Parentheses

You might have noticed we said "Unless overridden with parentheses" prior to presenting Table 3.1 on operator precedence. That's because you can change the order of operation explicitly by wrapping parentheses around the sections you want evaluated first.

Changing the Order of Operation

Let's return to the previous price example. The following code snippet contains the same values and operators, in the same order, but with two sets of parentheses added:

```
int price = 2 * ((5 + 3) * 4 - 8);
```

This time you would evaluate the addition operator 5 + 3, which reduces the expression to the following:

```
int price = 2 * (8 * 4 - 8);
```

You can further reduce this expression by multiplying the first two values within the parentheses:

```
int price = 2 * (32 - 8);
```

Next, you subtract the values within the parentheses before applying terms outside the parentheses:

```
int price = 2 * 24;
```

Finally, you would multiply the result by 2, resulting in a value of 48 for price.

Parentheses can appear in nearly any question on the exam involving numeric values, so make sure you understand how they are changing the order of operation when you see them.

Verifying Parentheses Syntax

When working with parentheses, you need to make sure they are always valid and balanced. Consider the following examples:

```
long pigeon = 1 + ((3 * 5) / 3;       // DOES NOT COMPILE
int blueJay = (9 + 2) + 3) / (2 * 4;  // DOES NOT COMPILE
short robin = 3 + [(4 * 2) + 4];      // DOES NOT COMPILE
```

The first example does not compile because the parentheses are not balanced. There is a left-parenthesis with no matching right-parenthesis. The second example has an equal number of left and right parentheses, but they are not balanced properly. When reading from left to right, a new right-parenthesis must match a previous left-parenthesis. Likewise, all left-parentheses must be closed by right-parentheses before the end of the expression. The last example does not compile because Java, unlike some other programming languages, does not allow brackets, [], to be used in place of parentheses. If you replace the brackets with parentheses, the last example will compile just fine.

Division and Modulus Operators

Although we are sure you have seen most of the arithmetic operators before, the modulus operator, %, may be new to you. The modulus operator, often called the *remainder operator*, is simply the remainder when two numbers are divided. For example, 9 divided by 3 divides evenly and has no remainder; therefore, the result of 9 % 3 is 0. On the other hand, 11 divided by 3 does not divide evenly; therefore, the result of 11 % 3, is 2.

The following examples illustrate this distinction:

```
System.out.println(9 / 3);    // 3
System.out.println(9 % 3);    // 0

System.out.println(10 / 3);   // 3
System.out.println(10 % 3);   // 1

System.out.println(11 / 3);   // 3
System.out.println(11 % 3);   // 2

System.out.println(12 / 3);   // 4
System.out.println(12 % 3);   // 0
```

As you can see, the division results increase only when the value on the left side goes from 11 to 12, whereas the modulus remainder value increases by 1 each time the left side is increased until it wraps around to zero. For a given divisor y, which is 3 in these examples, the modulus operation results in a value between 0 and (y - 1) for positive dividends. This means that the result of this modulus operation is always 0, 1, or 2.

Be sure to understand the difference between arithmetic division and modulus. For integer values, division results in the floor value of the nearest integer that fulfills the operation, whereas modulus is the remainder value. If you hear the phrase *floor value*, it just means the value without anything after the decimal point. For example, the floor value is 4 for each of the values 4.0, 4.5, and 4.9999999. Unlike rounding, which we'll cover in Chapter 5, you just take the value before the decimal point, regardless of what is after the decimal point.

The modulus operation is not limited to positive integer values in Java; it may also be applied to negative integers and floating-point numbers. For example, if the divisor is 5, then the modulus value of a negative number is between -4 and 0. For the exam, though, you are not required to be able to take the modulus of a negative integer or a floating-point number.

Numeric Promotion

Now that you understand the basics of arithmetic operators, it is vital to talk about primitive *numeric promotion*, as Java may do things that seem unusual to you at first. As we showed in Chapter 2, "Java Building Blocks," each primitive numeric type has a bit-length. You don't need to know the exact size of these types for the exam, but you should know which are bigger than others. For example, you should know that a long takes up more space than an int, which in turn takes up more space than a short, and so on.

You need to memorize certain rules Java will follow when applying operators to data types:

Numeric Promotion Rules

1. If two values have different data types, Java will automatically promote one of the values to the larger of the two data types.

2. If one of the values is integral and the other is floating-point, Java will automatically promote the integral value to the floating-point value's data type.

3. Smaller data types, namely, byte, short, and char, are first promoted to int any time they're used with a Java binary arithmetic operator, even if neither of the operands is int.

4. After all promotion has occurred and the operands have the same data type, the resulting value will have the same data type as its promoted operands.

The last two rules are the ones most people have trouble with and the ones likely to trip you up on the exam. For the third rule, note that unary operators are excluded from this rule. For example, applying ++ to a short value results in a short value.

Let's tackle some examples for illustrative purposes:

▪   What is the data type of x * y?

```
int x = 1;
long y = 33;
var z = x * y;
```

If we follow the first rule, since one of the values is long and the other is int and since long is larger than int, then the int value is promoted to a long, and the resulting value is long.

- What is the data type of x + y?

```
double x = 39.21;
float y = 2.1;
var z = x + y;
```

This is actually a trick question, as this code will not compile! As you may remember from Chapter 2, floating-point literals are assumed to be double, unless postfixed with an f, as in 2.1f. If the value of y was set properly to 2.1f, then the promotion would be similar to the previous example, with both operands being promoted to a double, and the result would be a double value.

- What is the data type of x * y?

```
short x = 10;
short y = 3;
var z = x * y;
```

On the last line, we must apply the third rule, namely, that x and y will both be promoted to int before the binary multiplication operation, resulting in an output of type int. If you were to try to assign the value to a short variable without casting, the code would not compile. Pay close attention to the fact that the resulting output is not a short, as we'll come back to this example in the upcoming "Assigning Values" section.

- What is the data type of w * x / y?

```
short w = 14;
float x = 13;
double y = 30;
var z = w * x / y;
```

In this case, we must apply all of the rules. First, w will automatically be promoted to int solely because it is a short and it is being used in an arithmetic binary operation. The promoted w value will then be automatically promoted to a float so that it can be multiplied with x. The result of w * x will then be automatically promoted to a double so that it can be divided by y, resulting in a double value.

When working arithmetic operators in Java, you should always be aware of the data type of variables, intermediate values, and resulting values. You should apply operator precedence and parentheses and work outward, promoting data types along the way. In the next section, we'll discuss the intricacies of assigning these values to variables of a particular type.

Assigning Values

Compilation errors from assignment operators are often overlooked on the exam, in part because of how subtle these errors can be. To master the assignment operators, you should be fluent in understanding how the compiler handles numeric promotion and when casting is required. Being able to spot these issues is critical to passing the exam, as assignment operators appear in nearly every question with a code snippet.

Assignment Operator

An *assignment operator* is a binary operator that modifies, or *assigns*, the variable on the left side of the operator, with the result of the value on the right side of the equation. The simplest assignment operator is the = assignment, which you have seen already:

```
int herd = 1;
```

This statement assigns the herd variable the value of 1.

Java will automatically promote from smaller to larger data types, as you saw in the previous section on arithmetic operators, but it will throw a compiler exception if it detects that you are trying to convert from larger to smaller data types without casting. Table 3.4 lists the first assignment operator that you need to know for the exam. We will present additional assignment operators later in this section.

TABLE 3.4 Simple assignment operator

Operator	Description
=	Assigns the value on the right to the variable on the left

Casting Values

Seems easy so far, right? Well, we can't really talk about the assignment operator in detail until we've covered casting. *Casting* is a unary operation where one data type is explicitly interpreted as another data type. Casting is optional and unnecessary when converting to a larger or widening data type, but it is required when converting to a smaller or narrowing data type. Without casting, the compiler will generate an error when trying to put a larger data type inside a smaller one.

Casting is performed by placing the data type, enclosed in parentheses, to the left of the value you want to cast. Here are some examples of casting:

```
int fur = (int)5;
int hair = (short) 2;
String type = (String) "Bird";
```

```
short tail = (short)(4 + 10);
long feathers = 10(long);  // DOES NOT COMPILE
```

Spaces between the cast and the value are optional. As shown in the second-to-last example, it is common for the right side to also be in parentheses. Since casting is a unary operation, it would only be applied to the 4 if we didn't enclose 4 + 10 in parentheses. The last example does not compile because the type is on the wrong side of the value.

On the one hand, it is convenient that the compiler automatically casts smaller data types to larger ones. On the other hand, it makes for great exam questions when they do the opposite to see whether you are paying attention. See if you can figure out why none of the following lines of code compile:

```
float egg = 2.0 / 9;        // DOES NOT COMPILE
int tadpole = (int)5 * 2L;  // DOES NOT COMPILE
short frog = 3 - 2.0;       // DOES NOT COMPILE
```

All of these examples involve putting a larger value into a smaller data type. Don't worry if you don't follow this yet; we will be covering many examples like these in this part of the chapter.

In this chapter, casting is primarily concerned with converting numeric data types into other data types. As you will see in later chapters, casting can also be applied to objects and references. In those cases, though, no conversion is performed, as casting is allowed only if the underlying object is already a member of the class or interface.

And during the exam, remember to keep track of parentheses and return types any time casting is involved!

Reviewing Primitive Assignments

Let's return to some examples similar to what you saw in Chapter 2 to show how casting can resolve these issues:

```
int fish = 1.0;         // DOES NOT COMPILE
short bird = 1921222;   // DOES NOT COMPILE
int mammal = 9f;        // DOES NOT COMPILE
long reptile = 192301398193810323;  // DOES NOT COMPILE
```

The first statement does not compile because you are trying to assign a double 1.0 to an integer value. Even though the value is a mathematic integer, by adding .0, you're instructing the compiler to treat it as a double. The second statement does not compile because the literal value 1921222 is outside the range of short and the compiler detects this. The third statement does not compile because of the f added to the end of the number that instructs the compiler to treat the number as a floating-point value, but the assignment is to an int. Finally, the last statement does not compile because Java interprets the literal as an int and notices that the value is larger than int allows. The literal would need a postfix L or l to be considered a long.

Applying Casting

We can fix the previous set of examples by casting the results to a smaller data type. Remember, casting primitives is required any time you are going from a larger numerical data type to a smaller numerical data type, or converting from a floating-point number to an integral value.

```
int trainer = (int)1.0;
short ticketTaker = (short)1921222;   // Stored as 20678
int usher = (int)9f;
long manager = 192301398193810323L;
```

Overflow and Underflow

The expressions in the previous example now compile, although there's a cost. The second value, 1,921,222, is too large to be stored as a short, so numeric overflow occurs and it becomes 20,678. *Overflow* is when a number is so large that it will no longer fit within the data type, so the system "wraps around" to the lowest negative value and counts up from there, similar to how modulus arithmetic works. There's also an analogous *underflow*, when the number is too low to fit in the data type, such as storing -200 in a byte field.

This is beyond the scope of the exam, but something to be careful of in your own code. For example, the following statement outputs a negative number:

```
System.out.print(2147483647+1);   // -2147483648
```

Since 2147483647 is the maximum int value, adding any strictly positive value to it will cause it to wrap to the smallest negative number.

Let's return to a similar example from the "Numeric Promotion" section earlier in the chapter.

```
short mouse = 10;
short hamster = 3;
short capybara = mouse * hamster;   // DOES NOT COMPILE
```

Based on everything you have learned up until now about numeric promotion and casting, do you understand why the last line of this statement will not compile? As you may remember, short values are automatically promoted to int when applying any arithmetic operator, with the resulting value being of type int. Trying to assign a short variable with an int value results in a compiler error, as Java thinks you are trying to implicitly convert from a larger data type to a smaller one.

We can fix this expression by casting, as there are times that you may want to override the compiler's default behavior. In this example, we know the result of 10 * 3 is 30, which can easily fit into a short variable, so we can apply casting to convert the result back to a short.

```
short mouse = 10;
short hamster = 3;
short capybara = (short)(mouse * hamster);
```

By casting a larger value into a smaller data type, you are instructing the compiler to ignore its default behavior. In other words, you are telling the compiler that you have taken additional steps to prevent overflow or underflow. It is also possible that in your particular application and scenario, overflow or underflow would result in acceptable values.

Last but not least, casting can appear anywhere in an expression, not just on the assignment. For example, let's take a look at a modified form of the previous example:

```
short mouse = 10;
short hamster = 3;
short capybara = (short)mouse * hamster;         // DOES NOT COMPILE
short gerbil = 1 + (short)(mouse * hamster);  // DOES NOT COMPILE
```

So, what's going on in the last two lines? Well, remember when we said casting was a unary operation? That means the cast in the first line is applied to mouse, and mouse alone. After the cast is complete, both operands are promoted to int since they are used with the binary multiplication operator (*), making the result an int and causing a compiler error.

In the second example, casting is performed successfully, but the resulting value is automatically promoted to int because it is used with the binary arithmetic operator (+).

Compound Assignment Operators

Besides the simple assignment operator (=) Java supports numerous *compound assignment operators*. For the exam, you should be familiar with the compound operators in Table 3.5.

TABLE 3.5 Compound assignment operators

Operator	Description
+=	Adds the value on the right to the variable on the left and assigns the sum to the variable
-=	Subtracts the value on the right from the variable on the left and assigns the difference to the variable
*=	Multiplies the value on the right with the variable on the left and assigns the product to the variable
/=	Divides the variable on the left by the value on the right and assigns the quotient to the variable

Complex operators are really just glorified forms of the simple assignment operator, with a built-in arithmetic or logical operation that applies the left and right sides of the statement and stores the resulting value in the variable on the left side of the statement. For example, the following two statements after the declaration of camel and giraffe are equivalent when run independently:

```
int camel = 2, giraffe = 3;
camel = camel * giraffe;    // Simple assignment operator
camel *= giraffe;           // Compound assignment operator
```

The left side of the compound operator can be applied only to a variable that is already defined and cannot be used to declare a new variable. In this example, if camel were not already defined, then the expression camel *= giraffe would not compile.

Compound operators are useful for more than just shorthand—they can also save us from having to explicitly cast a value. For example, consider the following example. Can you figure out why the last line does not compile?

```
long goat = 10;
int sheep = 5;
sheep = sheep * goat;    // DOES NOT COMPILE
```

From the previous section, you should be able to spot the problem in the last line. We are trying to assign a long value to an int variable. This last line could be fixed with an explicit cast to (int), but there's a better way using the compound assignment operator:

```
long goat = 10;
int sheep = 5;
sheep *= goat;
```

The compound operator will first cast sheep to a long, apply the multiplication of two long values, and then cast the result to an int. Unlike the previous example, in which the compiler reported an error, in this example we see that the compiler will automatically cast the resulting value to the data type of the value on the left side of the compound operator.

Assignment Operator Return Value

One final thing to know about assignment operators is that the result of an assignment is an expression in and of itself, equal to the value of the assignment. For example, the following snippet of code is perfectly valid, if not a little odd-looking:

```
long wolf = 5;
long coyote = (wolf=3);
System.out.println(wolf);    // 3
System.out.println(coyote);  // 3
```

The key here is that (wolf=3) does two things. First, it sets the value of the variable wolf to be 3. Second, it returns a value of the assignment, which is also 3.

The exam creators are fond of inserting the assignment operator (=) in the middle of an expression and using the value of the assignment as part of a more complex expression. For example, don't be surprised if you see an if statement on the exam similar to the following:

```
boolean healthy = false;
if(healthy = true)
    System.out.print("Good!");
```

While this may look like a test if healthy is true, it's actually assigning healthy a value of true. The result of the assignment is the value of the assignment, which is true, resulting in this snippet printing Good!. We'll cover this in more detail in the upcoming "Equality Operators" section.

Comparing Values

The last set of binary operators revolves around comparing values. They can be used to check if two values are the same, check if one numeric value is less than or greater than another, and perform boolean arithmetic. Chances are you have used many of the operators in this section in your development experience.

Equality Operators

Determining equality in Java can be a nontrivial endeavor as there's a semantic difference between "two objects are the same" and "two objects are equivalent." It is further complicated by the fact that for numeric and boolean primitives, there is no such distinction.

Table 3.6 lists the equality operators. The equals operator (==) and not equals operator (!=) compare two operands and return a boolean value determining whether the expressions or values are equal or not equal, respectively.

TABLE 3.6 Equality operators

Operator	Apply to primitives	Apply to objects
==	Returns true if the two values represent the same value	Returns true if the two values reference the same object
!=	Returns true if the two values represent different values	Returns true if the two values do not reference the same object

The equality operators are used in one of three scenarios:

- Comparing two numeric or character primitive types. If the numeric values are of different data types, the values are automatically promoted. For example, 5 == 5.00 returns true since the left side is promoted to a double.

- Comparing two boolean values

- Comparing two objects, including null and String values

The comparisons for equality are limited to these three cases, so you cannot mix and match types. For example, each of the following would result in a compiler error:

```
boolean monkey = true == 3;       // DOES NOT COMPILE
boolean ape = false != "Grape";   // DOES NOT COMPILE
boolean gorilla = 10.2 == "Koko"; // DOES NOT COMPILE
```

Pay close attention to the data types when you see an equality operator on the exam. As we mentioned in the previous section, the exam creators also have a habit of mixing assignment operators and equality operators.

```
boolean bear = false;
boolean polar = (bear = true);
System.out.println(polar);  // true
```

At first glance, you might think the output should be false, and if the expression were (bear == true), then you would be correct. In this example, though, the expression is assigning the value of true to bear, and as you saw in the section on assignment operators, the assignment itself has the value of the assignment. Therefore, polar is also assigned a value of true, and the output is true.

For object comparison, the equality operator is applied to the references to the objects, not the objects they point to. Two references are equal if and only if they point to the same object or both point to null. Let's take a look at some examples:

```
File monday = new File("schedule.txt");
File tuesday = new File("schedule.txt");
File wednesday = tuesday;
System.out.println(monday == tuesday);    // false
System.out.println(tuesday == wednesday); // true
```

Even though all of the variables point to the same file information, only two references, tuesday and wednesday, are equal in terms of == since they point to the same object.

NOTE   Wait, what's the File class? In this example, as well as during the exam, you may be presented with class names that are unfamiliar, such as File. Many times you can answer questions about these classes without knowing the specific details of these classes. In the previous example, you should be able to answer questions that indicate monday and tuesday are two separate and distinct objects because the new keyword is used, even if you are not familiar with the data types of these objects.

In some languages, comparing `null` with any other value is always `false`, although this is not the case in Java.

```
System.out.print(null == null);  // true
```

In Chapter 5, we'll continue the discussion of object equality by introducing what it means for two different objects to be equivalent. We'll also cover `String` equality and show how this can be a nontrivial topic.

Relational Operators

We now move on to *relational operators*, which compare two expressions and return a `boolean` value. Table 3.7 describes the relational operators you need to know for the exam.

TABLE 3.7 Relational operators

Operator	Description
<	Returns `true` if the value on the left is strictly less than the value on the right
<=	Returns `true` if the value on the left is less than or equal to the value on the right
>	Returns `true` if the value on the left is strictly greater than the value on the right
>=	Returns `true` if the value on the left is greater than or equal to the value on the right
a instanceof *b*	Returns `true` if the reference that a points to is an instance of a class, subclass, or class that implements a particular interface, as named in b

Numeric Comparison Operators

The first four relational operators in Table 3.7 apply only to numeric values. If the two numeric operands are not of the same data type, the smaller one is promoted as previously discussed.

Let's look at examples of these operators in action:

```
int gibbonNumFeet = 2, wolfNumFeet = 4, ostrichNumFeet = 2;
System.out.println(gibbonNumFeet < wolfNumFeet);      // true
System.out.println(gibbonNumFeet <= wolfNumFeet);     // true
System.out.println(gibbonNumFeet >= ostrichNumFeet);  // true
System.out.println(gibbonNumFeet > ostrichNumFeet);   // false
```

Notice that the last example outputs `false`, because although `gibbonNumFeet` and `ostrichNumFeet` have the same value, `gibbonNumFeet` is not strictly greater than `ostrichNumFeet`.

instanceof Operator

The final relational operator you need to know for the exam is the `instanceof` operator, shown in Table 3.7. It is useful for determining whether an arbitrary object is a member of a particular class or interface at runtime.

Why wouldn't you know what class or interface an object is? As we will get into in Chapter 8, "Class Design," Java supports polymorphism. For now, that just means some objects can be passed around using a variety of references. For example, all classes inherit from `java.lang.Object`. This means that any instance can be assigned to an `Object` reference. For example, how many objects are created and used in the following code snippet?

```
Integer zooTime = Integer.valueOf(9);
Number num = zooTime;
Object obj = zooTime;
```

In this example, there is only one object created in memory but three different references to it because `Integer` inherits both `Number` and `Object`. This means that you can call `instanceof` on any of these references with three different data types and it would return `true` for each of them.

Where polymorphism often comes into play is when you create a method that takes a data type with many possible subclasses. For example, imagine we have a function that opens the zoo and prints the time. As input, it takes a `Number` as an input parameter.

```
public void openZoo(Number time) {}
```

Now, we want the function to add `O'clock` to the end of output if the value is a whole number type, such as an `Integer`; otherwise, it just prints the value.

```
public static void openZoo(Number time) {
   if(time instanceof Integer)
      System.out.print((Integer)time + " O'clock");
   else
      System.out.print(time);
}
```

We now have a method that can intelligently handle both `Integer` and other values. A good exercise left for the reader is to add checks for other numeric data types.

Notice that we cast the `Integer` value in this example. It is common to use casting and `instanceof` together when working with objects that can be various different types, since it can give you access to fields available only in the more specific classes. It is considered a good coding practice to use the `instanceof` operator prior to casting from one object to a narrower type.

Invalid *instanceof*

One area the exam might try to trip you up on is using `instanceof` with incompatible types. For example, `Number` cannot possibly hold a `String` value, so the following would cause a compilation error:

```
public static void openZoo(Number time) {
   if(time instanceof String) // DOES NOT COMPILE
   ...
```

It gets even more complicated as the previous rule applies to classes, but not interfaces. Don't worry if this is all new to you; we will go into more detail when we discuss polymorphism in Chapter 9, "Advanced Class Design."

null and the *instanceof* operator

What happens if you call `instanceof` on a `null` variable? For the exam, you should know that calling `instanceof` on the `null` literal or a `null` reference always returns `false`.

```
System.out.print(null instanceof Object);

Object noObjectHere = null;
System.out.print(noObjectHere instanceof String);
```

The preceding examples both print `false`. It almost doesn't matter what the right side of the expression is. We say "almost" because there are exceptions. The last example does not compile, since `null` is used on the right side of the `instanceof` operator:

```
System.out.print(null instanceof null);   // DOES NOT COMPILE
```

Logical Operators

If you have studied computer science, you may have already come across logical operators before. If not, no need to panic—we'll be covering them in detail in this section.

The logical operators, (&), (|), and (^), may be applied to both numeric and `boolean` data types; they are listed in Table 3.8. When they're applied to `boolean` data types, they're referred to as *logical operators*. Alternatively, when they're applied to numeric data types, they're referred to as *bitwise operators*, as they perform bitwise comparisons of the bits that compose the number. For the exam, though, you don't need to know anything about numeric bitwise comparisons, so we'll leave that educational aspect to other books.

TABLE 3.8 Logical operators

Operator	Description
&	Logical AND is true only if both values are true.
|	Inclusive OR is true if at least one of the values is true.
^	Exclusive XOR is true only if one value is true and the other is false.

You should familiarize yourself with the truth tables in Figure 3.1, where x and y are assumed to be boolean data types.

FIGURE 3.1 The logical truth tables for &, |, and ^

x & y (AND)	y = true	y = false
x = true	true	false
x = false	false	false

x | y (INCLUSIVE OR)	y = true	y = false
x = true	true	true
x = false	true	false

x ^ y (EXCLUSIVE OR)	y = true	y = false
x = true	false	true
x = false	true	false

Here are some tips to help you remember this table:

- AND is only true if both operands are true.
- Inclusive OR is only false if both operands are false.
- Exclusive OR is only true if the operands are different.

Let's take a look at some examples:

```java
boolean eyesClosed = true;
boolean breathingSlowly = true;

boolean resting = eyesClosed | breathingSlowly;
boolean asleep = eyesClosed & breathingSlowly;
boolean awake = eyesClosed ^ breathingSlowly;
System.out.println(resting);   // true
System.out.println(asleep);    // true
System.out.println(awake);     // false
```

You should try these out yourself, changing the values of eyesClosed and breathingSlowly and studying the results.

Short-Circuit Operators

Next, we present the conditional operators, && and ||, which are often referred to as *short-circuit operators* and are shown in Table 3.9.

TABLE 3.9 Short-circuit operators

Operator	Description
&&	Short-circuit AND is true only if both values are true. If the left side is false, then the right side will not be evaluated.
||	Short-circuit OR is true if at least one of the values is true. If the left side is true, then the right side will not be evaluated.

The *short-circuit operators* are nearly identical to the logical operators, & and |, except that the right side of the expression may never be evaluated if the final result can be determined by the left side of the expression. For example, consider the following statement:

```
int hour = 10;
boolean zooOpen = true || (hour < 4);
System.out.println(zooOpen);   // true
```

Referring to the truth tables, the value zooOpen can be false only if both sides of the expression are false. Since we know the left side is true, there's no need to evaluate the right side, since no value of hour will ever make this code print false. In other words, hour could have been -10 or 892; the output would have been the same. Try it yourself with different values for hour!

Avoiding a NullPointerException

A more common example of where short-circuit operators are used is checking for null objects before performing an operation. In the following example, if duck is null, then the program will throw a NullPointerException at runtime:

```
if(duck!=null & duck.getAge()<5) { // Could throw a NullPointerException
    // Do something
}
```

The issue is that the logical AND (&) operator evaluates both sides of the expression. We could add a second if statement, but this could get unwieldy if we have a lot of variables to check. An easy-to-read solution is to use the short-circuit AND operator (&&):

```
if(duck!=null && duck.getAge()<5) {
    // Do something
}
```

In this example, if duck was null, then the short-circuit prevents a NullPointerException from ever being thrown, since the evaluation of duck.getAge() < 5 is never reached.

Checking for Unperformed Side Effects

Be wary of short-circuit behavior on the exam, as questions are known to alter a variable on the right side of the expression that may never be reached. This is referred to as an *unperformed side effect*. For example, what is the output of the following code?

```
int rabbit = 6;
boolean bunny = (rabbit >= 6) || (++rabbit <= 7);
System.out.println(rabbit);
```

Because rabbit >= 6 is true, the increment operator on the right side of the expression is never evaluated, so the output is 6.

Making Decisions with the Ternary Operator

The final operator you should be familiar with for the exam is the conditional operator, ? :, otherwise known as the *ternary operator*. It is notable in that it is the only operator that takes three operands. The ternary operator has the following form:

```
booleanExpression ? expression₁ : expression₂
```

The first operand must be a boolean expression, and the second and third operands can be any expression that returns a value. The ternary operation is really a condensed form of a combined if and else statement that returns a value. We will be covering if/else statements in a lot more detail in Chapter 4, "Making Decisions," so for now we will just use simple examples.

For example, consider the following code snippet that calculates the food amount for an owl:

```java
int owl = 5;
int food;
if(owl < 2) {
    food = 3;
} else {
    food = 4;
}
System.out.println(food);  // 4
```

Compare the previous code snippet with the following ternary operator code snippet:

```java
int owl = 5;
int food = owl < 2 ? 3 : 4;
System.out.println(food); // 4
```

These two code snippets are equivalent to each other. Note that it is often helpful for readability to add parentheses around the expressions in ternary operations, although it is certainly not required.

```java
int food = (owl < 2) ? 3 : 4;
```

For the exam, you should know that there is no requirement that second and third expressions in ternary operations have the same data types, although it does come into play when combined with the assignment operator. Compare the two statements following the variable declaration:

```java
int stripes = 7;

System.out.print((stripes > 5) ? 21 : "Zebra");

int animal = (stripes < 9) ? 3 : "Horse";  // DOES NOT COMPILE
```

Both expressions evaluate similar boolean values and return an `int` and a `String`, although only the first one will compile. `System.out.print()` does not care that the expressions are completely different types, because it can convert both to `Object` values and call `toString()` on them. On the other hand, the compiler does know that `"Horse"` is of the wrong data type and cannot be assigned to an `int`; therefore, it will not allow the code to be compiled.

Ternary Expression and Unperformed Side Effects

Like we saw with the short-circuit operator, a ternary expression can contain an unperformed side effect, as only one of the expressions on the right side will be evaluated at runtime. Let's illustrate this principle with the following example:

```
int sheep = 1;
int zzz = 1;
int sleep = zzz<10 ? sheep++ : zzz++;
System.out.print(sheep+","+zzz);  // 2,1
```

Notice that since the left-hand boolean expression was true, only sheep was incremented. Contrast the preceding example with the following modification:

```
int sheep = 1;
int zzz = 1;
int sleep = sheep>=10 ? sheep++ : zzz++;
System.out.print(sheep+","+zzz);  // 1,2
```

Now that the left-hand boolean expression evaluates to false, only zzz was incremented. In this manner, we see how the expressions in a ternary operator may not be applied if the particular expression is not used.

For the exam, be wary of any question that includes a ternary expression in which a variable is modified in one of the right-hand side expressions.

Summary

This chapter covered a wide variety of Java operator topics for unary, binary, and ternary operators. Hopefully, most of these operators were review for you. If not, you'll need to study them in detail. It is important that you understand how to use all of the required Java operators covered in this chapter and know how operator precedence and parentheses influence the way a particular expression is interpreted.

There will likely be numerous questions on the exam that appear to test one thing, such as StringBuilder or exception handling, when in fact the answer is related to the misuse of a particular operator that causes the application to fail to compile. When you see an operator involving numbers on the exam, always check that the appropriate data types are used and that they match each other where applicable.

Operators are used throughout the exam, in nearly every code sample, so the better you understand this chapter, the more prepared you will be for the exam.

Exam Essentials

Be able to write code that uses Java operators.   This chapter covered a wide variety of operator symbols. Go back and review them several times so that you are familiar with them throughout the rest of the book.

Be able to recognize which operators are associated with which data types.   Some operators may be applied only to numeric primitives, some only to boolean values, and some only to objects. It is important that you notice when an operator and operand(s) are mismatched, as this issue is likely to come up in a couple of exam questions.

Understand when casting is required or numeric promotion occurs.   Whenever you mix operands of two different data types, the compiler needs to decide how to handle the resulting data type. When you're converting from a smaller to a larger data type, numeric promotion is automatically applied. When you're converting from a larger to a smaller data type, casting is required.

Understand Java operator precedence.   Most Java operators you'll work with are binary, but the number of expressions is often greater than two. Therefore, you must understand the order in which Java will evaluate each operator symbol.

Be able to write code that uses parentheses to override operator precedence.   You can use parentheses in your code to manually change the order of precedence.

Review Questions

1. Which of the following Java operators can be used with `boolean` variables? (Choose all that apply.)

   A. `==`

   B. `+`

   C. `--`

   D. `!`

   E. `%`

   F. `<=`

   G. Cast with `(boolean)`

2. What data type (or types) will allow the following code snippet to compile? (Choose all that apply.)

   ```
   byte apples = 5;
   short oranges = 10;
   _____ bananas = apples + oranges;
   ```

   A. `int`

   B. `long`

   C. `boolean`

   D. `double`

   E. `short`

   F. `byte`

3. What change, when applied independently, would allow the following code snippet to compile? (Choose all that apply.)

   ```
   3: long ear = 10;
   4: int hearing = 2 * ear;
   ```

   A. No change; it compiles as is.

   B. Cast ear on line 4 to `int`.

   C. Change the data type of ear on line 3 to `short`.

   D. Cast `2 * ear` on line 4 to `int`.

   E. Change the data type of hearing on line 4 to `short`.

   F. Change the data type of hearing on line 4 to `long`.

4. What is the output of the following code snippet?

   ```
   3: boolean canine = true, wolf = true;
   4: int teeth = 20;
   ```

```
5: canine = (teeth != 10) ^ (wolf=false);
6: System.out.println(canine+", "+teeth+", "+wolf);
```

A. true, 20, true

B. true, 20, false

C. false, 10, true

D. false, 20, false

E. The code will not compile because of line 5.

F. None of the above

5. Which of the following operators are ranked in increasing or the same order of precedence? Assume the + operator is binary addition, not the unary form. (Choose all that apply.)

A. +, *, %, --

B. ++, (int), *

C. =, ==, !

D. (short), =, !, *

E. *, /, %, +, ==

F. !, ||, &

G. ^, +, =, +=

6. What is the output of the following program?

```
1: public class CandyCounter {
2:     static long addCandy(double fruit, float vegetables) {
3:         return (int)fruit+vegetables;
4:     }
5:
6:     public static void main(String[] args) {
7:         System.out.print(addCandy(1.4, 2.4f) + "-");
8:         System.out.print(addCandy(1.9, (float)4) + "-");
9:         System.out.print(addCandy((long)(int)(short)2, (float)4)); } }
```

A. 4-6-6.0

B. 3-5-6

C. 3-6-6

D. 4-5-6

E. The code does not compile because of line 9.

F. None of the above

7. What is the output of the following code snippet?

```
int ph = 7, vis = 2;
boolean clear = vis > 1 & (vis < 9 || ph < 2);
boolean safe = (vis > 2) && (ph++ > 1);
boolean tasty = 7 <= --ph;
System.out.println(clear+"-"+safe+"-"+tasty);
```

- **A.** true-true-true
- **B.** true-true-false
- **C.** true-false-true
- **D.** true-false-false
- **E.** false-true-true
- **F.** false-true-false
- **G.** false-false-true
- **H.** false-false-false

8. What is the output of the following code snippet?

```
4: int pig = (short)4;
5: pig = pig++;
6: long goat = (int)2;
7: goat -= 1.0;
8: System.out.print(pig + " - " + goat);
```

- **A.** 4 - 1
- **B.** 4 - 2
- **C.** 5 - 1
- **D.** 5 - 2
- **E.** The code does not compile due to line 7.
- **F.** None of the above

9. What are the unique outputs of the following code snippet? (Choose all that apply.)

```
int a = 2, b = 4, c = 2;
System.out.println(a > 2 ? --c : b++);
System.out.println(b = (a!=c ? a : b++));
System.out.println(a > b ? b < c ? b : 2 : 1);
```

- **A.** 1
- **B.** 2
- **C.** 3

D. 4

E. 5

F. 6

G. The code does not compile.

10. What are the unique outputs of the following code snippet? (Choose all that apply.)

```
short height = 1, weight = 3;
short zebra = (byte) weight * (byte) height;
double ox = 1 + height * 2 + weight;
long giraffe = 1 + 9 % height + 1;
System.out.println(zebra);
System.out.println(ox);
System.out.println(giraffe);
```

A. 1

B. 2

C. 3

D. 4

E. 5

F. 6

G. The code does not compile.

11. What is the output of the following code?

```
1: public class ArithmeticSample {
2:    public static void main(String[] args) {
3:        int sample1 = (2 * 4) % 3;
4:        int sample2 = 3 * 2 % 3;
5:        int sample3 = 5 * (1 % 2);
6:        System.out.println(sample1+"-"+sample2+"-"+sample3);
7: }}
```

A. 0-0-5

B. 1-2-10

C. 2-1-5

D. 2-0-5

E. 3-1-10

F. 3-2-6

G. The code does not compile.

12. The _____ operator increases a value and returns the original value, while the _____ operator decreases a value and returns the new value.

A. post-increment, post-increment

B. pre-decrement, post-decrement

C. post-increment, post-increment

D. post-increment, pre-decrement

E. pre-increment, pre-decrement

F. pre-increment, post-decrement

13. What is the output of the following code snippet?

```
boolean sunny = true, raining = false, sunday = true;
boolean goingToTheStore = sunny & raining ^ sunday;
boolean goingToTheZoo = sunday && !raining;
boolean stayingHome = !(goingToTheStore && goingToTheZoo);
System.out.println(goingToTheStore + "-" + goingToTheZoo
    + "-" +stayingHome);
```

A. true-false-false

B. false-true-false

C. true-true-true

D. false-true-true

E. false-false-false

F. true-true-false

G. None of the above

14. Which of the following statements are correct? (Choose all that apply.)

A. The return value of an assignment operation expression can be void.

B. The inequality operator (!=) can be used to compare objects.

C. The equality operator (==) can be used to compare a boolean value with a numeric value.

D. During runtime, the && and | operators may cause only the left side of the expression to be evaluated.

E. The return value of an assignment operation expression is the value of the newly assigned variable.

F. In Java, 0 and false may be used interchangeably.

G. The logical complement operator (!) cannot be used to flip numeric values.

15. Which operators take three operands or values? (Choose all that apply.)

A. =

B. &&

C. *=

D. ? :

E. &

F. ++

G. /

16. How many lines of the following code contain compiler errors?

```
int note = 1 * 2 + (long)3;
short melody = (byte)(double)(note *= 2);
double song = melody;
float symphony = (float)((song == 1_000f) ? song * 2L : song);
```

A. 0

B. 1

C. 2

D. 3

E. 4

17. Given the following code snippet, what is the value of the variables after it is executed? (Choose all that apply.)

```
int ticketsTaken = 1;
int ticketsSold = 3;
ticketsSold += 1 + ticketsTaken++;
ticketsTaken *= 2;
ticketsSold += (long)1;
```

A. ticketsSold is 8

B. ticketsTaken is 2

C. ticketsSold is 6

D. ticketsTaken is 6

E. ticketsSold is 7

F. ticketsTaken is 4

G. The code does not compile.

18. Which of the following can be used to change the order of operation in an expression? (Choose all that apply.)

    A. [ ]

    B. < >

    C. ( )

    D. \ /

    E. { }

    F. " "

19. What is the result of executing the following code snippet? (Choose all that apply.)

    ```
    3: int start = 7;
    4: int end = 4;
    5: end += ++start;
    6: start = (byte)(Byte.MAX_VALUE + 1);
    ```

    A. start is 0

    B. start is -128

    C. start is 127

    D. end is 8

    E. end is 11

    F. end is 12

    G. The code does not compile.

    H. The code compiles but throws an exception at runtime.

20. Which of the following statements about unary operators are true? (Choose all that apply.)

    A. Unary operators are always executed before any surrounding binary or ternary operators.

    B. The - operator can be used to flip a boolean value.

    C. The pre-increment operator (++) returns the value of the variable before the increment is applied.

    D. The post-decrement operator (--) returns the value of the variable before the decrement is applied.

    E. The ! operator cannot be used on numeric values.

    F. None of the above

Chapter

4

Making Decisions

OCP EXAM OBJECTIVES COVERED IN THIS CHAPTER:

✓ **Using Operators and Decision Constructs**

- Use Java control statements including if, if/else, switch

- Create and use do/while, while, for and for each loops, including nested loops, use break and continue statements

Like many programming languages, Java is composed primarily of variables, operators, and statements put together in some logical order. Previously, we covered how to create and manipulate variables. Writing software is about more than managing variables, though; it is about creating applications that can make intelligent decisions. In this chapter, we present the various decision-making statements available to you within the language. This knowledge will allow you to build complex functions and class structures that you'll see throughout this book.

Creating Decision-Making Statements

Java operators allow you to create a lot of complex expressions, but they're limited in the manner in which they can control program flow. Imagine you want a method to be executed only under certain conditions that cannot be evaluated until runtime. For example, on rainy days, a zoo should remind patrons to bring an umbrella, or on a snowy day, the zoo might need to close. The software doesn't change, but the behavior of the software should, depending on the inputs supplied in the moment. In this section, we will discuss decision-making statements including `if`, `else`, and `switch` statements.

Statements and Blocks

As you may recall from Chapter 2, "Java Building Blocks," a Java *statement* is a complete unit of execution in Java, terminated with a semicolon (;). For the remainder of the chapter, we'll be introducing you to various Java control flow statements. *Control flow statements* break up the flow of execution by using decision-making, looping, and branching, allowing the application to selectively execute particular segments of code.

These statements can be applied to single expressions as well as a block of Java code. As described in Chapter 2, a *block* of code in Java is a group of zero or more statements between balanced braces ({}) and can be used anywhere a single statement is allowed. For example, the following two snippets are equivalent, with the first being a single expression and the second being a block of statements:

```
// Single statement
patrons++;

// Statement inside a block
{
    patrons++;
}
```

A statement or block often functions as the target of a decision-making statement. For example, we can prepend the decision-making if statement to these two examples:

```
// Single statement
if(ticketsTaken > 1)
   patrons++;

// Statement inside a block
if(ticketsTaken > 1)
{
   patrons++;
}
```

Again, both of these code snippets are equivalent. Just remember that the target of a decision-making statement can be a single statement or block of statements. For the rest of the chapter, we will use both forms to better prepare you for what you will see on the exam.

 While both of the previous examples are equivalent, stylistically the second form is often preferred, even if the block has only one statement. The second form has the advantage that you can quickly insert new lines of code into the block, without modifying the surrounding structure. While either of these forms is correct, it might explain why you often see developers who always use blocks with all decision-making statements.

The *if* Statement

Oftentimes, we want to execute a block of code only under certain circumstances. The *if* statement, as shown in Figure 4.1, accomplishes this by allowing our application to execute a particular block of code if and only if a boolean expression evaluates to true at runtime.

FIGURE 4.1   The structure of an if statement

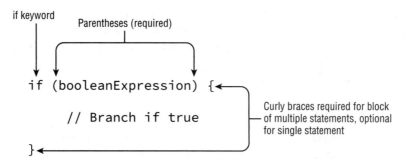

For example, imagine we had a function that used the hour of day, an integer value from 0 to 23, to display a message to the user:

```
if(hourOfDay < 11)
    System.out.println("Good Morning");
```

If the hour of the day is less than 11, then the message will be displayed. Now let's say we also wanted to increment some value, morningGreetingCount, every time the greeting is printed. We could write the if statement twice, but luckily Java offers us a more natural approach using a block:

```
if(hourOfDay < 11) {
    System.out.println("Good Morning");
    morningGreetingCount++;
}
```

The block allows multiple statements to be executed based on the if evaluation. Notice that the first statement didn't contain a block around the print section, but it easily could have. As discussed in the previous section, it is often considered good coding practice to put blocks around the execution component of if statements, as well as many other control flow statements, although it is certainly not required.

Watch Indentation and Braces

One area where the exam writers will try to trip you up is on if statements without braces ({}). For example, take a look at this slightly modified form of our example:

```
if(hourOfDay < 11)
    System.out.println("Good Morning");
    morningGreetingCount++;
```

Based on the indentation, you might be inclined to think the variable morningGreetingCount is only going to be incremented if the hourOfDay is less than 11, but that's not what this code does. It will execute the print statement only if the condition is met, but it will always execute the increment operation.

Remember that in Java, unlike some other programming languages, tabs are just whitespace and are not evaluated as part of the execution. When you see a control flow statement in a question, be sure to trace the open and close braces of the block, ignoring any indentation you may come across.

The *else* Statement

Let's expand our example a little. What if we want to display a different message if it is 11 a.m. or later? Could we do it using only the tools we have? Of course we can!

```
if(hourOfDay < 11) {
    System.out.println("Good Morning");
```

```
}
if(hourOfDay >= 11) {
   System.out.println("Good Afternoon");
}
```

This seems a bit redundant, though, since we're performing an evaluation on hourOfDay twice. It's also wasteful because in some circumstances the cost of the boolean expression we're evaluating could be computationally expensive. Luckily, Java offers us a more useful approach in the form of an else statement, as shown in Figure 4.2.

FIGURE 4.2   The structure of an else statement

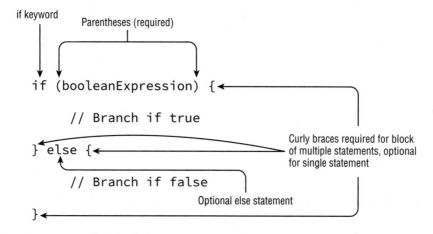

Let's return to this example:

```
if(hourOfDay < 11) {
   System.out.println("Good Morning");
} else {
   System.out.println("Good Afternoon");
}
```

Now our code is truly branching between one of the two possible options, with the boolean evaluation happening only once. The else operator takes a statement or block of statements, in the same manner as the if statement does. Similarly, we can append additional if statements to an else block to arrive at a more refined example:

```
if(hourOfDay < 11) {
   System.out.println("Good Morning");
} else if(hourOfDay < 15) {
   System.out.println("Good Afternoon");
} else {
   System.out.println("Good Evening");
}
```

In this example, the Java process will continue execution until it encounters an if state-ment that evaluates to true. If neither of the first two expressions is true, it will execute the final code of the else block. One thing to keep in mind in creating complex if and else statements is that order is important. For example, see what happens if we reorder the previous snippet of code as follows:

```java
if(hourOfDay < 15) {
    System.out.println("Good Afternoon");
} else if(hourOfDay < 11) {
    System.out.println("Good Morning");  // COMPILES BUT IS UNREACHABLE
} else {
    System.out.println("Good Evening");
}
```

For hours of the day less than 11, this code behaves very differently than the previous set of code. Do you see why the second block can never be executed regardless of the value of hourOfDay?

If a value is less than 11, then it must be also less than 15 by definition. Therefore, if the second branch in the example can be reached, the first branch can also be reached. Since exe-cution of each branch is mutually exclusive in this example (that is, only one branch can be executed), then if the first branch is executed, the second cannot be executed. Therefore, there is no way the second branch will ever be executed, and the code is deemed unreachable.

Verifying That the *if* Statement Evaluates to a Boolean Expression

Another common place the exam may try to lead you astray is by providing code where the boolean expression inside the if statement is not actually a boolean expression. For example, take a look at the following lines of code:

```java
int hourOfDay = 1;
if(hourOfDay) {  // DOES NOT COMPILE
    ...
}
```

This statement may be valid in some other programming and scripting languages, but not in Java, where 0 and 1 are not considered boolean values.

Also, like you saw in Chapter 3, "Operators," be wary of assignment operators being used as if they were equals (==) operators in if statements:

```java
int hourOfDay = 1;
if(hourOfDay = 5) {  // DOES NOT COMPILE
    ...
}
```

The *switch* Statement

What if we have a lot of possible branches for a single value? For example, we might want to print a different message based on the day of the week. We could certainly accomplish this with a combination of seven if or else statements, but that tends to create code that is long, difficult to read, and often not fun to maintain. For example, the following code prints a different value based on the day of the week using various different styles for each decision statement:

```java
int dayOfWeek = 5;

if(dayOfWeek == 0) System.out.print("Sunday");
else if(dayOfWeek == 1)
{
   System.out.print("Monday");
}
else if(dayOfWeek == 2) {
   System.out.print("Tuesday");
} else if(dayOfWeek == 3)
   System.out.print("Wednesday");
...
```

Luckily, Java, along with many other languages, provides a cleaner approach. A *switch* statement, as shown in Figure 4.3, is a complex decision-making structure in which a single value is evaluated and flow is redirected to the first matching branch, known as a *case* statement. If no such case statement is found that matches the value, an optional *default* statement will be called. If no such default option is available, the entire switch statement will be skipped.

FIGURE 4.3   The structure of a switch statement

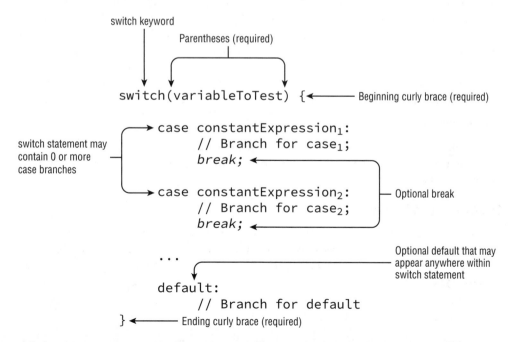

Proper Switch Syntax

Because switch statements can be longer than most decision-making statements, the exam may present invalid switch syntax to see whether you are paying attention. See if you can figure out why each of the following switch statements does not compile:

```
int month = 5;

switch month {  // DOES NOT COMPILE
   case 1: System.out.print("January");
}

switch (month)  // DOES NOT COMPILE
   case 1: System.out.print("January");

switch (month) {
   case 1: 2: System.out.print("January"); // DOES NOT COMPILE
}

switch (month) {
   case 1 || 2: System.out.print("January"); // DOES NOT COMPILE
}
```

The first switch statement does not compile because it is missing parentheses around the switch variable. The second statement does not compile because it is missing braces around the switch body. The third statement does not compile because the case keyword is missing before the 2: label. Each case statement requires the keyword case, followed by a value and a colon (:).

Finally, the last switch statement does not compile because 1 || 2 uses the short-circuit boolean operator, which cannot be applied to numeric values. A single bitwise operator (|) would have allowed the code to compile, although the interpretation of this might not be what you expect. It would then only match a value of month that is the bitwise result of 1 | 2, which is 3, and would *not* match month having a value 1 or 2. You don't need to know bitwise arithmetic for the exam, but you do need to know proper syntax for case statements.

Notice that these last two statements both try to combine case statements in ways that are not valid. One last note you should be aware of for the exam: a switch statement is not required to contain any case statements. For example, this statement is perfectly valid:

```
switch (month) {}
```

For the exam, make sure you memorize the syntax used in Figure 4.3. As you will see in the next section, while some aspects of switch statements have changed over the years, many things have not changed.

Switch Data Types

As shown in Figure 4.3, a switch statement has a target variable that is not evaluated until runtime. Prior to Java 5.0, this variable could only be int values or those values that could be promoted to int, specifically byte, short, char, or int, which we refer to as *primitive numeric types*.

The switch statement also supports any of the wrapper class versions of these primitive numeric types, such as Byte, Short, Character, or Integer. Don't worry if you haven't seen numeric wrapper classes—we'll be covering them in Chapter 5, "Core Java APIs." For now, you just need to know that they are objects that can store primitive values.

> Notice that boolean, long, float, and double are excluded from switch statements, as are their associated Boolean, Long, Float, and Double classes. The reasons are varied, such as boolean having too small a range of values and floating-point numbers having quite a wide range of values. For the exam, though, you just need to know that they are not permitted in switch statements.

When enumeration, denoted enum, was added in Java 5.0, support was added to switch statements to support enum values. An enumeration is a fixed set of constant values, which can also include methods and class variables, similar to a class definition. For the exam, you do not need to know how to create enums, but you should be aware they can be used as the target of switch statements.

In Java 7, switch statements were further updated to allow matching on String values. In Java 10, if the type a var resolves to is one of the types supported by a switch statement, then var can be used in a switch statement too.

Switch History and Changes

As you can see, switch statements have been modified in numerous versions of Java. You don't have to worry about remembering the history—just know what types are now allowed. The history lesson is for experienced Java developers who have been using an older version of Java and may not be aware of the numerous changes to switch statements over the years.

But wait, there's more. Java 12 launched with a Preview release of a powerful new feature called Switch Expressions, a construct that combines switch statements with lambda expressions and allows switch statements to return a value. You won't need to know Switch Expressions for the exam, but it's just a sign that the writers of Java are far from done making enhancements to switch statements.

The following is a list of all data types supported by switch statements:

- int and Integer
- byte and Byte
- short and Short
- char and Character
- String
- enum values
- var (if the type resolves to one of the preceding types)

For the exam, we recommend you memorize this list. Remember, `boolean`, `long`, `float`, `double`, and each of their associated wrapper classes are not supported by `switch` statements.

Switch Control Flow

Let's look at a simple `switch` example using the day of the week, with 0 for Sunday, 1 for Monday, and so on:

```
int dayOfWeek = 5;
switch(dayOfWeek) {
    default:
        System.out.println("Weekday");
    break;
        case 0:
    System.out.println("Sunday");
        break;
    case 6:
        System.out.println("Saturday");
    break;
}
```

With a value of dayOfWeek of 5, this code will output the following:

```
Weekday
```

The first thing you may notice is that there is a break statement at the end of each `case` and `default` section. We'll discuss `break` statements in more detail when we discuss branching, but for now all you need to know is that they terminate the `switch` statement and return flow control to the enclosing statement. As you'll soon see, if you leave out the `break` statement, flow will continue to the next proceeding `case` or `default` block automatically.

Another thing you might notice is that the `default` block is not at the end of the `switch` statement. There is no requirement that the `case` or `default` statement be in a particular order, unless you are going to have pathways that reach multiple sections of the `switch` block in a single execution.

To illustrate both of the preceding points, consider the following variation:

```
var dayOfWeek = 5;
switch(dayOfWeek) {
    case 0:
        System.out.println("Sunday");
    default:
        System.out.println("Weekday");
    case 6:
        System.out.println("Saturday");
    break;
}
```

This code looks a lot like the previous example. Notice that we used a var for the switch variable, which is allowed because it resolves to an int by the compiler. Next, two of the break statements have been removed, and the order has been changed. This means that for the given value of dayOfWeek, 5, the code will jump to the default block and then execute all of the proceeding case statements in order until it finds a break statement or finishes the switch statement:

```
Weekday
Saturday
```

The order of the case and default statements is now important since placing the default statement at the end of the switch statement would cause only one word to be output.

What if the value of dayOfWeek was 6 in this example? Would the default block still be executed? The output of this example with dayOfWeek set to 6 would be as follows:

```
Saturday
```

Even though the default block was before the case block, only the case block was executed. If you recall the definition of the default block, it is branched to only if there is no matching case value for the switch statement, regardless of its position within the switch statement.

Finally, if the value of dayOfWeek was 0, all three statements would be output:

```
Sunday
Weekday
Saturday
```

Notice that in this last example, the default statement is executed since there was no break statement at the end of the preceding case block. While the code will not branch to the default statement if there is a matching case value within the switch statement, it will execute the default statement if it encounters it after a case statement for which there is no terminating break statement.

The exam creators are fond of switch *examples that are missing* break *statements!* When evaluating switch statements on the exam, always consider that multiple branches may be visited in a single execution.

Acceptable Case Values

We conclude our discussion of switch statements by talking about acceptable values for case statements, given a particular switch variable. Not just any variable or value can be used in a case statement!

First off, the values in each case statement must be compile-time constant values of the same data type as the switch value. This means you can use only literals, enum constants, or final constant variables of the same data type. By final constant, we mean that the variable must be marked with the final modifier and initialized with a literal value in the same expression in which it is declared. For example, you can't have a case statement value that requires executing a method at runtime, even if that method always returns the same value. For these reasons, only the first and last case statements in the following example compiles:

```java
final int getCookies() { return 4; }
void feedAnimals() {
   final int bananas = 1;
   int apples = 2;
   int numberOfAnimals = 3;
   final int cookies = getCookies();
   switch (numberOfAnimals) {
      case bananas:
      case apples:  // DOES NOT COMPILES
      case getCookies():  // DOES NOT COMPILE
      case cookies :  // DOES NOT COMPILE
      case 3 * 5 :
   }
}
```

The bananas variable is marked final, and its value is known at compile-time, so it is valid. The apples variable is not marked final, even though its value is known, so it is not permitted. The next two case statements, with values getCookies() and cookies, do not compile because methods are not evaluated until runtime, so they cannot be used as the value of a case statement, even if one of the values is stored in a final variable. The last case statement, with value 3 * 5, does compile, as expressions are allowed as case values, provided the value can be resolved at compile-time. They also must be able to fit in the switch data type without an explicit cast. We'll go into that in more detail shortly.

Next, the data type for case statements must all match the data type of the switch variable. For example, you can't have a case statement of type String, if the switch statement variable is of type int, since the types are incomparable.

A More Complex Example

We now present a large switch statement, not unlike what you could see on the exam, with numerous broken case statements. See if you can figure out why certain case statements compile and others do not.

```java
private int getSortOrder(String firstName, final String lastName) {
   String middleName = "Patricia";
   final String suffix = "JR";
   int id = 0;
   switch(firstName) {
      case "Test":
         return 52;
      case middleName:  // DOES NOT COMPILE
         id = 5;
         break;
      case suffix:
```

```
            id = 0;
            break;
        case lastName:     // DOES NOT COMPILE
            id = 8;
            break;
        case 5:            // DOES NOT COMPILE
            id = 7;
            break;
        case 'J':          // DOES NOT COMPILE
            id = 10;
            break;
        case java.time.DayOfWeek.SUNDAY:  // DOES NOT COMPILE
            id=15;
            break;
    }
    return id;
}
```

The first case statement, "Test", compiles without issue since it is a String literal and is a good example of how a return statement, like a break statement, can be used to exit the switch statement early. The second case statement does not compile because middleName is not a constant value, despite having a known value at this particular line of execution. If a final modifier was added to the declaration of middleName, this case statement would have compiled. The third case statement compiles without issue because suffix is a final constant variable.

In the fourth case statement, despite lastName being final, it is not constant as it is passed to the function; therefore, this line does not compile as well. Finally, the last three case statements do not compile because none of them has a matching type of String, the last one being an enum value.

Numeric Promotion and Casting

Last but not least, switch statements support numeric promotion that does not require an explicit cast. For example, see if you can understand why only one of these case statements compiles:

```
short size = 4;
final int small = 15;
final int big = 1_000_000;
switch(size) {
    case small:
    case 1+2 :
    case big:  // DOES NOT COMPILE
}
```

As you may recall from our discussion of numeric promotion and casting in Chapter 3, the compiler can easily cast small from int to short at compile-time because the value 15 is small enough to fit inside a short. This would not be permitted if small was not a compile-time constant. Likewise, it can convert the expression 1+2 from int to short at compile-time. On the other hand, 1_000_000 is too large to fit inside of short without an explicit cast, so the last case statement does not compile.

Writing *while* Loops

A common practice when writing software is the need to do the same task some number of times. You could use the decision structures we have presented so far to accomplish this, but that's going to be a pretty long chain of if or else statements, especially if you have to execute the same thing 100 times or more.

Enter loops! A *loop* is a repetitive control structure that can execute a statement of code multiple times in succession. By making use of variables being able to be assigned new values, each repetition of the statement may be different. In the following example, the loop increments a counter variable that causes the value of price to increase by 10 on each execution of the loop. The loop continues for a total of 10 times.

```
int counter = 0;
while (counter < 10) {
    double price = counter * 10;
    System.out.println(price);
    counter++;
}
```

If you don't follow this code, don't panic—we'll be covering it shortly. In this section, we're going to discuss the while loop and its two forms. In the next section, we'll move onto for loops, which have their roots in while loops.

The *while* Statement

The simplest repetitive control structure in Java is the while statement, described in Figure 4.4. Like all repetition control structures, it has a termination condition, implemented as a boolean expression, that will continue as long as the expression evaluates to true.

FIGURE 4.4   The structure of a while statement

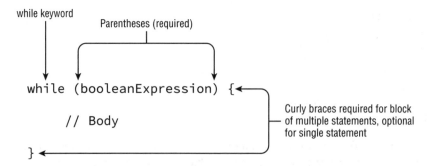

As shown in Figure 4.4, a `while` loop is similar to an `if` statement in that it is composed of a `boolean` expression and a statement, or a block of statements. During execution, the `boolean` expression is evaluated before each iteration of the loop and exits if the evaluation returns `false`.

Let's return to our mouse example from Chapter 2 and show how a loop can be used to model a mouse eating a meal.

```
int roomInBelly = 5;
public void eatCheese(int bitesOfCheese) {
    while (bitesOfCheese > 0 && roomInBelly > 0) {
        bitesOfCheese--;
        roomInBelly--;
    }
    System.out.println(bitesOfCheese+" pieces of cheese left");
}
```

This method takes an amount of food, in this case cheese, and continues until the mouse has no room in its belly or there is no food left to eat. With each iteration of the loop, the mouse "eats" one bite of food and loses one spot in its belly. By using a compound `boolean` statement, you ensure that the `while` loop can end for either of the conditions.

One thing to remember is that a `while` loop may terminate after its first evaluation of the `boolean` expression. For example, how many times is `Not full!` printed in the following example?

```
int full = 5;
while(full < 5) {
    System.out.println("Not full!");
    full++;
}
```

The answer? Zero! On the first iteration of the loop, the condition is reached, and the loop exits. This is why `while` loops are often used in places where you expect zero or more executions of the loop. Simply put, the body of the loop may not execute at all or may execute many times.

The *do/while* Statement

The second form a `while` loop can take is called a *do/while* loop, which like a `while` loop is a repetition control structure with a termination condition and statement, or a block of statements, as shown in Figure 4.5. Unlike a `while` loop, though, a do/while loop guarantees that the statement or block will be executed at least once. Whereas a `while` loop is executed zero or more times, a do/while loop is executed one or more times.

FIGURE 4.5   The structure of a do/while statement

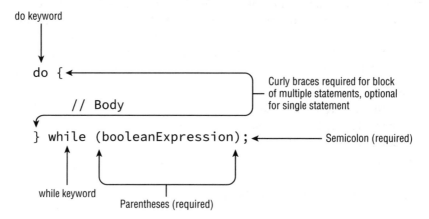

The primary difference between the syntactic structure of a do/while loop and a while loop is that a do/while loop purposely orders the body before the conditional expression so that the body will be executed at least once. For example, what is the output of the following statements?

```
int lizard = 0;
do {
    lizard++;
} while(false);
System.out.println(lizard);   // 1
```

Java will execute the statement block first and then check the loop condition. Even though the loop exits right away, the statement block is still executed once, and the program prints 1.

Comparing *while* and *do/while* Loops

In practice, it might be difficult to determine when you should use a while loop and when you should use a do/while loop. The short answer is that it does not actually matter. Any while loop can be converted to a do/while loop, and vice versa. For example, compare this while loop:

```
while(llama > 10) {
    System.out.println("Llama!");
    llama--;
}
```

and this do/while loop:

```
if(llama > 10) {
    do {
```

```
      System.out.println("Llama!");
      llama--;
   } while(llama > 10);
}
```

Although one of the loops is certainly easier to read, they are functionally equivalent. Think about it. If `llama` is less than or equal to 10 at the start, then both code snippets will exit without printing anything. If `llama` is greater than 10, say 15, then both loops will print `Llama!` exactly five times.

We recommend you use a `while` loop when the code will execute zero or more times and a do/while loop when the code will execute one or more times. To put it another way, you should use a do/while loop when you want your loop to execute at least once.

That said, determining whether you should use a `while` loop or a do/while loop in practice is sometimes about personal preference and about code readability.

For example, although the first statement in our previous example is shorter, the do/while statement has the advantage that you could leverage the existing `if` statement and perform some other operation in a new `else` branch, as shown in the following example:

```
if(llama > 10) {
   do {
      System.out.println("Llama!");
      llama--;
   } while(llama > 10);
} else {
   llama++;
}
```

For fun, try taking a do/while loop you've written in the past and convert it to a `while` loop, or vice versa.

Infinite Loops

The single most important thing you should be aware of when you are using any repetition control structure is to make sure they always terminate! Failure to terminate a loop can lead to numerous problems in practice including overflow exceptions, memory leaks, slow performance, and even bad data. Let's take a look at an example:

```
int pen = 2;
int pigs = 5;
while(pen < 10)
   pigs++;
```

You may notice one glaring problem with this statement: it will never end. The variable pen is never modified, so the expression (`pen < 10`) will always evaluate to true. The result is that the loop will never end, creating what is commonly referred to as an infinite loop. An *infinite loop* is a loop whose termination condition is never reached during runtime.

Anytime you write a loop, you should examine it to determine whether the termination condition is always eventually met under some condition. For example, a loop in which no variables are changing between two executions suggests that the termination condition may not be met. The loop variables should always be moving in a particular direction.

In other words, make sure the loop condition, or the variables the condition is dependent on, are changing between executions. Then, ensure that the termination condition will be eventually reached in all circumstances. As you'll see in the last section of this chapter, a loop may also exit under other conditions, such as a break statement.

 Real World Scenario

A Practical Use of an Infinite Loop

In practice, infinite loops can be used to monitor processes that exist for the life of the program—for example, a process that wakes up every 30 seconds to look for work to be done and then goes back to sleep afterward.

When creating an infinite loop like this, you need to make sure there are only a fixed number of them created by the application, or you could run out of memory. You also have to make sure that there is a way to stop them, often as part of the application shutting down. Finally, there are modern alternatives to creating infinite loops, such as using a scheduled thread executor, that are well beyond the scope of the exam.

If you're not familiar with how to create and execute multiple processes at once, don't worry, you don't need to be for this exam. When you continue on to exam 1Z0-816, you will study these topics as part of concurrency.

Constructing *for* Loops

Even though while and do/while statements are quite powerful, some tasks are so common in writing software that special types of loops were created—for example, iterating over a statement exactly 10 times or iterating over a list of names. You could easily accomplish these tasks with various while loops that you've seen so far, but they usually require writing multiple lines of code and managing variables manually. Wouldn't it be great if there was a looping structure that could do the same thing in a single line of code?

With that, we present the most convenient repetition control structure, for loops. There are two types of for loops, although both use the same for keyword. The first is referred to as the *basic* for loop, and the second is often called the *enhanced* for loop. For clarity, we'll refer to them as the for loop and the for-each loop, respectively, throughout the book.

The *for* Loop

A basic *for loop* has the same conditional boolean expression and statement, or block of statements, as the while loops, as well as two new sections: an *initialization block* and an *update* statement. Figure 4.6 shows how these components are laid out.

FIGURE 4.6   The structure of a basic for loop

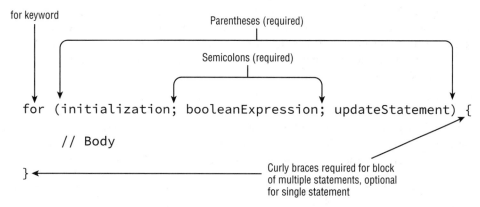

① Initialization statement executes
② If booleanExpression is true continue, else exit loop
③ Body executes
④ Execute updateStatement
⑤ Return to Step 2

Although Figure 4.6 might seem a little confusing and almost arbitrary at first, the organization of the components and flow allow us to create extremely powerful statements in a single line that otherwise would take multiple lines with a while loop. Note that each section is separated by a semicolon. Also, the initialization and update sections may contain multiple statements, separated by commas.

Variables declared in the initialization block of a for loop have limited scope and are accessible only within the for loop. Be wary of any exam questions in which a variable is declared within the initialization block of a for loop and then read outside the loop. For example, this code does not compile because the loop variable i is referenced outside the loop:

```
for(int i=0; i < 10; i++)
   System.out.print("Value is: "+i);
System.out.println(i);  // DOES NOT COMPILE
```

Alternatively, variables declared before the for loop and assigned a value in the initialization block may be used outside the for loop because their scope precedes the creation of the for loop.

Let's take a look at an example that prints the first five numbers, starting with zero:

```java
for(int i = 0; i < 5; i++) {
    System.out.print(i + " ");
}
```

The local variable i is initialized first to 0. The variable i is only in scope for the duration of the loop and is not available outside the loop once the loop has completed. Like a while loop, the boolean condition is evaluated on every iteration of the loop *before* the loop executes. Since it returns true, the loop executes and outputs the 0 followed by a space. Next, the loop executes the update section, which in this case increases the value of i to 1. The loop then evaluates the boolean expression a second time, and the process repeats multiple times, printing the following:

```
0 1 2 3 4
```

On the fifth iteration of the loop, the value of i reaches 4 and is incremented by 1 to reach 5. On the sixth iteration of the loop, the boolean expression is evaluated, and since (5 < 5) returns false, the loop terminates without executing the statement loop body.

 Real World Scenario

Why *i* in *for* Loops?

You may notice it is common practice to name a for loop variable i. Long before Java existed, programmers started using i as short for increment variable, and the practice exists today, even though many of those programming languages no longer do!

For double or triple loops, where i is already used, the next letters in the alphabet, j and k, are often used, respectively. One advantage of using a single-letter variable name in a for loop is that it doesn't take up a lot of space, allowing the for loop declaration to fit on a single line.

For the exam, and for your own coding experience, you should know that using a single-letter variable name is not required. That said, you are likely to encounter i in for loops throughout your professional software development experience.

Printing Elements in Reverse

Let's say you wanted to print the same first five numbers from zero as we did in the previous section, but this time in reverse order. The goal then is to print 4 3 2 1 0.

How would you do that? Starting with Java 10, you may now see var used in a for loop, so let's use that for this example. An initial implementation might look like the following:

```java
for (var counter = 5; counter > 0; counter--) {
    System.out.print(counter + " ");
}
```

First, how is `var` interpreted? Since it is assigned a value of 5, the compiler treats it as having a type of `int`. Next, what does the example output? While this snippet does output five distinct values and it resembles our first `for` loop example, it does not output the same five values. Instead, this is the output:

```
5 4 3 2 1
```

Wait, that's not what we wanted! We wanted 4 3 2 1 0. It starts with 5, because that is the first value assigned to it. Let's fix that by starting with 4 instead:

```
for (var counter = 4; counter > 0; counter--) {

    System.out.print(counter + " ");
}
```

What does this print now? This prints the following:

```
4 3 2 1
```

So close! The problem is it ends with 1, not 0, because we told it to exit as soon as the value was not strictly greater than 0. If we want to print the same 0 through 4 as our first example, we need to update the termination condition, like this:

```
for (var counter = 4; counter >= 0; counter--) {
    System.out.print(counter + " ");
}
```

Finally! We have code that now prints 4 3 2 1 0 and matches the reverse of our `for` loop example in the previous section. We could have instead used `counter > -1` as the loop termination condition in this example, although `counter >= 0` tends to be more readable.

 For the exam, you are going to have to know how to read forward and backward for loops. When you see a for loop on the exam, pay close attention to the loop variable and operations if the decrement operator, `--`, is used. While incrementing from 0 in a for loop is often straightforward, decrementing tends to be less intuitive. In fact, if you do see a for loop with a decrement operator on the exam, you should assume they are trying to test your knowledge of loop operations.

Working with *for* Loops

Although most for loops you are likely to encounter in your professional development experience will be well defined and similar to the previous examples, there are a number of variations and edge cases you could see on the exam. You should familiarize yourself with the following five examples; variations of these are likely to be seen on the exam.

Let's tackle some examples for illustrative purposes:

1. Creating an Infinite Loop

```
for( ; ; )
   System.out.println("Hello World");
```

Although this for loop may look like it does not compile, it will in fact compile and run without issue. It is actually an infinite loop that will print the same statement repeatedly. This example reinforces the fact that the components of the for loop are each optional. Note that the semicolons separating the three sections are required, as for( ) without any semicolons will not compile.

2. Adding Multiple Terms to the for Statement

```
int x = 0;
for(long y = 0, z = 4; x < 5 && y < 10; x++, y++) {
   System.out.print(y + " "); }
System.out.print(x + " ");
```

This code demonstrates three variations of the for loop you may not have seen. First, you can declare a variable, such as x in this example, before the loop begins and use it after it completes. Second, your initialization block, boolean expression, and update statements can include extra variables that may or may not reference each other. For example, z is defined in the initialization block and is never used. Finally, the update statement can modify multiple variables. This code will print the following when executed:

```
0 1 2 3 4 5
```

3. Redeclaring a Variable in the Initialization Block

```
int x = 0;
for(int x = 4; x < 5; x++) {    // DOES NOT COMPILE
   System.out.print(x + " ");
}
```

This example looks similar to the previous one, but it does not compile because of the initialization block. The difference is that x is repeated in the initialization block after already being declared before the loop, resulting in the compiler stopping because of a duplicate variable declaration. We can fix this loop by removing the declaration of x from the for loop as follows:

```
int x = 0;
for(x = 0; x < 5; x++) {
   System.out.print(x + " ");
}
```

Note that this variation will now compile because the initialization block simply assigns a value to x and does not declare it.

4. Using Incompatible Data Types in the Initialization Block

```
int x = 0;
for(long y = 0, int z = 4; x < 5; x++) {  // DOES NOT COMPILE
   System.out.print(y + " ");
}
```

Like the third example, this code will not compile, although this time for a different reason. The variables in the initialization block must all be of the same type. In the multiple terms example, y and z were both long, so the code compiled without issue, but in this example they have differing types, so the code will not compile.

5. Using Loop Variables Outside the Loop

```
for(long y = 0, x = 4; x < 5 && y < 10; x++, y++) {
   System.out.print(y + " ");
}
System.out.print(x);  // DOES NOT COMPILE
```

We covered this already at the start of this section, but this is so important for passing the exam that we discuss it again here. If you notice, x is defined in the initialization block of the loop and then used after the loop terminates. Since x was only scoped for the loop, using it outside the loop will cause a compiler error.

Modifying Loop Variables

What happens if you modify a variable in a for loop, or any other loop for that matter? Does Java even let you modify these variables? Take a look at the following three examples, and see whether you can determine what will happen if they are each run independently:

```
for(int i=0; i<10; i++)
   i = 0;

for(int j=1; j<10; j++)
   j--;

for(int k=0; k<10; )
   k++;
```

All three of these examples compile, as Java does let you modify loop variables, whether they be in for, while, or do/while loops. The first two examples create infinite loops, as loop conditions i<10 and j<10 are never reached, independently. In the first example, i is reset during every loop to 0, then incremented to 1, then reset to 0, and so on. In the second example, j is decremented to 0, then incremented to 1, then decremented to 0, and so on. The last example executes the loop exactly 10 times, so it is valid, albeit a little unusual.

Java does allow modification of loop variables, but you should be wary if you see questions on the exam that do this. While it is normally straightforward to look at a for loop and get an idea of how many times the loop will execute, once we start modifying loop variables, the behavior can be extremely erratic. This is especially true when nested loops are involved, which we cover later in this chapter.

There are also some special considerations when modifying a `Collection` object within a loop. For example, if you delete an element from a `List` while iterating over it, you could run into a `ConcurrentModificationException`. This topic is out of scope for the exam, though. You'll revisit this when studying for the 1Z0-816 exam.

> As a general rule, it is considered a poor coding practice to modify loop variables due to the unpredictability of the result. It also tends to make code difficult for other people to read. If you need to exit a loop early or change the flow, you can use `break`, `continue`, or `return`, which we'll discuss later in this chapter.

The for-each Loop

Let's say you want to iterate over a set of values, such as a list of names, and print each of them. Using a for loop, this can be accomplished with a counter variable:

```
public void printNames(String[] names) {
   for(int counter=0; counter<names.length; counter++)
      System.out.println(names[counter]);
}
```

This works, although it's a bit verbose. We're creating a counter variable, but we really don't care about its value—just that it loops through the array in order.

After almost 20 years of programming for loops like this, the writers of Java took a page from some other programming languages and added the enhanced for loop, or for-each loop as we like to call it. The *for-each* loop is a specialized structure designed to iterate over arrays and various Collection Framework classes, as presented in Figure 4.7.

FIGURE 4.7   The structure of an enhanced for-each loop

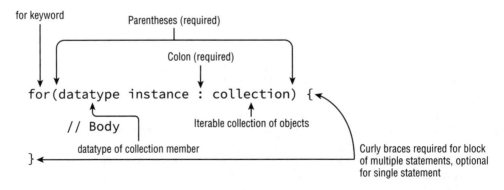

The for-each loop declaration is composed of an initialization section and an object to be iterated over. The right side of the for-each loop must be one of the following:

- A built-in Java array

- An object whose type implements `java.lang.Iterable`

We'll cover what implements means in Chapter 9, "Advanced Class Design," but for now you just need to know the right side must be an array or collection of items, such as a `List` or a `Set`. For the exam, you should know that this does not include all of the Collections Framework classes or interfaces, but only those that implement or extend that `Collection` interface. For example, `Map` is not supported in a for-each loop, although `Map` does include methods that return `Collection` instances.

In Chapter 5, we'll go into detail about how to create `List` objects and how they differ from traditional Java arrays. Likewise, `String` and `StringBuilder`, which you will also see in the next chapter, do not implement `Iterable` and cannot be used as the right side of a for-each statement.

The left side of the for-each loop must include a declaration for an instance of a variable whose type is compatible with the type of the array or collection on the right side of the statement. A `var` may also be used for the variable type declaration, with the specific type determined by the right side of the for-each statement. On each iteration of the loop, the named variable on the left side of the statement is assigned a new value from the array or collection on the right side of the statement.

Let's return to our previous example and see how we can apply a for-each loop to it.

```java
public void printNames(String[] names) {
    for(String name : names)
        System.out.println(name);
}
```

A lot shorter, isn't it? We no longer have a counter loop variable that we need to create, increment, and monitor. Like using a `for` loop in place of a `while` loop, for-each loops are meant to make code easier to read/write, freeing you to focus on the parts of your code that really matter.

Tackling the for-each Statement

Let's work with some examples:

- What will this code output?

```java
final String[] names = new String[3];
names[0] = "Lisa";
names[1] = "Kevin";
names[2] = "Roger";

for(String name : names) {
    System.out.print(name + ", ");
}
```

This is a simple one, with no tricks. The code will compile and print the following:

```
Lisa, Kevin, Roger,
```

▪ What will this code output?

```
List<String> values = new ArrayList<String>();
values.add("Lisa");
values.add("Kevin");
values.add("Roger");

for(var value : values) {
    System.out.print(value + ", ");
}
```

This code will compile and print the same values:

```
Lisa, Kevin, Roger,
```

Like the regular for loop, the for-each loop also accepts var for the loop variable, with the type implied by the data type being iterated over.

When you see a for-each loop on the exam, make sure the right side is an array or Iterable object and the left side has a matching type.

▪ Why does this fail to compile?

```
String names = "Lisa";
for(String name : names) {   // DOES NOT COMPILE
    System.out.print(name + " ");
}
```

In this example, the String names is not an array, nor does it define a list of items, so the compiler will throw an exception since it does not know how to iterate over the String. As a developer, you could iterate over each character of a String, but this would require using the charAt() method, which is not compatible with a for-each loop. The charAt() method, along with other String methods, will be covered in Chapter 5.

▪ Why does this fail to compile?

```
String[] names = new String[3];
for(int name : names) {  // DOES NOT COMPILE
    System.out.print(name + " ");
}
```

This code will fail to compile because the left side of the for-each statement does not define an instance of String. Notice that in this last example, the array is initialized with three null pointer values. In and of itself, that will not cause the code to not compile, as a corrected loop would just output null three times.

Switching Between *for* and for-each Loops

You may have noticed that in the previous for-each examples, there was an extra comma printed at the end of the list:

```
Lisa, Kevin, Roger,
```

While the for-each statement is convenient for working with lists in many cases, it does hide access to the loop iterator variable. If we wanted to print only the comma between names, we could convert the example into a standard for loop, as in the following example:

```
List<String> names = new ArrayList<String>();
names.add("Lisa");
names.add("Kevin");
names.add("Roger");

for(int i=0; i<names.size(); i++) {
   String name = names.get(i);
   if(i > 0) {
      System.out.print(", ");
   }
   System.out.print(name);
}
```

This sample code would output the following:

```
Lisa, Kevin, Roger
```

This is not as short as our for-each example, but it does create the output we wanted, without the extra comma.

It is also common to use a standard for loop over a for-each loop if comparing multiple elements in a loop within a single iteration, as in the following example:

```
int[] values = new int[3];
values[0] = 1;
values[1] = Integer.valueOf(3);
values[2] = 6;

for(int i=1; i<values.length; i++) {
   System.out.print((values[i]-values[i-1]) + ", ");
}
```

This sample code would output the following:

```
2, 3,
```

Notice that we skip the first index of the array, since value[-1] is not defined and would throw an IndexOutOfBoundsException error if called with i=0. When comparing n elements of a list with each other, our loop should be executed n-1 times.

Despite these examples, enhanced for-each loops are extremely convenient in a variety of circumstances. As a developer, though, you can always revert to a standard for loop if you need fine-grained control.

 Real World Scenario

Comparing *for* and for-each Loops

Since for and for-each both use the same keyword, you might be wondering how they are related. While this discussion is out of scope for the exam, let's take a moment to explore how for-each loops are converted to for loops by the compiler.

When for-each was introduced in Java 5, it was added as a compile-time enhancement. This means that Java actually converts the for-each loop into a standard for loop during compilation. For example, assuming names is an array of String as we saw in the first example, the following two loops are equivalent:

```
for(String name : names) {
    System.out.print(name + ", ");
}
for(int i=0; i < names.length; i++) {
    String name = names[i];
    System.out.print(name + ", ");
}
```

For objects that inherit Iterable, there is a different, but similar, conversion. For example, assuming values is an instance of List<Integer>, the following two loops are equivalent:

```
for(int value : values) {
    System.out.print(value + ", ");
}
for(Iterator<Integer> i = values.iterator(); i.hasNext(); ) {
    int value = i.next();
    System.out.print(value + ", ");
}
```

Notice that in the second version, there is no update statement in the for loop as next() both retrieves the next available value and moves the iterator forward.

Controlling Flow with Branching

The final type of control flow structures we will cover in this chapter are branching statements. Up to now, we have been dealing with single loops that ended only when their boolean expression evaluated to false. We'll now show you other ways loops could end, or branch, and you'll see that the path taken during runtime may not be as straightforward as in the previous examples.

Nested Loops

Before we move into branching statements, we need to introduce the concept of nested loops. A *nested loop* is a loop that contains another loop including while, do/while, for, and for-each loops. For example, consider the following code that iterates over a two-dimensional array, which is an array that contains other arrays as its members. We'll cover multidimensional arrays in detail in Chapter 5, but for now assume the following is how you would declare a two-dimensional array:

```java
int[][] myComplexArray = {{5,2,1,3},{3,9,8,9},{5,7,12,7}};

for(int[] mySimpleArray : myComplexArray) {
    for(int i=0; i<mySimpleArray.length; i++) {
        System.out.print(mySimpleArray[i]+"\t");
    }
    System.out.println();
}
```

Notice that we intentionally mix a for and for-each loop in this example. The outer loop will execute a total of three times. Each time the outer loop executes, the inner loop is executed four times. When we execute this code, we see the following output:

```
5       2       1       3
3       9       8       9
5       7       12      7
```

Nested loops can include while and do/while, as shown in this example. See whether you can determine what this code will output:

```java
int hungryHippopotamus = 8;
while(hungryHippopotamus>0) {
    do {
        hungryHippopotamus -= 2;
    } while (hungryHippopotamus>5);
    hungryHippopotamus--;
    System.out.print(hungryHippopotamus+", ");
}
```

The first time this loop executes, the inner loop repeats until the value of hungryHippopotamus is 4. The value will then be decremented to 3, and that will be the output at the end of the first iteration of the outer loop.

On the second iteration of the outer loop, the inner do/while will be executed once, even though hungryHippopotamus is already not greater than 5. As you may recall, do/while statements always execute the body at least once. This will reduce the value to 1, which will be further lowered by the decrement operator in the outer loop to 0. Once the value reaches 0, the outer loop will terminate. The result is that the code will output the following:

3, 0,

The examples in the rest of this section will include many nested loops. You will also encounter nested loops on the exam, so the more practice you have with them, the more prepared you will be.

Some of the most time-consuming questions you may see on the exam could involve nested loops with lots of branching. We recommend you try to answer the question right away, but if you start to think it is going to take too long, you should mark it and come back to it later. Remember, all questions on the exam are weighted evenly!

Adding Optional Labels

One thing we intentionally skipped when we presented if statements, switch statements, and loops is that they can all have optional labels. A *label* is an optional pointer to the head of a statement that allows the application flow to jump to it or break from it. It is a single identifier that is proceeded by a colon (:). For example, we can add optional labels to one of the previous examples:

```
int[][] myComplexArray = {{5,2,1,3},{3,9,8,9},{5,7,12,7}};

OUTER_LOOP:  for(int[] mySimpleArray : myComplexArray) {
    INNER_LOOP:  for(int i=0; i<mySimpleArray.length; i++) {
        System.out.print(mySimpleArray[i]+"\t");
    }
    System.out.println();
}
```

Labels follow the same rules for formatting as identifiers. For readability, they are commonly expressed using uppercase letters, with underscores between words, to distinguish them from regular variables. When dealing with only one loop, labels do not add any value, but as we'll see in the next section, they are extremely useful in nested structures.

The *break* Statement

As you saw when working with `switch` statements, a *break* statement transfers the flow of control out to the enclosing statement. The same holds true for a `break` statement that appears inside of a `while`, do/`while`, or `for` loop, as it will end the loop early, as shown in Figure 4.8.

FIGURE 4.8   The structure of a break statement

```
Optional reference to head of loop
                                              Colon (required if optionalLabel is present)

optionalLabel: while(booleanExpression) {

        // Body

        // Somewhere in loop
        break optionalLabel;
                                          Semicolon (required)
}
        break keyword
```

Notice in Figure 4.8 that the break statement can take an optional label parameter. Without a label parameter, the break statement will terminate the nearest inner loop it is currently in the process of executing. The optional label parameter allows us to break out of a higher-level outer loop. In the following example, we search for the first (x,y) array index position of a number within an unsorted two-dimensional array:

```
public class FindInMatrix {
    public static void main(String[] args) {
        int[][] list = {{1,13},{5,2},{2,2}};
        int searchValue = 2;
        int positionX = -1;
```

```
    int positionY = -1;

PARENT_LOOP: for(int i=0; i<list.length; i++) {
    for(int j=0; j<list[i].length; j++) {
        if(list[i][j]==searchValue) {
            positionX = i;
            positionY = j;
            break PARENT_LOOP;
        }
    }
}
if(positionX==-1 || positionY==-1) {
    System.out.println("Value "+searchValue+" not found");
} else {
    System.out.println("Value "+searchValue+" found at: " +
        "("+positionX+","+positionY+")");
}
    }
}
```

When executed, this code will output the following:

```
Value 2 found at: (1,1)
```

In particular, take a look at the statement break `PARENT_LOOP`. This statement will break out of the entire loop structure as soon as the first matching value is found. Now, imagine what would happen if we replaced the body of the inner loop with the following:

```
if(list[i][j]==searchValue) {
    positionX = i;
    positionY = j;
    break;
}
```

How would this change our flow, and would the output change? Instead of exiting when the first matching value is found, the program will now only exit the inner loop when the condition is met. In other words, the structure will now find the first matching value of the last inner loop to contain the value, resulting in the following output:

```
Value 2 found at: (2,0)
```

Finally, what if we removed the break altogether?

```
if(list[i][j]==searchValue) {
    positionX = i;
    positionY = j;
}
```

In this case, the code will search for the last value in the entire structure that has the matching value. The output will look like this:

```
Value 2 found at: (2,1)
```

You can see from this example that using a label on a break statement in a nested loop, or not using the break statement at all, can cause the loop structure to behave quite differently.

The *continue* Statement

Let's now extend our discussion of advanced loop control with the *continue* statement, a statement that causes flow to finish the execution of the current loop, as shown in Figure 4.9.

FIGURE 4.9   The structure of a continue statement

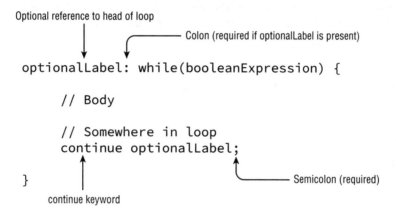

You may notice the syntax of the continue statement mirrors that of the break statement. In fact, the statements are identical in how they are used, but with different results. While the break statement transfers control to the enclosing statement, the continue statement transfers control to the boolean expression that determines if the loop should continue. In other words, it ends the current iteration of the loop. Also, like the break statement, the continue statement is applied to the nearest inner loop under execution using optional label statements to override this behavior.

Let's take a look at an example. Imagine we have a zookeeper who is supposed to clean the first leopard in each of four stables but skip stable b entirely.

```
1: public class CleaningSchedule {
2:     public static void main(String[] args) {
3:         CLEANING: for(char stables = 'a'; stables<='d'; stables++) {
4:             for(int leopard = 1; leopard<4; leopard++) {
5:                 if(stables=='b' || leopard==2) {
```

```
6:                     continue CLEANING;
7:                 }
8:                 System.out.println("Cleaning: "+stables+","+leopard);
9: } } } }
```

With the structure as defined, the loop will return control to the parent loop any time the first value is b or the second value is 2. On the first, third, and fourth executions of the outer loop, the inner loop prints a statement exactly once and then exits on the next inner loop when leopard is 2. On the second execution of the outer loop, the inner loop immediately exits without printing anything since b is encountered right away. The following is printed:

```
Cleaning: a,1
Cleaning: c,1
Cleaning: d,1
```

Now, imagine we removed the CLEANING label in the continue statement so that control is returned to the inner loop instead of the outer. Line 6 becomes the following:

```
6:                     continue;
```

This corresponds to the zookeeper skipping all leopards except those labeled 2 or in stable b. The output would then be the following:

```
Cleaning: a,1
Cleaning: a,3
Cleaning: c,1
Cleaning: c,3
Cleaning: d,1
Cleaning: d,3
```

Finally, if we remove the continue statement and associated if statement altogether by removing lines 5–7, we arrive at a structure that outputs all the values, such as this:

```
Cleaning: a,1
Cleaning: a,2
Cleaning: a,3
Cleaning: b,1
Cleaning: b,2
Cleaning: b,3
Cleaning: c,1
Cleaning: c,2
Cleaning: c,3
Cleaning: d,1
Cleaning: d,2
Cleaning: d,3
```

The *return* Statement

Given that this book shouldn't be your first foray into programming, we hope you've come across methods that contain return statements. Regardless, we'll be covering how to design and create methods that use them in detail in Chapter 7, "Methods and Encapsulation."

For now, though, you should be familiar with the idea that creating methods and using return statements can be used as an alternative to using labels and break statements. For example, take a look at this rewrite of our earlier FindInMatrix class:

```java
public class FindInMatrixUsingReturn {
    private static int[] searchForValue(int[][] list, int v) {
        for (int i = 0; i < list.length; i++) {
            for (int j = 0; j < list[i].length; j++) {
                if (list[i][j] == v) {
                    return new int[] {i,j};
                }
            }
        }
        return null;
    }

    public static void main(String[] args) {
        int[][] list = { { 1, 13 }, { 5, 2 }, { 2, 2 } };
        int searchValue = 2;
        int[] results = searchForValue(list,searchValue);

        if (results == null) {
            System.out.println("Value " + searchValue + " not found");
        } else {
            System.out.println("Value " + searchValue + " found at: " +
                "(" + results[0] + "," + results[1] + ")");
        }
    }
}
```

This class is functionally the same as the first FindInMatrix class we saw earlier using break. If you need finer-grained control of the loop with multiple break and continue statements, the first class is probably better. That said, we find code without labels and break statements a lot easier to read and debug. Also, making the search logic an independent function makes the code more reusable and the calling main() method a lot easier to read.

For the exam, you will need to know both forms. Just remember that return statements can be used to exit loops quickly and can lead to more readable code in practice, especially when used with nested loops.

Unreachable Code

One facet of break, continue, and return that you should be aware of is that any code placed immediately after them in the same block is considered unreachable and will not compile. For example, the following code snippet does not compile:

```
int checkDate = 0;
while(checkDate<10) {
    checkDate++;
    if(checkDate>100) {
        break;
        checkDate++;  // DOES NOT COMPILE
    }
}
```

Even though it is not logically possible for the if statement to evaluate to true in this code sample, the compiler notices that you have statements immediately following the break and will fail to compile with "unreachable code" as the reason. The same is true for continue and return statements too, as shown in the following two examples:

```
int minute = 1;
WATCH: while(minute>2) {
    if(minute++>2) {
        continue WATCH;
        System.out.print(minute);  // DOES NOT COMPILE
    }
}

int hour = 2;
switch(hour) {
    case 1: return; hour++;  // DOES NOT COMPILE
    case 2:
}
```

One thing to remember is that it does not matter if loop or decision structure actually visits the line of code. For example, the loop could execute zero or infinite times at runtime. Regardless of execution, the compiler will report an error if it finds any code it deems unreachable, in this case any statements immediately following a break, continue, or return statement.

Reviewing Branching

We conclude this section with Table 4.1, which will help remind you when labels, break, and continue statements are permitted in Java. Although for illustrative purposes our examples have included using these statements in nested loops, they can be used inside single loops as well.

TABLE 4.1   Advanced flow control usage

	Allows optional labels	Allows *break* statement	Allows *continue* statement
while	Yes	Yes	Yes
do while	Yes	Yes	Yes
for	Yes	Yes	Yes
switch	Yes	Yes	No

Last but not least, all testing centers should offer some form of scrap paper or dry-erase board to use during the exam. We strongly recommend you make use of these testing aids should you encounter complex questions involving nested loops and branching statements.

Summary

This chapter presented how to make intelligent decisions in Java. We covered basic decision-making constructs such as if, else, and switch statements and showed how to use them to change the path of process at runtime. Remember that the switch statement allows a lot of data types it did not in the past, such as String, enum, and in certain cases var.

We then moved our discussion to repetition control structures, starting with while and do/while loops. We showed how to use them to create processes that looped multiple times and also showed how it is important to make sure they eventually terminate. Remember that most of these structures require the evaluation of a particular boolean expression to complete.

Next, we covered the extremely convenient repetition control structures, for and for-each loops. While their syntax is more complex than the traditional while or do/while loops, they are extremely useful in everyday coding and allow you to create complex expressions in a single line of code. With a for-each loop you don't need to explicitly write a boolean expression, since the compiler builds one for you. For clarity, we referred to an enhanced for loop as a for-each loop, but syntactically both are written using the for keyword.

We concluded this chapter by discussing advanced control options and how flow can be enhanced through nested loops, coupled with break, continue, and return statements. Be wary of questions on the exam that use nested loops, especially ones with labels, and verify they are being used correctly.

This chapter is especially important because at least one component of this chapter will likely appear in every exam question with sample code. Many of the questions on the exam focus on proper syntactic use of the structures, as they will be a large source of questions that end in "Does not compile." You should be able to answer all of the review questions correctly or fully understand those that you answered incorrectly before moving on to later chapters.

Exam Essentials

Understand if and else decision control statements.   The if and else statements come up frequently throughout the exam in questions unrelated to decision control, so make sure you fully understand these basic building blocks of Java.

Understand switch statements and their proper usage.   You should be able to spot a poorly formed switch statement on the exam. The switch value and data type should be compatible with the case statements, and the values for the case statements must evaluate to compile-time constants. Finally, at runtime a switch statement branches to the first matching case, or default if there is no match, or exits entirely if there is no match and no default branch. The process then continues into any proceeding case or default statements until a break or return statement is reached.

Understand while loops.   Know the syntactical structure of all while and do/while loops. In particular, know when to use one versus the other.

Be able to use for loops.   You should be familiar with for and for-each loops and know how to write and evaluate them. Each loop has its own special properties and structures. You should know how to use for-each loops to iterate over lists and arrays.

Understand how break, continue, and return can change flow control.   Know how to change the flow control within a statement by applying a break, continue, or return statement. Also know which control statements can accept break statements and which can accept continue statements. Finally, you should understand how these statements work inside embedded loops or switch statements.

Review Questions

1. Which of the following data types can be used in a `switch` statement? (Choose all that apply.)

   A. enum

   B. int

   C. Byte

   D. long

   E. String

   F. char

   G. var

   H. double

2. What is the output of the following code snippet? (Choose all that apply.)

   ```
   3: int temperature = 4;
   4: long humidity = -temperature + temperature * 3;
   5: if (temperature>=4)
   6: if (humidity < 6) System.out.println("Too Low");
   7: else System.out.println("Just Right");
   8: else System.out.println("Too High");
   ```

   A. Too Low

   B. Just Right

   C. Too High

   D. A `NullPointerException` is thrown at runtime.

   E. The code will not compile because of line 7.

   F. The code will not compile because of line 8.

3. What is the output of the following code snippet?

   ```
   List<Integer> myFavoriteNumbers = new ArrayList<>();
   myFavoriteNumbers.add(10);
   myFavoriteNumbers.add(14);
   for (var a : myFavoriteNumbers) {
       System.out.print(a + ", ");
       break;
   }

   for (int b : myFavoriteNumbers) {
   ```

```
        continue;
        System.out.print(b + ", ");
    }

    for (Object c : myFavoriteNumbers)
        System.out.print(c + ", ");
```

A. It compiles and runs without issue but does not produce any output.

B. 10, 14,

C. 10, 10, 14,

D. 10, 10, 14, 10, 14,

E. Exactly one line of code does not compile.

F. Exactly two lines of code do not compile.

G. Three or more lines of code do not compile.

H. The code contains an infinite loop and does not terminate.

4. Which statements about decision structures are true? (Choose all that apply.)

   A. A for-each loop can be executed on any Collections Framework object.

   B. The body of a while loop is guaranteed to be executed at least once.

   C. The conditional expression of a for loop is evaluated before the first execution of the loop body.

   D. A switch statement with no matching case statement requires a default statement.

   E. The body of a do/while loop is guaranteed to be executed at least once.

   F. An if statement can have multiple corresponding else statements.

5. Assuming weather is a well-formed nonempty array, which code snippet, when inserted independently into the blank in the following code, prints all of the elements of weather? (Choose all that apply.)

```
private void print(int[] weather) {
    for(_____) {
        System.out.println(weather[i]);
    }
}
```

   A. int i=weather.length; i>0; i--

   B. int i=0; i<=weather.length-1; ++i

   C. var w : weather

   D. int i=weather.length-1; i>=0; i--

   E. int i=0, int j=3; i<weather.length; ++i

   F. int i=0; ++i<10 && i<weather.length;

   G. None of the above

6. Which statements, when inserted independently into the following blank, will cause the code to print 2 at runtime? (Choose all that apply.)

```
int count = 0;
BUNNY: for(int row = 1; row <=3; row++)
   RABBIT: for(int col = 0; col <3 ; col++) {
      if((col + row) % 2 == 0)
         _____;
      count++;
   }
System.out.println(count);
```

A. break BUNNY

B. break RABBIT

C. continue BUNNY

D. continue RABBIT

E. break

F. continue

G. None of the above, as the code contains a compiler error

7. Given the following method, how many lines contain compilation errors? (Choose all that apply.)

```
private DayOfWeek getWeekDay(int day, final int thursday) {
   int otherDay = day;
   int Sunday = 0;
   switch(otherDay) {
      default:
      case 1: continue;
      case thursday: return DayOfWeek.THURSDAY;
      case 2: break;
      case Sunday: return DayOfWeek.SUNDAY;
      case DayOfWeek.MONDAY: return DayOfWeek.MONDAY;
   }
   return DayOfWeek.FRIDAY;
}
```

A. None, the code compiles without issue.

B. 1

C. 2

D. 3

E. 4

F. 5

G. 6

H. The code compiles but may produce an error at runtime.

8.   What is the result of the following code snippet?

```
3: int sing = 8, squawk = 2, notes = 0;
4: while(sing > squawk) {
5:     sing--;
6:     squawk += 2;
7:     notes += sing + squawk;
8: }
9: System.out.println(notes);
```

A. 11

B. 13

C. 23

D. 33

E. 50

F. The code will not compile because of line 7.

9.   What is the output of the following code snippet?

```
2: boolean keepGoing = true;
3: int result = 15, meters = 10;
4: do {
5:     meters--;
6:     if(meters==8) keepGoing = false;
7:     result -= 2;
8: } while keepGoing;
9: System.out.println(result);
```

A. 7

B. 9

C. 10

D. 11

E. 15

F. The code will not compile because of line 6.

G. The code does not compile for a different reason.

10. Which statements about the following code snippet are correct? (Choose all that apply.)

```
for(var penguin : new int[2])
   System.out.println(penguin);

var ostrich = new Character[3];
for(var emu : ostrich)
   System.out.println(emu);

List parrots = new ArrayList();
for(var macaw  : parrots)
   System.out.println(macaw);
```

   A. The data type of penguin is Integer.
   B. The data type of penguin is int.
   C. The data type of emu is undefined.
   D. The data type of emu is Character.
   E. The data type of macaw is undefined.
   F. The data type of macaw is Object.
   G. None of the above, as the code does not compile

11. What is the result of the following code snippet?

```
final char a = 'A', e = 'E';
char grade = 'B';
switch (grade) {
   default:
   case a:
   case 'B': 'C': System.out.print("great ");
   case 'D': System.out.print("good "); break;
   case e:
   case 'F': System.out.print("not good ");
}
```

   A. great
   B. great good
   C. good
   D. not good
   E. The code does not compile because the data type of one or more case statements does not match the data type of the switch variable.
   F. None of the above

12. Given the following array, which code snippets print the elements in reverse order from how they are declared? (Choose all that apply.)

```
char[] wolf = {'W', 'e', 'b', 'b', 'y'};
```

A.
```
int q = wolf.length;
for( ; ; ) {
   System.out.print(wolf[--q]);
   if(q==0) break;
}
```

B.
```
for(int m=wolf.length-1; m>=0; --m)
   System.out.print(wolf[m]);
```

C.
```
for(int z=0; z<wolf.length; z++)
   System.out.print(wolf[wolf.length-z]);
```

D.
```
int x = wolf.length-1;
for(int j=0; x>=0 && j==0; x--)
   System.out.print(wolf[x]);
```

E.
```
final int r = wolf.length;
for(int w = r-1; r>-1; w = r-1)
   System.out.print(wolf[w]);
```

F.
```
for(int i=wolf.length; i>0; --i)
   System.out.print(wolf[i]);
```

G. None of the above

13. What distinct numbers are printed when the following method is executed? (Choose all that apply.)

```
private void countAttendees() {
   int participants = 4, animals = 2, performers = -1;

   while((participants = participants+1) < 10) {}
   do {} while (animals++ <= 1);
   for( ; performers<2; performers+=2) {}

   System.out.println(participants);
   System.out.println(animals);
   System.out.println(performers);
}
```

A. 6

B. 3

C. 4

D. 5

E. 10

F. 9

G. The code does not compile.

H. None of the above

14. What is the output of the following code snippet?

```
2: double iguana = 0;
3: do {
4:    int snake = 1;
5:    System.out.print(snake++ + " ");
6:    iguana--;
7: } while (snake <= 5);
8: System.out.println(iguana);
```

A. 1 2 3 4 -4.0

B. 1 2 3 4 -5.0

C. 1 2 3 4 5 -4.0

D. 0 1 2 3 4 5 -5.0

E. The code does not compile.

F. The code compiles but produces an infinite loop at runtime.

G. None of the above

15. Which statements, when inserted into the following blanks, allow the code to compile and run without entering an infinite loop? (Choose all that apply.)

```
4:   int height = 1;
5:   L1: while(height++ <10) {
6:      long humidity = 12;
7:      L2: do {
8:          if(humidity-- % 12 == 0) _____;
9:          int temperature = 30;
10:         L3: for( ; ; ) {
11:             temperature++;
12:             if(temperature>50) _____;
13:         }
14:     } while (humidity > 4);
15: }
```

A. break `L2` on line 8; continue `L2` on line 12

B. continue on line 8; continue on line 12

C. break `L3` on line 8; break `L1` on line 12

D. continue `L2` on line 8; continue `L3` on line 12

E. continue `L2` on line 8; continue `L2` on line 12

F. None of the above, as the code contains a compiler error.

16. What is the output of the following code snippet? (Choose all that apply.)

```
2: var tailFeathers = 3;
3: final var one = 1;
4: switch (tailFeathers) {
5:    case one: System.out.print(3 + " ");
6:    default: case 3: System.out.print(5 + " ");
7: }
8: while (tailFeathers > 1) {
9:    System.out.print(--tailFeathers + " "); }
```

A. 3

B. 5 1

C. 5 2

D. 3 5 1

E. 5 2 1

F. The code will not compile because of lines 3–5.

G. The code will not compile because of line 6.

17. What is the output of the following code snippet?

```
15: int penguin = 50, turtle = 75;
16: boolean older = penguin >= turtle;
17: if (older = true) System.out.println("Success");
18: else System.out.println("Failure");
19: else if(penguin != 50) System.out.println("Other");
```

A. Success

B. Failure

C. Other

D. The code will not compile because of line 17.

E. The code compiles but throws an exception at runtime.

F. None of the above

18. Which of the following are possible data types for `olivia` that would allow the code to compile? (Choose all that apply.)

```
for(var sophia : olivia) {
    System.out.println(sophia);
}
```

A. Set

B. Map

C. String

D. int[]

E. Collection

F. StringBuilder

G. None of the above

19. What is the output of the following code snippet?

```
6:  String instrument = "violin";
7:  final String CELLO = "cello";
8:  String viola = "viola";
9:  int p = -1;
10: switch(instrument) {
11:     case "bass" : break;
12:     case CELLO : p++;
13:     default: p++;
14:     case "VIOLIN": p++;
15:     case "viola" : ++p; break;
16: }
17: System.out.print(p);
```

A. -1

B. 0

C. 1

D. 2

E. 3

F. The code does not compile.

20. What is the output of the following code snippet? (Choose all that apply.)

```
9:  int w = 0, r = 1;
10: String name = "";
11: while(w < 2) {
12:     name += "A";
```

```
13:    do {
14:        name += "B";
15:        if(name.length()>0) name += "C";
16:        else break;
17:    } while (r <=1);
18:    r++; w++; }
19: System.out.println(name);
```

A. ABC

B. ABCABC

C. ABCABCABC

D. Line 15 contains a compilation error.

E. Line 18 contains a compilation error.

F. The code compiles but never terminates at runtime.

G. The code compiles but throws a `NullPointerException` at runtime.

Chapter

5

Core Java APIs

OCP EXAM OBJECTIVES COVERED IN THIS CHAPTER:

✓ **Working with Java Primitive Data Types and String APIs**

- ■ Create and manipulate Strings
- ■ Manipulate data using the StringBuilder class and its methods

✓ **Working with Java Arrays**

- ■ Declare, instantiate, initialize and use a one-dimensional array
- ■ Declare, instantiate, initialize and use a two-dimensional array

✓ **Programming Abstractly Through Interfaces**

- ■ Declare and use List and ArrayList instances

In the context of an Application Programming Interface (API), an interface refers to a group of classes or Java interface definitions giving you access to a service or functionality.

In this chapter, you will learn about many core data structures in Java, along with the most common APIs to access them. For example, String and StringBuilder, along with their associated APIs, are used to create and manipulate text data. An array, List, Set, or Map are used to manage often large groups of data. You'll also learn how to determine whether two objects are equivalent.

This chapter is long, so we recommend reading it in multiple sittings. On the bright side, it contains most of the APIs you need to know for the exam.

Creating and Manipulating Strings

The String class is such a fundamental class that you'd be hard-pressed to write code without it. After all, you can't even write a main() method without using the String class. A *string* is basically a sequence of characters; here's an example:

```
String name = "Fluffy";
```

As you learned in Chapter 2, "Java Building Blocks," this is an example of a reference type. You also learned that reference types are created using the new keyword. Wait a minute. Something is missing from the previous example: It doesn't have new in it! In Java, these two snippets both create a String:

```
String name = "Fluffy";
String name = new String("Fluffy");
```

Both give you a reference variable named name pointing to the String object "Fluffy". They are subtly different, as you'll see in the section "The *String* Pool" later in this chapter. For now, just remember that the String class is special and doesn't need to be instantiated with new.

Since a String is a sequence of characters, you probably won't be surprised to hear that it implements the interface CharSequence. This interface is a general way of representing several classes, including String and StringBuilder. You'll learn more about interfaces later in the book.

In this section, we'll look at concatenation, immutability, common methods, and method chaining.

Concatenation

In Chapter 3, "Operators," you learned how to add numbers. 1 + 2 is clearly 3. But what is "1" + "2"? It's actually "12" because Java combines the two String objects. Placing one String before the other String and combining them is called string *concatenation*. The exam creators like string concatenation because the + operator can be used in two ways within the same line of code. There aren't a lot of rules to know for this, but you have to know them well:

1. If both operands are numeric, + means numeric addition.

2. If either operand is a String, + means concatenation.

3. The expression is evaluated left to right.

Now let's look at some examples:

```
System.out.println(1 + 2);          // 3
System.out.println("a" + "b");      // ab
System.out.println("a" + "b" + 3);  // ab3
System.out.println(1 + 2 + "c");    // 3c
System.out.println("c" + 1 + 2);    // c12
```

The first example uses the first rule. Both operands are numbers, so we use normal addition. The second example is simple string concatenation, described in the second rule. The quotes for the String are only used in code—they don't get output.

The third example combines both the second and third rules. Since we start on the left, Java figures out what "a" + "b" evaluates to. You already know that one: It's "ab". Then Java looks at the remaining expression of "ab" + 3. The second rule tells us to concatenate since one of the operands is a String.

In the fourth example, we start with the third rule, which tells us to consider 1 + 2. Both operands are numeric, so the first rule tells us the answer is 3. Then we have 3 + "c", which uses the second rule to give us "3c". Notice all three rules get used in one line?

Finally, the fifth example shows the importance of the third rule. First we have "c" + 1, which uses the second rule to give us "c1". Then we have "c1" + 2, which uses the second rule again to give us "c12".

The exam takes this a step further and will try to trick you with something like this:

```
int three = 3;
String four = "4";
System.out.println(1 + 2 + three + four);
```

When you see this, just take it slow and remember the three rules—and be sure to check the variable types. In this example, we start with the third rule, which tells us to consider 1 + 2. The first rule gives us 3. Next we have 3 + three. Since three is of type int, we still use the first rule, giving us 6. Next we have 6 + four. Since four is of type String, we switch to the second rule and get a final answer of "64". When you see questions like this, just take your time and check the types. Being methodical pays off.

There is only one more thing to know about concatenation, but it is an easy one. In this example, you just have to remember what += does. s += "2" means the same thing as s = s + "2".

```
4: String s = "1";              // s currently holds "1"
5: s += "2";                    // s currently holds "12"
6: s += 3;                      // s currently holds "123"
7: System.out.println(s);       // 123
```

On line 5, we are "adding" two strings, which means we concatenate them. Line 6 tries to trick you by adding a number, but it's just like we wrote s = s + 3. We know that a string "plus" anything else means to use concatenation.

To review the rules one more time: Use numeric addition if two numbers are involved, use concatenation otherwise, and evaluate from left to right. Have you memorized these three rules yet? Be sure to do so before the exam!

Immutability

Once a String object is created, it is not allowed to change. It cannot be made larger or smaller, and you cannot change one of the characters inside it.

You can think of a String as a storage box you have perfectly full and whose sides can't bulge. There's no way to add objects, nor can you replace objects without disturbing the entire arrangement. The trade-off for the optimal packing is zero flexibility.

Mutable is another word for changeable. *Immutable* is the opposite—an object that can't be changed once it's created. On the exam, you need to know that String is immutable.

More on Immutability

You won't be asked to identify whether custom classes are immutable on the OCP part 1 exam, but it's helpful to see an example. Consider the following code:

```
class Mutable {
   private String s;
   public void setS(String newS){ s = newS; }   // Setter makes it mutable
   public String getS() { return s; }
}
final class Immutable {
   private String s = "name";
   public String getS() { return s; }
}
```

Immutable has only a getter. There's no way to change the value of s once it's set. Mutable has a setter. This allows the reference s to change to point to a different String

---

later. Note that even though the String class is immutable, it can still be used in a mutable class. You can even make the instance variable final so the compiler reminds you if you accidentally change s.

Also, immutable classes in Java are final, which prevents subclasses creation. You wouldn't want a subclass adding mutable behavior.

You learned that + is used to do String concatenation in Java. There's another way, which isn't used much on real projects but is great for tricking people on the exam. What does this print out?

```
String s1 = "1";
String s2 = s1.concat("2");
s2.concat("3");
System.out.println(s2);
```

Did you say "12"? Good. The trick is to see if you forget that the String class is immutable by throwing a method call at you.

Important *String* Methods

The String class has dozens of methods. Luckily, you need to know only a handful for the exam. The exam creators pick most of the methods developers use in the real world.

For all these methods, you need to remember that a string is a sequence of characters and Java counts from 0 when indexed. Figure 5.1 shows how each character in the string "animals" is indexed.

FIGURE 5.1   Indexing for a string

a	n	i	m	a	l	s
0	1	2	3	4	5	6

Let's look at a number of methods from the String class. Many of them are straightforward, so we won't discuss them at length. You need to know how to use these methods. We left out public from the signatures in the following sections so you can focus on the important parts.

length()

The method length() returns the number of characters in the String. The method signature is as follows:

```
int length()
```

The following code shows how to use `length()`:

```
String string = "animals";
System.out.println(string.length());  // 7
```

Wait. It outputs 7? Didn't we just tell you that Java counts from 0? The difference is that zero counting happens only when you're using indexes or positions within a list. When determining the total size or length, Java uses normal counting again.

charAt()

The method `charAt()` lets you query the string to find out what character is at a specific index. The method signature is as follows:

```
char charAt(int index)
```

The following code shows how to use `charAt()`:

```
String string = "animals";
System.out.println(string.charAt(0));  // a
System.out.println(string.charAt(6));  // s
System.out.println(string.charAt(7));  // throws exception
```

Since indexes start counting with 0, `charAt(0)` returns the "first" character in the sequence. Similarly, `charAt(6)` returns the "seventh" character in the sequence. `charAt(7)` is a problem. It asks for the "eighth" character in the sequence, but there are only seven characters present. When something goes wrong that Java doesn't know how to deal with, it throws an exception, as shown here. You'll learn more about exceptions in Chapter 10, "Exceptions."

```
java.lang.StringIndexOutOfBoundsException: String index out of range: 7
```

indexOf()

The method `indexOf()` looks at the characters in the string and finds the first index that matches the desired value. `indexOf` can work with an individual character or a whole `String` as input. It can also start from a requested position. Remember that a char can be passed to an int parameter type. On the exam, you'll only see a char passed to the parameters named ch. The method signatures are as follows:

```
int indexOf(int ch)
int indexOf(int ch, int fromIndex)
int indexOf(String str)
int indexOf(String str, int fromIndex)
```

The following code shows how to use `indexOf()`:

```
String string = "animals";
System.out.println(string.indexOf('a'));        // 0
System.out.println(string.indexOf("al"));       // 4
```

```
System.out.println(string.indexOf('a', 4));    // 4
System.out.println(string.indexOf("al", 5));    // -1
```

Since indexes begin with 0, the first 'a' matches at that position. The second statement looks for a more specific string, so it matches later. The third statement says Java shouldn't even look at the characters until it gets to index 4. The final statement doesn't find anything because it starts looking after the match occurred. Unlike charAt(), the indexOf() method doesn't throw an exception if it can't find a match. indexOf() returns −1 when no match is found. Because indexes start with 0, the caller knows that −1 couldn't be a valid index. This makes it a common value for a method to signify to the caller that no match is found.

substring()

The method substring() also looks for characters in a string. It returns parts of the string. The first parameter is the index to start with for the returned string. As usual, this is a zero-based index. There is an optional second parameter, which is the end index you want to stop at.

Notice we said "stop at" rather than "include." This means the endIndex parameter is allowed to be 1 past the end of the sequence if you want to stop at the end of the sequence. That would be redundant, though, since you could omit the second parameter entirely in that case. In your own code, you want to avoid this redundancy. Don't be surprised if the exam uses it, though. The method signatures are as follows:

```
String substring(int beginIndex)
String substring(int beginIndex, int endIndex)
```

It helps to think of indexes a bit differently for the substring methods. Pretend the indexes are right before the character they would point to. Figure 5.2 helps visualize this. Notice how the arrow with the 0 points to the character that would have index 0. The arrow with the 1 points between characters with indexes 0 and 1. There are seven characters in the String. Since Java uses zero-based indexes, this means the last character has an index of 6. The arrow with the 7 points immediately after this last character. This will help you remember that endIndex doesn't give an out-of-bounds exception when it is one past the end of the String.

FIGURE 5.2 Indexes for a substring

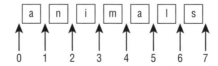

The following code shows how to use substring():

```
String string = "animals";
System.out.println(string.substring(3));                 // mals
System.out.println(string.substring(string.indexOf('m'))); // mals
```

```
System.out.println(string.substring(3, 4));                    // m
System.out.println(string.substring(3, 7));                    // mals
```

The substring() method is the trickiest String method on the exam. The first example says to take the characters starting with index 3 through the end, which gives us "mals". The second example does the same thing, but it calls indexOf() to get the index rather than hard-coding it. This is a common practice when coding because you may not know the index in advance.

The third example says to take the characters starting with index 3 until, but not including, the character at index 4—which is a complicated way of saying we want a String with one character: the one at index 3. This results in "m". The final example says to take the characters starting with index 3 until we get to index 7. Since index 7 is the same as the end of the string, it is equivalent to the first example.

We hope that wasn't too confusing. The next examples are less obvious:

```
System.out.println(string.substring(3, 3)); // empty string
System.out.println(string.substring(3, 2));  // throws exception
System.out.println(string.substring(3, 8)); // throws exception
```

The first example in this set prints an empty string. The request is for the characters starting with index 3 until you get to index 3. Since we start and end with the same index, there are *no* characters in between. The second example in this set throws an exception because the indexes can't be backward. Java knows perfectly well that it will never get to index 2 if it starts with index 3. The third example says to continue until the eighth character. There is no eighth position, so Java throws an exception. Granted, there is no seventh character either, but at least there is the "end of string" invisible position.

Let's review this one more time since substring() is so tricky. The method returns the string starting from the requested index. If an end index is requested, it stops right before that index. Otherwise, it goes to the end of the string.

toLowerCase() and *toUpperCase()*

Whew. After that mental exercise, it is nice to have methods that do exactly what they sound like! These methods make it easy to convert your data. The method signatures are as follows:

```
String toLowerCase()
String toUpperCase()
```

The following code shows how to use these methods:

```
String string = "animals";
System.out.println(string.toUpperCase());  // ANIMALS
System.out.println("Abc123".toLowerCase());  // abc123
```

These methods do what they say. toUpperCase() converts any lowercase characters to uppercase in the returned string. toLowerCase() converts any uppercase characters to lowercase in the returned string. These methods leave alone any characters other than letters. Also, remember that strings are immutable, so the original string stays the same.

equals() and *equalsIgnoreCase()*

The equals() method checks whether two String objects contain exactly the same characters in the same order. The equalsIgnoreCase() method checks whether two String objects contain the same characters with the exception that it will convert the characters' case if needed. The method signatures are as follows:

```
boolean equals(Object obj)
boolean equalsIgnoreCase(String str)
```

You might have noticed that equals() takes an Object rather than a String. This is because the method is the same for all objects. If you pass in something that isn't a String, it will just return false. By contrast, the equalsIgnoreCase method only applies to String objects so it can take the more specific type as the parameter.

The following code shows how to use these methods:

```
System.out.println("abc".equals("ABC"));  // false
System.out.println("ABC".equals("ABC"));  // true
System.out.println("abc".equalsIgnoreCase("ABC"));  // true
```

This example should be fairly intuitive. In the first example, the values aren't exactly the same. In the second, they are exactly the same. In the third, they differ only by case, but it is okay because we called the method that ignores differences in case.

startsWith() and *endsWith()*

The startsWith() and endsWith() methods look at whether the provided value matches part of the String. The method signatures are as follows:

```
boolean startsWith(String prefix)
boolean endsWith(String suffix)
```

The following code shows how to use these methods:

```
System.out.println("abc".startsWith("a")); // true
System.out.println("abc".startsWith("A")); // false
System.out.println("abc".endsWith("c")); // true
System.out.println("abc".endsWith("a")); // false
```

Again, nothing surprising here. Java is doing a case-sensitive check on the values provided.

replace()

The replace() method does a simple search and replace on the string. There's a version that takes char parameters as well as a version that takes CharSequence parameters. The method signatures are as follows:

```
String replace(char oldChar, char newChar)
String replace(CharSequence target, CharSequence replacement)
```

The following code shows how to use these methods:

```
System.out.println("abcabc".replace('a', 'A')); // AbcAbc
System.out.println("abcabc".replace("a", "A")); // AbcAbc
```

The first example uses the first method signature, passing in `char` parameters. The second example uses the second method signature, passing in `String` parameters.

contains()

The `contains()` method looks for matches in the `String`. It isn't as particular as `startsWith()` and `endsWith()`—the match can be anywhere in the `String`. The method signature is as follows:

```
boolean contains(CharSequence charSeq)
```

The following code shows how to use these methods:

```
System.out.println("abc".contains("b")); // true
System.out.println("abc".contains("B")); // false
```

Again, we have a case-sensitive search in the `String`. The `contains()` method is a convenience method so you don't have to write `str.indexOf(otherString) != -1`.

trim(), strip(), stripLeading(), and stripTrailing()

You've made it through almost all the `String` methods you need to know. Next up is removing blank space from the beginning and/or end of a `String`. The `strip()` and `trim()` methods remove whitespace from the beginning and end of a `String`. In terms of the exam, whitespace consists of spaces along with the `\t` (tab) and `\n` (newline) characters. Other characters, such as `\r` (carriage return), are also included in what gets trimmed. The `strip()` method is new in Java 11. It does everything that `trim()` does, but it supports Unicode.

> You don't need to know about Unicode for the exam. But if you want to test the difference, one of Unicode whitespace characters is as follows:
>
> ```
> char ch = '\u2000';
> ```

Additionally, the `stripLeading()` and `stripTrailing()` methods were added in Java 11. The `stripLeading()` method removes whitespace from the beginning of the `String` and leaves it at the end. The `stripTrailing()` method does the opposite. It removes whitespace from the end of the `String` and leaves it at the beginning.

The method signatures are as follows:

```
String strip()
String stripLeading()
String stripTrailing()
String trim()
```

The following code shows how to use these methods:

```java
System.out.println("abc".strip());                    // abc
System.out.println("\t    a b c\n".strip());          // a b c

String text = " abc\t ";
System.out.println(text.trim().length());             // 3
System.out.println(text.strip().length());            // 3
System.out.println(text.stripLeading().length());     // 5
System.out.println(text.stripTrailing().length());    // 4
```

First, remember that \t is a single character. The backslash escapes the t to represent a tab. The first example prints the original string because there are no whitespace characters at the beginning or end. The second example gets rid of the leading tab, subsequent spaces, and the trailing newline. It leaves the spaces that are in the middle of the string.

The remaining examples just print the number of characters remaining. You can see that both trim() and strip() leave the same three characters "abc" because they remove both the leading and trailing whitespace. The stripLeading() method only removes the one whitespace character at the beginning of the String. It leaves the tab and space at the end. The stripTrailing() method removes these two characters at the end but leaves the character at the beginning of the String.

intern()

The intern() method returns the value from the string pool if it is there. Otherwise, it adds the value to the string pool. We will explain about the string pool and give examples for intern() later in the chapter. The method signature is as follows:

```java
String intern()
```

Method Chaining

It is common to call multiple methods as shown here:

```java
String start = "AniMaL    ";
String trimmed = start.trim();                   // "AniMaL"
String lowercase = trimmed.toLowerCase();        // "animal"
String result = lowercase.replace('a', 'A');     // "AnimAl"
System.out.println(result);
```

This is just a series of String methods. Each time one is called, the returned value is put in a new variable. There are four String values along the way, and AnimAl is output.

However, on the exam there is a tendency to cram as much code as possible into a small space. You'll see code using a technique called method chaining. Here's an example:

```java
String result = "AniMaL    ".trim().toLowerCase().replace('a', 'A');
System.out.println(result);
```

This code is equivalent to the previous example. It also creates four String objects and outputs AnimAl. To read code that uses method chaining, start at the left and evaluate the first method. Then call the next method on the returned value of the first method. Keep going until you get to the semicolon.

Remember that String is immutable. What do you think the result of this code is?

```
5: String a = "abc";
6: String b = a.toUpperCase();
7: b = b.replace("B", "2").replace('C', '3');
8: System.out.println("a=" + a);
9: System.out.println("b=" + b);
```

On line 5, we set a to point to "abc" and never pointed a to anything else. Since we are dealing with an immutable object, none of the code on lines 6 and 7 changes a, and the value remains "abc".

b is a little trickier. Line 6 has b pointing to "ABC", which is straightforward. On line 7, we have method chaining. First, "ABC".replace("B", "2") is called. This returns "A2C". Next, "A2C".replace('C', '3') is called. This returns "A23". Finally, b changes to point to this returned String. When line 9 executes, b is "A23".

Using the *StringBuilder* Class

A small program can create a lot of String objects very quickly. For example, how many do you think this piece of code creates?

```
10: String alpha = "";
11: for(char current = 'a'; current <= 'z'; current++)
12:     alpha += current;
13: System.out.println(alpha);
```

The empty String on line 10 is instantiated, and then line 12 appends an "a". However, because the String object is immutable, a new String object is assigned to alpha, and the "" object becomes eligible for garbage collection. The next time through the loop, alpha is assigned a new String object, "ab", and the "a" object becomes eligible for garbage collection. The next iteration assigns alpha to "abc", and the "ab" object becomes eligible for garbage collection, and so on.

This sequence of events continues, and after 26 iterations through the loop, a total of 27 objects are instantiated, most of which are immediately eligible for garbage collection.

This is very inefficient. Luckily, Java has a solution. The StringBuilder class creates a String without storing all those interim String values. Unlike the String class, StringBuilder is not immutable.

```
15: StringBuilder alpha = new StringBuilder();
16: for(char current = 'a'; current <= 'z'; current++)
```

```
17:     alpha.append(current);
18: System.out.println(alpha);
```

On line 15, a new StringBuilder object is instantiated. The call to append() on line 17 adds a character to the StringBuilder object each time through the for loop appending the value of current to the end of alpha. This code reuses the same StringBuilder without creating an interim String each time.

In old code, you might see references to StringBuffer. It works the same way except it supports threads, which you'll learn about when preparing for the 1Z0-816 exam. StringBuffer is no longer on either exam. It performs slower than StringBuilder, so just use StringBuilder.

In this section, we'll look at creating a StringBuilder and using its common methods.

Mutability and Chaining

We're sure you noticed this from the previous example, but StringBuilder is not immutable. In fact, we gave it 27 different values in the example (blank plus adding each letter in the alphabet). The exam will likely try to trick you with respect to String and StringBuilder being mutable.

Chaining makes this even more interesting. When we chained String method calls, the result was a new String with the answer. Chaining StringBuilder methods doesn't work this way. Instead, the StringBuilder changes its own state and returns a reference to itself. Let's look at an example to make this clearer:

```
4: StringBuilder sb = new StringBuilder("start");
5: sb.append("+middle");                    // sb = "start+middle"
6: StringBuilder same = sb.append("+end");  // "start+middle+end"
```

Line 5 adds text to the end of sb. It also returns a reference to sb, which is ignored. Line 6 also adds text to the end of sb and returns a reference to sb. This time the reference is stored in same—which means sb and same point to the same object and would print out the same value.

The exam won't always make the code easy to read by having only one method per line. What do you think this example prints?

```
4: StringBuilder a = new StringBuilder("abc");
5: StringBuilder b = a.append("de");
6: b = b.append("f").append("g");
7: System.out.println("a=" + a);
8: System.out.println("b=" + b);
```

Did you say both print "abcdefg"? Good. There's only one StringBuilder object here. We know that because new StringBuilder() was called only once. On line 5, there are two variables referring to that object, which has a value of "abcde". On line 6, those two variables are still referring to that same object, which now has a value of "abcdefg".

Incidentally, the assignment back to b does absolutely nothing. b is already pointing to that `StringBuilder`.

Creating a *StringBuilder*

There are three ways to construct a `StringBuilder`:

```
StringBuilder sb1 = new StringBuilder();
StringBuilder sb2 = new StringBuilder("animal");
StringBuilder sb3 = new StringBuilder(10);
```

The first says to create a `StringBuilder` containing an empty sequence of characters and assign sb1 to point to it. The second says to create a `StringBuilder` containing a specific value and assign sb2 to point to it. For the first two, it tells Java to manage the implementation details. The final example tells Java that we have some idea of how big the eventual value will be and would like the `StringBuilder` to reserve a certain capacity, or number of slots, for characters.

Important *StringBuilder* Methods

As with `String`, we aren't going to cover every single method in the `StringBuilder` class. These are the ones you might see on the exam.

charAt(), indexOf(), length(), and substring()

These four methods work exactly the same as in the `String` class. Be sure you can identify the output of this example:

```
StringBuilder sb = new StringBuilder("animals");
String sub = sb.substring(sb.indexOf("a"), sb.indexOf("al"));
int len = sb.length();
char ch = sb.charAt(6);
System.out.println(sub + " " + len + " " + ch);
```

The correct answer is anim 7 s. The indexOf()method calls return 0 and 4, respectively. substring() returns the `String` starting with index 0 and ending right before index 4.

length() returns 7 because it is the number of characters in the `StringBuilder` rather than an index. Finally, charAt() returns the character at index 6. Here we do start with 0 because we are referring to indexes. If any of this doesn't sound familiar, go back and read the section on `String` again.

Notice that substring() returns a `String` rather than a `StringBuilder`. That is why sb is not changed. substring() is really just a method that inquires about what the state of the `StringBuilder` happens to be.

append()

The append() method is by far the most frequently used method in `StringBuilder`. In fact, it is so frequently used that we just started using it without comment. Luckily, this method does just what it sounds like: It adds the parameter to the `StringBuilder` and returns a reference to the current `StringBuilder`. One of the method signatures is as follows:

```
StringBuilder append(String str)
```

Notice that we said *one* of the method signatures. There are more than 10 method signatures that look similar but that take different data types as parameters. All those methods are provided so you can write code like this:

```
StringBuilder sb = new StringBuilder().append(1).append('c');
sb.append("-").append(true);
System.out.println(sb);        // 1c-true
```

Nice method chaining, isn't it? append() is called directly after the constructor. By having all these method signatures, you can just call append() without having to convert your parameter to a String first.

insert()

The insert() method adds characters to the `StringBuilder` at the requested index and returns a reference to the current `StringBuilder`. Just like append(), there are lots of method signatures for different types. Here's one:

```
StringBuilder insert(int offset, String str)
```

Pay attention to the offset in these examples. It is the index where we want to insert the requested parameter.

```
3: StringBuilder sb = new StringBuilder("animals");
4: sb.insert(7, "-");                // sb = animals-
5: sb.insert(0, "-");                // sb = -animals-
6: sb.insert(4, "-");                // sb = -ani-mals-
7: System.out.println(sb);
```

Line 4 says to insert a dash at index 7, which happens to be the end of the sequence of characters. Line 5 says to insert a dash at index 0, which happens to be the very beginning. Finally, line 6 says to insert a dash right before index 4. The exam creators will try to trip you up on this. As we add and remove characters, their indexes change. When you see a question dealing with such operations, draw what is going on so you won't be confused.

delete() and deleteCharAt()

The delete() method is the opposite of the insert() method. It removes characters from the sequence and returns a reference to the current `StringBuilder`. The deleteCharAt() method is convenient when you want to delete only one character. The method signatures are as follows:

```
StringBuilder delete(int startIndex, int endIndex)
StringBuilder deleteCharAt(int index)
```

The following code shows how to use these methods:

```
StringBuilder sb = new StringBuilder("abcdef");
sb.delete(1, 3);                  // sb = adef
sb.deleteCharAt(5);               // throws an exception
```

First, we delete the characters starting with index 1 and ending right before index 3. This gives us adef. Next, we ask Java to delete the character at position 5. However, the remaining value is only four characters long, so it throws a StringIndexOutOfBoundsException.

The delete() method is more flexible than some others when it comes to array indexes. If you specify a second parameter that is past the end of the StringBuilder, Java will just assume you meant the end. That means this code is legal:

```
StringBuilder sb = new StringBuilder("abcdef");
sb.delete(1, 100);                     // sb = a
```

replace()

The replace() method works differently for StringBuilder than it did for String. The method signature is as follows:

```
StringBuilder replace(int startIndex, int endIndex, String newString)
```

The following code shows how to use this method:

```
StringBuilder builder = new StringBuilder("pigeon dirty");
builder.replace(3, 6, "sty");
System.out.println(builder);  // pigsty dirty
```

First, Java deletes the characters starting with index 3 and ending right before index 6. This gives us pig dirty. Then Java inserts to the value "sty" in that position.

In this example, the number of characters removed and inserted is the same. However, there is no reason that it has to be. What do you think this does?

```
StringBuilder builder = new StringBuilder("pigeon dirty");
builder.replace(3, 100, "");
System.out.println(builder);
```

It actually prints "pig". Remember the method is first doing a logical delete. The replace() method allows specifying a second parameter that is past the end of the StringBuilder. That means only the first three characters remain.

reverse()

After all that, it's time for a nice, easy method. The reverse() method does just what it sounds like: it reverses the characters in the sequences and returns a reference to the current StringBuilder. The method signature is as follows:

```
StringBuilder reverse()
```

The following code shows how to use this method:

```
StringBuilder sb = new StringBuilder("ABC");
sb.reverse();
System.out.println(sb);
```

As expected, this prints CBA. This method isn't that interesting. Maybe the exam creators like to include it to encourage you to write down the value rather than relying on memory for indexes.

toString()

The last method converts a StringBuilder into a String. The method signature is as follows:

```
String toString()
```

The following code shows how to use this method:

```
StringBuilder sb = new StringBuilder("ABC");
String s = sb.toString();
```

Often StringBuilder is used internally for performance purposes, but the end result needs to be a String. For example, maybe it needs to be passed to another method that is expecting a String.

Understanding Equality

In Chapter 3, you learned how to use == to compare numbers and that object references refer to the same object. In this section, we will look at what it means for two objects to be equivalent or the same. We will also look at the impact of the String pool on equality.

Comparing equals() and ==

Consider the following code that uses == with objects:

```
StringBuilder one = new StringBuilder();
StringBuilder two = new StringBuilder();
StringBuilder three = one.append("a");
System.out.println(one == two); // false
System.out.println(one == three); // true
```

Since this example isn't dealing with primitives, we know to look for whether the references are referring to the same object. one and two are both completely separate StringBuilder objects, giving us two objects. Therefore, the first print statement gives us false. three is more interesting. Remember how StringBuilder methods like to return the current reference for chaining? This means one and three both point to the same object, and the second print statement gives us true.

You saw earlier that you can say you want logical equality rather than object equality for String objects:

```
String x = "Hello World";
String z = " Hello World".trim();
System.out.println(x.equals(z)); // true
```

This works because the authors of the String class implemented a standard method called equals to check the values inside the String rather than the string reference itself. If a class doesn't have an equals method, Java determines whether the references point to the same object—which is exactly what == does.

In case you are wondering, the authors of StringBuilder did not implement equals(). If you call equals() on two StringBuilder instances, it will check reference equality. You can call toString() on StringBuilder to get a String to check for equality instead.

The exam will test you on your understanding of equality with objects they define too. For example, the following Tiger class works just like StringBuilder but is easier to understand:

```
1:  public class Tiger {
2:      String name;
3:      public static void main(String[] args) {
4:          Tiger t1 = new Tiger();
5:          Tiger t2 = new Tiger();
6:          Tiger t3 = t1;
7:          System.out.println(t1 == t3);        // true
8:          System.out.println(t1 == t2);        // false
9:          System.out.println(t1.equals(t2));   // false
10: } }
```

The first two statements check object reference equality. Line 7 prints true because we are comparing references to the same object. Line 8 prints false because the two object references are different. Line 9 prints false since Tiger does not implement equals(). Don't worry—you aren't expected to know how to implement equals() for this exam.

Finally, the exam might try to trick you with a question like this. Can you guess why the code doesn't compile?

```
String string = "a";
StringBuilder builder = new StringBuilder("a");
System.out.println(string == builder); //DOES NOT COMPILE
```

Remember that == is checking for object reference equality. The compiler is smart enough to know that two references can't possibly point to the same object when they are completely different types.

The *String* Pool

Since strings are everywhere in Java, they use up a lot of memory. In some production applications, they can use a large amount of memory in the entire program. Java realizes that many strings repeat in the program and solves this issue by reusing common ones. The *string pool*, also known as the intern pool, is a location in the Java virtual machine (JVM) that collects all these strings.

The string pool contains literal values and constants that appear in your program. For example, "name" is a literal and therefore goes into the string pool. myObject.toString() is a string but not a literal, so it does not go into the string pool.

Let's now visit the more complex and confusing scenario, String equality, made so in part because of the way the JVM reuses String literals.

```
String x = "Hello World";
String y = "Hello World";
System.out.println(x == y);     // true
```

Remember that Strings are immutable and literals are pooled. The JVM created only one literal in memory. x and y both point to the same location in memory; therefore, the statement outputs true. It gets even trickier. Consider this code:

```
String x = "Hello World";
String z = " Hello World".trim();
System.out.println(x == z); // false
```

In this example, we don't have two of the same String literal. Although x and z happen to evaluate to the same string, one is computed at runtime. Since it isn't the same at compile-time, a new String object is created. Let's try another one. What do you think is output here?

```
String singleString = "hello world";
String oneLine = "hello " + "world";
String concat = " hello";
concat += "world";
System.out.println(singleString == oneLine);
System.out.println(singleString == concat);
```

Both print false. Concatenation is just like calling a method and results in a new String. You can even force the issue by creating a new String:

```
String x = "Hello World";
String y = new String("Hello World");
System.out.println(x == y); // false
```

The former says to use the string pool normally. The second says "No, JVM, I really don't want you to use the string pool. Please create a new object for me even though it is less efficient."

You can also do the opposite and tell Java to use the string pool. The `intern()` method will use an object in the string pool if one is present. If the literal is not yet in the string pool, Java will add it at this time.

```
String name = "Hello World";
String name2 = new String("Hello World").intern();
System.out.println(name == name2);      // true
```

First we tell Java to use the string pool normally for name. Then for name2, we tell Java to create a new object using the constructor but to intern it and use the string pool anyway. Since both variables point to the same reference in the string pool, we can use the == operator.

Let's try another one. What do you think this prints out? Be careful. It is tricky.

```
15: String first = "rat" + 1;
16: String second = "r" + "a" + "t" + "1";
17: String third = "r" + "a" + "t" + new String("1");
18: System.out.println(first == second);
19: System.out.println(first == second.intern());
20: System.out.println(first == third);
21: System.out.println(first == third.intern());
```

On line 15, we have a compile-time constant that automatically gets placed in the string pool as "rat1". On line 16, we have a more complicated expression that is also a compile-time constant. Therefore, first and second share the same string pool reference. This makes line 18 and 19 print true.

On line 17, we have a String constructor. This means we no longer have a compile-time constant, and third does not point to a reference in the string pool. Therefore, line 20 prints false. On line 21, the `intern()` call looks in the string pool. Java notices that first points to the same String and prints true.

When you write programs, you wouldn't want to create a String of a String or use the `intern()` method. For the exam, you need to know that both are allowed and how they behave.

Remember to never use `intern()` or == to compare `String` objects in your code. The only time you should have to deal with these is on the exam.

Understanding Java Arrays

Up to now, we've been referring to the `String` and `StringBuilder` classes as a "sequence of characters." This is true. They are implemented using an *array* of characters. An array is an area of memory on the heap with space for a designated number of elements. A `String` is implemented as an array with some methods that you might want to use when dealing with characters specifically. A `StringBuilder` is implemented as an array where the array object is replaced with a new bigger array object when it runs out of space to store all the characters. A big difference is that an array can be of any other Java type. If we didn't want to use a `String` for some reason, we could use an array of `char` primitives directly:

```
char[] letters;
```

This wouldn't be very convenient because we'd lose all the special properties `String` gives us, such as writing `"Java"`. Keep in mind that `letters` is a reference variable and not a primitive. `char` is a primitive. But `char` is what goes into the array and not the type of the array itself. The array itself is of type `char[]`. You can mentally read the brackets (`[]`) as "array."

In other words, an array is an ordered list. It can contain duplicates. In this section, we'll look at creating an array of primitives and objects, sorting, searching, varargs, and multidimensional arrays.

Creating an Array of Primitives

The most common way to create an array looks like this:

```
int[] numbers1 = new int[3];
```

The basic parts are shown in Figure 5.3. It specifies the type of the array (`int`) and the size (3). The brackets tell you this is an array.

FIGURE 5.3   The basic structure of an array

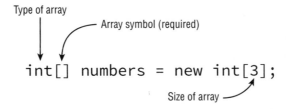

When you use this form to instantiate an array, all elements are set to the default value for that type. As you learned in Chapter 2, the default value of an `int` is 0. Since `numbers1` is a reference variable, it points to the array object, as shown in Figure 5.4. As you can see, the default value for all the elements is 0. Also, the indexes start with 0 and count up, just as they did for a `String`.

FIGURE 5.4   An empty array

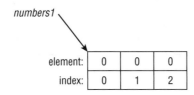

Another way to create an array is to specify all the elements it should start out with:

```
int[] numbers2 = new int[] {42, 55, 99};
```

In this example, we also create an int array of size 3. This time, we specify the initial values of those three elements instead of using the defaults. Figure 5.5 shows what this array looks like.

FIGURE 5.5 An initialized array

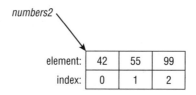

Java recognizes that this expression is redundant. Since you are specifying the type of the array on the left side of the equal sign, Java already knows the type. And since you are specifying the initial values, it already knows the size. As a shortcut, Java lets you write this:

```
int[] numbers2 = {42, 55, 99};
```

This approach is called an *anonymous array*. It is anonymous because you don't specify the type and size.

Finally, you can type the [] before or after the name, and adding a space is optional. This means that all five of these statements do the exact same thing:

```
int[] numAnimals;
int [] numAnimals2;
int []numAnimals3;
int numAnimals4[];
int numAnimals5 [];
```

Most people use the first one. You could see any of these on the exam, though, so get used to seeing the brackets in odd places.

Multiple "Arrays" in Declarations

What types of reference variables do you think the following code creates?

```
int[] ids, types;
```

The correct answer is two variables of type int[]. This seems logical enough. After all, int a, b; created two int variables. What about this example?

```
int ids[], types;
```

All we did was move the brackets, but it changed the behavior. This time we get one variable of type int[] and one variable of type int. Java sees this line of code and thinks something like this: "They want two variables of type int. The first one is called ids[]. This one is an int[] called ids. The second one is just called types. No brackets, so it is a regular integer."

Needless to say, you shouldn't write code that looks like this. But you do need to understand it for the exam.

Creating an Array with Reference Variables

You can choose any Java type to be the type of the array. This includes classes you create yourself. Let's take a look at a built-in type with String:

```java
public class ArrayType {
    public static void main(String args[]) {
        String [] bugs = { "cricket", "beetle", "ladybug" };
        String [] alias = bugs;
        System.out.println(bugs.equals(alias));      // true
        System.out.println(
            bugs.toString()); //[Ljava.lang.String;@160bc7c0
} }
```

We can call equals() because an array is an object. It returns true because of reference equality. The equals() method on arrays does not look at the elements of the array. Remember, this would work even on an int[] too. int is a primitive; int[] is an object.

The second print statement is even more interesting. What on earth is [Ljava.lang .String;@160bc7c0? You don't have to know this for the exam, but [L means it is an array, java.lang.String is the reference type, and 160bc7c0 is the hash code. You'll get different numbers and letters each time you run it since this is a reference.

    Since Java 5, Java has provided a method that prints an array nicely: Arrays.toString(bugs) would print [cricket, beetle, ladybug].

Make sure you understand Figure 5.6. The array does not allocate space for the String objects. Instead, it allocates space for a reference to where the objects are really stored.

FIGURE 5.6   An array pointing to strings

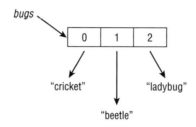

As a quick review, what do you think this array points to?

```
class Names {
    String names[];
}
```

You got us. It was a review of Chapter 2 and not our discussion on arrays. The answer is null. The code never instantiated the array, so it is just a reference variable to null. Let's try that again—what do you think this array points to?

```
class Names {
    String names[] = new String[2];
}
```

It is an array because it has brackets. It is an array of type String since that is the type mentioned in the declaration. It has two elements because the length is 2. Each of those two slots currently is null but has the potential to point to a String object.

Remember casting from the previous chapter when you wanted to force a bigger type into a smaller type? You can do that with arrays too:

```
3: String[] strings = { "stringValue" };
4: Object[] objects = strings;
5: String[] againStrings = (String[]) objects;
6: againStrings[0] = new StringBuilder();   // DOES NOT COMPILE
7: objects[0] = new StringBuilder();         // careful!
```

Line 3 creates an array of type String. Line 4 doesn't require a cast because Object is a broader type than String. On line 5, a cast is needed because we are moving to a more specific type. Line 6 doesn't compile because a String[] only allows String objects and StringBuilder is not a String.

Line 7 is where this gets interesting. From the point of view of the compiler, this is just fine. A StringBuilder object can clearly go in an Object[]. The problem is that we don't actually have an Object[]. We have a String[] referred to from an Object[] variable. At runtime, the code throws an ArrayStoreException. You don't need to memorize the name of this exception, but you do need to know that the code will throw an exception.

Using an Array

Now that you know how to create an array, let's try accessing one:

```
4: String[] mammals = {"monkey", "chimp", "donkey"};
5: System.out.println(mammals.length);        // 3
6: System.out.println(mammals[0]);            // monkey
7: System.out.println(mammals[1]);            // chimp
8: System.out.println(mammals[2]);            // donkey
```

Line 4 declares and initializes the array. Line 5 tells us how many elements the array can hold. The rest of the code prints the array. Notice elements are indexed starting with 0. This should be familiar from String and StringBuilder, which also start counting with 0. Those classes also counted length as the number of elements. Note that there are no parentheses after length since it is not a method.

To make sure you understand how length works, what do you think this prints?

```
String[] birds = new String[6];
System.out.println(birds.length);
```

The answer is 6. Even though all six elements of the array are null, there are still six of them. length does not consider what is in the array; it only considers how many slots have been allocated.

It is very common to use a loop when reading from or writing to an array. This loop sets each element of numbers to five higher than the current index:

```
5: int[] numbers = new int[10];
6: for (int i = 0; i < numbers.length; i++)
7:     numbers[i] = i + 5;
```

Line 5 simply instantiates an array with 10 slots. Line 6 is a for loop that uses an extremely common pattern. It starts at index 0, which is where an array begins as well. It keeps going, one at a time, until it hits the end of the array. Line 7 sets the current element of numbers.

The exam will test whether you are being observant by trying to access elements that are not in the array. Can you tell why each of these throws an ArrayIndexOutOfBoundsException for our array of size 10?

```
numbers[10] = 3;
numbers[numbers.length] = 5;
for (int i = 0; i <= numbers.length; i++) numbers[i] = i + 5;
```

The first one is trying to see whether you know that indexes start with 0. Since we have 10 elements in our array, this means only numbers[0] through numbers[9] are valid. The second example assumes you are clever enough to know 10 is invalid and disguises it by using the length field. However, the length is always one more than the maximum valid index. Finally, the for loop incorrectly uses <= instead of <, which is also a way of referring to that 10th element.

Sorting

Java makes it easy to sort an array by providing a sort method—or rather, a bunch of sort methods. Just like StringBuilder allowed you to pass almost anything to append(), you can pass almost any array to Arrays.sort().

Arrays is the first class provided by Java we have used that requires an import. To use it, you must have either of the following two statements in your class:

```
import java.util.*;        // import whole package including Arrays
import java.util.Arrays;   // import just Arrays
```

There is one exception, although it doesn't come up often on the exam. You can write java.util.Arrays every time it is used in the class instead of specifying it as an import.

Remember that if you are shown a code snippet with a line number that doesn't begin with 1, you can assume the necessary imports are there. Similarly, you can assume the imports are present if you are shown a snippet of a method.

This simple example sorts three numbers:

```
int[] numbers = { 6, 9, 1 };
Arrays.sort(numbers);
for (int i = 0; i < numbers.length; i++)
    System.out.print(numbers[i] +  "  ");
```

The result is 1 6 9, as you should expect it to be. Notice that we looped through the output to print the values in the array. Just printing the array variable directly would give the annoying hash of [I@2bd9c3e7. Alternatively, we could have printed Arrays .toString(numbers) instead of using the loop. That would have output [1, 6, 9].

Try this again with String types:

```
String[] strings = { "10", "9", "100" };
Arrays.sort(strings);
for (String string : strings)
    System.out.print(string + " ");
```

This time the result might not be what you expect. This code outputs 10 100 9. The problem is that String sorts in alphabetic order, and 1 sorts before 9. (Numbers sort before letters, and uppercase sorts before lowercase, in case you were wondering.) For the 1Z0-816 exam, you'll learn how to create custom sort orders using something called a *comparator*.

Did you notice we snuck in the enhanced for loop in this example? Since we aren't using the index, we don't need the traditional for loop. That won't stop the exam creators from using it, though, so we'll be sure to use both to keep you sharp!

Searching

Java also provides a convenient way to search—but only if the array is already sorted. Table 5.1 covers the rules for binary search.

TABLE 5.1   Binary search rules

Scenario	Result
Target element found in sorted array	Index of match
Target element not found in sorted array	Negative value showing one smaller than the negative of the index, where a match needs to be inserted to preserve sorted order
Unsorted array	A surprise—this result isn't predictable

Let's try these rules with an example:

```
3: int[] numbers = {2,4,6,8};
4: System.out.println(Arrays.binarySearch(numbers, 2)); // 0
5: System.out.println(Arrays.binarySearch(numbers, 4)); // 1
6: System.out.println(Arrays.binarySearch(numbers, 1)); // -1
7: System.out.println(Arrays.binarySearch(numbers, 3)); // -2
8: System.out.println(Arrays.binarySearch(numbers, 9)); // -5
```

Take note of the fact that line 3 is a sorted array. If it wasn't, we couldn't apply either of the other rules. Line 4 searches for the index of 2. The answer is index 0. Line 5 searches for the index of 4, which is 1.

Line 6 searches for the index of 1. Although 1 isn't in the list, the search can determine that it should be inserted at element 0 to preserve the sorted order. Since 0 already means something for array indexes, Java needs to subtract 1 to give us the answer of –1. Line 7 is similar. Although 3 isn't in the list, it would need to be inserted at element 1 to preserve the sorted order. We negate and subtract 1 for consistency, getting –1 –1, also known as –2. Finally, line 8 wants to tell us that 9 should be inserted at index 4. We again negate and subtract 1, getting –4 –1, also known as –5.

What do you think happens in this example?

```
5: int[] numbers = new int[] {3,2,1};
6: System.out.println(Arrays.binarySearch(numbers, 2));
7: System.out.println(Arrays.binarySearch(numbers, 3));
```

Note that on line 5, the array isn't sorted. This means the output will not be predictable. When testing this example, line 6 correctly gave 1 as the output. However, line 7 gave the wrong answer. The exam creators will not expect you to know what incorrect values come out. As soon as you see the array isn't sorted, look for an answer choice about unpredictable output.

On the exam, you need to know what a binary search returns in various scenarios. Oddly, you don't need to know why "binary" is in the name. In case you are curious, a binary search splits the array into two equal pieces (remember 2 is binary) and determines which half the target is in. It repeats this process until only one element is left.

Comparing

Java also provides methods to compare two arrays to determine which is "smaller." First we will cover the compare() method and then go on to mismatch().

compare()

There are a bunch of rules you need to know before calling compare(). Luckily, these are the same rules you'll need to know for the 1Z0-816 exam when writing a Comparator.

First you need to learn what the return value means. You do not need to know the exact return values, but you do need to know the following:

- A negative number means the first array is smaller than the second.

- A zero means the arrays are equal.

- A positive number means the first array is larger than the second.

    Here's an example:

```
System.out.println(Arrays.compare(new int[] {1}, new int[] {2}));
```

This code prints a negative number. It should be pretty intuitive that 1 is smaller than 2, making the first array smaller.

Now that you know how to compare a single value, let's look at how to compare arrays of different lengths:

- If both arrays are the same length and have the same values in each spot in the same order, return zero.

- If all the elements are the same but the second array has extra elements at the end, return a negative number.

- If all the elements are the same but the first array has extra elements at the end, return a positive number.

- If the first element that differs is smaller in the first array, return a negative number.

- If the first element that differs is larger in the first array, return a positive number.

    Finally, what does smaller mean? Here are some more rules that apply here and to compareTo(), which you'll see in Chapter 6, "Lambdas and Functional Interfaces":

- null is smaller than any other value.
- For numbers, normal numeric order applies.
- For strings, one is smaller if it is a prefix of another.
- For strings/characters, numbers are smaller than letters.
- For strings/characters, uppercase is smaller than lowercase.

Table 5.2 shows examples of these rules in action.

TABLE 5.2   `Arrays.compare()` examples

First array	Second array	Result	Reason
`new int[] {1, 2}`	`new int[] {1}`	Positive number	The first element is the same, but the first array is longer.
`new int[] {1, 2}`	`new int[] {1, 2}`	Zero	Exact match
`new String[] {"a"}`	`new String[] {"aa"}`	Negative number	The first element is a substring of the second.
`new String[] {"a"}`	`new String[] {"A"}`	Positive number	Uppercase is smaller than lowercase.
`new String[] {"a"}`	`new String[] {null}`	Positive number	null is smaller than a letter.

Finally, this code does not compile because the types are different. When comparing two arrays, they must be the same array type.

```
System.out.println(Arrays.compare(
   new int[] {1}, new String[] {"a"})); // DOES NOT COMPILE
```

mismatch()

Now that you are familiar with `compare()`, it is time to learn about `mismatch()`. If the arrays are equal, `mismatch()` returns -1. Otherwise, it returns the first index where they differ. Can you figure out what these print?

```
System.out.println(Arrays.mismatch(new int[] {1}, new int[] {1}));
System.out.println(Arrays.mismatch(new String[] {"a"},
   new String[] {"A"}));
System.out.println(Arrays.mismatch(new int[] {1, 2}, new int[] {1}));
```

In the first example, the arrays are the same, so the result is -1. In the second example, the entries at element 0 are not equal, so the result is 0. In the third example, the entries at element 0 are equal, so we keep looking. The element at index 1 is not equal. Or more specifically, one array has an element at index 1, and the other does not. Therefore, the result is 1.

To make sure you understand the compare() and mismatch() methods, study Table 5.3. If you don't understand why all of the values are there, please go back and study this section again.

TABLE 5.3   Equality vs. comparison vs. mismatch

Method	When arrays are the same	When arrays are different
equals()	true	false
compare()	0	Positive or negative number
mismatch()	-1	Zero or positive index

Varargs

When you're creating an array yourself, it looks like what we've seen thus far. When one is passed to your method, there is another way it can look. Here are three examples with a main() method:

```
public static void main(String[] args)
public static void main(String args[])
public static void main(String... args) // varargs
```

The third example uses a syntax called *varargs* (variable arguments), which you saw in Chapter 1, "Welcome to Java." You'll learn how to call a method using varargs in Chapter 7, "Methods and Encapsulation." For now, all you need to know is that you can use a variable defined using varargs as if it were a normal array. For example, args.length and args[0] are legal.

Multidimensional Arrays

Arrays are objects, and of course array components can be objects. It doesn't take much time, rubbing those two facts together, to wonder whether arrays can hold other arrays, and of course they can.

Creating a Multidimensional Array

Multiple array separators are all it takes to declare arrays with multiple dimensions. You can locate them with the type or variable name in the declaration, just as before:

```
int[][] vars1;          // 2D array
int vars2 [][];         // 2D array
int[] vars3[];          // 2D array
int[] vars4 [], space [][];  // a 2D AND a 3D array
```

The first two examples are nothing surprising and declare a two-dimensional (2D) array. The third example also declares a 2D array. There's no good reason to use this style other than to confuse readers with your code. The final example declares two arrays on the same line. Adding up the brackets, we see that the vars4 is a 2D array and space is a 3D array. Again, there's no reason to use this style other than to confuse readers of your code. The exam creators like to try to confuse you, though. Luckily, you are on to them and won't let this happen to you!

You can specify the size of your multidimensional array in the declaration if you like:

```
String [][] rectangle = new String[3][2];
```

The result of this statement is an array rectangle with three elements, each of which refers to an array of two elements. You can think of the addressable range as [0][0] through [2][1], but don't think of it as a structure of addresses like [0,0] or [2,1].

Now suppose we set one of these values:

```
rectangle[0][1] = "set";
```

You can visualize the result as shown in Figure 5.7. This array is sparsely populated because it has a lot of null values. You can see that rectangle still points to an array of three elements and that we have three arrays of two elements. You can also follow the trail from reference to the one value pointing to a String. First you start at index 0 in the top array. Then you go to index 1 in the next array.

FIGURE 5.7   A sparsely populated multidimensional array

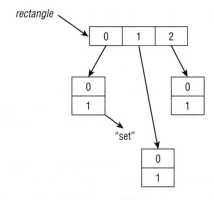

While that array happens to be rectangular in shape, an array doesn't need to be. Consider this one:

```
int[][] differentSizes = {{1, 4}, {3}, {9,8,7}};
```

We still start with an array of three elements. However, this time the elements in the next level are all different sizes. One is of length 2, the next length 1, and the last length 3 (see Figure 5.8). This time the array is of primitives, so they are shown as if they are in the array themselves.

FIGURE 5.8 An asymmetric multidimensional array

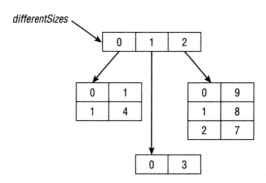

Another way to create an asymmetric array is to initialize just an array's first dimension and define the size of each array component in a separate statement:

```
int [][] args = new int[4][];
args[0] = new int[5];
args[1] = new int[3];
```

This technique reveals what you really get with Java: arrays of arrays that, properly managed, offer a multidimensional effect.

Using a Multidimensional Array

The most common operation on a multidimensional array is to loop through it. This example prints out a 2D array:

```
int[][] twoD = new int[3][2];
for (int i = 0; i < twoD.length; i++) {
   for (int j = 0; j < twoD[i].length; j++)
      System.out.print(twoD[i][j] + " "); // print element
   System.out.println();                  // time for a new row
}
```

We have two loops here. The first uses index i and goes through the first subarray for twoD. The second uses a different loop variable j. It is important that these be different variable names so the loops don't get mixed up. The inner loop looks at how many elements are in the second-level array. The inner loop prints the element and leaves a space for readability. When the inner loop completes, the outer loop goes to a new line and repeats the process for the next element.

This entire exercise would be easier to read with the enhanced for loop.

```
for (int[] inner : twoD) {
    for (int num : inner)
        System.out.print(num + " ");
    System.out.println();
}
```

We'll grant you that it isn't fewer lines, but each line is less complex, and there aren't any loop variables or terminating conditions to mix up.

Understanding an *ArrayList*

An array has one glaring shortcoming: You have to know how many elements will be in the array when you create it, and then you are stuck with that choice. Just like a StringBuilder, an ArrayList can change capacity at runtime as needed. Like an array, an ArrayList is an ordered sequence that allows duplicates.

As when we used Arrays.sort, ArrayList requires an import. To use it, you must have either of the following two statements in your class:

```
import java.util.*;          // import whole package
import java.util.ArrayList; // import just ArrayList
```

In this section, we'll look at creating an ArrayList, common methods, autoboxing, conversion, and sorting.

Experienced programmers, take note: This section is simplified and doesn't cover a number of topics that are out of scope for this exam.

Creating an *ArrayList*

As with StringBuilder, there are three ways to create an ArrayList:

```
ArrayList list1 = new ArrayList();
ArrayList list2 = new ArrayList(10);
ArrayList list3 = new ArrayList(list2);
```

The first says to create an ArrayList containing space for the default number of elements but not to fill any slots yet. The second says to create an ArrayList containing a specific number of slots, but again not to assign any. The final example tells Java that we want to make a copy of another ArrayList. We copy both the size and contents of that ArrayList. Granted, list2 is empty in this example, so it isn't particularly interesting.

Although these are the only three constructors you need to know, you do need to learn some variants of it. The previous examples were the old pre–Java 5 way of creating an ArrayList. They still work, and you still need to know they work. You also need to know the new and improved way. Java 5 introduced *generics*, which allow you to specify the type of class that the `ArrayList` will contain.

```
ArrayList<String> list4 = new ArrayList<String>();
ArrayList<String> list5 = new ArrayList<>();
```

Java 5 allows you to tell the compiler what the type would be by specifying it between < and >. Starting in Java 7, you can even omit that type from the right side. The < and > are still required, though. This is called the *diamond operator* because <> looks like a diamond.

Using `var` with `ArrayList`

Now that var can be used to obscure data types, there is a whole new group of questions that can be asked with generics. Consider this code mixing the two:

```
var strings = new ArrayList<String>();
strings.add("a");
for (String s: strings) {  }
```

The type of var is `ArrayList<String>`. This means you can add a `String` or loop through the `String` objects. What if we use the diamond operator with var?

```
var list = new ArrayList<>();
```

Believe it or not, this does compile. The type of the var is `ArrayList<Object>`. Since there isn't a type specified for the generic, Java has to assume the ultimate superclass. This is a bit silly and unexpected, so please don't write this. But if you see it on the exam, you'll know what to expect. Now can you figure out why this doesn't compile?

```
var list = new ArrayList<>();
list.add("a");
for (String s: list) { } // DOES NOT COMPILE
```

The type of var is `ArrayList<Object>`. Since there isn't a type in the diamond operator, Java has to assume the most generic option it can. Therefore, it picks `Object`, the ultimate superclass. Adding a `String` to the list is fine. You can add any subclass of `Object`. However, in the loop, we need to use the `Object` type rather than `String`.

Just when you thought you knew everything about creating an `ArrayList`, there is one more thing you need to know. `ArrayList` implements an interface called `List`. In other words, an `ArrayList` is a `List`. You will learn about interfaces later in the book. In the meantime, just know that you can store an `ArrayList` in a `List` reference variable but not vice versa. The reason is that `List` is an interface and interfaces can't be instantiated.

```
List<String> list6 = new ArrayList<>();
ArrayList<String> list7 = new List<>(); // DOES NOT COMPILE
```

Using an *ArrayList*

ArrayList has many methods, but you only need to know a handful of them—even fewer than you did for String and StringBuilder.

Before reading any further, you are going to see something new in the method signatures: a "class" named E. Don't worry—it isn't really a class. E is used by convention in generics to mean "any class that this array can hold." If you didn't specify a type when creating the ArrayList, E means Object. Otherwise, it means the class you put between < and >.

You should also know that ArrayList implements toString(), so you can easily see the contents just by printing it. Arrays do not produce such pretty output by default.

add()

The add() methods insert a new value in the ArrayList. The method signatures are as follows:

```
boolean add(E element)
void add(int index, E element)
```

Don't worry about the boolean return value. It always returns true. As we'll see later in the chapter, it is there because other classes in the Collections family need a return value in the signature when adding an element.

Since add() is the most critical ArrayList method you need to know for the exam, we are going to show a few examples for it. Let's start with the most straightforward case:

```
ArrayList list = new ArrayList();
list.add("hawk");             // [hawk]
list.add(Boolean.TRUE);       // [hawk, true]
System.out.println(list);     // [hawk, true]
```

add() does exactly what we expect: It stores the String in the no longer empty ArrayList. It then does the same thing for the Boolean. This is okay because we didn't specify a type for ArrayList; therefore, the type is Object, which includes everything except primitives. It may not have been what we intended, but the compiler doesn't know that. Now, let's use generics to tell the compiler we only want to allow String objects in our ArrayList:

```
ArrayList<String> safer = new ArrayList<>();
safer.add("sparrow");
safer.add(Boolean.TRUE);     // DOES NOT COMPILE
```

This time the compiler knows that only String objects are allowed in and prevents the attempt to add a Boolean. Now let's try adding multiple values to different positions.

```
4: List<String> birds = new ArrayList<>();
5: birds.add("hawk");          // [hawk]
6: birds.add(1, "robin");      // [hawk, robin]
7: birds.add(0, "blue jay");   // [blue jay, hawk, robin]
8: birds.add(1, "cardinal");   // [blue jay, cardinal, hawk, robin]
9: System.out.println(birds);  // [blue jay, cardinal, hawk, robin]
```

When a question has code that adds objects at indexed positions, draw it so that you won't lose track of which value is at which index. In this example, line 5 adds "hawk" to the end of birds. Then line 6 adds "robin" to index 1 of birds, which happens to be the end. Line 7 adds "blue jay" to index 0, which happens to be the beginning of birds. Finally, line 8 adds "cardinal" to index 1, which is now near the middle of birds.

remove()

The remove() methods remove the first matching value in the ArrayList or remove the element at a specified index. The method signatures are as follows:

```
boolean remove(Object object)
E remove(int index)
```

This time the boolean return value tells us whether a match was removed. The E return type is the element that actually got removed. The following shows how to use these methods:

```
3: List<String> birds = new ArrayList<>();
4: birds.add("hawk");      // [hawk]
5: birds.add("hawk");      // [hawk, hawk]
6: System.out.println(birds.remove("cardinal")); // prints false
7: System.out.println(birds.remove("hawk"));     // prints true
8: System.out.println(birds.remove(0));          // prints hawk
9: System.out.println(birds);                    // []
```

Line 6 tries to remove an element that is not in birds. It returns false because no such element is found. Line 7 tries to remove an element that is in birds and so returns true. Notice that it removes only one match. Line 8 removes the element at index 0, which is the last remaining element in the ArrayList.

Since calling remove() with an int uses the index, an index that doesn't exist will throw an exception. For example, birds.remove(100) throws an IndexOutOfBoundsException.

There is also a removeIf() method. We'll cover it in the next chapter because it uses lambda expressions (a topic in that chapter).

set()

The set() method changes one of the elements of the ArrayList without changing the size. The method signature is as follows:

```
E set(int index, E newElement)
```

The E return type is the element that got replaced. The following shows how to use this method:

```
15: List<String> birds = new ArrayList<>();
16: birds.add("hawk");                  // [hawk]
17: System.out.println(birds.size());   // 1
18: birds.set(0, "robin");              // [robin]
19: System.out.println(birds.size());   // 1
20: birds.set(1, "robin");              // IndexOutOfBoundsException
```

Line 16 adds one element to the array, making the size 1. Line 18 replaces that one element, and the size stays at 1. Line 20 tries to replace an element that isn't in the `ArrayList`. Since the size is 1, the only valid index is 0. Java throws an exception because this isn't allowed.

isEmpty() and size()

The `isEmpty()` and `size()` methods look at how many of the slots are in use. The method signatures are as follows:

```
boolean isEmpty()
int size()
```

The following shows how to use these methods:

```
List<String> birds = new ArrayList<>();
System.out.println(birds.isEmpty());   // true
System.out.println(birds.size());      // 0
birds.add("hawk");                     // [hawk]
birds.add("hawk");                     // [hawk, hawk]
System.out.println(birds.isEmpty());   // false
System.out.println(birds.size());      // 2
```

At the beginning, `birds` has a size of 0 and is empty. It has a capacity that is greater than 0. However, as with `StringBuilder`, we don't use the capacity in determining size or length. After adding elements, the size becomes positive, and it is no longer empty. Notice how `isEmpty()` is a convenience method for `size() == 0`.

clear()

The `clear()` method provides an easy way to discard all elements of the `ArrayList`. The method signature is as follows:

```
void clear()
```

The following shows how to use this method:

```
List<String> birds = new ArrayList<>();
birds.add("hawk");                  // [hawk]
birds.add("hawk");                  // [hawk, hawk]
```

```
System.out.println(birds.isEmpty());   // false
System.out.println(birds.size());      // 2
birds.clear();                         // []
System.out.println(birds.isEmpty());   // true
System.out.println(birds.size());      // 0
```

After we call clear(), birds is back to being an empty ArrayList of size 0.

contains()

The contains() method checks whether a certain value is in the ArrayList. The method signature is as follows:

```
boolean contains(Object object)
```

The following shows how to use this method:

```
List<String> birds = new ArrayList<>();
birds.add("hawk");                             // [hawk]
System.out.println(birds.contains("hawk"));    // true
System.out.println(birds.contains("robin"));   // false
```

This method calls equals() on each element of the ArrayList to see whether there are any matches. Since String implements equals(), this works out well.

equals()

Finally, ArrayList has a custom implementation of equals(),so you can compare two lists to see whether they contain the same elements in the same order.

```
boolean equals(Object object)
```

The following shows an example:

```
31: List<String> one = new ArrayList<>();
32: List<String> two = new ArrayList<>();
33: System.out.println(one.equals(two));   // true
34: one.add("a");                          // [a]
35: System.out.println(one.equals(two));   // false
36: two.add("a");                          // [a]
37: System.out.println(one.equals(two));   // true
38: one.add("b");                          // [a,b]
39: two.add(0, "b");                       // [b,a]
40: System.out.println(one.equals(two));   // false
```

On line 33, the two ArrayList objects are equal. An empty list is certainly the same elements in the same order. On line 35, the ArrayList objects are not equal because the size is different. On line 37, they are equal again because the same one element is in each. On line

40, they are not equal. The size is the same and the values are the same, but they are not in the same order.

Wrapper Classes

Up to now, we've only put String objects in the ArrayList. What happens if we want to put primitives in? Each primitive type has a wrapper class, which is an object type that corresponds to the primitive. Table 5.4 lists all the wrapper classes along with how to create them.

TABLE 5.4   Wrapper classes

Primitive type	Wrapper class	Example of creating
boolean	Boolean	Boolean.valueOf(true)
byte	Byte	Byte.valueOf((byte) 1)
short	Short	Short.valueOf((short) 1)
int	Integer	Integer.valueOf(1)
long	Long	Long.valueOf(1)
float	Float	Float.valueOf((float) 1.0)
double	Double	Double.valueOf(1.0)
char	Character	Character.valueOf('c')

Each wrapper class also has a constructor. It works the same way as valueOf() but isn't recommended for new code. The valueOf() allows object caching. Remember how a String could be shared when the value is the same? The wrapper classes are immutable and take advantage of some caching as well.

The wrapper classes also have a method that converts back to a primitive. You don't need to know much about the valueOf() or intValue() type methods for the exam because autoboxing has removed the need for them (see the next section). You just need to be able to read the code and not look for tricks in it.

There are also methods for converting a String to a primitive or wrapper class. You do need to know these methods. The parse methods, such as parseInt(), return a primitive, and the valueOf() method returns a wrapper class. This is easy to remember because the name of the returned primitive is in the method name. Here's an example:

```
int primitive = Integer.parseInt("123");
Integer wrapper = Integer.valueOf("123");
```

The first line converts a `String` to an `int` primitive. The second converts a `String` to an `Integer` wrapper class. If the `String` passed in is not valid for the given type, Java throws an exception. In these examples, letters and dots are not valid for an integer value:

```
int bad1 = Integer.parseInt("a");        // throws NumberFormatException
Integer bad2 = Integer.valueOf("123.45"); // throws NumberFormatException
```

Before you worry, the exam won't make you recognize that the method `parseInt()` is used rather than `parseInteger()`. You simply need to be able to recognize the methods when put in front of you. Also, the `Character` class doesn't participate in the `parse/valueOf` methods. Since a `String` consists of characters, you can just call `charAt()` normally.

Table 5.5 lists the methods you need to recognize for creating a primitive or wrapper class object from a `String`. In real coding, you won't be so concerned about which is returned from each method due to autoboxing.

TABLE 5.5 Converting from a `String`

Wrapper class	Converting `String` to a primitive	Converting `String` to a wrapper class
Boolean	Boolean.parseBoolean("true")	Boolean.valueOf("TRUE")
Byte	Byte.parseByte("1")	Byte.valueOf("2")
Short	Short.parseShort("1")	Short.valueOf("2")
Integer	Integer.parseInt("1")	Integer.valueOf("2")
Long	Long.parseLong("1")	Long.valueOf("2")
Float	Float.parseFloat("1")	Float.valueOf("2.2")
Double	Double.parseDouble("1")	Double.valueOf("2.2")
Character	None	None

Wrapper Classes and Null

When we presented numeric primitives in Chapter 2, we mentioned they could not be used to store `null` values. One advantage of a wrapper class over a primitive is that because it's an object, it can be used to store a `null` value. While `null` values aren't particularly useful for numeric calculations, they are quite useful in data-based services. For example, if you are storing a user's location data using (latitude,longitude), it would be a bad idea to store a missing point as (0,0) since that refers to an actual location off the coast of Africa where the user could theoretically be.

Autoboxing and Unboxing

Why won't you need to be concerned with whether a primitive or wrapper class is returned, you ask? Since Java 5, you can just type the primitive value, and Java will convert it to the relevant wrapper class for you. This is called *autoboxing*. The reverse conversion of wrapper class to primitive value is called *unboxing*. Let's look at an example:

```
3: List<Integer> weights = new ArrayList<>();
4: Integer w = 50;
5: weights.add(w);                   // [50]
6: weights.add(Integer.valueOf(60));    // [50, 60]
7: weights.remove(50);              // [60]
8: double first = weights.get(0);   // 60.0
```

Line 4 autoboxes the int primitive into an Integer object, and line 5 adds that to the List. Line 6 shows that you can still write code the long way and pass in a wrapper object. Line 7 again autoboxes into the wrapper object and passes it to remove(). Line 8 retrieves the first Integer in the list, unboxes it as a primitive and implicitly casts it to double.

What do you think happens if you try to unbox a null?

```
3: List<Integer> heights = new ArrayList<>();
4: heights.add(null);
5: int h = heights.get(0);          // NullPointerException
```

On line 4, we add a null to the list. This is legal because a null reference can be assigned to any reference variable. On line 5, we try to unbox that null to an int primitive. This is a problem. Java tries to get the int value of null. Since calling any method on null gives a NullPointerException, that is just what we get. Be careful when you see null in relation to autoboxing.

Also be careful when autoboxing into Integer. What do you think this code outputs?

```
List<Integer> numbers = new ArrayList<>();
numbers.add(1);
numbers.add(2);
numbers.remove(1);
System.out.println(numbers);
```

It actually outputs [1]. After adding the two values, the List contains [1, 2]. We then request the element with index 1 be removed. That's right: index 1. Because there's already a remove() method that takes an int parameter, Java calls that method rather than autoboxing. If you want to remove the 1, you can write numbers.remove(new Integer(1)) to force wrapper class use.

Converting Between *array* and *List*

You should know how to convert between an array and a List. Let's start with turning an ArrayList into an array:

```
13: List<String> list = new ArrayList<>();
14: list.add("hawk");
15: list.add("robin");
16: Object[] objectArray = list.toArray();
17: String[] stringArray = list.toArray(new String[0]);
18: list.clear();
19: System.out.println(objectArray.length);     // 2
20: System.out.println(stringArray.length);     // 2
```

Line 16 shows that an ArrayList knows how to convert itself to an array. The only problem is that it defaults to an array of class Object. This isn't usually what you want. Line 17 specifies the type of the array and does what we actually want. The advantage of specifying a size of 0 for the parameter is that Java will create a new array of the proper size for the return value. If you like, you can suggest a larger array to be used instead. If the ArrayList fits in that array, it will be returned. Otherwise, a new one will be created.

Also, notice that line 18 clears the original List. This does not affect either array. The array is a newly created object with no relationship to the original List. It is simply a copy.

Converting from an array to a List is more interesting. We will show you two methods to do this conversion. Note that you aren't guaranteed to get a java.util.ArrayList from either. This means each has special behavior to learn about.

One option is to create a List that is linked to the original array. When a change is made to one, it is available in the other. It is a fixed-size list and is also known as a backed List because the array changes with it. Pay careful attention to the values here:

```
20: String[] array = { "hawk", "robin" };     // [hawk, robin]
21: List<String> list = Arrays.asList(array); // returns fixed size list
22: System.out.println(list.size());          // 2
23: list.set(1, "test");                       // [hawk, test]
24: array[0] = "new";                          // [new, test]
25: System.out.print(Arrays.toString(array)); // [new, test]
26: list.remove(1);     // throws UnsupportedOperationException
```

Line 21 converts the array to a List. Note that it isn't the java.util.ArrayList we've grown used to. It is a fixed-size, backed version of a List. Line 23 is okay because set() merely replaces an existing value. It updates both array and list because they point to the same data store. Line 24 also changes both array and list. Line 25 shows the array has changed to [new, test]. Line 26 throws an exception because we are not allowed to change the size of the list.

Another option is to create an immutable List. That means you cannot change the values or the size of the List. You can change the original array, but changes will not be reflected in the immutable List. Again, pay careful attention to the values:

```
32: String[] array = { "hawk", "robin" };        // [hawk, robin]
33: List<String> list = List.of(array);          // returns immutable list
34: System.out.println(list.size());             // 2
```

```
35: array[0] = "new";
36: System.out.println(Arrays.toString(array)); // [new, robin]
37: System.out.println(list);                    // [hawk, robin]
38: list.set(1, "test");      // throws UnsupportedOperationException
```

Line 33 creates the immutable List. It contains the two values that array happened to contain at the time the List was created. On line 35, there is a change to the array. Line 36 shows that array has changed. Line 37 shows that list still has the original values. This is because it is an immutable copy of the original array. Line 38 shows that changing a list value in an immutable list is not allowed.

Using Varargs to Create a List

Using varargs allows you to create a List in a cool way:

```
List<String> list1 = Arrays.asList("one", "two");
List<String> list2 = List.of("one", "two");
```

Both of these methods take varargs, which let you pass in an array or just type out the String values. This is handy when testing because you can easily create and populate a List on one line. Both methods create fixed-size arrays. If you will need to later add or remove elements, you'll still need to create an ArrayList using the constructor. There's a lot going on here, so let's study Table 5.6.

TABLE 5.6　　Array and list conversions

	toArray()	Arrays.asList()	List.of()
Type converting from	List	Array (or varargs)	Array (or varargs)
Type created	Array	List	List
Allowed to remove values from created object	No	No	No
Allowed to change values in the created object	Yes	Yes	No
Changing values in the created object affects the original or vice versa.	No	Yes	N/A

Notice that none of the options allows you to change the number of elements. If you want to do that, you'll need to actually write logic to create the new object. Here's an example:

```
List<String> fixedSizeList  = Arrays.asList("a", "b", "c");
List<String> expandableList = new ArrayList<>(fixedSizeList);
```

Sorting

Sorting an `ArrayList` is similar to sorting an array. You just use a different helper class:

```
List<Integer> numbers = new ArrayList<>();
numbers.add(99);
numbers.add(5);
numbers.add(81);
Collections.sort(numbers);
System.out.println(numbers); // [5, 81, 99]
```

As you can see, the numbers got sorted, just like you'd expect. Isn't it nice to have something that works just like you think it will?

Creating Sets and Maps

Although advanced collections topics are not covered until the 1Z0-816 exam, you should still know the basics of `Set` and `Map` now.

Introducing Sets

A `Set` is a collection of objects that cannot contain duplicates. If you try to add a duplicate to a set, the API will not fulfill the request. You can imagine a set as shown in Figure 5.9.

FIGURE 5.9 Example of a Set

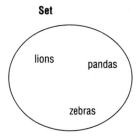

All the methods you learned for `ArrayList` apply to a `Set` with the exception of those taking an index as a parameter. Why is this? Well, a `Set` isn't ordered, so it wouldn't make sense to talk about the first element. This means you cannot call `set(index, value)` or `remove(index)`. You can call other methods like `add(value)` or `remove(value)`.

Do you remember that `boolean` return value on `add()` that always returned `true` for an `ArrayList`? `Set` is a reason it needs to exist. When trying to add a duplicate value, the method returns `false` and does not add the value.

There are two common classes that implement Set that you might see on the exam. HashSet is the most common. TreeSet is used when sorting is important.

To make sure you understand a Set, follow along with this code:

```
3: Set<Integer> set = new HashSet<>();
4: System.out.println(set.add(66)); // true
5: System.out.println(set.add(66)); // false
6: System.out.println(set.size()); // 1
7: set.remove(66);
8: System.out.println(set.isEmpty()); // true
```

Line 3 creates a new set that declares only unique elements are allowed. Both lines 4 and 5 attempt to add the same value. Only the first one is allowed, making line 4 print true and line 5 false. Line 6 confirms there is only one value in the set. Removing an element on line 7 works normally, and the set is empty on line 8.

Introducing Maps

A Map uses a key to identify values. For example, when you use the contact list on your phone, you look up "George" rather than looking through each phone number in turn. Figure 5.10 shows how to visualize a Map.

FIGURE 5.10   Example of a Map

George	555-555-5555
Mary	777-777-7777

The most common implementation of Map is HashMap. Some of the methods are the same as those in ArrayList like clear(), isEmpty(), and size().

There are also methods specific to dealing with key and value pairs. Table 5.7 shows these minimal methods you need to know.

TABLE 5.7   Common Map methods

Method	Description
V get(Object key)	Returns the value mapped by key or null if none is mapped
V getOrDeafult(Object key, V other)	Returns the value mapped by key or other if none is mapped
V put(K key, V value)	Adds or replaces key/value pair. Returns previous value or null

TABLE 5.7   Common Map methods *(continued)*

Method	Description
V remove(Object key)	Removes and returns value mapped to key. Returns null if none
boolean containsKey(Object key)	Returns whether key is in map
boolean containsValue(Object key)	Returns whether value is in map
Set<K> keySet()	Returns set of all keys
Collection<V> values()	Returns Collection of all values

Now let's look at an example to confirm this is clear:

```
8:  Map<String, String> map = new HashMap<>();
9:  map.put("koala", "bamboo");
10: String food = map.get("koala"); // bamboo
11: String other = map.getOrDefault("ant", "leaf"); // leaf
12: for (String key: map.keySet())
13:    System.out.println(key + " " + map.get(key)); // koala bamboo
```

In this example, we create a new map and store one key/value pair inside. Line 10 gets this value by key. Line 11 looks for a key that isn't there, so it returns the second parameter leaf as the default value. Lines 12 and 13 list all the key and value pairs.

Calculating with Math APIs

It should come as no surprise that computers are good at computing numbers. Java comes with a powerful Math class with many methods to make your life easier. We will just cover a few common ones here that are most likely to appear on the exam. When doing your own projects, look at the Math Javadoc to see what other methods can help you.

Pay special attention to return types in math questions. They are an excellent opportunity for trickery!

min() and max()

The min() and max() methods compare two values and return one of them.

The method signatures for min() are as follows:

```
double min(double a, double b)
float min(float a, float b)
```

```
int min(int a, int b)
long min(long a, long b)
```

There are four overloaded methods, so you always have an API available with the same type. Each method returns whichever of a or b is smaller. The max() method works the same way except it returns the larger value.

The following shows how to use these methods:

```
int first = Math.max(3, 7);  // 7
int second = Math.min(7, -9);  // -9
```

The first line returns 7 because it is larger. The second line returns -9 because it is smaller. Remember from school that negative values are smaller than positive ones.

round()

The round() method gets rid of the decimal portion of the value, choosing the next higher number if appropriate. If the fractional part is .5 or higher, we round up.

The method signatures for round() are as follows:

```
long round(double num)
int round(float num)
```

There are two overloaded methods to ensure there is enough room to store a rounded double if needed. The following shows how to use this method:

```
long low = Math.round(123.45); // 123
long high = Math.round(123.50); // 124
int fromFloat = Math.round(123.45f); // 123
```

The first line returns 123 because .45 is smaller than a half. The second line returns 124 because the fractional part is just barely a half. The final line shows that an explicit float triggers the method signature that returns an int.

pow()

The pow() method handles exponents. As you may recall from your elementary school math class, 3^2 means three squared. This is 3 * 3 or 9. Fractional exponents are allowed as well. Sixteen to the .5 power means the square root of 16, which is 4. (Don't worry, you won't have to do square roots on the exam.)

The method signature is as follows:

```
double pow(double number, double exponent)
```

The following shows how to use this method:

```
double squared = Math.pow(5, 2); // 25.0
```

Notice that the result is 25.0 rather than 25 since it is a double. (Again, don't worry, the exam won't ask you to do any complicated math.)

random()

The random() method returns a value greater than or equal to 0 and less than 1. The method signature is as follows:

```
double random()
```

The following shows how to use this method:

```
double num = Math.random();
```

Since it is a random number, we can't know the result in advance. However, we can rule out certain numbers. For example, it can't be negative because that's less than 0. It can't be 1.0 because that's not less than 1.

Summary

In this chapter, you learned that Strings are immutable sequences of characters. The new operator is optional. The concatenation operator (+) creates a new String with the content of the first String followed by the content of the second String. If either operand involved in the + expression is a String, concatenation is used; otherwise, addition is used. String literals are stored in the string pool. The String class has many methods.

StringBuilders are mutable sequences of characters. Most of the methods return a reference to the current object to allow method chaining. The StringBuilder class has many methods.

Calling == on String objects will check whether they point to the same object in the pool. Calling == on StringBuilder references will check whether they are pointing to the same StringBuilder object. Calling equals() on String objects will check whether the sequence of characters is the same. Calling equals() on StringBuilder objects will check whether they are pointing to the same object rather than looking at the values inside.

An array is a fixed-size area of memory on the heap that has space for primitives or pointers to objects. You specify the size when creating it—for example, int[] a = new int[6];. Indexes begin with 0, and elements are referred to using a[0]. The Arrays.sort() method sorts an array. Arrays.binarySearch() searches a sorted array and returns the index of a match. If no match is found, it negates the position where the element would need to be inserted and subtracts 1. Arrays.compare() and Arrays .mismatch() check whether two arrays are the equivalent. Methods that are passed varargs (…) can be used as if a normal array was passed in. In a multidimensional array, the second-level arrays and beyond can be different sizes.

An ArrayList can change size over its life. It can be stored in an ArrayList or List reference. Generics can specify the type that goes in the ArrayList. Although an ArrayList is not allowed to contain primitives, Java will autobox parameters passed in to the proper wrapper type. Collections.sort() sorts an ArrayList.

A Set is a collection with unique values. A Map consists of key/value pairs. The Math class provides many static methods to facilitate programming.

Exam Essentials

Be able to determine the output of code using String. Know the rules for concatenating Strings and how to use common String methods. Know that Strings are immutable. Pay special attention to the fact that indexes are zero-based and that substring() gets the string up until right before the index of the second parameter.

Be able to determine the output of code using StringBuilder. Know that StringBuilder is mutable and how to use common StringBuilder methods. Know that substring() does not change the value of a StringBuilder, whereas append(), delete(), and insert() do change it. Also note that most StringBuilder methods return a reference to the current instance of StringBuilder.

Understand the difference between == and equals(). == checks object equality. equals() depends on the implementation of the object it is being called on. For Strings, equals() checks the characters inside of it.

Be able to determine the output of code using arrays. Know how to declare and instantiate one-dimensional and multidimensional arrays. Be able to access each element and know when an index is out of bounds. Recognize correct and incorrect output when searching and sorting.

Be able to determine the output of code using ArrayList. Know that ArrayList can increase in size. Be able to identify the different ways of declaring and instantiating an ArrayList. Identify correct output from ArrayList methods, including the impact of autoboxing.

Review Questions

1. What is output by the following code? (Choose all that apply.)

```
1: public class Fish {
2:     public static void main(String[] args) {
3:         int numFish = 4;
4:         String fishType = "tuna";
5:         String anotherFish = numFish + 1;
6:         System.out.println(anotherFish + " " + fishType);
7:         System.out.println(numFish + " " + 1);
8: } }
```

   A. 4 1
   B. 5
   C. 5 tuna
   D. 5tuna
   E. 51tuna
   F. The code does not compile.

2. Which of the following are output by this code? (Choose all that apply.)

```
3: var s = "Hello";
4: var t = new String(s);
5: if ("Hello".equals(s)) System.out.println("one");
6: if (t == s) System.out.println("two");
7: if (t.intern() == s) System.out.println("three");
8: if ("Hello" == s) System.out.println("four");
9: if ("Hello".intern() == t) System.out.println("five");
```

   A. one
   B. two
   C. three
   D. four
   E. five
   F. The code does not compile.
   G. None of the above

3. Which statements about the following code snippet are correct? (Choose all that apply.)

```
List<String> gorillas = new ArrayList<>();
for(var koko : gorillas)
```

```
System.out.println(koko);

var monkeys = new ArrayList<>();
for(var albert : monkeys)
    System.out.println(albert);

List chimpanzees = new ArrayList<Integer>();
for(var ham : chimpanzees)
    System.out.println(ham);
```

A. The data type of koko is `String`.

B. The data type of koko is `Object`.

C. The data type of albert is `Object`.

D. The data type of albert is undefined.

E. The data type of ham is `Integer`.

F. The data type of ham is `Object`.

G. None of the above, as the code does not compile

4. What is the result of the following code?

```
7: StringBuilder sb = new StringBuilder();
8: sb.append("aaa").insert(1, "bb").insert(4, "ccc");
9: System.out.println(sb);
```

A. abbaaccc

B. abbaccca

C. bbaaaccc

D. bbaaccca

E. An empty line

F. The code does not compile.

5. What is the result of the following code?

```
12: int count = 0;
13: String s1 = "java";
14: String s2 = "java";
15: StringBuilder s3 = new StringBuilder("java");
16: if (s1 == s2) count++;
17: if (s1.equals(s2)) count++;
18: if (s1 == s3) count++;
19: if (s1.equals(s3)) count++;
20: System.out.println(count);
```

A. 0

B. 1

C. 2

D. 3

E. 4

F. An exception is thrown.

G. The code does not compile.

6. What is the result of the following code?

```java
public class Lion {
    public void roar(String roar1, StringBuilder roar2) {
        roar1.concat("!!!");
        roar2.append("!!!");
    }
    public static void main(String[] args) {
        String roar1 = "roar";
        StringBuilder roar2 = new StringBuilder("roar");
        new Lion().roar(roar1, roar2);
        System.out.println(roar1 + " " + roar2);
    }
}
```

A. roar roar

B. roar roar!!!

C. roar!!! roar

D. roar!!! roar!!!

E. An exception is thrown.

F. The code does not compile.

7. Which of the following return the number 5 when run independently? (Choose all that apply.)

```java
var string = "12345";
var builder = new StringBuilder("12345");
```

A. builder.charAt(4)

B. builder.replace(2, 4, "6").charAt(3)

C. builder.replace(2, 5, "6").charAt(2)

D. string.charAt(5)

E. string.length

F. string.replace("123", "1").charAt(2)

G. None of the above

8. What is output by the following code? (Choose all that apply.)

```java
String numbers = "012345678";
System.out.println(numbers.substring(1, 3));
System.out.println(numbers.substring(7, 7));
```

```
System.out.println(numbers.substring(7));
```

A. 12

B. 123

C. 7

D. 78

E. A blank line

F. The code does not compile.

G. An exception is thrown.

9. What is the result of the following code? (Choose all that apply.)

```
14: String s1 = "purr";
15: String s2 = "";
16:
17: s1.toUpperCase();
18: s1.trim();
19: s1.substring(1, 3);
20: s1 += "two";
21:
22: s2 += 2;
23: s2 += 'c';
24: s2 += false;
25:
26: if ( s2 == "2cfalse") System.out.println("==");
27: if ( s2.equals("2cfalse")) System.out.println("equals");
28: System.out.println(s1.length());
```

A. 2

B. 4

C. 7

D. 10

E. ==

F. equals

G. An exception is thrown.

H. The code does not compile.

10. Which of these statements are true? (Choose all that apply.)

```
var letters = new StringBuilder("abcdefg");
```

A. `letters.substring(1, 2)` returns a single character String.

B. `letters.substring(2, 2)` returns a single character String.

C. `letters.substring(6, 5)` returns a single character String.

    D. `letters.substring(6, 6)` returns a single character `String`.

    E. `letters.substring(1, 2)` throws an exception.

    F. `letters.substring(2, 2)` throws an exception.

    G. `letters.substring(6, 5)` throws an exception.

    H. `letters.substring(6, 6)` throws an exception.

11. What is the result of the following code?

```
StringBuilder numbers = new StringBuilder("0123456789");
numbers.delete(2,  8);
numbers.append("-").insert(2, "+");
System.out.println(numbers);
```

    A. `01+89-`

    B. `012+9-`

    C. `012+-9`

    D. `0123456789`

    E. An exception is thrown.

    F. The code does not compile.

12. What is the result of the following code?

```
StringBuilder b = "rumble";
b.append(4).deleteCharAt(3).delete(3, b.length() - 1);
System.out.println(b);
```

    A. `rum`

    B. `rum4`

    C. `rumb4`

    D. `rumble4`

    E. An exception is thrown.

    F. The code does not compile.

13. Which of the following can replace line 4 to print `"avaJ"`? (Choose all that apply.)

```
3: var puzzle = new StringBuilder("Java");
4: // INSERT CODE HERE
5: System.out.println(puzzle);
```

    A. `puzzle.reverse();`

    B. `puzzle.append("vaJ$").substring(0, 4);`

    C. `puzzle.append("vaJ$").delete(0, 3).deleteCharAt(puzzle.length() - 1);`

    D. `puzzle.append("vaJ$").delete(0, 3).deleteCharAt(puzzle.length());`

    E. None of the above

14. Which of these array declarations is not legal? (Choose all that apply.)

A. `int[][] scores = new int[5][];`

B. `Object[][][] cubbies = new Object[3][0][5];`

C. `String beans[] = new beans[6];`

D. `java.util.Date[] dates[] = new java.util.Date[2][];`

E. `int[][] types = new int[];`

F. `int[][] java = new int[][];`

15. Which of the following can fill in the blanks so the code compiles? (Choose two.)

```
6: char[]c = new char[2];
7: ArrayList l = new ArrayList();
8: int length = _____ + _____;
```

A. `c.length`

B. `c.length()`

C. `c.size`

D. `c.size()`

E. `l.length`

F. `l.length()`

G. `l.size`

H. `l.size()`

16. Which of the following are true? (Choose all that apply.)

A. An array has a fixed size.

B. An `ArrayList` has a fixed size.

C. An array is immutable.

D. An `ArrayList` is immutable.

E. Calling `equals()` on two arrays returns `true`.

F. Calling `equals()` on two `ArrayList` objects returns `true`.

G. If you call `remove(0)` using an empty `ArrayList` object, it will compile successfully.

H. If you call `remove(0)` using an empty `ArrayList` object, it will run successfully.

17. What is the result of the following statements?

```
6:  var list = new ArrayList<String>();
7:  list.add("one");
8:  list.add("two");
9:  list.add(7);
10: for(var s : list)  System.out.print(s);
```

A. onetwo

B. onetwo7

  C. onetwo followed by an exception

  D. Compiler error on line 6

  E. Compiler error on line 7

  F. Compiler error on line 9

  G. Compiler error on line 10

18. Which of the following pairs fill in the blanks to output 6?

```
3: var values = new _____<Integer>();
4: values.add(4);
5: values.add(4);
6: values._____;
7: values.remove(0);
8: for (var v : values) System.out.print(v);
```

  A. ArrayList and put(1, 6)

  B. ArrayList and replace(1, 6)

  C. ArrayList and set(1, 6)

  D. HashSet and put(1, 6)

  E. HashSet and replace(1, 6)

  F. HashSet and set(1, 6)

  G. The code does not compile with any of these options.

19. What is output by the following? (Choose all that apply.)

```
8:  List<Integer> list = Arrays.asList(10, 4, -1, 5);
9:  int[] array = { 6, -4, 12, 0, -10 };
10: Collections.sort(list);
11:
12: Integer converted[] = list.toArray(new Integer[4]);
13: System.out.println(converted[0]);
14: System.out.println(Arrays.binarySearch(array, 12));
```

  A. -1

  B. 2

  C. 4

  D. 6

  E. 10

  F. One of the outputs is undefined.

  G. An exception is thrown.

  H. The code does not compile.

20. Which of the lines contain a compiler error? (Choose all that apply.)

```
23: double one = Math.pow(1, 2);
24: int two = Math.round(1.0);
25: float three = Math.random();
26: var doubles = new double[] { one, two, three};
27:
28: String [] names = {"Tom", "Dick", "Harry"};
29: List<String> list = names.asList();
30: var other = Arrays.asList(names);
31: other.set(0, "Sue");
```

A. Line 23

B. Line 24

C. Line 25

D. Line 26

E. Line 29

F. Line 30

G. Line 31

21. What is the result of the following?

```
List<String> hex = Arrays.asList("30", "8", "3A", "FF");
Collections.sort(hex);
int x = Collections.binarySearch(hex, "8");
int y = Collections.binarySearch(hex, "3A");
int z = Collections.binarySearch(hex, "4F");
System.out.println(x + " " + y + " " + z);
```

A. 0 1 -2

B. 0 1 -3

C. 2 1 -2

D. 2 1 -3

E. None of the above

F. The code doesn't compile.

22. Which of the following are true statements about the following code? (Choose all that apply.)

```
4: List<Integer> ages = new ArrayList<>();
5: ages.add(Integer.parseInt("5"));
6: ages.add(Integer.valueOf("6"));
7: ages.add(7);
8: ages.add(null);
9: for (int age : ages) System.out.print(age);
```

A. The code compiles.

B. The code throws a runtime exception.

C. Exactly one of the add statements uses autoboxing.

D. Exactly two of the add statements use autoboxing.

E. Exactly three of the add statements use autoboxing.

23. What is the result of the following?

```java
List<String> one = new ArrayList<String>();
one.add("abc");
List<String> two = new ArrayList<>();
two.add("abc");
if (one == two)
    System.out.println("A");
else if (one.equals(two))
    System.out.println("B");
else
    System.out.println("C");
```

A. A

B. B

C. C

D. An exception is thrown.

E. The code does not compile.

24. Which statements are true about the following code? (Choose all that apply.)

```java
public void run(Integer[] ints, Double[] doubles) {
    List<Integer> intList = Arrays.asList(ints);
    List<Double> doubleList = List.of(doubles);
    // more code
}
```

A. Adding an element to doubleList is allowed.

B. Adding an element to intList is allowed.

C. Changing the first element in doubleList changes the first element in doubles.

D. Changing the first element in intList changes the first element in ints.

E. doubleList is immutable.

F. intList is immutable.

25. Which of the following statements are true of the following code? (Choose all that apply.)

```
String[] s1 = { "Camel", "Peacock", "Llama"};
String[] s2 = { "Camel", "Llama", "Peacock"};
String[] s3 = { "Camel"};
String[] s4 = { "Camel", null};
```

A. `Arrays.compare(s1, s2)` returns a positive integer.

B. `Arrays.mismatch(s1, s2)` returns a positive integer.

C. `Arrays.compare(s3, s4)` returns a positive integer.

D. `Arrays.mismatch(s3, s4)` returns a positive integer.

E. `Arrays.compare(s4, s4)` returns a positive integer.

F. `Arrays.mismatch(s4, s4)` returns a positive integer.

Chapter

6

Lambdas and Functional Interfaces

OCP EXAM OBJECTIVES COVERED IN THIS CHAPTER:

✓ **Programming Abstractly Through Interfaces**

- Declare and use List and ArrayList instances

- Understanding Lambda Expressions

When we covered the Java APIs in the previous chapter, we didn't cover the ones that use lambda syntax. This chapter remedies that! You'll learn what a lambda is used for, about common functional interfaces, how to write a lambda with variables, and the APIs on the exam that rely on lambdas.

Writing Simple Lambdas

Java is an object-oriented language at heart. You've seen plenty of objects by now. In Java 8, the language added the ability to write code using another style.

Functional programming is a way of writing code more declaratively. You specify what you want to do rather than dealing with the state of objects. You focus more on expressions than loops.

Functional programming uses lambda expressions to write code. A *lambda expression* is a block of code that gets passed around. You can think of a lambda expression as an unnamed method. It has parameters and a body just like full-fledged methods do, but it doesn't have a name like a real method. Lambda expressions are often referred to as *lambdas* for short. You might also know them as closures if Java isn't your first language. If you had a bad experience with closures in the past, don't worry. They are far simpler in Java.

In other words, a lambda expression is like a method that you can pass as if it were a variable. For example, there are different ways to calculate age. One human year is equivalent to seven dog years. You want to write a method that takes an age() method as input. To do this in an object-oriented program, you'd need to define a Human subclass and a Dog subclass. With lambdas, you can just pass in the relevant expression to calculate age.

Lambdas allow you to write powerful code in Java. Only the simplest lambda expressions are on this exam. The goal is to get you comfortable with the syntax and the concepts. You'll see lambdas again on the 1Z0-816 exam.

In this section, we'll cover an example of why lambdas are helpful and the syntax of lambdas.

Lambda Example

Our goal is to print out all the animals in a list according to some criteria. We'll show you how to do this without lambdas to illustrate how lambdas are useful. We start out with the Animal class:

```
public class Animal {
   private String species;
   private boolean canHop;
   private boolean canSwim;
   public Animal(String speciesName, boolean hopper, boolean swimmer){
      species = speciesName;
      canHop = hopper;
      canSwim = swimmer;
   }
   public boolean canHop() { return canHop; }
   public boolean canSwim() { return canSwim; }
   public String toString() { return species; }
}
```

The Animal class has three instance variables, which are set in the constructor. It has two methods that get the state of whether the animal can hop or swim. It also has a toString() method so we can easily identify the Animal in programs.

We plan to write a lot of different checks, so we want an interface. You'll learn more about interfaces in Chapter 9, "Advanced Class Design." For now, it is enough to remember that an interface specifies the methods that our class needs to implement:

```
public interface CheckTrait {
   boolean test(Animal a);
}
```

The first thing we want to check is whether the Animal can hop. We provide a class that can check this:

```
public class CheckIfHopper implements CheckTrait {
   public boolean test(Animal a) {
      return a.canHop();
   }
}
```

This class may seem simple—and it is. This is actually part of the problem that lambdas solve. Just bear with us for a bit. Now we have everything that we need to write our code to find the Animals that hop:

```
1:  import java.util.*;
2:  public class TraditionalSearch {
3:     public static void main(String[] args) {
4:
```

```
5:        // list of animals
6:        List<Animal> animals = new ArrayList<Animal>();
7:        animals.add(new Animal("fish", false, true));
8:        animals.add(new Animal("kangaroo", true, false));
9:        animals.add(new Animal("rabbit", true, false));
10:       animals.add(new Animal("turtle", false, true));
11:
12:       // pass class that does check
13:       print(animals, new CheckIfHopper());
14:    }
15:    private static void print(List<Animal> animals,
16:       CheckTrait checker) {
17:       for (Animal animal : animals) {
18:
19:          // the general check
20:          if (checker.test(animal))
21:             System.out.print(animal + " ");
22:       }
23:       System.out.println();
24:    }
25: }
```

The print() method on line 13 method is very general—it can check for any trait. This is good design. It shouldn't need to know what specifically we are searching for in order to print a list of animals.

Now what happens if we want to print the Animals that swim? Sigh. We need to write another class, CheckIfSwims. Granted, it is only a few lines. Then we need to add a new line under line 13 that instantiates that class. That's two things just to do another check.

Why can't we just specify the logic we care about right here? Turns out that we can with lambda expressions. We could repeat that whole class here and make you find the one line that changed. Instead, we'll just show you. We could replace line 13 with the following, which uses a lambda:

```
13:    print(animals, a -> a.canHop());
```

Don't worry that the syntax looks a little funky. You'll get used to it, and we'll describe it in the next section. We'll also explain the bits that look like magic. For now, just focus on how easy it is to read. We are telling Java that we only care about Animals that can hop.

It doesn't take much imagination to figure out how we would add logic to get the Animals that can swim. We only have to add one line of code—no need for an extra class to do something simple. Here's that other line:

```
print(animals, a -> a.canSwim());
```

How about Animals that cannot swim?

```
print(animals, a -> ! a.canSwim());
```

The point here is that it is really easy to write code that uses lambdas once you get the basics in place. This code uses a concept called deferred execution. *Deferred execution* means that code is specified now but will run later. In this case, later is when the print() method calls it.

Lambda Syntax

One of the simplest lambda expressions you can write is the one you just saw:

```
a -> a.canHop()
```

Lambdas work with interfaces that have only one abstract method. In this case, Java looks at the CheckTrait interface that has one method. The lambda indicates that Java should call a method with an Animal parameter that returns a boolean value that's the result of a.canHop(). We know all this because we wrote the code. But how does Java know?

Java relies on context when figuring out what lambda expressions mean. We are passing this lambda as the second parameter of the print() method. That method expects a CheckTrait as the second parameter. Since we are passing a lambda instead, Java tries to map our lambda to that interface:

```
boolean test(Animal a);
```

Since that interface's method takes an Animal, that means the lambda parameter has to be an Animal. And since that interface's method returns a boolean, we know the lambda returns a boolean.

The syntax of lambdas is tricky because many parts are optional. These two lines do the exact same thing:

```
a -> a.canHop()
```

```
(Animal a) -> { return a.canHop(); }
```

Let's look at what is going on here. The first example, shown in Figure 6.1, has three parts:

- A single parameter specified with the name a
- The arrow operator to separate the parameter and body
- A body that calls a single method and returns the result of that method

FIGURE 6.1 Lambda syntax omitting optional parts

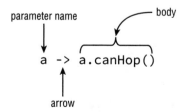

The second example shows the most verbose form of a lambda that returns a boolean (see Figure 6.2):

- A single parameter specified with the name a and stating the type is Animal
- The arrow operator to separate the parameter and body
- A body that has one or more lines of code, including a semicolon and a return statement

FIGURE 6.2   Lambda syntax, including optional parts

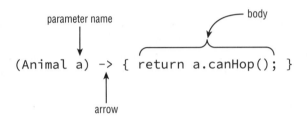

The parentheses can be omitted only if there is a single parameter and its type is not explicitly stated. Java does this because developers commonly use lambda expressions this way and they can do as little typing as possible.

It shouldn't be news to you that we can omit braces when we have only a single statement. We did this with if statements and loops already. What is different here is that the rules change when you omit the braces. Java doesn't require you to type return or use a semicolon when no braces are used. This special shortcut doesn't work when we have two or more statements. At least this is consistent with using {} to create blocks of code elsewhere.

    Here's a fun fact: s -> {} is a valid lambda. If there is no code on the right side of the expression, you don't need the semicolon or return statement.

Table 6.1 shows examples of valid lambdas that return a boolean.

TABLE 6.1   Valid lambdas

Lambda	# parameters
() -> true	0
a -> a.startsWith("test")	1
(String a) -> a.startsWith("test")	1
(a, b) -> a.startsWith("test")	2
(String a, String b) -> a.startsWith("test")	2

Notice that all of these examples have parentheses around the parameter list except the one that takes only one parameter and doesn't specify the type. The first row takes zero parameters and always returns the boolean value `true`. The second row takes one parameter and calls a method on it, returning the result. The third row does the same except that it explicitly defines the type of the variable. The final two rows take two parameters and ignore one of them—there isn't a rule that says you must use all defined parameters.

Now let's make sure you can identify invalid syntax for each row in Table 6.2 where each is supposed to return a `boolean`. Make sure you understand what's wrong with each of these.

TABLE 6.2   Invalid lambdas that return boolean

Invalid lambda	Reason
`a, b -> a.startsWith("test")`	Missing parentheses
`a -> { a.startsWith("test"); }`	Missing return
`a -> { return a.startsWith("test") }`	Missing semicolon

Remember that the parentheses are optional *only* when there is one parameter and it doesn't have a type declared.

Introducing Functional Interfaces

In our earlier example, we created an interface with one method:

```
boolean test(Animal a);
```

Lambdas work with interfaces that have only one abstract method. These are called *functional interfaces*. (It's actually more complicated than this, but for this exam the simplified definition is fine. On the 1Z0-816 exam, you'll get to deal with the full definition of a functional interface.)

We mentioned that a functional interface has only one abstract method. Your friend Sam can help you remember this because it is officially known as a *Single Abstract Method (SAM)* rule.

    Java provides an annotation @FunctionalInterface on some, but not all, functional interfaces. This annotation means the authors of the interface promise it will be safe to use in a lambda in the future. However, just because you don't see the annotation doesn't mean it's not a functional interface. Remember that having exactly one abstract method is what makes it a functional interface, not the annotation.

There are four functional interfaces you are likely to see on the exam. The next sections take a look at Predicate, Consumer, Supplier, and Comparator.

Predicate

You can imagine that we'd have to create lots of interfaces like this to use lambdas. We want to test Animals and Strings and Plants and anything else that we come across.

Luckily, Java recognizes that this is a common problem and provides such an interface for us. It's in the package java.util.function and the gist of it is as follows:

```
public interface Predicate<T> {
    boolean test(T t);
}
```

That looks a lot like our test(Animal) method. The only difference is that it uses the type T instead of Animal. That's the syntax for generics. It's like when we created an ArrayList and got to specify any type that goes in it.

This means we don't need our own interface anymore and can put everything related to our search in one class:

```
1:  import java.util.*;
2:  import java.util.function.*;
3:  public class PredicateSearch {
4:     public static void main(String[] args) {
5:        List<Animal> animals = new ArrayList<Animal>();
6:        animals.add(new Animal("fish", false, true));
7:
8:        print(animals, a -> a.canHop());
9:     }
10:    private static void print(List<Animal> animals,
11:       Predicate<Animal>  checker) {
12:       for (Animal animal : animals) {
13:          if (checker.test(animal))
14:             System.out.print(animal + " ");
15:       }
16:       System.out.println();
17:    }
18: }
```

This time, line 11 is the only one that changed. We expect to have a Predicate passed in that uses type Animal. Pretty cool. We can just use it without having to write extra code.

Consumer

The Consumer functional interface has one method you need to know:

```
void accept(T t)
```

Why might you want to receive a value and not return it? A common reason is when printing a message:

```
Consumer<String> consumer = x -> System.out.println(x);
```

We've declared functionality to print out the value we were given. It's okay that we don't have a value yet. When the consumer is called, the value will be provided and printed then. Let's take a look at code that uses a Consumer:

```
public static void main(String[] args) {
    Consumer<String> consumer = x -> System.out.println(x);
    print(consumer, "Hello World");
}
private static void print(Consumer<String> consumer, String value) {
    consumer.accept(value);
}
```

This code prints Hello World. It's a more complicated version than the one you learned as your first program. The print() method accepts a Consumer that knows how to print a value. When the accept() method is called, the lambda actually runs, printing the value.

Supplier

The Supplier functional interface has only one method:

```
T get()
```

A good use case for a Supplier is when generating values. Here are two examples:

```
Supplier<Integer> number = () ->  42;
Supplier<Integer> random = () ->  new Random().nextInt();
```

The first example returns 42 each time the lambda is called. The second generates a random number each time it is called. It could be the same number but is likely to be a different one. After all, it's random. Let's take a look at code that uses a Supplier:

```
public static void main(String[] args) {
    Supplier<Integer> number = () ->  42;
    System.out.println(returnNumber(number));
}

private static int returnNumber(Supplier<Integer> supplier) {
    return supplier.get();
}
```

When the returnNumber() method is called, it invokes the lambda to get the desired value. In this case, the method returns 2.

Comparator

In Chapter 5, "Core Java APIs," we compared numbers. We didn't supply a Comparator because we were using the default sort order. We did learn the rules. A negative number means the first value is smaller, zero means they are equal, and a positive number means the first value is bigger. The method signature is as follows:

```
int compare(T o1, T o2)
```

This interface is a functional interface since it has only one unimplemented method. It has many static and default methods to facilitate writing complex comparators.

> The Comparator interface existed prior to lambdas being added to Java. As a result, it is in a different package. You can find Comparator in java.util.

You only have to know compare() for the exam. Can you figure out whether this sorts in ascending or descending order?

```
Comparator<Integer> ints = (i1, i2) -> i1 - i2;
```

The ints comparator uses natural sort order. If the first number is bigger, it will return a positive number. Try it. Suppose we are comparing 5 and 3. The comparator subtracts 5-3 and gets 2. This is a positive number that means the first number is bigger and we are sorting in ascending order.

Let's try another one. Do you think these two statements would sort in ascending or descending order?

```
Comparator<String> strings = (s1, s2) -> s2.compareTo(s1);
Comparator<String> moreStrings = (s1, s2) -> - s1.compareTo(s2);
```

Both of these comparators actually do the same thing: sort in descending order. In the first example, the call to compareTo() is "backwards," making it descending. In the second example, the call uses the default order; however, it applies a negative sign to the result, which reverses it.

Be sure you understand Table 6.3 to identify what type of lambda you are looking at.

TABLE 6.3 Basic functional interfaces

Functional interface	# parameters	Return type
Comparator	Two	int
Consumer	One	void
Predicate	One	boolean
Supplier	None	One (type varies)

Working with Variables in Lambdas

Variables can appear in three places with respect to lambdas: the parameter list, local variables declared inside the lambda body, and variables referenced from the lambda body. All three of these are opportunities for the exam to trick you. We will explore each one so you'll be alert when tricks show up!

Parameter List

Earlier in this chapter, you learned that specifying the type of parameters is optional. Additionally, var can be used in place of the specific type. That means that all three of these statements are interchangeable:

```
Predicate<String> p = x -> true;
Predicate<String> p = (var x) -> true;
Predicate<String> p = (String x) -> true;
```

The exam might ask you to identify the type of the lambda parameter. In our example, the answer is String. How did we figure that out? A lambda infers the types from the surrounding context. That means you get to do the same.

In this case, the lambda is being assigned to a Predicate that takes a String. Another place to look for the type is in a method signature. Let's try another example. Can you figure out the type of x?

```
public void whatAmI() {
    consume((var x) -> System.out.print(x), 123);
}
public void consume(Consumer<Integer> c, int num) {
    c.accept(num);
}
```

If you guessed Integer, you were right. The whatAmI() method creates a lambda to be passed to the consume() method. Since the consume() method expects an Integer as the generic, we know that is what the inferred type of x will be.

But wait; there's more. In some cases, you can determine the type without even seeing the method signature. What do you think the type of x is here?

```
public void counts(List<Integer> list) {
    list.sort((var x, var y) -> x.compareTo(y));
}
```

The answer is again Integer. Since we are sorting a list, we can use the type of the list to determine the type of the lambda parameter.

Local Variables inside the Lambda Body

While it is most common for a lambda body to be a single expression, it is legal to define a block. That block can have anything that is valid in a normal Java block, including local variable declarations.

The following code does just that. It creates a local variable named c that is scoped to the lambda block.

```
(a, b) -> { int c = 0; return 5;}
```

 When writing your own code, a lambda block with a local variable is a good hint that you should extract that code into a method.

Now let's try another one. Do you see what's wrong here?

```
(a, b) -> { int a = 0; return 5;}      // DOES NOT COMPILE
```

We tried to redeclare a, which is not allowed. Java doesn't let you create a local variable with the same name as one already declared in that scope. Now let's try a hard one. How many syntax errors do you see in this method?

```
11: public void variables(int a) {
12:     int b = 1;
13:     Predicate<Integer> p1 = a -> {
14:         int b = 0;
15:         int c = 0;
16:         return b == c;}
17: }
```

There are three syntax errors. The first is on line 13. The variable a was already used in this scope as a method parameter, so it cannot be reused. The next syntax error comes on line 14 where the code attempts to redeclare local variable b. The third syntax error is quite subtle and on line 16. See it? Look really closely.

The variable p1 is missing a semicolon at the end. There is a semicolon before the }, but that is inside the block. While you don't normally have to look for missing semicolons, lambdas are tricky in this space, so beware!

Variables Referenced from the Lambda Body

Lambda bodies are allowed to reference some variables from the surrounding code. The following code is legal:

```
public class Crow {
    private String color;
    public void caw(String name) {
        String volume = "loudly";
        Consumer<String> consumer = s ->
            System.out.println(name + " says "
                + volume + " that she is " + color);
    }
}
```

This shows that lambda can access an instance variable, method parameter, or local variable under certain conditions. Instance variables (and class variables) are always allowed.

Method parameters and local variables are allowed to be referenced if they are *effectively final*. This means that the value of a variable doesn't change after it is set, regardless of whether it is explicitly marked as `final`. If you aren't sure whether a variable is effectively final, add the `final` keyword. If the code would still compile, the variable is effectively final. You can think of it as if we had written this:

```java
public class Crow {
    private String color;
    public void caw(final String name) {
        final String volume = "loudly";
        Consumer<String> consumer = s ->
            System.out.println(name + " says "
                + volume + " that she is " + color);
    }
}
```

It gets even more interesting when you look at where the compiler errors occur when the variables are not effectively final.

```java
2:  public class Crow {
3:      private String color;
4:      public void caw(String name) {
5:          String volume = "loudly";
6:          name = "Caty";
7:          color = "black";
8:
9:          Consumer<String> consumer = s ->
10:             System.out.println(name + " says "
11:                 + volume + " that she is " + color);
12:         volume = "softly";
13:     }
14: }
```

In this example, `name` is not effectively final because it is set on line 6. However, the compiler error occurs on line 10. It's not a problem to assign a value to a nonfinal variable. However, once the lambda tries to use it, we do have a problem. The variable is no longer effectively final, so the lambda is not allowed to use the variable.

The variable `volume` is not effectively final either since it is updated on line 12. In this case, the compiler error is on line 11. That's before the assignment! Again, the act of assigning a value is only a problem from the point of view of the lambda. Therefore, the lambda has to be the one to generate the compiler error.

To review, make sure you've memorized Table 6.4.

TABLE 6.4   Rules for accessing a variable from a lambda body inside a method

Variable type	Rule
Instance variable	Allowed
Static variable	Allowed
Local variable	Allowed if effectively final
Method parameter	Allowed if effectively final
Lambda parameter	Allowed

Calling APIs with Lambdas

Now that you are familiar with lambdas and functional interfaces, we can look at the most common methods that use them on the exam. The 1Z0-816 will cover streams and many more APIs that use lambdas.

removeIf()

List and Set declare a removeIf() method that takes a Predicate. Imagine we have a list of names for pet bunnies. We decide we want to remove all of the bunny names that don't begin with the letter h because our little cousin really wants us to choose an h name. We could solve this problem by writing a loop. Or we could solve it in one line:

```
3: List<String> bunnies = new ArrayList<>();
4: bunnies.add("long ear");
5: bunnies.add("floppy");
6: bunnies.add("hoppy");
7: System.out.println(bunnies);    // [long ear, floppy, hoppy]
8: bunnies.removeIf(s -> s.charAt(0) != 'h');
9: System.out.println(bunnies);    // [hoppy]
```

Line 8 takes care of everything for us. It defines a predicate that takes a String and returns a boolean. The removeIf() method does the rest.

The removeIf() method works the same way on a Set. It removes any values in the set that match the Predicate. There isn't a removeIf() method on a Map. Remember that maps have both keys and values. It wouldn't be clear what one was removing!

sort()

While you can call `Collections.sort(list)`, you can now sort directly on the list object.

```
3: List<String> bunnies = new ArrayList<>();
4: bunnies.add("long ear");
5: bunnies.add("floppy");
6: bunnies.add("hoppy");
7: System.out.println(bunnies);       // [long ear, floppy, hoppy]
8: bunnies.sort((b1, b2) -> b1.compareTo(b2));
9: System.out.println(bunnies);       // [floppy, hoppy, long ear]
```

On line 8, we sort the list alphabetically. The `sort()` method takes `Comparator` that provides the sort order. Remember that `Comparator` takes two parameters and returns an `int`. If you need a review of what the return value of a `compare()` operation means, check the `Comparator` section in this chapter or the Comparing section in Chapter 5. This is really important to memorize!

There is not a sort method on `Set` or `Map`. Neither of those types has indexing, so it wouldn't make sense to sort them.

forEach()

Our final method is `forEach()`. It takes a `Consumer` and calls that lambda for each element encountered.

```
3: List<String> bunnies = new ArrayList<>();
4: bunnies.add("long ear");
5: bunnies.add("floppy");
6: bunnies.add("hoppy");
7:
8: bunnies.forEach(b -> System.out.println(b));
9: System.out.println(bunnies);
```

This code prints the following:

```
long ear
floppy
hoppy
[long ear, floppy, hoppy]
```

The method on line 8 prints one entry per line. The method on line 9 prints the entire list on one line.

We can use `forEach()` with a `Set` or `Map`. For a `Set`, it works the same way as a `List`.

```
Set<String> bunnies = Set.of("long ear", "floppy", "hoppy");
bunnies.forEach(b -> System.out.println(b));
```

For a Map, you have to choose whether you want to go through the keys or values:

```
Map<String, Integer> bunnies =  new HashMap<>();
bunnies.put("long ear", 3);
bunnies.put("floppy", 8);
bunnies.put("hoppy", 1);
bunnies.keySet().forEach(b -> System.out.println(b));
bunnies.values().forEach(b -> System.out.println(b));
```

It turns out the keySet() and values() methods each return a Set. Since we know how to use forEach() with a Set, this is easy!

 Real World Scenario

Using *forEach()* with a Map Directly

You don't need to know this for the exam, but Java has a functional interface called BiConsumer. It works just like Consumer except it can take two parameters. This functional interface allows you to use forEach() with key/value pairs from Map.

```
Map<String, Integer> bunnies = new HashMap<>();
bunnies.put("long ear", 3);
bunnies.put("floppy", 8);
bunnies.put("hoppy", 1);
bunnies.forEach((k, v) -> System.out.println(k + " " + v));
```

Summary

Lambda expressions, or lambdas, allow passing around blocks of code. The full syntax looks like this:

```
(String a, String b) -> { return a.equals(b); }
```

The parameter types can be omitted. When only one parameter is specified without a type the parentheses can also be omitted. The braces and return statement can be omitted for a single statement, making the short form as follows:

```
a -> a.equals(b)
```

Lambdas are passed to a method expecting an instance of a functional interface.

A functional interface is one with a single abstract method. Predicate is a common interface that returns a boolean and takes any type. Consumer takes any type and doesn't return a value. Supplier returns a value and does not take any parameters. Comparator takes two parameters and returns an int.

A lambda can define parameters or variables in the body as long as their names are different from existing local variables. The body of a lambda is allowed to use any instance or class variables. Additionally, it can use any local variables or method parameters that are effectively final.

We covered three common APIs that use lambdas. The removeIf() method on a List and a Set takes a Predicate. The sort() method on a List interface takes a Comparator. The forEach() methods on a List and a Set interface both take a Consumer.

Exam Essentials

Write simple lambda expressions.   Look for the presence or absence of optional elements in lambda code. Parameter types are optional. Braces and the return keyword are optional when the body is a single statement. Parentheses are optional when only one parameter is specified and the type is implicit.

Identify common functional interfaces.   From a code snippet, identify whether the lambda is a Comparator, Consumer, Predicate, or Supplier. You can use the number of parameters and return type to tell them apart.

Determine whether a variable can be used in a lambda body.   Local variables and method parameters must be effectively final to be referenced. This means the code must compile if you were to add the final keyword to these variables. Instance and class variables are always allowed.

Use common APIs with lambdas.   Be able to read and write code using forEach(), removeIf(), and sort().

Review Questions

1. What is the result of the following class?

```
1:  import java.util.function.*;
2:
3:  public class Panda {
4:      int age;
5:      public static void main(String[] args) {
6:          Panda p1 = new Panda();
7:          p1.age = 1;
8:          check(p1, p -> p.age < 5);
9:      }
10:     private static void check(Panda panda,
11:         Predicate<Panda> pred) {
12:         String result =
13:             pred.test(panda) ? "match" : "not match";
14:         System.out.print(result);
15: } }
```

   A. match

   B. not match

   C. Compiler error on line 8.

   D. Compiler error on lines 10 and 11.

   E. Compiler error on lines 12 and 13.

   F. A runtime exception is thrown.

2. What is the result of the following code?

```
1:  interface Climb {
2:      boolean isTooHigh(int height, int limit);
3:  }
4:
5:  public class Climber {
6:      public static void main(String[] args) {
7:          check((h, m) -> h.append(m).isEmpty(), 5);
8:      }
9:      private static void check(Climb climb, int height) {
10:         if (climb.isTooHigh(height, 10))
11:             System.out.println("too high");
12:         else
```

```
13:           System.out.println("ok");
14:     }
15: }
```

A. ok

B. too high

C. Compiler error on line 7.

D. Compiler error on line 10.

E. Compiler error on a different line.

F. A runtime exception is thrown.

3. Which of the following lambda expressions can fill in the blank? (Choose all that apply.)

```
List<String> list = new ArrayList<>();
list.removeIf(_____);
```

A. s -> s.isEmpty()

B. s -> {s.isEmpty()}

C. s -> {s.isEmpty();}

D. s -> {return s.isEmpty();}

E. String s -> s.isEmpty()

F. (String s) -> s.isEmpty()

4. Which lambda can replace the MySecret class to return the same value? (Choose all that apply.)

```
interface Secret {
    String magic(double d);
}

class MySecret implements Secret {
    public String magic(double d) {
        return "Poof";
    }
}
```

A. (e) -> "Poof"

B. (e) -> {"Poof"}

C. (e) -> { String e = ""; "Poof" }

D. (e) -> { String e = ""; return "Poof"; }

E. (e) -> { String e = ""; return "Poof" }

F. (e) -> { String f = ""; return "Poof"; }

5. Which of the following lambda expressions can be passed to a function of `Predicate<String>` type? (Choose all that apply.)

A. `() -> s.isEmpty()`

B. `s -> s.isEmpty()`

C. `String s -> s.isEmpty()`

D. `(String s) -> s.isEmpty()`

E. `(s1) -> s.isEmpty()`

F. `(s1, s2) -> s1.isEmpty()`

6. Which of these statements is true about the following code?

```
public void method() {
    x((var x) -> {}, (var x, var y) -> 0);
}
public void x(Consumer<String> x, Comparator<Boolean> y) {
}
```

A. The code does not compile because of one of the variables named x.

B. The code does not compile because of one of the variables named y.

C. The code does not compile for another reason.

D. The code compiles, and the var in each lambda refers to the same type.

E. The code compiles, and the var in each lambda refers to a different type.

7. Which of the following will compile when filling in the blank? (Choose all that apply.)

```
List list = List.of(1, 2, 3);
Set set = Set.of(1, 2, 3);
Map map = Map.of(1, 2, 3, 4);

_____.forEach(x -> System.out.println(x));
```

A. `list`

B. `set`

C. `map`

D. `map.keys()`

E. `map.keySet()`

F. `map.values()`

G. `map.valueSet()`

8. Which statements are true?

A. The `Consumer` interface is best for printing out an existing value.

B. The `Supplier` interface is best for printing out an existing value.

C. The `Comparator` interface returns an `int`.

D. The `Predicate` interface returns an `int`.

E. The `Comparator` interface has a method named `test()`.

F. The `Predicate` interface has a method named `test()`.

9. Which of the following can be inserted without causing a compilation error? (Choose all that apply.)

```
public void remove(List<Character> chars) {
    char end = 'z';
    chars.removeIf(c -> {
        char start = 'a'; return start <= c && c <= end; });
        // INSERT LINE HERE
}
```

A. `char start = 'a';`

B. `char c = 'x';`

C. `chars = null;`

D. `end = '1';`

E. None of the above

10. How many lines does this code output?

```
Set<String> set = Set.of("mickey", "minnie");
List<String> list = new ArrayList<>(set);

set.forEach(s -> System.out.println(s));
list.forEach(s -> System.out.println(s));
```

A. 0

B. 2

C. 4

D. The code does not compile.

E. A runtime exception is thrown.

11. What is the output of the following code?

```
List<String> cats = new ArrayList<>();
cats.add("leo");
cats.add("Olivia");

cats.sort((c1, c2) -> -c1.compareTo(c2)); // line X
System.out.println(cats);
```

A. `[leo, Olivia]`

B. `[Olivia, leo]`

C. The code does not compile because of line X.

D. The code does not compile for another reason.

E. A runtime exception is thrown.

12. Which pieces of code can fill in the blanks? (Choose all that apply.)

```
_____ first = () -> Set.of(1.23);
_____ second = x -> true;
```

    A.   Consumer<Set<Double>>

    B.   Consumer<Set<Float>>

    C.   Predicate<Set<Double>>

    D.   Predicate<Set<Float>>

    E.   Supplier<Set<Double>>

    F.   Supplier<Set<Float>>

13. Which is true of the following code?

```
int length = 3;

for (int i = 0; i<3; i++) {
   if (i%2 == 0) {
      Supplier<Integer> supplier = () -> length; // A
      System.out.println(supplier.get());        // B
   } else {
      int j = i;
      Supplier<Integer> supplier = () -> j;     // C
      System.out.println(supplier.get());        // D
   }
}
```

    A.   The first compiler error is on line A.

    B.   The first compiler error is on line B.

    C.   The first compiler error is on line C.

    D.   The first compiler error is on line D.

    E.   The code compiles successfully.

14. Which of the following can be inserted without causing a compilation error? (Choose all that apply.)

```
public void remove(List<Character> chars) {
   char end = 'z';
   // INSERT LINE HERE
   chars.removeIf(c -> {
      char start = 'a'; return start <= c && c <= end; });
}
```

    A.   char start = 'a';

    B.   char c = 'x';

C. `chars = null;`

D. `end = '1';`

E. None of the above

15. What is the output of the following code?

```
Set<String> cats = new HashSet<>();
cats.add("leo");
cats.add("Olivia");

cats.sort((c1, c2) -> -c1.compareTo(c2)); // line X
System.out.println(cats);
```

A. `[leo, Olivia]`

B. `[Olivia, leo]`

C. The code does not compile because of line X.

D. The code does not compile for another reason.

E. A runtime exception is thrown.

16. Which variables are effectively final? (Choose all that apply.)

```
public void isIt(String param1, String param2) {
    String local1 = param1 + param2;
    String local2 = param1 + param2;

    param1 = null;
    local2 = null;
}
```

A. `local1`

B. `local2`

C. `param1`

D. `param2`

E. None of the above

17. What is the result of the following class?

```
1:  import java.util.function.*;
2:
3:  public class Panda {
4:      int age;
5:      public static void main(String[] args) {
6:          Panda p1 = new Panda();
7:          p1.age = 1;
8:          check(p1, p -> {p.age < 5});
9:      }
```

```
10:    private static void check(Panda panda,
11:        Predicate<Panda> pred) {
12:        String result = pred.test(panda)
13:            ? "match" : "not match";
14:        System.out.print(result);
15: } }
```

A. match

B. not match

C. Compiler error on line 8.

D. Compiler error on line 10.

E. Compile error on line 12.

F. A runtime exception is thrown.

18. How many lines does this code output?

```
Set<String> s = Set.of("mickey", "minnie");
List<String> x = new ArrayList<>(s);

s.forEach(s -> System.out.println(s));
x.forEach(x -> System.out.println(x));
```

A. 0

B. 2

C. 4

D. The code does not compile.

E. A runtime exception is thrown.

19. Which lambda can replace the MySecret class? (Choose all that apply.)

```
interface Secret {
    String concat(String a, String b);
}

class MySecret implements Secret {
    public String concat(String a, String b) {
        return a + b;
    }
}
```

A. (a, b) -> a + b

B. (String a, b) -> a + b

C. (String a, String b) -> a + b

D. (a, b) , a + b

E. (String a, b) , a + b

F. (String a, String b) , a + b

20. Which of the following lambda expressions can be passed to a function of Predicate<String> type? (Choose all that apply.)

A. s -> s.isEmpty()

B. s --> s.isEmpty()

C. (String s) -> s.isEmpty()

D. (String s) --> s.isEmpty()

E. (StringBuilder s) -> s.isEmpty()

F. (StringBuilder s) --> s.isEmpty()

Chapter

7

Methods and Encapsulation

OCP EXAM OBJECTIVES COVERED IN THIS CHAPTER:

✓ **Creating and Using Methods**

- Create methods and constructors with arguments and return values

- Create and invoke overloaded methods

- Apply the static keyword to methods and fields

✓ **Applying Encapsulation**

- Apply access modifiers

- Apply encapsulation principles to a class

In previous chapters, you learned how to use methods without examining them in detail. In this chapter, you'll explore methods in depth, including overloading. This chapter discusses instance variables, access modifiers, and encapsulation.

Designing Methods

Every interesting Java program we've seen has had a `main()` method. You can write other methods, too. For example, you can write a basic method to take a nap, as shown in Figure 7.1.

FIGURE 7.1 Method declaration

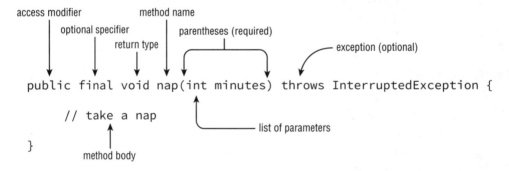

This is called a *method declaration*, which specifies all the information needed to call the method. There are a lot of parts, and we'll cover each one in more detail. Two of the parts—the method name and parameter list—are called the *method signature*.

Table 7.1 is a brief reference to the elements of a method declaration. Don't worry if it seems like a lot of information—by the time you finish this chapter, it will all fit together.

TABLE 7.1 Parts of a method declaration

Element	Value in nap() example	Required?
Access modifier	`public`	No
Optional specifier	`final`	No

Element	Value in nap() example	Required?
Return type	void	Yes
Method name	nap	Yes
Parameter list	(int minutes)	Yes, but can be empty parentheses
Optional exception list	throws InterruptedException	No

Method body*	{
	  // take a nap
	}
		Yes, but can be empty braces

* Body omitted for abstract methods, which we will cover in the later in the book.

To call this method, just type its name, followed by a single int value in parentheses:

nap(10);

Let's start by taking a look at each of these parts of a basic method.

Access Modifiers

Java offers four choices of access modifier:

private   The private modifier means the method can be called only from within the same class.

Default (Package-Private) Access   With default access, the method can be called only from classes in the same package. This one is tricky because there is no keyword for default access. You simply omit the access modifier.

protected   The protected modifier means the method can be called only from classes in the same package or subclasses. You'll learn about subclasses in Chapter 8, "Class Design."

public   The public modifier means the method can be called from any class.

 There's a default keyword in Java. You saw it in the switch statement in Chapter 4, "Making Decisions," and you'll see it again in the Chapter 9, "Advanced Class Design," when I discuss interfaces. It's not used for access control.

We'll explore the impact of the various access modifiers later in this chapter. For now, just master identifying valid syntax of methods. The exam creators like to trick you by putting method elements in the wrong order or using incorrect values.

We'll see practice examples as we go through each of the method elements in this section. Make sure you understand why each of these is a valid or invalid method declaration. Pay attention to the access modifiers as you figure out what is wrong with the ones that don't compile when inserted into a class:

```
public void walk1() {}
default void walk2() {} // DOES NOT COMPILE
void public walk3() {}  // DOES NOT COMPILE
void walk4() {}
```

The walk1() method is a valid declaration with public access. The walk4() method is a valid declaration with default access. The walk2() method doesn't compile because default is not a valid access modifier. The walk3() method doesn't compile because the access modifier is specified after the return type.

Optional Specifiers

There are a number of optional specifiers, but most of them aren't on the exam. Optional specifiers come from the following list. Unlike with access modifiers, you can have multiple specifiers in the same method (although not all combinations are legal). When this happens, you can specify them in any order. And since these specifiers are optional, you are allowed to not have any of them at all. This means you can have zero or more specifiers in a method declaration.

static   The static modifier is used for class methods and will be covered later in this chapter.

abstract   The abstract modifier is used when a method body is not provided. It will be covered in Chapter 9.

final   The final modifier is used when a method is not allowed to be overridden by a subclass. It will also be covered in Chapter 8.

synchronized   The synchronized modifier is used with multithreaded code. It is on the 1Z0-816 exam, but not the 1Z0-815 exam.

native   The native modifier is used when interacting with code written in another language such as C++. It is not on either OCP 11 exam.

strictfp   The strictfp modifier is used for making floating-point calculations portable. It is not on either OCP 11 exam.

Again, just focus on syntax for now. Do you see why these compile or don't compile?

```
public void walk1() {}
public final void walk2() {}
public static final void walk3() {}
public final static void walk4() {}
public modifier void walk5() {}        // DOES NOT COMPILE
public void final walk6() {}           // DOES NOT COMPILE
final public void walk7() {}
```

The walk1() method is a valid declaration with no optional specifier. This is okay—it is optional after all. The walk2() method is a valid declaration, with final as the optional specifier. The walk3() and walk4() methods are valid declarations with both final and static as optional specifiers. The order of these two keywords doesn't matter. The walk5() method doesn't compile because modifier is not a valid optional specifier. The walk6() method doesn't compile because the optional specifier is after the return type.

The walk7() method does compile. Java allows the optional specifiers to appear before the access modifier. This is a weird case and not one you need to know for the exam. We are mentioning it so you don't get confused when practicing.

Return Type

The next item in a method declaration is the return type. The return type might be an actual Java type such as String or int. If there is no return type, the void keyword is used. This special return type comes from the English language: *void* means without contents. In Java, there is no type there.

> **NOTE**   Remember that a method must have a return type. If no value is returned, the return type is void. You cannot omit the return type.

When checking return types, you also have to look inside the method body. Methods with a return type other than void are required to have a return statement inside the method body. This return statement must include the primitive or object to be returned. Methods that have a return type of void are permitted to have a return statement with no value returned or omit the return statement entirely.

Ready for some examples? Can you explain why these methods compile or don't?

```
public void walk1() {}
public void walk2() { return; }
public String walk3() { return ""; }
public String walk4() {}                    // DOES NOT COMPILE
public walk5() {}                           // DOES NOT COMPILE
public String int walk6() { }               // DOES NOT COMPILE
String walk7(int a) { if (a == 4) return ""; } // DOES NOT COMPILE
```

Since the return type of the walk1() method is void, the return statement is optional. The walk2() method shows the optional return statement that correctly doesn't return anything. The walk3() method is a valid declaration with a String return type and a return statement that returns a String. The walk4() method doesn't compile because the return statement is missing. The walk5() method doesn't compile because the return type is missing. The walk6() method doesn't compile because it attempts to use two return types. You get only one return type.

The walk7() method is a little tricky. There is a return statement, but it doesn't always get run. If a is 6, the return statement doesn't get executed. Since the String always needs to be returned, the compiler complains.

When returning a value, it needs to be assignable to the return type. Imagine there is a local variable of that type to which it is assigned before being returned. Can you think of how to add a line of code with a local variable in these two methods?

```
int integer() {
   return 9;
}
int longMethod() {
   return 9L; // DOES NOT COMPILE
}
```

It is a fairly mechanical exercise. You just add a line with a local variable. The type of the local variable matches the return type of the method. Then you return that local variable instead of the value directly:

```
int integerExpanded() {
   int temp = 9;
   return temp;
}
int longExpanded() {
   int temp = 9L; // DOES NOT COMPILE
   return temp;
}
```

This shows more clearly why you can't return a long primitive in a method that returns an int. You can't stuff that long into an int variable, so you can't return it directly either.

Method Name

Method names follow the same rules as we practiced with variable names in Chapter 2, "Java Building Blocks." To review, an identifier may only contain letters, numbers, $, or _. Also, the first character is not allowed to be a number, and reserved words are not allowed. Finally, the single underscore character is not allowed. By convention, methods begin with a lowercase letter but are not required to. Since this is a review of Chapter 2, we can jump right into practicing with some examples:

```
public void walk1() {}
public void 2walk() {}    // DOES NOT COMPILE
public walk3 void() {}    // DOES NOT COMPILE
public void Walk_$() {}
public _() {}             // DOES NOT COMPILE
public void() {}          // DOES NOT COMPILE
```

The walk1() method is a valid declaration with a traditional name. The 2walk() method doesn't compile because identifiers are not allowed to begin with numbers. The walk3() method doesn't compile because the method name is before the return type. The Walk_$() method is a valid declaration. While it certainly isn't good practice to start a method name with a capital letter and end with punctuation, it is legal. The _ method is not allowed since it consists of a single underscore. The final line of code doesn't compile because the method name is missing.

Parameter List

Although the parameter list is required, it doesn't have to contain any parameters. This means you can just have an empty pair of parentheses after the method name, as follows:

```
void nap(){}
```

If you do have multiple parameters, you separate them with a comma. There are a couple more rules for the parameter list that you'll see when we cover varargs shortly. For now, let's practice looking at method declaration with "regular" parameters:

```
public void walk1() {}
public void walk2 {}                  // DOES NOT COMPILE
public void walk3(int a) {}
public void walk4(int a; int b) {}  // DOES NOT COMPILE
public void walk5(int a, int b) {}
```

The walk1() method is a valid declaration without any parameters. The walk2() method doesn't compile because it is missing the parentheses around the parameter list. The walk3() method is a valid declaration with one parameter. The walk4() method doesn't compile because the parameters are separated by a semicolon rather than a comma. Semicolons are for separating statements, not for parameter lists. The walk5() method is a valid declaration with two parameters.

Optional Exception List

In Java, code can indicate that something went wrong by throwing an exception. We'll cover this in Chapter 10, "Exceptions." For now, you just need to know that it is optional and where in the method declaration it goes if present. For example, InterruptedException is a type of Exception. You can list as many types of exceptions as you want in this clause separated by commas. Here's an example:

```
public void zeroExceptions() {}
public void oneException() throws IllegalArgumentException {}
public void twoExceptions() throws
    IllegalArgumentException, InterruptedException {}
```

You might be wondering what methods do with these exceptions. The calling method can throw the same exceptions or handle them. You'll learn more about this in Chapter 10.

Method Body

The final part of a method declaration is the method body (except for abstract methods and interfaces, but you don't need to know about either of those yet). A method body is simply a code block. It has braces that contain zero or more Java statements. We've spent several chapters looking at Java statements by now, so you should find it easy to figure out why these compile or don't:

```
public void walk1() {}
public void walk2()      // DOES NOT COMPILE
public void walk3(int a) { int name = 5; }
```

The walk1() method is a valid declaration with an empty method body. The walk2() method doesn't compile because it is missing the braces around the empty method body. The walk3() method is a valid declaration with one statement in the method body.

You've made it through the basics of identifying correct and incorrect method declarations. Now you can delve into more detail.

Working with Varargs

As you saw in Chapter 5, "Core Java APIs," a method may use a varargs parameter (variable argument) as if it is an array. It is a little different than an array, though. A varargs parameter must be the last element in a method's parameter list. This means you are allowed to have only one varargs parameter per method.

Can you identify why each of these does or doesn't compile? (Yes, there is a lot of practice in this chapter. You have to be really good at identifying valid and invalid methods for the exam.)

```
public void walk1(int... nums) {}
public void walk2(int start, int... nums) {}
public void walk3(int... nums, int start) {}    // DOES NOT COMPILE
public void walk4(int... start, int... nums) {} // DOES NOT COMPILE
```

The walk1() method is a valid declaration with one varargs parameter. The walk2() method is a valid declaration with one int parameter and one varargs parameter. The walk3() and walk4() methods do not compile because they have a varargs parameter in a position that is not the last one.

When calling a method with a varargs parameter, you have a choice. You can pass in an array, or you can list the elements of the array and let Java create it for you. You can even omit the varargs values in the method call and Java will create an array of length zero for you.

Finally! You get to do something other than identify whether method declarations are valid. Instead, you get to look at method calls. Can you figure out why each method call outputs what it does?

```
15: public static void walk(int start, int... nums) {
16:     System.out.println(nums.length);
17: }
18: public static void main(String[] args) {
19:     walk(1);                    // 0
20:     walk(1, 2);                 // 1
21:     walk(1, 2, 3);              // 2
22:     walk(1, new int[] {4, 5});  // 2
23: }
```

Line 19 passes 1 as start but nothing else. This means Java creates an array of length 0 for nums. Line 20 passes 1 as start and one more value. Java converts this one value to an array of length 1. Line 21 passes 1 as start and two more values. Java converts these two values to an array of length 2. Line 22 passes 1 as start and an array of length 2 directly as nums.

You've seen that Java will create an empty array if no parameters are passed for a vararg. However, it is still possible to pass null explicitly:

```
walk(1, null);     // throws a NullPointerException in walk()
```

Since null isn't an int, Java treats it as an array reference that happens to be null. It just passes on the null array object to walk. Then the walk() method throws an exception because it tries to determine the length of null.

Accessing a varargs parameter is just like accessing an array. It uses array indexing. Here's an example:

```
16: public static void run(int... nums) {
17:     System.out.println(nums[1]);
18: }
19: public static void main(String[] args) {
20:     run(11, 22);     // 22
21: }
```

Line 20 calls a varargs method with two parameters. When the method gets called, it sees an array of size 2. Since indexes are 0 based, 22 is printed.

Applying Access Modifiers

You already saw that there are four access modifiers: public, private, protected, and default access. We are going to discuss them in order from most restrictive to least restrictive:

- **private:** Only accessible within the same class
- **Default (package-private) access:** private plus other classes in the same package
- **protected:** Default access plus child classes
- **public:** protected plus classes in the other packages

We will explore the impact of these four levels of access on members of a class. As you learned in Chapter 1, "Welcome to Java," a member is an instance variable or instance method.

Private Access

Private access is easy. Only code in the same class can call private methods or access private fields.

First, take a look at Figure 7.2. It shows the classes you'll use to explore private and default access. The big boxes are the names of the packages. The smaller boxes inside them are the classes in each package. You can refer back to this figure if you want to quickly see how the classes relate.

FIGURE 7.2   Classes used to show private and default access

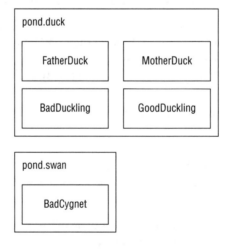

This is perfectly legal code because everything is one class:

```
1: package pond.duck;
2: public class FatherDuck {
3:     private String noise = "quack";
4:     private void quack() {
5:         System.out.println(noise);      // private access is ok
6:     }
7:     private void makeNoise() {
8:         quack();                        // private access is ok
9:     } }
```

So far, so good. FatherDuck makes a call to private method quack() on line 8 and uses private instance variable noise on line 5.

Now we add another class:

```
1: package pond.duck;
2: public class BadDuckling {
3:     public void makeNoise() {
4:         FatherDuck duck = new FatherDuck();
5:         duck.quack();                       // DOES NOT COMPILE
6:         System.out.println(duck.noise);     // DOES NOT COMPILE
7:     } }
```

BadDuckling is trying to access an instance variable and a method it has no business touching. On line 5, it tries to access a private method in another class. On line 6, it tries to access a private instance variable in another class. Both generate compiler errors. Bad duckling!

Our bad duckling is only a few days old and doesn't know better yet. Luckily, you know that accessing private members of other classes is not allowed and you need to use a different type of access.

Default (Package-Private) Access

Luckily, MotherDuck is more accommodating about what her ducklings can do. She allows classes in the same package to access her members. When there is no access modifier, Java uses the default, which is package-private access. This means that the member is "private" to classes in the same package. In other words, only classes in the package may access it.

```
package pond.duck;
public class MotherDuck {
    String noise = "quack";
    void quack() {
        System.out.println(noise);      // default access is ok
```

```
   }
   private void makeNoise() {
      quack();                          // default access is ok
   }
}
```

MotherDuck can refer to noise and call quack(). After all, members in the same class are certainly in the same package. The big difference is MotherDuck lets other classes in the same package access members (due to being package-private), whereas FatherDuck doesn't (due to being private). GoodDuckling has a much better experience than BadDuckling:

```
package pond.duck;
public class GoodDuckling {
   public void makeNoise() {
      MotherDuck duck = new MotherDuck();
      duck.quack();                          // default access
      System.out.println(duck.noise);        // default access
   }
}
```

GoodDuckling succeeds in learning to quack() and make noise by copying its mother. Notice that all the classes covered so far are in the same package pond.duck. This allows default (package-private) access to work.

In this same pond, a swan just gave birth to a baby swan. A baby swan is called a *cygnet*. The cygnet sees the ducklings learning to quack and decides to learn from MotherDuck as well.

```
package pond.swan;
import pond.duck.MotherDuck;               // import another package
public class BadCygnet {
   public void makeNoise() {
      MotherDuck duck = new MotherDuck();
      duck.quack();                     // DOES NOT COMPILE
      System.out.println(duck.noise);   // DOES NOT COMPILE
   }
}
```

Oh no! MotherDuck only allows lessons to other ducks by restricting access to the pond.duck package. Poor little BadCygnet is in the pond.swan package, and the code doesn't compile.

Remember that when there is no access modifier on a member, only classes in the same package can access the member.

Protected Access

Protected access allows everything that default (package-private) access allows and more. The protected access modifier adds the ability to access members of a parent class. We'll cover creating subclasses in depth in Chapter 8. For now, we'll cover the simplest possible use of a child class.

Figure 7.3 shows the many classes we will create in this section. There are a number of classes and packages, so don't worry about keeping them all in your head. Just check back with this figure as you go.

FIGURE 7.3   Classes used to show protected access

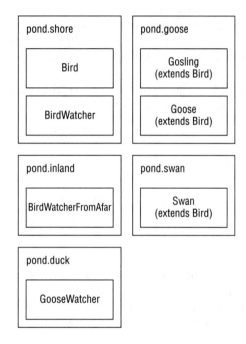

First, create a Bird class and give protected access to its members:

```
package pond.shore;
public class Bird {
   protected String text = "floating";          // protected access
   protected void floatInWater() {              // protected access
      System.out.println(text);
   }
}
```

Next, we create a subclass:

```
package pond.goose;
import pond.shore.Bird;                // in a different package
public class Gosling extends Bird {    // extends means create subclass
   public void swim() {
      floatInWater();                  // calling protected member
      System.out.println(text);        // accessing protected member
   }
}
```

This is a simple subclass. It *extends* the Bird class. Extending means creating a subclass that has access to any protected or public members of the parent class. Running this code prints floating twice: once from calling floatInWater(), and once from the print statement in swim(). Since Gosling is a subclass of Bird, it can access these members even though it is in a different package.

Remember that protected also gives us access to everything that default access does. This means that a class in the same package as Bird can access its protected members.

```
package pond.shore;                    // same package as Bird
public class BirdWatcher {
   public void watchBird() {
      Bird bird = new Bird();
      bird.floatInWater();             // calling protected member
      System.out.println(bird.text);   // accessing protected member
   }
}
```

Since Bird and BirdWatcher are in the same package, BirdWatcher can access members of the bird variable. The definition of protected allows access to subclasses and classes in the same package. This example uses the same package part of that definition.

Now let's try the same thing from a different package:

```
package pond.inland;
import pond.shore.Bird;                // different package than Bird
public class BirdWatcherFromAfar {
   public void watchBird() {
      Bird bird = new Bird();
      bird.floatInWater();             // DOES NOT COMPILE
      System.out.println(bird.text);   // DOES NOT COMPILE
   }
}
```

BirdWatcherFromAfar is not in the same package as Bird, and it doesn't inherit from Bird. This means that it is not allowed to access protected members of Bird.

Got that? Subclasses and classes in the same package are the only ones allowed to access protected members.

There is one gotcha for protected access. Consider this class:

```
1:  package pond.swan;
2:  import pond.shore.Bird;      // in different package than Bird
3:  public class Swan extends Bird {      // but subclass of Bird
4:      public void swim() {
5:          floatInWater();                // subclass access to superclass
6:          System.out.println(text);      // subclass access to superclass
7:      }
8:      public void helpOtherSwanSwim() {
9:          Swan other = new Swan();
10:         other.floatInWater();          // subclass access to superclass
11:         System.out.println(other.text);  // subclass access
12:                                          // to superclass
13:     }
14:     public void helpOtherBirdSwim() {
15:         Bird other = new Bird();
16:         other.floatInWater();            // DOES NOT COMPILE
17:         System.out.println(other.text);  // DOES NOT COMPILE
18:     }
19: }
```

Take a deep breath. This is interesting. Swan is not in the same package as Bird but does extend it—which implies it has access to the protected members of Bird since it is a subclass. And it does. Lines 5 and 6 refer to protected members via inheriting them.

Lines 10 and 11 also successfully use protected members of Bird. This is allowed because these lines refer to a Swan object. Swan inherits from Bird, so this is okay. It is sort of a two-phase check. The Swan class is allowed to use protected members of Bird, and we are referring to a Swan object. Granted, it is a Swan object created on line 9 rather than an inherited one, but it is still a Swan object.

Lines 16 and 17 do *not* compile. Wait a minute. They are almost exactly the same as lines 10 and 11! There's one key difference. This time a Bird reference is used rather than inheritance. It is created on line 15. Bird is in a different package, and this code isn't inheriting from Bird, so it doesn't get to use protected members. Say what now? We just got through saying repeatedly that Swan inherits from Bird. And it does. However, the variable reference isn't a Swan. The code just happens to be in the Swan class.

It's okay to be confused. This is arguably one of the most confusing points on the exam. Looking at it a different way, the protected rules apply under two scenarios:

- A member is used without referring to a variable. This is the case on lines 5 and 6. In this case, we are taking advantage of inheritance and protected access is allowed.

- A member is used through a variable. This is the case on lines 10, 11, 16, and 17. In this case, the rules for the reference type of the variable are what matter. If it is a subclass, protected access is allowed. This works for references to the same class or a subclass.

We're going to try this again to make sure you understand what is going on. Can you figure out why these examples don't compile?

```
package pond.goose;
import pond.shore.Bird;
public class Goose extends Bird {
   public void helpGooseSwim() {
      Goose other = new Goose();
      other.floatInWater();
      System.out.println(other.text);
   }
   public void helpOtherGooseSwim() {
      Bird other = new Goose();
      other.floatInWater();          // DOES NOT COMPILE
      System.out.println(other.text); // DOES NOT COMPILE
   }
}
```

The first method is fine. In fact, it is equivalent to the Swan example. Goose extends Bird. Since we are in the Goose subclass and referring to a Goose reference, it can access protected members. The second method is a problem. Although the object happens to be a Goose, it is stored in a Bird reference. We are not allowed to refer to members of the Bird class since we are not in the same package and the reference type of other is not a subclass of Goose.

What about this one?

```
package pond.duck;
import pond.goose.Goose;
public class GooseWatcher {
   public void watch() {
      Goose goose = new Goose();
      goose.floatInWater();     // DOES NOT COMPILE
   }
}
```

This code doesn't compile because we are not in the goose object. The floatInWater() method is declared in Bird. GooseWatcher is not in the same package as Bird, nor does it extend Bird. Goose extends Bird. That only lets Goose refer to floatInWater() and not callers of Goose.

If this is still puzzling, try it. Type in the code and try to make it compile. Then reread this section. Don't worry—it wasn't obvious to us the first time either!

Public Access

Protected access was a tough concept. Luckily, the last type of access modifier is easy: public means anyone can access the member from anywhere.

The Java module system redefines "anywhere," and it becomes possible to restrict access to public code. When given a code sample, you can assume it isn't in a module unless explicitly stated otherwise.

Let's create a class that has public members:

```
package pond.duck;
public class DuckTeacher {
    public String name = "helpful";     // public access
    public void swim() {                 // public access
        System.out.println("swim");
    }
}
```

DuckTeacher allows access to any class that wants it. Now we can try it:

```
package pond.goose;
import pond.duck.DuckTeacher;
public class LostDuckling {
    public void swim() {
        DuckTeacher teacher = new DuckTeacher();
        teacher.swim();                                    // allowed
        System.out.println("Thanks" + teacher.name);       // allowed
    }
}
```

LostDuckling is able to refer to swim() and name on DuckTeacher because they are public. The story has a happy ending. LostDuckling has learned to swim and can find its parents—all because DuckTeacher made members public.

To review access modifiers, make sure you know why everything in Table 7.2 is true. Remember that a member is a method or field.

TABLE 7.2   Access modifiers

A method in _____ can access a _____ member	private	Default (package-private)	protected	public
the same class	Yes	Yes	Yes	Yes
another class in the same package	No	Yes	Yes	Yes
in a subclass in a different package	No	No	Yes	Yes
an unrelated class in a different package	No	No	No	Yes

Applying the *static* Keyword

When the static keyword is applied to a variable, method, or class, it applies to the class rather than a specific instance of the class. In this section, you will see that the static keyword can also be applied to import statements.

Designing *static* Methods and Fields

Except for the main() method, we've been looking at instance methods. static methods don't require an instance of the class. They are shared among all users of the class. You can think of a static variable as being a member of the single class object that exists independently of any instances of that class.

You have seen one static method since Chapter 1. The main() method is a static method. That means you can call it using the class name:

```
public class Koala {
    public static int count = 0;              // static variable
    public static void main(String[] args) {  // static method
        System.out.println(count);
    }
}
```

Here the JVM basically calls Koala.main() to get the program started. You can do this too. We can have a KoalaTester that does nothing but call the main() method:

```
public class KoalaTester {
    public static void main(String[] args) {
        Koala.main(new String[0]);            // call static method
    }
}
```

Quite a complicated way to print 0, isn't it? When we run KoalaTester, it makes a call to the main() method of Koala, which prints the value of count. The purpose of all these examples is to show that main() can be called just like any other static method.

In addition to main() methods, static methods have two main purposes:

- For utility or helper methods that don't require any object state. Since there is no need to access instance variables, having static methods eliminates the need for the caller to instantiate an object just to call the method.

- For state that is shared by all instances of a class, like a counter. All instances must share the same state. Methods that merely use that state should be static as well.

In the following sections, we will look at some examples covering other static concepts.

Accessing a *static* Variable or Method

Usually, accessing a static member like count is easy. You just put the class name before the method or variable and you are done. Here's an example:

```
System.out.println(Koala.count);
Koala.main(new String[0]);
```

Both of these are nice and easy. There is one rule that is trickier. You can use an instance of the object to call a static method. The compiler checks for the type of the reference and uses that instead of the object—which is sneaky of Java. This code is perfectly legal:

```
5: Koala k = new Koala();
6: System.out.println(k.count);        // k is a Koala
7: k = null;
8: System.out.println(k.count);        // k is still a Koala
```

Believe it or not, this code outputs 0 twice. Line 6 sees that k is a Koala and count is a static variable, so it reads that static variable. Line 8 does the same thing. Java doesn't care that k happens to be null. Since we are looking for a static, it doesn't matter.

Remember to look at the reference type for a variable when you see a static method or variable. The exam creators will try to trick you into thinking a NullPointerException is thrown because the variable happens to be null. Don't be fooled!

One more time because this is really important: what does the following output?

```
Koala.count = 4;
Koala koala1 = new Koala();
Koala koala2 = new Koala();
koala1.count = 6;
koala2.count = 5;
System.out.println(Koala.count);
```

We hope you answered 5. There is only one count variable since it is static. It is set to 4, then 6, and finally winds up as 5. All the Koala variables are just distractions.

Static vs. Instance

There's another way the exam creators will try to trick you regarding static and instance members. A static member cannot call an instance member without referencing an instance of the class. This shouldn't be a surprise since static doesn't require any instances of the class to even exist.

The following is a common mistake for rookie programmers to make:

```
public class Static {
    private String name = "Static class";
    public static void first() {  }
    public static void second() {  }
    public void third() {  System.out.println(name); }
    public static void main(String args[]) {
        first();
        second();
        third();          // DOES NOT COMPILE
    }
}
```

The compiler will give you an error about making a static reference to a nonstatic method. If we fix this by adding static to third(), we create a new problem. Can you figure out what it is?

All this does is move the problem. Now, third() is referring to nonstatic name. Adding static to name as well would solve the problem. Another solution would have been to call third as an instance method—for example, new Static().third();.

The exam creators like this topic. A static method or instance method can call a static method because static methods don't require an object to use. Only an instance method can call another instance method on the same class without using a reference variable, because instance methods do require an object. Similar logic applies for the instance and static variables.

Suppose we have a Giraffe class:

```
public class Giraffe {
    public void eat(Giraffe g) {}
    public void drink() {};
    public static void allGiraffeGoHome(Giraffe g) {}
    public static void allGiraffeComeOut() {}
}
```

Make sure you understand Table 7.3 before continuing.

TABLE 7.3   Static vs. instance calls

Type	Calling	Legal?
allGiraffeGoHome()	allGiraffeComeOut()	Yes
allGiraffeGoHome()	drink()	No
allGiraffeGoHome()	g.eat()	Yes
eat()	allGiraffeComeOut()	Yes
eat()	drink()	Yes
eat()	g.eat()	Yes

Let's try one more example so you have more practice at recognizing this scenario. Do you understand why the following lines fail to compile?

```
1:  public class Gorilla {
2:     public static int count;
3:     public static void addGorilla() { count++; }
4:     public void babyGorilla() { count++; }
5:     public void announceBabies() {
6:        addGorilla();
7:        babyGorilla();
8:     }
9:     public static void announceBabiesToEveryone() {
10:        addGorilla();
11:        babyGorilla();      // DOES NOT COMPILE
12:     }
13:     public int total;
14:     public static double average
15:        = total / count;  // DOES NOT COMPILE
16: }
```

Lines 3 and 4 are fine because both static and instance methods can refer to a static variable. Lines 5–8 are fine because an instance method can call a static method. Line 11 doesn't compile because a static method cannot call an instance method. Similarly, line 15 doesn't compile because a static variable is trying to use an instance variable.

A common use for static variables is counting the number of instances:

```java
public class Counter {
    private static int count;
    public Counter() { count++; }
    public static void main(String[] args) {
        Counter c1 = new Counter();
        Counter c2 = new Counter();
        Counter c3 = new Counter();
        System.out.println(count);          // 3
    }
}
```

Each time the constructor gets called, it increments count by 1. This example relies on the fact that static (and instance) variables are automatically initialized to the default value for that type, which is 0 for int. See Chapter 2 to review the default values.

Also notice that we didn't write Counter.count. We could have. It isn't necessary because we are already in that class so the compiler can infer it.

Does Each Instance Have Its Own Copy of the Code?

Each object has a copy of the instance variables. There is only one copy of the code for the instance methods. Each instance of the class can call it as many times as it would like. However, each call of an instance method (or any method) gets space on the stack for method parameters and local variables.

The same thing happens for static methods. There is one copy of the code. Parameters and local variables go on the stack.

Just remember that only data gets its "own copy." There is no need to duplicate copies of the code itself.

---

static Variables

Some static variables are meant to change as the program runs. Counters are a common example of this. We want the count to increase over time. Just as with instance variables, you can initialize a static variable on the line it is declared:

```java
public class Initializers {
    private static int counter = 0;          // initialization
}
```

Other static variables are meant to never change during the program. This type of variable is known as a *constant*. It uses the final modifier to ensure the variable never changes. Constants use the modifier static final and a different naming convention than other variables. They use all uppercase letters with underscores between "words." Here's an example:

```
public class Initializers {
   private static final int NUM_BUCKETS = 45;
   public static void main(String[] args) {
      NUM_BUCKETS = 5;  // DOES NOT COMPILE
   }
}
```

The compiler will make sure that you do not accidentally try to update a final variable. This can get interesting. Do you think the following compiles?

```
private static final ArrayList<String> values = new ArrayList<>();
public static void main(String[] args) {
   values.add("changed");
}
```

It actually does compile since values is a reference variable. We are allowed to call methods on reference variables. All the compiler can do is check that we don't try to reassign the final values to point to a different object.

Static Initialization

In Chapter 2, we covered instance initializers that looked like unnamed methods—just code inside braces. Static initializers look similar. They add the static keyword to specify they should be run when the class is first loaded. Here's an example:

```
private static final int NUM_SECONDS_PER_MINUTE;
private static final int NUM_MINUTES_PER_HOUR;
private static final int NUM_SECONDS_PER_HOUR;
static {
   NUM_SECONDS_PER_MINUTE = 60;
   NUM_MINUTES_PER_HOUR = 60;
}
static {
   NUM_SECONDS_PER_HOUR
      = NUM_SECONDS_PER_MINUTE * NUM_MINUTES_PER_HOUR;
}
```

All static initializers run when the class is first used in the order they are defined. The statements in them run and assign any static variables as needed. There is something interesting about this example. We just got through saying that `final` variables aren't allowed to be reassigned. The key here is that the static initializer is the first assignment. And since it occurs up front, it is okay.

Let's try another example to make sure you understand the distinction:

```
14: private static int one;
15: private static final int two;
16: private static final int three = 3;
17: private static final int four;     // DOES NOT COMPILE
18: static {
19:    one = 1;
20:    two = 2;
21:    three = 3;                       // DOES NOT COMPILE
22:    two = 4;                         // DOES NOT COMPILE
23: }
```

Line 14 declares a `static` variable that is not `final`. It can be assigned as many times as we like. Line 15 declares a `final` variable without initializing it. This means we can initialize it exactly once in a `static` block. Line 22 doesn't compile because this is the second attempt. Line 16 declares a `final` variable and initializes it at the same time. We are not allowed to assign it again, so line 21 doesn't compile. Line 17 declares a `final` variable that never gets initialized. The compiler gives a compiler error because it knows that the `static` blocks are the only place the variable could possibly get initialized. Since the programmer forgot, this is clearly an error.

Try to Avoid Static and Instance Initializers

Using static and instance initializers can make your code much harder to read. Everything that could be done in an instance initializer could be done in a constructor instead. Many people find the constructor approach is easier to read.

There is a common case to use a static initializer: when you need to initialize a static field and the code to do so requires more than one line. This often occurs when you want to initialize a collection like an ArrayList. When you do need to use a static initializer, put all the static initialization in the same block. That way, the order is obvious.

Static Imports

In Chapter 1, you saw that we could import a specific class or all the classes in a package:

```
import java.util.ArrayList;
import java.util.*;
```

We could use this technique to import two classes:

```
import java.util.List;
import java.util.Arrays;
public class Imports {
    public static void main(String[] args) {
        List<String> list = Arrays.asList("one", "two");
    }
}
```

Imports are convenient because you don't need to specify where each class comes from each time you use it. There is another type of import called a *static import*. Regular imports are for importing classes. Static imports are for importing `static` members of classes. Just like regular imports, you can use a wildcard or import a specific member. The idea is that you shouldn't have to specify where each `static` method or variable comes from each time you use it. An example of when static imports shine is when you are referring to a lot of constants in another class.

 In a large program, static imports can be overused. When importing from too many places, it can be hard to remember where each `static` member comes from.

The previous method has one `static` method call: `Arrays.asList`. Rewriting the code to use a static import yields the following:

```
import java.util.List;
import static java.util.Arrays.asList;          // static import
public class StaticImports {
    public static void main(String[] args) {
        List<String> list = asList("one", "two"); // no Arrays.
    }
}
```

In this example, we are specifically importing the `asList` method. This means that any time we refer to `asList` in the class, it will call `Arrays.asList()`.

An interesting case is what would happen if we created an `asList` method in our `StaticImports` class. Java would give it preference over the imported one, and the method we coded would be used.

The exam will try to trick you with misusing static imports. This example shows almost everything you can do wrong. Can you figure out what is wrong with each one?

```
1: import static java.util.Arrays;      // DOES NOT COMPILE
2: import static java.util.Arrays.asList;
3: static import java.util.Arrays.*;      // DOES NOT COMPILE
```

```
4: public class BadStaticImports {
5:    public static void main(String[] args) {
6:       Arrays.asList("one");          // DOES NOT COMPILE
7:    } }
```

Line 1 tries to use a static import to import a class. Remember that static imports are only for importing static members. Regular imports are for importing a class. Line 3 tries to see whether you are paying attention to the order of keywords. The syntax is import static and not vice versa. Line 6 is sneaky. The asList method is imported on line 2. However, the Arrays class is not imported anywhere. This makes it okay to write asList("one") but not Arrays.asList("one").

There's only one more scenario with static imports. In Chapter 1, you learned that importing two classes with the same name gives a compiler error. This is true of static imports as well. The compiler will complain if you try to explicitly do a static import of two methods with the same name or two static variables with the same name. Here's an example:

```
import static statics.A.TYPE;
import static statics.B.TYPE;     // DOES NOT COMPILE
```

Luckily, when this happens, we can just refer to the static members via their class name in the code instead of trying to use a static import.

Passing Data among Methods

Java is a "pass-by-value" language. This means that a copy of the variable is made and the method receives that copy. Assignments made in the method do not affect the caller. Let's look at an example:

```
2: public static void main(String[] args) {
3:    int num = 4;
4:    newNumber(num);
5:    System.out.println(num);     // 4
6: }
7: public static void newNumber(int num) {
8:    num = 8;
9: }
```

On line 3, num is assigned the value of 4. On line 4, we call a method. On line 8, the num parameter in the method gets set to 8. Although this parameter has the same name as the variable on line 3, this is a coincidence. The name could be anything. The exam will often use the same name to try to confuse you. The variable on line 3 never changes because no assignments are made to it.

Now that you've seen primitives, let's try an example with a reference type. What do you think is output by the following code?

```
public static void main(String[] args) {
   String name = "Webby";
   speak(name);
   System.out.println(name);
}
public static void speak(String name) {
   name = "Sparky";
}
```

The correct answer is Webby. Just as in the primitive example, the variable assignment is only to the method parameter and doesn't affect the caller.

Notice how we keep talking about variable assignments. This is because we can call methods on the parameters. As an example, here is code that calls a method on the StringBuilder passed into the method:

```
public static void main(String[] args) {
   StringBuilder name = new StringBuilder();
   speak(name);
   System.out.println(name); // Webby
}
public static void speak(StringBuilder s) {
   s.append("Webby");
}
```

In this case, the output is Webby because the method merely calls a method on the parameter. It doesn't reassign name to a different object. In Figure 7.4, you can see how pass-by-value is still used. The variable s is a copy of the variable name. Both point to the same StringBuilder, which means that changes made to the StringBuilder are available to both references.

FIGURE 7.4 Copying a reference with pass-by-value

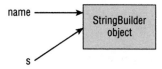

Real World Scenario

Pass-by-Value vs. Pass-by-Reference

Different languages handle parameters in different ways. Pass-by-value is used by many languages, including Java. In this example, the swap method does not change the original values. It only changes a and b within the method.

```java
public static void main(String[] args) {
    int original1 = 1;
    int original2 = 2;
    swap(original1, original2);
    System.out.println(original1);     // 1
    System.out.println(original2);     // 2
}
public static void swap(int a, int b) {
    int temp = a;
    a = b;
    b = temp;
}
```

The other approach is pass-by-reference. It is used by default in a few languages, such as Perl. We aren't going to show you Perl code here because you are studying for the Java exam and we don't want to confuse you. The following example is in a made-up language that shows pass-by-reference:

```
original1 = 1;
original2 = 2;
swapByReference(original1, original2);
print(original1);      // 2 (not in Java)
print(original2);      // 1 (not in Java)

swapByReference(a, b) {
    temp = a;
    a = b;
    b = temp;
}
```

See the difference? In our made-up language, the caller is affected by variable assignments made in the method.

To review, Java uses pass-by-value to get data into a method. Assigning a new primitive or reference to a parameter doesn't change the caller. Calling methods on a reference to an object can affect the caller.

Getting data back from a method is easier. A copy is made of the primitive or reference and returned from the method. Most of the time, this returned value is used. For example, it might be stored in a variable. If the returned value is not used, the result is ignored. Watch for this on the exam. Ignored returned values are tricky.

Let's try an example. Pay attention to the return types.

```
1:  public class ReturningValues {
2:      public static void main(String[] args) {
3:          int number = 1;                            // number=1
4:          String letters = "abc";                    // letters=abc
5:          number(number);                            // number=1
6:          letters = letters(letters);                // letters=abcd
7:          System.out.println(number + letters);      // 1abcd
8:      }
9:      public static int number(int number) {
10:          number++;
11:          return number;
12:      }
13:      public static String letters(String letters) {
14:          letters += "d";
15:          return letters;
16:      }
17: }
```

This is a tricky one because there is a lot to keep track of. When you see such questions on the exam, write down the values of each variable. Lines 3 and 4 are straightforward assignments. Line 5 calls a method. Line 10 increments the method parameter to 2 but leaves the number variable in the main() method as 1. While line 11 returns the value, the caller ignores it. The method call on line 6 doesn't ignore the result, so letters becomes "abcd". Remember that this is happening because of the returned value and not the method parameter.

Overloading Methods

Now that you are familiar with the rules for declaring methods, it is time to look at creating methods with the same name in the same class. *Method overloading* occurs when methods have the same name but different method signatures, which means they differ by method parameters. (Overloading differs from overriding, which you'll learn about in Chapter 8.)

We've been showing how to call overloaded methods for a while. `System.out.println` and `StringBuilder`'s append methods provide many overloaded versions, so you can pass just about anything to them without having to think about it. In both of these examples, the only change was the type of the parameter. Overloading also allows different numbers of parameters.

Everything other than the method name can vary for overloading methods. This means there can be different access modifiers, specifiers (like `static`), return types, and exception lists.

These are all valid overloaded methods:

```
public void fly(int numMiles) {}
public void fly(short numFeet) {}
public boolean fly() { return false; }
void fly(int numMiles, short numFeet) {}
public void fly(short numFeet, int numMiles) throws Exception {}
```

As you can see, we can overload by changing anything in the parameter list. We can have a different type, more types, or the same types in a different order. Also notice that the return type, access modifier, and exception list are irrelevant to overloading.

Now let's look at an example that is not valid overloading:

```
public void fly(int numMiles) {}
public int fly(int numMiles) {}      // DOES NOT COMPILE
```

This method doesn't compile because it differs from the original only by return type. The parameter lists are the same, so they are duplicate methods as far as Java is concerned.

What about these two? Why does the second not compile?

```
public void fly(int numMiles) {}
public static void fly(int numMiles) {}      // DOES NOT COMPILE
```

Again, the parameter list is the same. You cannot have methods where the only difference is that one is an instance method and one is a `static` method.

Calling overloaded methods is easy. You just write code and Java calls the right one. For example, look at these two methods:

```
public void fly(int numMiles) {
   System.out.println("int");
}
public void fly(short numFeet) {
   System.out.println("short");
}
```

The call `fly((short) 1)` prints `short`. It looks for matching types and calls the appropriate method. Of course, it can be more complicated than this.

Now that you know the basics of overloading, let's look at some more complex scenarios that you may encounter on the exam.

Varargs

Which method do you think is called if we pass an `int[]`?

```
public void fly(int[] lengths) {}
public void fly(int... lengths) {}        // DOES NOT COMPILE
```

Trick question! Remember that Java treats varargs as if they were an array. This means that the method signature is the same for both methods. Since we are not allowed to overload methods with the same parameter list, this code doesn't compile. Even though the code doesn't look the same, it compiles to the same parameter list.

Now that we've just gotten through explaining that they are the same, it is time to mention how they are not the same. It shouldn't be a surprise that you can call either method by passing an array:

```
fly(new int[] { 1, 2, 3 });
```

However, you can only call the varargs version with stand-alone parameters:

```
fly(1, 2, 3);
```

Obviously, this means they don't compile *exactly* the same. The parameter list is the same, though, and that is what you need to know with respect to overloading for the exam.

Autoboxing

In Chapter 5, you saw how Java will convert a primitive `int` to an object `Integer` to add it to an `ArrayList` through the wonders of autoboxing. This works for code you write too.

```
public void fly(Integer numMiles) {}
```

This means calling `fly(3)` will call the previous method as expected. However, what happens if you have both a primitive and an integer version?

```
public void fly(int numMiles) {}
public void fly(Integer numMiles) {}
```

Java will match the `int numMiles` version. Java tries to use the most specific parameter list it can find. When the primitive `int` version isn't present, it will autobox. However, when the primitive `int` version is provided, there is no reason for Java to do the extra work of autoboxing.

Reference Types

Given the rule about Java picking the most specific version of a method that it can, what do you think this code outputs?

```
public class ReferenceTypes {
   public void fly(String s) {
```

```
        System.out.print("string");
    }

    public void fly(Object o) {
        System.out.print("object");
    }
    public static void main(String[] args) {
        ReferenceTypes r = new ReferenceTypes();
        r.fly("test");
        System.out.print("-");
        r.fly(56);
    }
}
```

The answer is string-object. The first call is a String and finds a direct match. There's no reason to use the Object version when there is a nice String parameter list just waiting to be called. The second call looks for an int parameter list. When it doesn't find one, it autoboxes to Integer. Since it still doesn't find a match, it goes to the Object one.

Let's try another one. What does this print?

```
public static void print(Iterable i) {
    System.out.print("I");
}
public static void print(CharSequence c) {
    System.out.print("C");
}
public static void print(Object o) {
    System.out.print("O");
}
public static void main(String[] args){
    print("abc");
    print(new ArrayList<>());
    print(LocalDate.of(2019, Month.JULY, 4));
}
```

The answer is CIO. The code is due for a promotion! The first call to print() passes a String. As you learned in Chapter 5, String and StringBuilder implement the CharSequence interface.

The second call to print() passes an ArrayList. Remember that you get to assume unknown APIs do what they sound like. In this case, Iterable is an interface for classes you can iterate over.

The final call to print() passes a LocalDate. This is another class you might not know, but that's okay. It clearly isn't a sequence of characters or something to loop through. That means the Object method signature is used.

Primitives

Primitives work in a way that's similar to reference variables. Java tries to find the most specific matching overloaded method. What do you think happens here?

```java
public class Plane {
    public void fly(int i) {
        System.out.print("int");
    }
    public void fly(long l) {
        System.out.print("long");
    }
    public static void main(String[] args) {
        Plane p = new Plane();
        p.fly(123);
        System.out.print("-");
        p.fly(123L);
    }
}
```

The answer is int-long. The first call passes an int and sees an exact match. The second call passes a long and also sees an exact match. If we comment out the overloaded method with the int parameter list, the output becomes long-long. Java has no problem calling a larger primitive. However, it will not do so unless a better match is not found.

Note that Java can only accept wider types. An int can be passed to a method taking a long parameter. Java will not automatically convert to a narrower type. If you want to pass a long to a method taking an int parameter, you have to add a cast to explicitly say narrowing is okay.

Generics

You might be surprised to learn that these are not valid overloads:

```java
public void walk(List<String> strings) {}
public void walk(List<Integer> integers) {}    // DOES NOT COMPILE
```

Java has a concept called *type erasure* where generics are used only at compile time. That means the compiled code looks like this:

```java
public void walk(List strings) {}
public void walk(List integers) {}    // DOES NOT COMPILE
```

We clearly can't have two methods with the same method signature, so this doesn't compile. Remember that method overloads must differ in at least one of the method parameters.

Arrays

Unlike the previous example, this code is just fine:

```
public static void walk(int[] ints) {}
public static void walk(Integer[] integers) {}
```

Arrays have been around since the beginning of Java. They specify their actual types and don't participate in type erasure.

Putting It All Together

So far, all the rules for when an overloaded method is called should be logical. Java calls the most specific method it can. When some of the types interact, the Java rules focus on backward compatibility. A long time ago, autoboxing and varargs didn't exist. Since old code still needs to work, this means autoboxing and varargs come last when Java looks at overloaded methods. Ready for the official order? Table 7.4 lays it out for you.

TABLE 7.4   The order that Java uses to choose the right overloaded method

Rule	Example of what will be chosen for `glide(1,2)`
Exact match by type	`String glide(int i, int j)`
Larger primitive type	`String glide(long i, long j)`
Autoboxed type	`String glide(Integer i, Integer j)`
Varargs	`String glide(int... nums)`

Let's give this a practice run using the rules in Table 7.4. What do you think this outputs?

```
public class Glider2 {
    public static String glide(String s) {
        return "1";
    }
    public static String glide(String... s) {
        return "2";
    }
    public static String glide(Object o) {
        return "3";
    }
    public static String glide(String s, String t) {
```

```
        return "4";
    }
    public static void main(String[] args) {
        System.out.print(glide("a"));
        System.out.print(glide("a", "b"));
        System.out.print(glide("a", "b", "c"));
    }
}
```

It prints out 142. The first call matches the signature taking a single `String` because that is the most specific match. The second call matches the signature, taking two `String` parameters since that is an exact match. It isn't until the third call that the varargs version is used since there are no better matches.

As accommodating as Java is with trying to find a match, it will do only one conversion:

```
public class TooManyConversions {
    public static void play(Long l) {}
    public static void play(Long... l) {}
    public static void main(String[] args) {
        play(4);        // DOES NOT COMPILE
        play(4L);       // calls the Long version
    }
}
```

Here we have a problem. Java is happy to convert the `int` 4 to a `long` 4 or an `Integer` 4. It cannot handle converting to a `long` and then to a `Long`. If we had `public static void play(Object o) {}`, it would match because only one conversion would be necessary: from `int` to `Integer`. Remember, if a variable is not a primitive, it is an `Object`, as you'll see in Chapter 8.

Encapsulating Data

In Chapter 2, you saw an example of a class with a field that wasn't private:

```
public class Swan {
    int numberEggs;      // instance variable
}
```

Why do we care? Since there is default (package-private) access, that means any class in the package can set `numberEggs`. We no longer have control of what gets set in your own class. A caller could even write this:

```
mother.numberEggs = -1;
```

This is clearly no good. We do not want the mother Swan to have a negative number of eggs!

Encapsulation to the rescue. *Encapsulation* means only methods in the class with the variables can refer to the instance variables. Callers are required to use these methods. Let's take a look at the newly encapsulated Swan class:

```
1: public class Swan {
2:    private int numberEggs;                    // private
3:    public int getNumberEggs() {               // getter
4:       return numberEggs;
5:    }
6:    public void setNumberEggs(int newNumber) { // setter
7:       if (newNumber >= 0)                      // guard condition
8:          numberEggs = newNumber;
9:    } }
```

Note that numberEggs is now private on line 2. This means only code within the class can read or write the value of numberEggs. Since we wrote the class, we know better than to set a negative number of eggs. We added a method on lines 3–5 to read the value, which is called an *accessor method* or a getter. We also added a method on lines 6–9 to update the value, which is called a *mutator method* or a setter. The setter has an if statement in this example to prevent setting the instance variable to an invalid value. This guard condition protects the instance variable.

For encapsulation, remember that data (an instance variable) is private and getters/setters are public. Java defines a naming convention for getters and setters listed in Table 7.5.

TABLE 7.5   Naming conventions for getters and setters

Rule	Example

Getter methods most frequently begin with is if the property is a boolean.	`public boolean isHappy() {`
	`   return happy;`
	`}`

Getter methods begin with get if the property is not a boolean.	`public int getNumberEggs() {`
	`   return numberEggs;`
	`}`

Setter methods begin with set.	`public void setHappy(boolean _happy) {`
	`   happy = _happy;`
	`}`

In the last example in Table 7.5, you probably noticed that you can name the method parameter to anything you want. Only the method name and property name have naming conventions here.

It's time for some practice. See whether you can figure out which lines follow these naming conventions:

```
12: private boolean playing;
13: private String name;
14: public boolean isPlaying() { return playing; }
15: public String name() { return name; }
16: public void updateName(String n) { name = n; }
17: public void setName(String n) { name = n; }
```

Lines 12 and 13 are good. They are private instance variables. Line 14 is correct. Since `playing` is a `boolean`, line 14 is a correct getter. Line 15 doesn't follow the naming conventions because it should be called `getName()`. Line 16 does not follow the naming convention for a setter, but line 17 does.

For data to be encapsulated, you don't have to provide getters and setters. As long as the instance variables are `private`, you are good. For example, this is a well-encapsulated class:

```
public class Swan {
    private int numEggs;
    public void layEgg() {
        numEggs++;
    }
    public void printEggCount() {
        System.out.println(numEggs);
    }
}
```

To review, you can tell it is a well-encapsulated class because the `numEggs` instance variable is `private`. Only methods can retrieve and update the value.

Summary

As you learned in this chapter, Java methods start with an access modifier of `public`, `private`, `protected`, or blank (default access). This is followed by an optional specifier such as `static`, `final`, or `abstract`. Next comes the return type, which is `void` or a Java type. The method name follows, using standard Java identifier rules. Zero or more parameters go in parentheses as the parameter list. Next come any optional exception types. Finally, zero or more statements go in braces to make up the method body.

Using the `private` keyword means the code is only available from within the same class. Default (package-private) access means the code is available only from within the same package. Using the `protected` keyword means the code is available from the same package or subclasses. Using the `public` keyword means the code is available from anywhere. Both `static` methods and `static` variables are shared by all instances of the class. When referenced from outside the class, they are called using the classname—for example, `StaticClass.method()`. Instance members are allowed to call `static` members, but `static` members are not allowed to call instance members. Static imports are used to import `static` members.

Java uses pass-by-value, which means that calls to methods create a copy of the parameters. Assigning new values to those parameters in the method doesn't affect the caller's variables. Calling methods on objects that are method parameters changes the state of those objects and is reflected in the caller.

Overloaded methods are methods with the same name but a different parameter list. Java calls the most specific method it can find. Exact matches are preferred, followed by wider primitives. After that comes autoboxing and finally varargs.

Encapsulation refers to preventing callers from changing the instance variables directly. This is done by making instance variables `private` and getters/setters `public`.

Exam Essentials

Be able to identify correct and incorrect method declarations.   A sample method declaration is `public static void method(String... args) throws Exception {}`.

Identify when a method or field is accessible.   Recognize when a method or field is accessed when the access modifier (`private`, `protected`, `public`, or default access) does not allow it.

Recognize valid and invalid uses of static imports.   Static imports import `static` members. They are written as `import static`, not *static import*. Make sure they are importing `static` methods or variables rather than class names.

State the output of code involving methods.   Identify when to call `static` rather than instance methods based on whether the class name or object comes before the method. Recognize that instance methods can call `static` methods and that `static` methods need an instance of the object in order to call an instance method.

Recognize the correct overloaded method.   Exact matches are used first, followed by wider primitives, followed by autoboxing, followed by varargs. Assigning new values to method parameters does not change the caller, but calling methods on them does.

Identify properly encapsulated classes.   Instance variables in encapsulated classes are `private`. All code that retrieves the value or updates it uses methods. These methods are allowed to be `public`.

Review Questions

1. Which of the following can fill in the blank in this code to make it compile? (Choose all that apply.)

```
public class Ant {
    _____ void method() {}
}
```

   A. default
   B. final
   C. private
   D. Public
   E. String
   F. zzz:

2. Which of the following methods compile? (Choose all that apply.)
   A. final static void method4() {}
   B. public final int void method() {}
   C. private void int method() {}
   D. static final void method3() {}
   E. void final method() {}
   F. void public method() {}

3. Which of the following methods compile? (Choose all that apply.)
   A. public void methodA() { return;}
   B. public int methodB() { return null;}
   C. public void methodC() {}
   D. public int methodD() { return 9;}
   E. public int methodE() { return 9.0;}
   F. public int methodF() { return;}

4. Which of the following methods compile? (Choose all that apply.)
   A. public void moreA(int... nums) {}
   B. public void moreB(String values, int... nums) {}
   C. public void moreC(int... nums, String values) {}
   D. public void moreD(String... values, int... nums) {}
   E. public void moreE(String[] values, ...int nums) {}
   F. public void moreG(String[] values, int[] nums) {}

5. Given the following method, which of the method calls return 2? (Choose all that apply.)

```
public int howMany(boolean b, boolean... b2) {
 return b2.length;
}
```

A. `howMany();`

B. `howMany(true);`

C. `howMany(true, true);`

D. `howMany(true, true, true);`

E. `howMany(true, {true, true});`

F. `howMany(true, new boolean[2]);`

6. Which of the following statements is true?

A. Package-private access is more lenient than protected access.

B. A `public` class that has private fields and package-private methods is not visible to classes outside the package.

C. You can use access modifiers so only some of the classes in a package see a particular package-private class.

D. You can use access modifiers to allow access to all methods and not any instance variables.

E. You can use access modifiers to restrict access to all classes that begin with the word Test.

7. Given the following `my.school.Classroom` and `my.city.School` class definitions, which line numbers in `main()` generate a compiler error? (Choose all that apply.)

```
1: package my.school;
2: public class Classroom {
3:     private int roomNumber;
4:     protected static String teacherName;
5:     static int globalKey = 54321;
6:     public static int floor = 3;
7:     Classroom(int r, String t) {
8:         roomNumber = r;
9:         teacherName = t; } }
```

```
1: package my.city;
2: import my.school.*;
3: public class School {
4:     public static void main(String[] args) {
5:         System.out.println(Classroom.globalKey);
6:         Classroom room = new Classroom(101, "Mrs. Anderson");
7:         System.out.println(room.roomNumber);
```

```
8:          System.out.println(Classroom.floor);
9:          System.out.println(Classroom.teacherName); } }
```

A. None, the code compiles fine.

B. Line 5

C. Line 6

D. Line 7

E. Line 8

F. Line 9

8. Which of the following are true about encapsulation? (Choose all that apply.)

   A. It allows getters.

   B. It allows setters.

   C. It requires specific naming conventions.

   D. It uses package-private instance variables.

   E. It uses private instance variables.

9. Which pairs of methods are valid overloaded pairs? (Choose all that apply.)

   A.
   ```
   public void hiss(Iterable i) {}
   ```
   and
   ```
   public int hiss(Iterable i) { return 0; }
   ```
   B.
   ```
   public void baa(CharSequence c) {}
   ```
   and
   ```
   public void baa(String s) {}
   ```
   C.
   ```
   public var meow(List<String> l) {}
   ```
   and
   ```
   public var meow(String s) {}
   ```
   D.
   ```
   public void moo(Object o) {}
   ```
   and
   ```
   public void moo(String s) {}
   ```
   E.
   ```
   public void roar(List<Boolean> b) {}
   ```
   and
   ```
   public void roar(List<Character> c) {}
   ```
   F.
   ```
   public void woof(boolean[] b1) {}
   ```
   and
   ```
   public void woof(Boolean[] b) {}
   ```

10. What is the output of the following code?

```
1: package rope;
2: public class Rope {
3:    public static int LENGTH = 5;
4:    static {
5:       LENGTH = 10;
6:    }
7:    public static void swing() {
8:       System.out.print("swing ");
9:    } }
```

```
1: import rope.*;
2: import static rope.Rope.*;
3: public class Chimp {
4:    public static void main(String[] args) {
5:       Rope.swing();
6:       new Rope().swing();
7:       System.out.println(LENGTH);
8:    } }
```

A. swing swing 5

B. swing swing 10

C. Compiler error on line 2 of Chimp

D. Compiler error on line 5 of Chimp

E. Compiler error on line 6 of Chimp

F. Compiler error on line 7 of Chimp

11. Which statements are true of the following code? (Choose all that apply.)

```
1:  public class Rope {
2:     public static void swing() {
3:        System.out.print("swing");
4:     }
5:     public void climb() {
6:        System.out.println("climb");
7:     }
8:     public static void play() {
9:        swing();
10:       climb();
11:    }
12:    public static void main(String[] args) {
13:       Rope rope = new Rope();
```

```
14:        rope.play();
15:        Rope rope2 = null;
16:        System.out.println("-");
17:        rope2.play();
18:    } }
```

A. The code compiles as is.

B. There is exactly one compiler error in the code.

C. There are exactly two compiler errors in the code.

D. If the line(s) with compiler errors are removed, the output is swing-climb.

E. If the line(s) with compiler errors are removed, the output is swing-swing.

F. If the line(s) with compile errors are removed, the code throws a NullPointerException.

12. What is the output of the following code?

```
import rope.*;
import static rope.Rope.*;
public class RopeSwing {
    private static Rope rope1 = new Rope();
    private static Rope rope2 = new Rope();
    {
        System.out.println(rope1.length);
    }
    public static void main(String[] args) {
        rope1.length = 2;
        rope2.length = 8;
        System.out.println(rope1.length);
    }
}

package rope;
public class Rope {
    public static int length = 0;
}
```

A. 02

B. 08

C. 2

D. 8

E. The code does not compile.

F. An exception is thrown.

13. How many lines in the following code have compiler errors?

```
1:  public class RopeSwing {
2:      private static final String leftRope;
3:      private static final String rightRope;
4:      private static final String bench;
5:      private static final String name = "name";
6:      static {
7:          leftRope = "left";
8:          rightRope = "right";
9:      }
10:     static {
11:         name = "name";
12:         rightRope = "right";
13:     }
14:     public static void main(String[] args) {
15:         bench = "bench";
16:     }
17: }
```

A. 0

B. 1

C. 2

D. 3

E. 4

F. 5

14. Which of the following can replace line 2 to make this code compile? (Choose all that apply.)

```
1: import java.util.*;
2: // INSERT CODE HERE
3: public class Imports {
4:     public void method(ArrayList<String> list) {
5:         sort(list);
6:     }
7: }
```

A. import static java.util.Collections;

B. import static java.util.Collections.*;

C. import static java.util.Collections.sort(ArrayList<String>);

D. static import java.util.Collections;

E. static import java.util.Collections.*;

F. static import java.util.Collections.sort(ArrayList<String>);

15. What is the result of the following statements?

```
1:  public class Test {
2:      public void print(byte x) {
3:          System.out.print("byte-");
4:      }
5:      public void print(int x) {
6:          System.out.print("int-");
7:      }
8:      public void print(float x) {
9:          System.out.print("float-");
10:     }
11:     public void print(Object x) {
12:         System.out.print("Object-");
13:     }
14:     public static void main(String[] args) {
15:         Test t = new Test();
16:         short s = 123;
17:         t.print(s);
18:         t.print(true);
19:         t.print(6.789);
20:     }
21: }
```

A. byte-float-Object-

B. int-float-Object-

C. byte-Object-float-

D. int-Object-float-

E. int-Object-Object-

F. byte-Object-Object-

16. What is the result of the following program?

```
1:  public class Squares {
2:      public static long square(int x) {
3:          var y = x * (long) x;
4:          x = -1;
5:          return y;
6:      }
7:      public static void main(String[] args) {
8:          var value = 9;
9:          var result = square(value);
10:         System.out.println(value);
11:     } }
```

A. -1

B. 9

C. 81

D. Compiler error on line 9

E. Compiler error on a different line

17. Which of the following are output by the following code? (Choose all that apply.)

```java
public class StringBuilders {
    public static StringBuilder work(StringBuilder a,
        StringBuilder b) {
        a = new StringBuilder("a");
        b.append("b");
        return a;
    }
    public static void main(String[] args) {
        var s1 = new StringBuilder("s1");
        var s2 = new StringBuilder("s2");
        var s3 = work(s1, s2);
        System.out.println("s1 = " + s1);
        System.out.println("s2 = " + s2);
        System.out.println("s3 = " + s3);
    }
}
```

A. s1 = a

B. s1 = s1

C. s2 = s2

D. s2 = s2b

E. s3 = a

F. The code does not compile.

18. Which of the following will compile when independently inserted in the following code? (Choose all that apply.)

```java
1: public class Order3 {
2:     final String value1 = "red";
3:     static String value2 = "blue";
4:     String value3 = "yellow";
5:     {
6:         // CODE SNIPPET 1
7:     }
```

```
8:      static {
9:         // CODE SNIPPET 2
10:     } }
```

A. Insert at line 6: value1 = "green";

B. Insert at line 6: value2 = "purple";

C. Insert at line 6: value3 = "orange";

D. Insert at line 9: value1 = "magenta";

E. Insert at line 9: value2 = "cyan";

F. Insert at line 9: value3 = "turquoise";

19. Which of the following are true about the following code? (Choose all that apply.)

```java
public class Run {
    static void execute() {
        System.out.print("1-");
    }
    static void execute(int num) {
        System.out.print("2-");
    }
    static void execute(Integer num) {
        System.out.print("3-");
    }
    static void execute(Object num) {
        System.out.print("4-");
    }
    static void execute(int... nums) {
        System.out.print("5-");
    }
    public static void main(String[] args) {
        Run.execute(100);
        Run.execute(100L);
    }
}
```

A. The code prints out 2-4-.

B. The code prints out 3-4-.

C. The code prints out 4-2-.

D. The code prints out 4-4-.

E. The code prints 3-4- if you remove the method static void execute(int num).

F. The code prints 4-4- if you remove the constructor static void execute(int num).

20. Which pairs of methods are valid overloaded pairs? (Choose all that apply.)

A.
```
public void hiss(Set<String> s) {}
```
and
```
public void hiss(List<String> l) {}
```

B.
```
public void baa(var c) {}
```
and
```
public void baa(String s) {}
```

C.
```
public void meow(char ch) {}
```
and
```
public void meow(String s) {}
```

D.
```
public void moo(char ch) {}
```
and
```
public void moo(char ch) {}
```

E.
```
public void roar(long... longs){}
```
and
```
public void roar(long long) {}
```

F.
```
public void woof(char... chars) {}
```
and
```
public void woof(Character c) {}
```

21. Which can fill in the blank to create a properly encapsulated class? (Choose all that apply.)

```
public class Rabbits {
    _____ int numRabbits = 0;
    _____ void multiply() {
      numRabbits *= 6;
  }
    _____ int getNumberOfRabbits() {
      return numRabbits;
  }
}
```

A. private, public, and public

B. private, protected, and private

C. private, private, and protected

D. public, public, and public

E. None of the above since multiply() does not begin with set

F. None of the above for a reason other than the multiply() method

Chapter

8

Class Design

OCP EXAM OBJECTIVES COVERED IN THIS CHAPTER:

✓ **Creating and Using Methods**

- Create methods and constructors with arguments and return values

✓ **Reusing Implementations Through Inheritance**

- Create and use subclasses and superclasses

- Enable polymorphism by overriding methods

- Utilize polymorphism to cast and call methods, differentiating object type versus reference type

- Distinguish overloading, overriding, and hiding

In Chapter 2, "Java Building Blocks," we introduced the basic definition for a class in Java. In Chapter 7, "Methods and Encapsulation," we delved into methods and modifiers and showed how you can use them to build more structured classes. In this chapter, we'll take things one step further and show how class structure and inheritance is one of the most powerful features in the Java language.

At its core, proper Java class design is about code reusability, increased functionality, and standardization. For example, by creating a new class that extends an existing class, you may gain access to a slew of inherited primitives, objects, and methods, which increases code reuse. Through polymorphism, you may also gain access to a dynamic hierarchy that supports replacing method implementations in subclasses at runtime.

This chapter is the culmination of some of the most important topics in Java including class design, constructor overloading and inheritance, order of initialization, overriding/hiding methods, and polymorphism. Read this chapter carefully and make sure you understand all of the topics well. This chapter forms the basis of Chapter 9, "Advanced Class Design," in which we will expand our discussion of types to include abstract classes and interfaces.

Understanding Inheritance

When creating a new class in Java, you can define the class as inheriting from an existing class. *Inheritance* is the process by which a subclass automatically includes any public or protected members of the class, including primitives, objects, or methods, defined in the parent class.

For illustrative purposes, we refer to any class that inherits from another class as a *subclass* or *child class*, as it is considered a descendant of that class. Alternatively, we refer to the class that the child inherits from as the *superclass* or *parent class*, as it is considered an ancestor of the class. And inheritance is transitive. If child class X inherits from parent class Y, which in turn inherits from a parent class Z, then class X would be considered a subclass, or descendant, of class Z. By comparison, X is a direct descendant only of class Y, and Y is a direct descendant only of class Z.

In the last chapter, you learned that there are four access levels: public, protected, package-private, and private. When one class inherits from a parent class, all public and protected members are automatically available as part of the child class. Package-private members are available if the child class is in the same package as the parent class. Last but not least, private members are restricted to the class they are defined in and are never available via inheritance. This doesn't mean the parent class doesn't have private members that can hold data or modify an object; it just means the child class has no direct reference to them.

Let's take a look at a simple example with the BigCat and Jaguar classes. In this example, Jaguar is a subclass or child of BigCat, making BigCat a superclass or parent of Jaguar.

```java
public class BigCat {
    public double size;
}

public class Jaguar extends BigCat {
    public Jaguar() {
        size = 10.2;
    }
    public void printDetails() {
        System.out.println(size);
    }
}
```

In the Jaguar class, size is accessible because it is marked public. Via inheritance, the Jaguar subclass can read or write size as if it were its own member.

Single vs. Multiple Inheritance

Java supports *single inheritance*, by which a class may inherit from only one direct parent class. Java also supports multiple levels of inheritance, by which one class may extend another class, which in turn extends another class. You can have any number of levels of inheritance, allowing each descendant to gain access to its ancestor's members.

To truly understand single inheritance, it may helpful to contrast it with *multiple inheritance*, by which a class may have multiple direct parents. By design, Java doesn't support multiple inheritance in the language because multiple inheritance can lead to complex, often difficult-to-maintain data models. Java does allow one exception to the single inheritance rule that you'll see in Chapter 9—a class may implement multiple interfaces.

Figure 8.1 illustrates the various types of inheritance models. The items on the left are considered single inheritance because each child has exactly one parent. You may notice that single inheritance doesn't preclude parents from having multiple children. The right side shows items that have multiple inheritance. As you can see, a Dog object has multiple parent designations. Part of what makes multiple inheritance complicated is determining which parent to inherit values from in case of a conflict. For example, if you have an object or method defined in all of the parents, which one does the child inherit? There is no natural ordering for parents in this example, which is why Java avoids these issues by disallowing multiple inheritance altogether.

FIGURE 8.1   Types of inheritance

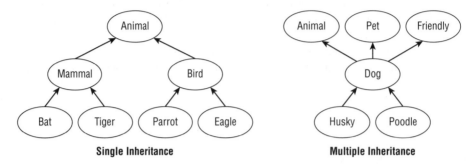

It is possible in Java to prevent a class from being extended by marking the class with the final modifier. If you try to define a class that inherits from a final class, then the class will fail to compile. Unless otherwise specified, throughout this chapter you can assume the classes we work with are not marked final.

Inheriting *Object*

Throughout our discussion of Java in this book, we have thrown around the word *object* numerous times—and with good reason. In Java, all classes inherit from a single class: java.lang.Object, or Object for short. Furthermore, Object is the only class that doesn't have a parent class.

You might be wondering, "None of the classes I've written so far extend Object, so how do all classes inherit from it?" The answer is that the compiler has been automatically inserting code into any class you write that doesn't extend a specific class. For example, consider the following two equivalent class definitions:

```
public class Zoo { }
```

```
public class Zoo extends java.lang.Object { }
```

The key is that when Java sees you define a class that doesn't extend another class, it automatically adds the syntax extends java.lang.Object to the class definition. The result is that every class gains access to any accessible methods in the Object class. For example, the toString() and equals() methods are available in Object; therefore, they are accessible in all classes. Without being overridden in a subclass, though, they may not be particularly useful. We will cover overriding methods later in this chapter.

On the other hand, when you define a new class that extends an existing class, Java does not automatically extend the Object class. Since all classes inherit from Object, extending an existing class means the child already inherits from Object by definition. If you look at the inheritance structure of any class, it will always end with Object on the top of the tree, as shown in Figure 8.2.

FIGURE 8.2 Java object inheritance

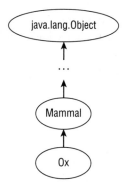

java.lang.Object
...
Mammal
Ox
All objects inherit java.lang.Object

Primitive types such as `int` and `boolean` do not inherit from `Object`, since they are not classes. As you learned in Chapter 5, "Core Java APIs," through autoboxing they can be assigned or passed as an instance of an associated wrapper class, which does inherit `Object`.

Creating Classes

Now that we've established how inheritance works in Java, we can use it to define and create complex class relationships. In this section, we will review the basics for creating and working with classes.

Extending a Class

The full syntax of defining and extending a class using the `extends` keyword is shown in Figure 8.3.

FIGURE 8.3 Defining and extending a class

public or default (package-private) access modifier
Class name (required)
abstract or final keyword (optional)
extends parent class (optional)
class keyword (required)
public abstract class ElephantSeal extends Seal {
// Methods and Variables defined here
}

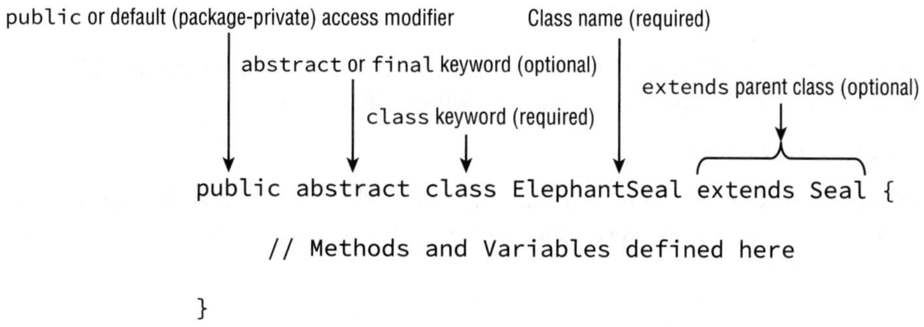

Remember that final means a class cannot be extended. We'll discuss what it means for a class to be abstract in Chapter 9.

Let's create two files, Animal.java and Lion.java, in which the Lion class extends the Animal class. Assuming they are in the same package, an import statement is not required in Lion.java to access the Animal class.

Here are the contents of Animal.java:

```java
public class Animal {
   private int age;
   protected String name;
   public int getAge() {
      return age;
   }
   public void setAge(int newAge) {
      age = newAge;
   }
}
```

And here are the contents of Lion.java:

```java
public class Lion extends Animal {
   public void setProperties(int age, String n) {
      setAge(age);
      name = n;
   }
   public void roar() {
      System.out.print(name + ", age " + getAge() + ", says: Roar!");
   }
   public static void main(String[] args) {
      var lion = new Lion();
      lion.setProperties(3, "kion");
      lion.roar();
   }
}
```

The extends keyword is used to express that the Lion class inherits the Animal class. When executed, the Lion program prints the following:

```
kion, age 3, says: Roar!
```

Let's take a look at the members of the Lion class. The instance variable age is marked as private and is not directly accessible from the subclass Lion. Therefore, the following would not compile:

```
public class Lion extends Animal {
   ...
   public void roar() {
      System.out.print("Lions age: "+age);  // DOES NOT COMPILE
   }
   ...
}
```

The age variable can be accessed indirectly through the getAge() and setAge() methods, which are marked as public in the Animal class. The name variable can be accessed directly in the Lion class since it is marked as protected in the Animal class.

Applying Class Access Modifiers

You already know that you can apply access modifiers to both methods and variables. It probably comes as little surprise that you can also apply access modifiers to class definitions, since we have been adding the public access modifier to most classes up to now.

In Java, a *top-level class* is a class that is not defined inside another class. Most of the classes in this book are top-level classes. They can only have public or package-private access. Applying public access to a class indicates that it can be referenced and used in any class. Applying default (package-private) access, which you'll remember is the lack of any access modifier, indicates the class can be accessed only by a class within the same package.

> An *inner class* is a class defined inside of another class and is the opposite of a top-level class. In addition to public and package-private access, inner classes can also have protected and private access. We will discuss inner classes in Chapter 9.

As you might recall, a Java file can have many top-level classes but at most one public top-level class. In fact, it may have no public class at all. There's also no requirement that the single public class be the first class in the file. One benefit of using the package-private access is that you can define many classes within the same Java file. For example, the following definition could appear in a single Java file named Groundhog.java, since it contains only one public class:

```
class Rodent {}

public class Groundhog extends Rodent {}
```

If we were to update the Rodent class with the public access modifier, the Groundhog.java file would not compile unless the Rodent class was moved to its own Rodent.java file.

> For simplicity, any time you see multiple public classes or interfaces defined in the same code sample in this book, assume each class is defined in its own Java file.

Accessing the *this* Reference

What happens when a method parameter has the same name as an existing instance variable? Let's take a look at an example. What do you think the following program prints?

```java
public class Flamingo {
   private String color;
   public void setColor(String color) {
      color = color;
   }
   public static void main(String... unused) {
      Flamingo f = new Flamingo();
      f.setColor("PINK");
      System.out.println(f.color);
   }
}
```

If you said null, then you'd be correct. Java uses the most granular scope, so when it sees color = color, it thinks you are assigning the method parameter value to itself. The assignment completes successfully within the method, but the value of the instance variable color is never modified and is null when printed in the main() method.

The fix when you have a local variable with the same name as an instance variable is to use the this reference or keyword. The this reference refers to the current instance of the class and can be used to access any member of the class, including inherited members. It can be used in any instance method, constructor, and instance initializer block. It cannot be used when there is no implicit instance of the class, such as in a static method or static initializer block. We apply this to our previous method implementation as follows:

```java
public void setColor(String color) {
   this.color = color;
}
```

The corrected code will now print PINK as expected. In many cases, the this reference is optional. If Java encounters a variable or method it cannot find, it will check the class hierarchy to see if it is available.

Now let's look at some examples that aren't common but that you might see on the exam.

```java
1:  public class Duck {
2:      private String color;
3:      private int height;
4:      private int length;
5:
6:      public void setData(int length, int theHeight) {
7:          length = this.length;  // Backwards - no good!
```

```
8:          height = theHeight;    // Fine because a different name
9:          this.color = "white";  // Fine, but this. not necessary
10:     }
11:
12:     public static void main(String[] args) {
13:         Duck b = new Duck();
14:         b.setData(1,2);
15:         System.out.print(b.length + " " + b.height + " " + b.color);
16:     } }
```

This code compiles and prints the following:

```
0 2 white
```

This might not be what you expected, though. Line 7 is incorrect, and you should watch for it on the exam. The instance variable length starts out with a 0 value. That 0 is assigned to the method parameter length. The instance variable stays at 0. Line 8 is more straightforward. The parameter theHeight and instance variable height have different names. Since there is no naming collision, this is not required. Finally, line 9 shows that a variable assignment is allowed to use this even when there is no duplication of variable names.

Calling the *super* Reference

In Java, a variable or method can be defined in both a parent class and a child class. When this happens, how do we reference the version in the parent class instead of the current class?

To achieve this, you can use the super reference or keyword. The super reference is similar to the this reference, except that it excludes any members found in the current class. In other words, the member must be accessible via inheritance. The following class shows how to apply super to use two variables with the same name in a method:

```
class Mammal {
    String type = "mammal";
}

public class Bat extends Mammal {
    String type = "bat";
    public String getType() {
        return super.type + ":" + this.type;
    }
    public static void main(String... zoo) {
        System.out.print(new Bat().getType());
    }
}
```

The program prints mammal:bat. What do you think would happen if the super reference was dropped? The program would then print bat:bat. Java uses the narrowest scope
it can—in this case, the type variable defined in the Bat class. Note that the this reference
in the previous example was optional, with the program printing the same output as it
would if this was dropped.

Let's see if you've gotten the hang of this and super. What does the following program
output?

```
1:  class Insect {
2:      protected int numberOfLegs = 4;
3:      String label = "buggy";
4:  }
5:
6:  public class Beetle extends Insect {
7:      protected int numberOfLegs = 6;
8:      short age = 3;
9:      public void printData() {
10:         System.out.print(this.label);
11:         System.out.print(super.label);
12:         System.out.print(this.age);
13:         System.out.print(super.age);
14:         System.out.print(numberOfLegs);
15:     }
16:     public static void main(String []n) {
17:         new Beetle().printData();
18:     }
19: }
```

That was a trick question—this program code would not compile! Let's review each line
of the printData() method. Since label is defined in the parent class, it is accessible via
both this and super references. For this reason, lines 10 and 11 compile and would both
print buggy if the class compiled. On the other hand, the variable age is defined only in the
current class, making it accessible via this but not super. For this reason, line 12 compiles, but line 13 does not. Remember, while this includes current and inherited members,
super only includes inherited members. In this example, line 12 would print 3 if the code
compiled.

Last but least, what would line 14 print if line 13 was commented out? Even though
both numberOfLegs variables are accessible in Beetle, Java checks outward starting with
the narrowest scope. For this reason, the value of numberOfLegs in the Beetle class is used
and 6 would be printed. In this example, this.numberOfLegs and super.numberOfLegs
refer to different variables with distinct values.

Since this includes inherited members, you often only use super when you have a naming conflict via inheritance. For example, you have a method or variable defined in the

current class that matches a method or variable in a parent class. This commonly comes up in method overriding and variable hiding, which will be discussed later in this chapter.

Declaring Constructors

As you learned in Chapter 2, a constructor is a special method that matches the name of the class and has no return type. It is called when a new instance of the class is created. For the exam, you'll need to know a lot of rules about constructors. In this section, we'll show how to create a constructor. Then, we'll look at default constructors, overloading constructors, calling parent constructors, final fields, and the order of initialization in a class.

Creating a Constructor

Let's start with a simple constructor:

```java
public class Bunny {
    public Bunny() {
        System.out.println("constructor");
    }
}
```

The name of the constructor, Bunny, matches the name of the class, Bunny, and there is no return type, not even void. That makes this a constructor. Can you tell why these two are not valid constructors for the Bunny class?

```java
public class Bunny {
    public bunny() { }       // DOES NOT COMPILE
    public void Bunny() { }
}
```

The first one doesn't match the class name because Java is case sensitive. Since it doesn't match, Java knows it can't be a constructor and is supposed to be a regular method. However, it is missing the return type and doesn't compile. The second method is a perfectly good method but is not a constructor because it has a return type.

Like method parameters, constructor parameters can be any valid class, array, or primitive type, including generics, but may not include var. The following does not compile:

```java
class Bonobo {
    public Bonobo(var food) { // DOES NOT COMPILE
    }
}
```

A class can have multiple constructors, so long as each constructor has a unique signature. In this case, that means the constructor parameters must be distinct. Like methods with the same name but different signatures, declaring multiple constructors with different signatures is referred to as *constructor overloading*. The following Turtle class has four distinct overloaded constructors:

```
public class Turtle {
   private String name;
   public Turtle() {
      name = "John Doe";
   }
   public Turtle(int age) {}
   public Turtle(long age) {}
   public Turtle(String newName, String... favoriteFoods) {
      name = newName;
   }
}
```

Constructors are used when creating a new object. This process is called *instantiation* because it creates a new instance of the class. A constructor is called when we write new followed by the name of the class we want to instantiate. Here's an example:

```
new Turtle()
```

When Java sees the new keyword, it allocates memory for the new object. It then looks for a constructor with a matching signature and calls it.

Default Constructor

Every class in Java has a constructor whether you code one or not. If you don't include any constructors in the class, Java will create one for you without any parameters. This Java-created constructor is called the *default constructor* and is added anytime a class is declared without any constructors. We often refer to it as the default no-argument constructor for clarity. Here's an example:

```
public class Rabbit {
   public static void main(String[] args) {
      Rabbit rabbit = new Rabbit();     // Calls default constructor
   }
}
```

In the Rabbit class, Java sees no constructor was coded and creates one. This default constructor is equivalent to typing this:

```
public Rabbit() {}
```

The default constructor has an empty parameter list and an empty body. It is fine for you to type this in yourself. However, since it doesn't do anything, Java is happy to generate it for you and save you some typing.

We keep saying *generated*. This happens during the compile step. If you look at the file with the .java extension, the constructor will still be missing. It is only in the compiled file with the .class extension that it makes an appearance.

Remember that a default constructor is only supplied if there are no constructors present. Which of these classes do you think has a default constructor?

```
public class Rabbit1 {}

public class Rabbit2 {
   public Rabbit2() {}
}

public class Rabbit3 {
   public Rabbit3(boolean b) {}
}

public class Rabbit4 {
   private Rabbit4() {}
}
```

Only Rabbit1 gets a default no-argument constructor. It doesn't have a constructor coded, so Java generates a default no-argument constructor. Rabbit2 and Rabbit3 both have public constructors already. Rabbit4 has a private constructor. Since these three classes have a constructor defined, the default no-argument constructor is not inserted for you.

Let's take a quick look at how to call these constructors:

```
1: public class RabbitsMultiply {
2:    public static void main(String[] args) {
3:       Rabbit1 r1 = new Rabbit1();
4:       Rabbit2 r2 = new Rabbit2();
5:       Rabbit3 r3 = new Rabbit3(true);
6:       Rabbit4 r4 = new Rabbit4();  // DOES NOT COMPILE
7:    } }
```

Line 3 calls the generated default no-argument constructor. Lines 4 and 5 call the user-provided constructors. Line 6 does not compile. Rabbit4 made the constructor private so that other classes could not call it.

Having only private constructors in a class tells the compiler not to provide a default no-argument constructor. It also prevents other classes from instantiating the class. This is useful when a class has only static methods or the developer wants to have full control of all calls to create new instances of the class. Remember, static methods in the class, including a main() method, may access private members, including private constructors.

Calling Overloaded Constructors with *this()*

Remember, a single class can have multiple constructors. This is referred to as constructor overloading because all constructors have the same inherent name but a different signature. Let's take a look at this in more detail using a `Hamster` class.

```java
public class Hamster {
   private String color;
   private int weight;
   public Hamster(int weight) {                   // First constructor
      this.weight = weight;
      color = "brown";
   }
   public Hamster(int weight, String color) {   // Second constructor
      this.weight = weight;
      this.color = color;
   }
}
```

One of the constructors takes a single `int` parameter. The other takes an `int` and a `String`. These parameter lists are different, so the constructors are successfully overloaded. There is a problem here, though.

There is a bit of duplication, as `this.weight` is assigned twice in the same way in both constructors. In programming, even a bit of duplication tends to turn into a lot of duplication as we keep adding "just one more thing." For example, imagine we had 20 variables being set like `this.weight`, rather than just one. What we really want is for the first constructor to call the second constructor with two parameters. So, how can you have a constructor call another constructor? You might be tempted to write this:

```java
public Hamster(int weight) {
   Hamster(weight, "brown");     // DOES NOT COMPILE
}
```

This will not work. Constructors can be called only by writing `new` before the name of the constructor. They are not like normal methods that you can just call. What happens if we stick `new` before the constructor name?

```java
public Hamster(int weight) {
   new Hamster(weight, "brown");  // Compiles, but incorrect
}
```

This attempt does compile. It doesn't do what we want, though. When this constructor is called, it creates a new object with the default `weight` and `color`. It then constructs a different object with the desired `weight` and `color` and ignores the new object. In this manner, we end up with two objects, with one being discarded after it is created. That's not what we want. We want weight and color set on the object we are trying to instantiate in the first place.

Java provides a solution: this()—yes, the same keyword we used to refer to instance members. When this() is used with parentheses, Java calls another constructor on the same instance of the class.

```java
public Hamster(int weight) {
    this(weight, "brown");
}
```

Success! Now Java calls the constructor that takes two parameters, with weight and color set as expected.

Calling this() has one special rule you need to know. If you choose to call it, the this() call must be the first statement in the constructor. The side effect of this is that there can be only one call to this() in any constructor.

```java
3:    public Hamster(int weight) {
4:        System.out.println("in constructor");
5:        // Set weight and default color
6:        this(weight, "brown");     // DOES NOT COMPILE
7:    }
```

Even though a print statement on line 4 doesn't change any variables, it is still a Java statement and is not allowed to be inserted before the call to this(). The comment on line 5 is just fine. Comments aren't considered statements and are allowed anywhere.

There's one last rule for overloaded constructors you should be aware of. Consider the following definition of the Gopher class:

```java
public class Gopher {
    public Gopher(int dugHoles) {
        this(5);  // DOES NOT COMPILE
    }
}
```

The compiler is capable of detecting that this constructor is calling itself infinitely. Since this code can never terminate, the compiler stops and reports this as an error. Likewise, this also does not compile:

```java
public class Gopher {
    public Gopher() {
        this(5);  // DOES NOT COMPILE
    }
    public Gopher(int dugHoles) {
        this();   // DOES NOT COMPILE
    }
}
```

In this example, the constructors call each other, and the process continues infinitely. Since the compiler can detect this, it reports this as an error.

---

this vs. _this()_

Despite using the same keyword, this and this() are very different. The first, this, refers to an instance of the class, while the second, this(), refers to a constructor call within the class. The exam may try to trick you by using both together, so make sure you know which one to use and why.

Calling Parent Constructors with _super()_

In Java, the first statement of every constructor is either a call to another constructor within the class, using this(), or a call to a constructor in the direct parent class, using super(). If a parent constructor takes arguments, then the super() call also takes arguments. For simplicity in this section, we refer to the super() command as any parent constructor, even those that take arguments. Let's take a look at the Animal class and its subclass Zebra and see how their constructors can be properly written to call one another:

```java
public class Animal {
    private int age;
    public Animal(int age) {
        super();      // Refers to constructor in java.lang.Object
        this.age = age;
    }
}

public class Zebra extends Animal {
    public Zebra(int age) {
        super(age);   // Refers to constructor in Animal
    }
    public Zebra() {
        this(4);      // Refers to constructor in Zebra with int argument
    }
}
```

In the first class, Animal, the first statement of the constructor is a call to the parent constructor defined in java.lang.Object, which takes no arguments. In the second class, Zebra, the first statement of the first constructor is a call to Animal's constructor, which takes a single argument. The class Zebra also includes a second no-argument constructor that doesn't call super() but instead calls the other constructor within the Zebra class using this(4).

Like calling this(), calling super() can only be used as the first statement of the constructor. For example, the following two class definitions will not compile:

```
public class Zoo {
   public Zoo() {
      System.out.println("Zoo created");
      super();      // DOES NOT COMPILE
   }
}

public class Zoo {
   public Zoo() {
      super();
      System.out.println("Zoo created");
      super();      // DOES NOT COMPILE
   }
}
```

The first class will not compile because the call to the parent constructor must be the first statement of the constructor. In the second code snippet, super() is the first statement of the constructor, but it is also used as the third statement. Since super() can only be called once as the first statement of the constructor, the code will not compile.

If the parent class has more than one constructor, the child class may use any valid parent constructor in its definition, as shown in the following example:

```
public class Animal {
   private int age;
   private String name;
   public Animal(int age, String name) {
      super();
      this.age = age;
      this.name = name;
   }
   public Animal(int age) {
      super();
      this.age = age;
      this.name = null;
   }
}

public class Gorilla extends Animal {
   public Gorilla(int age) {
      super(age,"Gorilla");
```

```
    }
    public Gorilla() {
        super(5);
    }
}
```

In this example, the first child constructor takes one argument, age, and calls the parent constructor, which takes two arguments, age and name. The second child constructor takes no arguments, and it calls the parent constructor, which takes one argument, age. In this example, notice that the child constructors are not required to call matching parent constructors. Any valid parent constructor is acceptable as long as the appropriate input parameters to the parent constructor are provided.

---

super vs. *super()*

Like `this` and `this()`, super and `super()` are unrelated in Java. The first, super, is used to reference members of the parent class, while the second, `super()`, calls a parent constructor. Anytime you see the super keyword on the exam, make sure it is being used properly.

Understanding Compiler Enhancements

Wait a second, we said the first line of every constructor is a call to either `this()` or `super()`, but we've been creating classes and constructors throughout this book, and we've rarely done either. How did these classes compile? The answer is that the Java compiler automatically inserts a call to the no-argument constructor `super()` if you do not explicitly call `this()` or `super()` as the first line of a constructor. For example, the following three class and constructor definitions are equivalent, because the compiler will automatically convert them all to the last example:

```
public class Donkey {}
```

```
public class Donkey {
    public Donkey() {}
}
```

```
public class Donkey {
    public Donkey() {
        super();
    }
}
```

Make sure you understand the differences between these three Donkey class definitions and why Java will automatically convert them all to the last definition. Keep the process that the Java compiler performs in mind while reading the next section.

Are Classes with Only *private* Constructors Considered *final*?

Remember, a final class cannot be extended. What happens if you have a class that is not marked final but only contains private constructors—can you extend the class? The answer is "yes," but only an inner class defined in the class itself can extend it. An inner class is the only one that would have access to a private constructor and be able to call super(). Other top-level classes cannot extend such a class. Don't worry—knowing this fact is not required for the exam. We include it here for those who were curious about declaring only private constructors.

Missing a Default No-Argument Constructor

What happens if the parent class doesn't have a no-argument constructor? Recall that the default no-argument constructor is not required and is inserted by the compiler only if there is no constructor defined in the class. For example, do you see why the following Elephant class declaration does not compile?

```
public class Mammal {
    public Mammal(int age) {}
}
```

```
public class Elephant extends Mammal {  // DOES NOT COMPILE
}
```

Since Elephant does not define any constructors, the Java compiler will attempt to insert a default no-argument constructor. As a second compile-time enhancement, it will also auto-insert a call to super() as the first line of the default no-argument constructor. Our previous Elephant declaration is then converted by the compiler to the following declaration:

```
public class Elephant extends Mammal {
    public Elephant() {
        super();  // DOES NOT COMPILE
    }
}
```

Since the Mammal class has at least one constructor declared, the compiler does not insert a default no-argument constructor. Therefore, the super() call in the Elephant class declaration does not compile. In this case, the Java compiler will not help, and you must create at least one constructor in your child class that explicitly calls a parent constructor via the super() command. We can fix this by adding a call to a parent constructor that takes a fixed argument.

```
public class Elephant extends Mammal {
    public Elephant() {
        super(10);
    }
}
```

This code will compile because we have added a constructor with an explicit call to a parent constructor. Notice that the class Elephant now has a no-argument constructor even though its parent class Mammal doesn't. Subclasses may define explicit no-argument constructors even if their parent classes do not, provided the constructor of the child maps to a parent constructor via an explicit call of the super() command. This means that subclasses of the Elephant can rely on compiler enhancements. For example, the following class compiles because Elephant now has a no-argument constructor, albeit one defined explicitly:

```
public class AfricanElephant extends Elephant {}
```

You should be wary of any exam question in which a class defines a constructor that takes arguments and doesn't define a no-argument constructor. Be sure to check that the code compiles before answering a question about it, especially if any classes inherit it. For the exam, you should be able to spot right away why classes such as our first Elephant implementation did not compile.

---

super() Always Refers to the Most Direct Parent

A class may have multiple ancestors via inheritance. In our previous example, AfricanElephant is a subclass of Elephant, which in turn is a subclass of Mammal. For constructors, though, super() always refers to the most direct parent. In this example, calling super() inside the AfricanElephant class always refers to the Elephant class, and never the Mammal class.

Constructors and *final* Fields

As you might recall from Chapter 7, final static variables must be assigned a value exactly once. You saw this happen in the line of the declaration and in a static initializer. Instance variables marked final follow similar rules. They can be assigned values in the line in which they are declared or in an instance initializer.

```
public class MouseHouse {
    private final int volume;
```

```
   private final String name = "The Mouse House";
   {
      volume = 10;
   }
}
```

Like other final variables, once the value is assigned, it cannot be changed. There is one more place they can be assigned a value—the constructor. The constructor is part of the initialization process, so it is allowed to assign final instance variables in it. For the exam, you need to know one important rule. By the time the constructor completes, all final instance variables must be assigned a value. Let's try this out in an example:

```
public class MouseHouse {
   private final int volume;
   private final String type;
   public MouseHouse() {
      this.volume = 10;
      type = "happy";
   }
}
```

In our MouseHouse implementation, the values for volume and type are assigned in the constructor. Remember that the this keyword is optional since the instance variables are part of the class declaration, and there are no constructor parameters with the same name.

Unlike local final variables, which are not required to have a value unless they are actually used, final instance variables *must* be assigned a value. Default values are not used for these variables. If they are not assigned a value in the line where they are declared or in an instance initializer, then they must be assigned a value in the constructor declaration. Failure to do so will result in a compiler error on the line that declares the constructor.

```
public class MouseHouse {
   private final int volume;
   private final String type;
   {
      this.volume = 10;
   }
   public MouseHouse(String type) {
      this.type = type;
   }
   public MouseHouse() {   // DOES NOT COMPILE
      this.volume = 2;     // DOES NOT COMPILE
   }
}
```

In this example, the first constructor that takes a String argument compiles. Although a final instance variable can be assigned a value only once, each constructor is considered independently in terms of assignment. The second constructor does not compile for two reasons. First, the constructor fails to set a value for the type variable. The compiler detects that a value is never set for type and reports an error on the line where the constructor is declared. Second, the constructor sets a value for the volume variable, even though it was already assigned a value by the instance initializer. The compiler reports this error on the line where volume is set.

 On the exam, be wary of any instance variables marked final. Make sure they are assigned a value in the line where they are declared, in an instance initializer, or in a constructor. They should be assigned a value only once, and failure to assign a value is considered a compiler error in the constructor.

What about final instance variables when a constructor calls another constructor in the same class? In that case, you have to follow the constructor logic pathway carefully, making sure every final instance variable is assigned a value exactly once. We can replace our previous bad constructor with the following one that does compile:

```
public MouseHouse() {
    this(null);
}
```

This constructor does not perform any assignments to any final instance variables, but it calls the MouseHouse(String) constructor, which we observed compiles without issue. We use null here to demonstrate that the variable does not need to be an object value. We can assign a null value to final instance variables, so long as they are explicitly set.

Order of Initialization

In Chapter 2, we presented the order of initialization. With inheritance, though, the order of initialization for an instance gets a bit more complicated. We'll start with how to initialize the class and then expand to initializing the instance.

Class Initialization

First, you need to initialize the class, which involves invoking all static members in the class hierarchy, starting with the highest superclass and working downward. This is often referred to as loading the class. The JVM controls when the class is initialized, although you can assume the class is loaded before it is used. The class may be initialized when the program first starts, when a static member of the class is referenced, or shortly before an instance of the class is created.

The most important rule with class initialization is that it happens at most once for each class. The class may also never be loaded if it is not used in the program. We summarize the order of initialization for a class as follows:

Initialize Class X

1. If there is a superclass Y of X, then initialize class Y first.

2. Process all `static` variable declarations in the order they appear in the class.

3. Process all `static` initializers in the order they appear in the class.

Taking a look at an example, what does the following program print?

```
public class Animal {
   static { System.out.print("A"); }
}
```

```
public class Hippo extends Animal {
   static { System.out.print("B"); }
   public static void main(String[] grass) {
      System.out.print("C");
      new Hippo();
      new Hippo();
      new Hippo();
   }
}
```

It prints ABC exactly once. Since the main() method is inside the Hippo class, the class will be initialized first, starting with the superclass and printing AB. Afterward, the main() method is executed, printing C. Even though the main() method creates three instances, the class is loaded only once.

Why the Hippo Program Printed *C* After *AB*

In the previous example, the Hippo class was initialized before the main() method was executed. This happened because our main() method was inside the class being executed, so it had to be loaded on startup. What if you instead called Hippo inside another program?

```
public class HippoFriend {
   public static void main(String[] grass) {
      System.out.print("C");
      new Hippo();
   }
}
```

Assuming the class isn't referenced anywhere else, this program will likely print CAB, with the Hippo class not being loaded until it is needed inside the main() method. We say *likely*, because the rules for when classes are loaded are determined by the JVM at runtime. For the exam, you just need to know that a class must be initialized before it is referenced or used. Also, the class containing the program entry point, aka the main() method, is loaded before the main() method is executed.

Instance Initialization

An instance is initialized anytime the new keyword is used. In our previous example, there were three new Hippo() calls, resulting in three Hippo instances being initialized. Instance initialization is a bit more complicated than class initialization, because a class or super-class may have many constructors declared but only a handful used as part of instance initialization.

First, start at the lowest-level constructor where the new keyword is used. Remember, the first line of every constructor is a call to this() or super(), and if omitted, the compiler will automatically insert a call to the parent no-argument constructor super(). Then, progress upward and note the order of constructors. Finally, initialize each class starting with the superclass, processing each instance initializer and constructor in the reverse order in which it was called. We summarize the order of initialization for an instance as follows:

Initialize Instance of X

1. If there is a superclass Y of X, then initialize the instance of Y first.
2. Process all instance variable declarations in the order they appear in the class.
3. Process all instance initializers in the order they appear in the class.
4. Initialize the constructor including any overloaded constructors referenced with this().

Let's try a simple example with no inheritance. See if you can figure out what the following application outputs:

```
1:   public class ZooTickets {
2:       private String name = "BestZoo";
3:       { System.out.print(name+"-"); }
4:       private static int COUNT = 0;
5:       static { System.out.print(COUNT+"-"); }
6:       static { COUNT += 10; System.out.print(COUNT+"-"); }
7:
8:       public ZooTickets() {
9:           System.out.print("z-");
10:      }
11:
12:      public static void main(String... patrons) {
```

```
13:        new ZooTickets();
14:    }
15: }
```

The output is as follows:

```
0-10-BestZoo-z-
```

First, we have to initialize the class. Since there is no superclass declared, which means the superclass is Object, we can start with the static components of ZooTickets. In this case, lines 4, 5, and 6 are executed, printing 0- and 10-. Next, we initialize the instance. Again, since there is no superclass declared, we start with the instance components. Lines 2 and 3 are executed, which prints BestZoo-. Finally, we run the constructor on lines 8–10, which outputs z-.

Next, let's try a simple example with inheritance.

```
class Primate {
    public Primate() {
        System.out.print("Primate-");
    }
}

class Ape extends Primate {
    public Ape(int fur) {
        System.out.print("Ape1-");
    }
    public Ape() {
        System.out.print("Ape2-");
    }
}

public class Chimpanzee extends Ape {
    public Chimpanzee() {
        super(2);
        System.out.print("Chimpanzee-");
    }
    public static void main(String[] args) {
        new Chimpanzee();
    }
}
```

The compiler inserts the super() command as the first statement of both the Primate and Ape constructors. The code will execute with the parent constructors called first and yields the following output:

```
Primate-Ape1-Chimpanzee-
```

Notice that only one of the two Ape() constructors is called. You need to start with the call to new Chimpanzee() to determine which constructors will be executed. Remember, constructors are executed from the bottom up, but since the first line of every constructor is a call to another constructor, the flow actually ends up with the parent constructor executed before the child constructor.

The next example is a little harder. What do you think happens here?

```
1:  public class Cuttlefish {
2:      private String name = "swimmy";
3:      { System.out.println(name); }
4:      private static int COUNT = 0;
5:      static { System.out.println(COUNT); }
6:      { COUNT++; System.out.println(COUNT); }
7:
8:      public Cuttlefish() {
9:          System.out.println("Constructor");
10:     }
11:
12:     public static void main(String[] args) {
13:         System.out.println("Ready");
14:         new Cuttlefish();
15:     }
16: }
```

The output looks like this:

```
0
Ready
swimmy
1
Constructor
```

There is no superclass declared, so we can skip any steps that relate to inheritance. We first process the static variables and static initializers—lines 4 and 5, with line 5 printing 0. Now that the static initializers are out of the way, the main() method can run, which prints Ready. Lines 2, 3, and 6 are processed, with line 3 printing swimmy and line 6 printing 1. Finally, the constructor is run on lines 8–10, which print Constructor.

Ready for a more difficult example? What does the following output?

```
1:  class GiraffeFamily {
2:      static { System.out.print("A"); }
3:      { System.out.print("B"); }
4:
5:      public GiraffeFamily(String name) {
```

```
6:          this(1);
7:          System.out.print("C");
8:      }
9:
10:     public GiraffeFamily() {
11:         System.out.print("D");
12:     }
13:
14:     public GiraffeFamily(int stripes) {
15:         System.out.print("E");
16:     }
17: }
18: public class Okapi extends GiraffeFamily {
19:     static { System.out.print("F"); }
20:
21:     public Okapi(int stripes) {
22:         super("sugar");
23:         System.out.print("G");
24:     }
25:     { System.out.print("H"); }
26:
27:     public static void main(String[] grass) {
28:         new Okapi(1);
29:         System.out.println();
30:         new Okapi(2);
31:     }
32: }
```

The program prints the following:

```
AFBECHG
BECHG
```

Let's walk through it. Start with initializing the Okapi class. Since it has a superclass GiraffeFamily, initialize it first, printing A on line 2. Next, initialize the Okapi class, printing F on line 19.

After the classes are initialized, execute the main() method on line 27. The first line of the main() method creates a new Okapi object, triggering the instance initialization process. Per the first rule, the superclass instance of GiraffeFamily is initialized first. Per our third rule, the instance initializer in the superclass GiraffeFamily is called, and B is printed on line 3. Per the fourth rule, we initialize the constructors. In this case, this involves calling the constructor on line 5, which in turn calls the overloaded constructor on line 14. The result is that EC is printed, as the constructor bodies are unwound in the reverse order that they were called.

The process then continues with the initialization of the Okapi instance itself. Per the third and fourth rules, H is printed on line 25, and G is printed on line 23, respectively. The process is a lot simpler when you don't have to call any overloaded constructors. Line 29 then inserts a line break in the output. Finally, line 30 initializes a new Okapi object. The order and initialization are the same as line 28, sans the class initialization, so BECHG is printed again. Notice that D is never printed, as only two of the three constructors in the superclass GiraffeFamily are called.

This example is tricky for a few reasons. There are multiple overloaded constructors, lots of initializers, and a complex constructor pathway to keep track of. Luckily, questions like this are rare on the exam. If you see one, just write down what is going on as you read the code.

Reviewing Constructor Rules

Let's review some of the most important constructor rules that we covered in this part of the chapter.

1. The first statement of every constructor is a call to an overloaded constructor via this(), or a direct parent constructor via super().

2. If the first statement of a constructor is not a call to this() or super(), then the compiler will insert a no-argument super() as the first statement of the constructor.

3. Calling this() and super() after the first statement of a constructor results in a compiler error.

4. If the parent class doesn't have a no-argument constructor, then every constructor in the child class must start with an explicit this() or super() constructor call.

5. If the parent class doesn't have a no-argument constructor and the child doesn't define any constructors, then the child class will not compile.

6. If a class only defines private constructors, then it cannot be extended by a top-level class.

7. All final instance variables must be assigned a value exactly once by the end of the constructor. Any final instance variables not assigned a value will be reported as a compiler error on the line the constructor is declared.

Make sure you understand these rules. The exam will often provide code that breaks one or many of these rules and therefore doesn't compile.

When taking the exam, pay close attention to any question involving two or more classes related by inheritance. Before even attempting to answer the question, you should check that the constructors are properly defined using the previous set of rules. You should also verify the classes include valid access modifiers for members. Once those are verified, you can continue answering the question.

Inheriting Members

Now that we've created a class, what can we do with it? One of Java's biggest strengths is leveraging its inheritance model to simplify code. For example, let's say you have five animal classes that each extend from the Animal class. Furthermore, each class defines an eat() method with identical implementations. In this scenario, it's a lot better to define eat() once in the Animal class with the proper access modifiers than to have to maintain the same method in five separate classes. As you'll also see in this section, Java allows any of the five subclasses to replace, or override, the parent method implementation at runtime.

Calling Inherited Members

Java classes may use any public or protected member of the parent class, including methods, primitives, or object references. If the parent class and child class are part of the same package, then the child class may also use any package-private members defined in the parent class. Finally, a child class may never access a private member of the parent class, at least not through any direct reference. As you saw earlier in this chapter, a private member age was accessed indirectly via a public or protected method.

To reference a member in a parent class, you can just call it directly, as in the following example with the output function displaySharkDetails():

```java
class Fish {
    protected int size;
    private int age;

    public Fish(int age) {
        this.age = age;
    }

    public int getAge() {
        return age;
    }
}

public class Shark extends Fish {
    private int numberOfFins = 8;

    public Shark(int age) {
        super(age);
        this.size = 4;
    }

    public void displaySharkDetails() {
```

```
        System.out.print("Shark with age: "+getAge());
        System.out.print(" and "+size+" meters long");
        System.out.print(" with "+numberOfFins+" fins");
    }
}
```

In the child class, we use the `public` method `getAge()` and `protected` member `size` to access values in the parent class. Remember, you can use `this` to access visible members of the current or a parent class, and you can use `super` to access visible members of a parent class.

```
public void displaySharkDetails() {
    System.out.print("Shark with age: "+super.getAge());
    System.out.print(" and "+super.size+" meters long");
    System.out.print(" with "+this.numberOfFins+" fins");
}
```

In this example, `getAge()` and `size` can be accessed with `this` or `super` since they are defined in the parent class, while `numberOfFins` can only be accessed with `this` and not `super` since it is not an inherited property.

Inheriting Methods

Inheriting a class not only grants access to inherited methods in the parent class but also sets the stage for collisions between methods defined in both the parent class and the subclass. In this section, we'll review the rules for method inheritance and how Java handles such scenarios.

Overriding a Method

What if there is a method defined in both the parent and child classes with the same signature? For example, you may want to define a new version of the method and have it behave differently for that subclass. The solution is to override the method in the child class. In Java, *overriding* a method occurs when a subclass declares a new implementation for an inherited method with the same signature and compatible return type. Remember that a method signature includes the name of the method and method parameters.

When you override a method, you may reference the parent version of the method using the super keyword. In this manner, the keywords `this` and `super` allow you to select between the current and parent versions of a method, respectively. We illustrate this with the following example:

```
public class Canine {
    public double getAverageWeight() {
        return 50;
    }
}
```

```
public class Wolf extends Canine {
   public double getAverageWeight() {
      return super.getAverageWeight()+20;
   }
   public static void main(String[] args) {
      System.out.println(new Canine().getAverageWeight());
      System.out.println(new Wolf().getAverageWeight());
   }
}
```

In this example, in which the child class `Wolf` overrides the parent class `Canine`, the method `getAverageWeight()` runs, and the program displays the following:

```
50.0
70.0
```

Method Overriding and Recursive Calls

You might be wondering whether the use of `super` in the previous example was required. For example, what would the following code output if we removed the `super` keyword?

```
public double getAverageWeight() {
   return getAverageWeight()+20;  // StackOverflowError
}
```

In this example, the compiler would not call the parent `Canine` method; it would call the current `Wolf` method since it would think you were executing a recursive method call. A *recursive method* is one that calls itself as part of execution. It is common in programming but must have a termination condition that triggers the end to recursion at some point or depth. In this example, there is no termination condition; therefore, the application will attempt to call itself infinitely and produce a `StackOverflowError` at runtime.

To override a method, you must follow a number of rules. The compiler performs the following checks when you override a method:

1. The method in the child class must have the same signature as the method in the parent class.

2. The method in the child class must be at least as accessible as the method in the parent class.

3. The method in the child class may not declare a checked exception that is new or broader than the class of any exception declared in the parent class method.

4. If the method returns a value, it must be the same or a subtype of the method in the parent class, known as *covariant return types*.

Defining Subtype and Supertype

When discussing inheritance and polymorphism, we often use the word *subtype* rather than *subclass*, since Java includes interfaces. A *subtype* is the relationship between two types where one type inherits the other. If we define X to be a subtype of Y, then one of the following is true:

▪ X and Y are classes, and X is a subclass of Y.

▪ X and Y are interfaces, and X is a subinterface of Y.

▪ X is a class and Y is an interface, and X implements Y (either directly or through an inherited class).

Likewise, a *supertype* is the reciprocal relationship between two types where one type is the ancestor of the other. Remember, a subclass is a subtype, but not all subtypes are subclasses.

The first rule of overriding a method is somewhat self-explanatory. If two methods have the same name but different signatures, the methods are overloaded, not overridden. Overloaded methods are considered independent and do not share the same polymorphic properties as overridden methods.

Overloading vs. Overriding

Overloading and overriding a method are similar in that they both involve redefining a method using the same name. They differ in that an overloaded method will use a different list of method parameters. This distinction allows overloaded methods a great deal more freedom in syntax than an overridden method would have. For example, compare the overloaded fly() with the overridden eat() in the Eagle class.

```java
public class Bird {
   public void fly() {
      System.out.println("Bird is flying");
   }
   public void eat(int food) {
      System.out.println("Bird is eating "+food+" units of food");
   }
}

public class Eagle extends Bird {
   public int fly(int height) {
      System.out.println("Bird is flying at "+height+" meters");
```

```
        return height;
    }
    public int eat(int food) {  // DOES NOT COMPILE
        System.out.println("Bird is eating "+food+" units of food");
        return food;
    }
}
```

The fly() method is overloaded in the subclass Eagle, since the signature changes from a no-argument method to a method with one int argument. Because the method is being overloaded and not overridden, the return type can be changed from void to int.

The eat() method is overridden in the subclass Eagle, since the signature is the same as it is in the parent class Bird—they both take a single argument int. Because the method is being overridden, the return type of the method in the Eagle class must be compatible with the return type for the method in the Bird class. In this example, the return type int is not a subtype of void; therefore, the compiler will throw an exception on this method definition.

Any time you see a method on the exam with the same name as a method in the parent class, determine whether the method is being overloaded or overridden first; doing so will help you with questions about whether the code will compile.

What's the purpose of the second rule about access modifiers? Let's try an illustrative example:

```
public class Camel {
    public int getNumberOfHumps() {
        return 1;
    }
}

public class BactrianCamel extends Camel {
    private int getNumberOfHumps() {  // DOES NOT COMPILE
        return 2;
    }
}

public class Rider {
    public static void main(String[] args) {
        Camel c = new BactrianCamel();
        System.out.print(c.getNumberOfHumps());
    }
}
```

In this example, BactrianCamel attempts to override the getNumberOfHumps() method defined in the parent class but fails because the access modifier private is more restrictive than the one defined in the parent version of the method. Let's say BactrianCamel was allowed to compile, though. Would the call to getNumberOfHumps() in Rider.main() succeed or fail? As you will see when we get into polymorphism later in this chapter, the answer is quite ambiguous. The reference type for the object is Camel, where the method is declared public, but the object is actually an instance of type BactrianCamel, which is declared private. Java avoids these types of ambiguity problems by limiting overriding a method to access modifiers that are as accessible or more accessible than the version in the inherited method.

The third rule says that overriding a method cannot declare new checked exceptions or checked exceptions broader than the inherited method. This is done for similar polymorphic reasons as limiting access modifiers. In other words, you could end up with an object that is more restrictive than the reference type it is assigned to, resulting in a checked exception that is not handled or declared. We will discuss what it means for an exception to be checked in Chapter 10, "Exceptions." For now, you should just recognize that if a broader checked exception is declared in the overriding method, the code will not compile. Let's try an example:

```
public class Reptile {
    protected void sleepInShell() throws IOException {}

    protected void hideInShell() throws NumberFormatException {}

    protected void exitShell() throws FileNotFoundException {}
}

public class GalapagosTortoise extends Reptile {
    public void sleepInShell() throws FileNotFoundException {}

    public void hideInShell() throws IllegalArgumentException {}

    public void exitShell() throws IOException {} // DOES NOT COMPILE
}
```

In this example, we have three overridden methods. These overridden methods use the more accessible public modifier, which is allowed per our second rule over overridden methods. The overridden sleepInShell() method declares FileNotFoundException, which is a subclass of the exception declared in the inherited method, IOException. Per our third rule of overridden methods, this is a successful override since the exception is narrower in the overridden method.

The overridden hideInShell() method declares an IllegalArgumentException, which is a superclass of the exception declared in the inherited method, NumberFormatException. While this seems like an invalid override since the overridden method uses a broader exception, both of these exceptions are unchecked, so the third rule does not apply.

The third overridden exitShell() method declares IOException, which is a superclass of the exception declared in the inherited method, FileNotFoundException. Since these are checked exceptions and IOException is broader, the overridden exitShell() method does not compile in the GalapagosTortoise class. We'll revisit these exception classes, including memorizing which ones are subclasses of each other, in Chapter 10.

The fourth and final rule around overriding a method is probably the most complicated, as it requires knowing the relationships between the return types. The overriding method must use a return type that is covariant with the return type of the inherited method.

Let's try an example for illustrative purposes:

```
public class Rhino {
    protected CharSequence getName() {
        return "rhino";
    }
    protected String getColor() {
        return "grey, black, or white";
    }
}

class JavanRhino extends Rhino {
    public String getName() {
        return "javan rhino";
    }
    public CharSequence getColor() {  // DOES NOT COMPILE
        return "grey";
    }
}
```

The subclass JavanRhino attempts to override two methods from Rhino: getName() and getColor(). Both overridden methods have the same name and signature as the inherited methods. The overridden methods also have a broader access modifier, public, than the inherited methods. Per the second rule, a broader access modifier is acceptable.

From Chapter 5, you should already know that String implements the CharSequence interface, making String a subtype of CharSequence. Therefore, the return type of getName() in JavanRhino is covariant with the return type of getName() in Rhino.

On the other hand, the overridden getColor() method does not compile because CharSequence is not a subtype of String. To put it another way, all String values are CharSequence values, but not all CharSequence values are String values. For example, a StringBuilder is a CharSequence but not a String. For the exam, you need to know if the return type of the overriding method is the same or a subtype of the return type of the inherited method.

> A simple test for covariance is the following: Given an inherited return type A and an overriding return type B, can you assign an instance of B to a reference variable for A without a cast? If so, then they are covariant. This rule applies to primitive types and object types alike. If one of the return types is void, then they both must be void, as nothing is covariant with void except itself.

The last three rules of overriding a method may seem arbitrary or confusing at first, but as you'll see later in this chapter when we discuss polymorphism, they are needed for consistency. Without these rules in place, it is possible to create contradictions within the Java language.

Overriding a Generic Method

Overriding methods is complicated enough, but add generics to it and things only get more challenging. In this section, we'll provide a discussion of the aspects of overriding generic methods that you'll need to know for the exam.

Review of Overloading a Generic Method

In Chapter 7, you learned that you cannot overload methods by changing the generic type due to type erasure. To review, only one of the two methods is allowed in a class because type erasure will reduce both sets of arguments to (List input).

```
public class LongTailAnimal {
   protected void chew(List<Object> input) {}
   protected void chew(List<Double> input) {}  // DOES NOT COMPILE
}
```

For the same reason, you also can't overload a generic method in a parent class.

```
public class LongTailAnimal {
   protected void chew(List<Object> input) {}
}

public class Anteater extends LongTailAnimal {
   protected void chew(List<Double> input) {}  // DOES NOT COMPILE
}
```

Both of these examples fail to compile because of type erasure. In the compiled form, the generic type is dropped, and it appears as an invalid overloaded method.

Generic Method Parameters

On the other hand, you can override a method with generic parameters, but you must match the signature including the generic type exactly. For example, this version of the

Anteater class does compile because it uses the same generic type in the overridden method as the one defined in the parent class:

```
public class LongTailAnimal {
    protected void chew(List<String> input) {}
}

public class Anteater extends LongTailAnimal {
    protected void chew(List<String> input) {}
}
```

The generic type parameters have to match, but what about the generic class or interface? Take a look at the following example. From what you know so far, do you think these classes will compile?

```
public class LongTailAnimal {
    protected void chew(List<Object> input) {}
}

public class Anteater extends LongTailAnimal {
    protected void chew(ArrayList<Double> input) {}
}
```

Yes, these classes do compile. However, they are considered overloaded methods, not overridden methods, because the signature is not the same. Type erasure does not change the fact that one of the method arguments is a List and the other is an ArrayList.

Generics and Wildcards

Java includes support for generic wildcards using the question mark (?) character. It even supports bounded wildcards.

```
void sing1(List<?> v) {}                // unbounded wildcard
void sing2(List<? super String> v) {}   // lower bounded wildcard
void sing3(List<? extends String> v) {} // upper bounded wildcard
```

Using generics with wildcards, overloaded methods, and overridden methods can get quite complicated. Luckily, wildcards are out of scope for the 1Z0-815 exam. They are required knowledge, though, when you take the 1Z0-816 exam.

Generic Return Types

When you're working with overridden methods that return generics, the return values must be covariant. In terms of generics, this means that the return type of the class or interface declared in the overriding method must be a subtype of the class defined in the parent class. The generic parameter type must match its parent's type exactly.

Given the following declaration for the `Mammal` class, which of the two subclasses, `Monkey` and `Goat`, compile?

```
public class Mammal {
    public List<CharSequence> play() { ... }
    public CharSequence sleep() { ... }
}

public class Monkey extends Mammal {
    public ArrayList<CharSequence> play() { ... }
}

public class Goat extends Mammal {
    public List<String> play() { ... }  // DOES NOT COMPILE
    public String sleep() { ... }
}
```

The `Monkey` class compiles because `ArrayList` is a subtype of `List`. The `play()` method in the `Goat` class does not compile, though. For the return types to be covariant, the generic type parameter must match. Even though `String` is a subtype of `CharSequence`, it does not exactly match the generic type defined in the `Mammal` class. Therefore, this is considered an invalid override.

Notice that the `sleep()` method in the `Goat` class does compile since `String` is a subtype of `CharSequence`. This example shows that covariance applies to the return type, just not the generic parameter type.

For the exam, it might be helpful for you to apply type erasure to questions involving generics to ensure that they compile properly. Once you've determined which methods are overridden and which are being overloaded, work backward, making sure the generic types match for overridden methods. And remember, generic methods cannot be overloaded by changing the generic parameter type only.

Redeclaring *private* Methods

What happens if you try to override a `private` method? In Java, you can't override `private` methods since they are not inherited. Just because a child class doesn't have access to the parent method doesn't mean the child class can't define its own version of the method. It just means, strictly speaking, that the new method is not an overridden version of the parent class's method.

Java permits you to redeclare a new method in the child class with the same or modified signature as the method in the parent class. This method in the child class is a separate and independent method, unrelated to the parent version's method, so none of the rules for overriding methods is invoked. Let's return to the Camel example we used in the previous section and show two related classes that define the same method:

```
public class Camel {
    private String getNumberOfHumps() {
        return "Undefined";
    }
}

public class DromedaryCamel extends Camel {
    private int getNumberOfHumps() {
        return 1;
    }
}
```

This code compiles without issue. Notice that the return type differs in the child method from String to int. In this example, the method getNumberOfHumps() in the parent class is redeclared, so the method in the child class is a new method and not an override of the method in the parent class. As you saw in the previous section, if the method in the parent class were public or protected, the method in the child class would not compile because it would violate two rules of overriding methods. The parent method in this example is private, so there are no such issues.

Hiding Static Methods

A *hidden method* occurs when a child class defines a static method with the same name and signature as an inherited static method defined in a parent class. Method hiding is similar but not exactly the same as method overriding. The previous four rules for overriding a method must be followed when a method is hidden. In addition, a new rule is added for hiding a method:

5. The method defined in the child class must be marked as static if it is marked as static in a parent class.

Put simply, it is method hiding if the two methods are marked static, and method overriding if they are not marked static. If one is marked static and the other is not, the class will not compile.

Let's review some examples of the new rule:

```
public class Bear {
    public static void eat() {
        System.out.println("Bear is eating");
    }
}

public class Panda extends Bear {
```

```
   public static void eat() {
      System.out.println("Panda is chewing");
   }
   public static void main(String[] args) {
      eat();
   }
}
```

In this example, the code compiles and runs. The eat() method in the Panda class hides the eat() method in the Bear class, printing "Panda is chewing" at runtime. Because they are both marked as static, this is not considered an overridden method. That said, there is still some inheritance going on. If you remove the eat() method in the Panda class, then the program prints "Bear is eating" at runtime.

Let's contrast this with an example that violates the fifth rule:

```
public class Bear {
   public static void sneeze() {
      System.out.println("Bear is sneezing");
   }
   public void hibernate() {
      System.out.println("Bear is hibernating");
   }
   public static void laugh() {
      System.out.println("Bear is laughing");
   }
}

public class Panda extends Bear {
   public void sneeze() {              // DOES NOT COMPILE
      System.out.println("Panda sneezes quietly");
   }
   public static void hibernate() { // DOES NOT COMPILE
      System.out.println("Panda is going to sleep");
   }
   protected static void laugh() {  // DOES NOT COMPILE
      System.out.println("Panda is laughing");
   }
}
```

In this example, sneeze() is marked static in the parent class but not in the child class. The compiler detects that you're trying to override using an instance method. However, sneeze() is a static method that should be hidden, causing the compiler to generate an error. In the second method, hibernate() is an instance member in the parent class but a static method in the child class. In this scenario, the compiler thinks that you're trying to hide a static method. Because hibernate() is an instance method that should be overridden, the compiler generates an error. Finally, the laugh() method does not compile. Even though both versions of method are marked static, the version in Panda has a more restrictive access modifier than the one it inherits, and it breaks the second rule for overriding methods. Remember, the four rules for overriding methods must be followed when hiding static methods.

Creating *final* Methods

We conclude our discussion of method inheritance with a somewhat self-explanatory rule—final methods cannot be replaced.

By marking a method final, you forbid a child class from replacing this method. This rule is in place both when you override a method and when you hide a method. In other words, you cannot hide a static method in a child class if it is marked final in the parent class.

Let's take a look at an example:

```
public class Bird {
   public final boolean hasFeathers() {
      return true;
   }
   public final static void flyAway() {}
}

public class Penguin extends Bird {
   public final boolean hasFeathers() {  // DOES NOT COMPILE
      return false;
   }
   public final static void flyAway() {}  // DOES NOT COMPILE
}
```

In this example, the instance method hasFeathers() is marked as final in the parent class Bird, so the child class Penguin cannot override the parent method, resulting in a compiler error. The static method flyAway() is also marked final, so it cannot be hidden in the subclass. In this example, whether or not the child method used the final keyword is irrelevant—the code will not compile either way.

This rule applies only to inherited methods. For example, if the two methods were marked private in the parent Bird class, then the Penguin class, as defined, would compile. In that case, the private methods would be redeclared, not overridden or hidden.

Real World Scenario

Why Mark a Method as *final*?

Although marking methods as final prevents them from being overridden, it does have advantages in practice. For example, you'd mark a method as final when you're defining a parent class and want to guarantee certain behavior of a method in the parent class, regardless of which child is invoking the method.

In the previous example with Bird, the author of the parent class may want to ensure the method hasFeathers() always returns true, regardless of the child class instance on which it is invoked. The author is confident that there is no example of a Bird in which feathers are not present.

The reason methods are not commonly marked as final in practice, though, is that it may be difficult for the author of a parent class method to consider all of the possible ways her child class may be used. For example, although all adult birds have feathers, a baby chick doesn't; therefore, if you have an instance of a Bird that is a chick, it would not have feathers. For this reason, the final modifier is often used when the author of the parent class wants to guarantee certain behavior at the cost of limiting polymorphism.

Hiding Variables

As you saw with method overriding, there are a lot of rules when two methods have the same signature and are defined in both the parent and child classes. Luckily, the rules for variables with the same name in the parent and child classes are a lot simpler. In fact, Java doesn't allow variables to be overridden. Variables can be hidden, though.

A *hidden variable* occurs when a child class defines a variable with the same name as an inherited variable defined in the parent class. This creates two distinct copies of the variable within an instance of the child class: one instance defined in the parent class and one defined in the child class.

As when hiding a static method, you can't override a variable; you can only hide it. Let's take a look at a hidden variable. What do you think the following application prints?

```
class Carnivore {
    protected boolean hasFur = false;
}

public class Meerkat extends Carnivore {
    protected boolean hasFur = true;

    public static void main(String[] args) {
        Meerkat m = new Meerkat();
        Carnivore c = m;
        System.out.println(m.hasFur);
```

```
        System.out.println(c.hasFur);
    }
}
```

It prints `true` followed by `false`. Confused? Both of these classes define a `hasFur` variable, but with different values. Even though there is only one object created by the `main()` method, both variables exist independently of each other. The output changes depending on the reference variable used.

If you didn't understand the last example, don't worry. The next section on polymorphism will expand on how overriding and hiding differ. For now, you just need to know that overriding a method replaces the parent method on all reference variables (other than super), whereas hiding a method or variable replaces the member only if a child reference type is used.

Understanding Polymorphism

Java supports *polymorphism*, the property of an object to take on many different forms. To put this more precisely, a Java object may be accessed using a reference with the same type as the object, a reference that is a superclass of the object, or a reference that defines an interface the object implements, either directly or through a superclass. Furthermore, a cast is not required if the object is being reassigned to a super type or interface of the object.

Interface Primer

We'll be discussing interfaces in detail in the next chapter. For this chapter, you need to know the following:

- An interface can define `abstract` methods.

- A class can implement any number of interfaces.

- A class implements an interface by overriding the inherited `abstract` methods.

- An object that implements an interface can be assigned to a reference for that interface.

As you'll see in the next chapter, the same rules for overriding methods and polymorphism apply.

Let's illustrate this polymorphism property with the following example:

```
public class Primate {
    public boolean hasHair() {
        return true;
```

```
      }
}
public interface HasTail {
    public abstract boolean isTailStriped();
}
public class Lemur extends Primate implements HasTail {
    public boolean isTailStriped() {
        return false;
    }
    public int age = 10;
    public static void main(String[] args) {
        Lemur lemur = new Lemur();
        System.out.println(lemur.age);

        HasTail hasTail = lemur;
        System.out.println(hasTail.isTailStriped());

        Primate primate = lemur;
        System.out.println(primate.hasHair());
    }
}
```

This code compiles and prints the following output:

```
10
false
true
```

The most important thing to note about this example is that only one object, Lemur, is created and referenced. Polymorphism enables an instance of Lemur to be reassigned or passed to a method using one of its supertypes, such as Primate or HasTail.

Once the object has been assigned to a new reference type, only the methods and variables available to that reference type are callable on the object without an explicit cast. For example, the following snippets of code will not compile:

```
        HasTail hasTail = lemur;
        System.out.println(hasTail.age);          // DOES NOT COMPILE

        Primate primate = lemur;
        System.out.println(primate.isTailStriped()); // DOES NOT COMPILE
```

In this example, the reference hasTail has direct access only to methods defined with the HasTail interface; therefore, it doesn't know the variable age is part of the object. Likewise, the reference primate has access only to methods defined in the Primate class, and it doesn't have direct access to the isTailStriped() method.

Object vs. Reference

In Java, all objects are accessed by reference, so as a developer you never have direct access to the object itself. Conceptually, though, you should consider the object as the entity that exists in memory, allocated by the Java runtime environment. Regardless of the type of the reference you have for the object in memory, the object itself doesn't change. For example, since all objects inherit java.lang.Object, they can all be reassigned to java.lang.Object, as shown in the following example:

```
Lemur lemur = new Lemur();

Object lemurAsObject = lemur;
```

Even though the Lemur object has been assigned to a reference with a different type, the object itself has not changed and still exists as a Lemur object in memory. What has changed, then, is our ability to access methods within the Lemur class with the lemurAsObject reference. Without an explicit cast back to Lemur, as you'll see in the next section, we no longer have access to the Lemur properties of the object.

We can summarize this principle with the following two rules:

1. The type of the object determines which properties exist within the object in memory.

2. The type of the reference to the object determines which methods and variables are accessible to the Java program.

It therefore follows that successfully changing a reference of an object to a new reference type may give you access to new properties of the object, but remember, those properties existed before the reference change occurred.

Let's illustrate this property using the previous example in Figure 8.4.

FIGURE 8.4   Object vs. reference

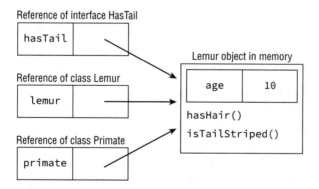

As you can see in the figure, the same object exists in memory regardless of which reference is pointing to it. Depending on the type of the reference, we may only have access to certain methods. For example, the hasTail reference has access to the method isTailStriped() but doesn't have access to the variable age defined in the Lemur class.

As you'll learn in the next section, it is possible to reclaim access to the variable age by explicitly casting the hasTail reference to a reference of type Lemur.

Casting Objects

In the previous example, we created a single instance of a Lemur object and accessed it via superclass and interface references. Once we changed the reference type, though, we lost access to more specific members defined in the subclass that still exist within the object. We can reclaim those references by casting the object back to the specific subclass it came from:

```
Primate primate = new Lemur();   // Implicit Cast

Lemur lemur2 = primate;          // DOES NOT COMPILE
System.out.println(lemur2.age);

Lemur lemur3 = (Lemur)primate;   // Explicit Cast
System.out.println(lemur3.age);
```

In this example, we first create a Lemur object and implicitly cast it to a Primate reference. Since Lemur is a subclass of Primate, this can be done without a cast operator. Next, we try to convert the primate reference back to a lemur reference, lemur2, without an explicit cast. The result is that the code will not compile. In the second example, though, we explicitly cast the object to a subclass of the object Primate, and we gain access to all the methods and fields available to the Lemur class.

Casting objects is similar to casting primitives, as you saw in Chapter 3, "Operators." When casting objects, you do not need a cast operator if the current reference is a subtype of the target type. This is referred to as an implicit cast or type conversion. Alternatively, if the current reference is not a subtype of the target type, then you need to perform an explicit cast with a compatible type. If the underlying object is not compatible with the type, then a ClassCastException will be thrown at runtime.

We summarize these concepts into a set of rules for you to memorize for the exam:

1. Casting a reference from a subtype to a supertype doesn't require an explicit cast.

2. Casting a reference from a supertype to a subtype requires an explicit cast.

3. The compiler disallows casts to an unrelated class.

4. At runtime, an invalid cast of a reference to an unrelated type results in a ClassCastException being thrown.

The third rule is important; the exam may try to trick you with a cast that the compiler doesn't allow. In our previous example, we were able to cast a Primate reference to a Lemur reference, because Lemur is a subclass of Primate and therefore related. Consider this example instead:

```
public class Bird {}

public class Fish {
    public static void main(String[] args) {
```

```
        Fish fish = new Fish();
        Bird bird = (Bird)fish;  // DOES NOT COMPILE
    }
}
```

In this example, the classes `Fish` and `Bird` are not related through any class hierarchy that the compiler is aware of; therefore, the code will not compile. While they both extend `Object` implicitly, they are considered unrelated types since one cannot be a subtype of the other.

 While the compiler can enforce rules about casting to unrelated types for classes, it cannot do the same for interfaces, since a subclass may implement the interface. We'll revisit this topic in the next chapter. For now, you just need to know the third rule on casting applies to class types only, not interfaces.

Casting is not without its limitations. Even though two classes share a related hierarchy, that doesn't mean an instance of one can automatically be cast to another. Here's an example:

```
public class Rodent {}

public class Capybara extends Rodent {
    public static void main(String[] args) {
        Rodent rodent = new Rodent();
        Capybara capybara = (Capybara)rodent;  // ClassCastException
    }
}
```

This code creates an instance of `Rodent` and then tries to cast it to a subclass of `Rodent`, `Capybara`. Although this code will compile, it will throw a `ClassCastException` at runtime since the object being referenced is not an instance of the `Capybara` class. The thing to keep in mind in this example is the `Rodent` object created does not inherit the `Capybara` class in any way.

When reviewing a question on the exam that involves casting and polymorphism, be sure to remember what the instance of the object actually is. Then, focus on whether the compiler will allow the object to be referenced with or without explicit casts.

The *instanceof* Operator

In Chapter 3, we presented the `instanceof` operator, which can be used to check whether an object belongs to a particular class or interface and to prevent `ClassCastExceptions` at runtime. Unlike the previous example, the following code snippet doesn't throw an exception at runtime and performs the cast only if the instanceof operator returns true:

```
if(rodent instanceof Capybara) {
    Capybara capybara = (Capybara)rodent;
}
```

Just as the compiler does not allow casting an object to unrelated types, it also does not allow instanceof to be used with unrelated types. We can demonstrate this with our unrelated Bird and Fish classes:

```
public static void main(String[] args) {
    Fish fish = new Fish();
    if (fish instanceof Bird) {  // DOES NOT COMPILE
        Bird bird = (Bird) fish;  // DOES NOT COMPILE
    }
}
```

In this snippet, neither the instanceof operator nor the explicit cast operation compile.

Polymorphism and Method Overriding

In Java, polymorphism states that when you override a method, you replace all calls to it, even those defined in the parent class. As an example, what do you think the following code snippet outputs?

```
class Penguin {
    public int getHeight() { return 3; }
    public void printInfo() {
        System.out.print(this.getHeight());
    }
}

public class EmperorPenguin extends Penguin {
    public int getHeight() { return 8; }
    public static void main(String []fish) {
        new EmperorPenguin().printInfo();
    }
}
```

If you said 8, then you are well on your way to understanding polymorphism. In this example, the object being operated on in memory is an EmperorPenguin. The getHeight() method is overridden in the subclass, meaning all calls to it are replaced at runtime. Despite printInfo() being defined in the Penguin class, calling getHeight() on the object calls the method associated with the precise object in memory, not the current reference type where it is called. Even using the this reference, which is optional in this example, does not call the parent version because the method has been replaced.

The facet of polymorphism that replaces methods via overriding is one of the most important properties in all of Java. It allows you to create complex inheritance models, with subclasses that have their own custom implementation of overridden methods. It also means the parent class does not need to be updated to use the custom or overridden method. If the method is properly overridden, then the overridden version will be used in all places that it is called.

Remember, you can choose to limit polymorphic behavior by marking methods final, which prevents them from being overridden by a subclass.

Calling the Parent Version of an Overridden Method

As you saw earlier in the chapter, there is one exception to overriding a method where the parent method can still be called, and that is when the super reference is used. How can you modify our EmperorPenguin example to print 3, as defined in the Penguin getHeight() method? You could try calling super.getHeight() in the printInfo() method of the Penguin class.

```
class Penguin {
   ...
   public void printInfo() {
      System.out.print(super.getHeight());  // DOES NOT COMPILE
   }
}
```

Unfortunately, this does not compile, as super refers to the superclass of Penguin, in this case Object. The solution is to override printInfo() in the EmperorPenguin class and use super there.

```
public class EmperorPenguin extends Penguin {
   ...
   public void printInfo() {
      System.out.print(super.getHeight());
   }
   ...
}
```

This new version of EmperorPenguin uses the getHeight() method declared in the parent class and prints 3.

Overriding vs. Hiding Members

While method overriding replaces the method everywhere it is called, static method and variable hiding does not. Strictly speaking, hiding members is not a form of polymorphism since the methods and variables maintain their individual properties. Unlike method overriding, hiding members is very sensitive to the reference type and location where the member is being used.

Let's take a look at an example:

```
class Penguin {
    public static int getHeight() { return 3; }
    public void printInfo() {
        System.out.println(this.getHeight());
    }
}
public class CrestedPenguin extends Penguin {
    public static int getHeight() { return 8; }
    public static void main(String... fish) {
        new CrestedPenguin().printInfo();
    }
}
```

The CrestedPenguin example is nearly identical to our previous EmporerPenguin example, although as you probably already guessed, it prints 3 instead of 8. The getHeight() method is static and is therefore hidden, not overridden. The result is that calling getHeight() in CrestedPenguin returns a different value than calling it in the Penguin, even if the underlying object is the same. Contrast this with overriding a method, where it returns the same value for an object regardless of which class it is called in.

What about the fact that we used this to access a static method in this.getHeight()? As discussed in Chapter 7, while you are permitted to use an instance reference to access a static variable or method, it is often discouraged. In fact, the compiler will warn you when you access static members in a non-static way. In this case, the this reference had no impact on the program output.

Besides the location, the reference type can also determine the value you get when you are working with hidden members. Ready? Let's try a more complex example:

```
class Marsupial {
    protected int age = 2;
    public static boolean isBiped() {
        return false;
    }
}

public class Kangaroo extends Marsupial {
```

```
    protected int age = 6;
    public static boolean isBiped() {
        return true;
    }

    public static void main(String[] args) {
        Kangaroo joey = new Kangaroo();
        Marsupial moey = joey;
        System.out.println(joey.isBiped());
        System.out.println(moey.isBiped());
        System.out.println(joey.age);
        System.out.println(moey.age);
    }
}
```

The program prints the following:

```
true
false
6
2
```

Remember, in this example, only *one object*, of type Kangaroo, is created and stored in memory. Since static methods can only be hidden, not overridden, Java uses the reference type to determine which version of isBiped() should be called, resulting in joey.isBiped() printing true and moey.isBiped() printing false.

Likewise, the age variable is hidden, not overridden, so the reference type is used to determine which value to output. This results in joey.age returning 6 and moey.age returning 2.

 Real World Scenario

Don't Hide Members in Practice

Although Java allows you to hide variables and static methods, it is considered an extremely poor coding practice. As you saw in the previous example, the value of the variable or method can change depending on what reference is used, making your code very confusing, difficult to follow, and challenging for others to maintain. This is further compounded when you start modifying the value of the variable in both the parent and child methods, since it may not be clear which variable you're updating.

When you're defining a new variable or static method in a child class, it is considered good coding practice to select a name that is not already used by an inherited member. Redeclaring private methods and variables is considered less problematic, though, because the child class does not have access to the variable in the parent class to begin with.

For the exam, make sure you understand these examples as they show how hidden and overridden methods are fundamentally different. In practice, overriding methods is the cornerstone of polymorphism and is an extremely powerful feature.

Summary

This chapter took the basic class structures we've presented throughout the book and expanded them by introducing the notion of inheritance. Java classes follow a multilevel single-inheritance pattern in which every class has exactly one direct parent class, with all classes eventually inheriting from java.lang.Object.

Inheriting a class gives you access to all of the public and protected members of the class. It also gives you access to package-private members of the class if the classes are in the same package. All instance methods, constructors, and instance initializers have access to two special reference variables: this and super. Both this and super provide access to all inherited members, with only this providing access to all members in the current class declaration.

Constructors are special methods that use the class name and do not have a return type. They are used to instantiate new objects. Declaring constructors requires following a number of important rules. If no constructor is provided, the compiler will automatically insert a default no-argument constructor in the class. The first line of every constructor is a call to an overloaded constructor, this(), or a parent constructor, super(); otherwise, the compiler will insert a call to super() as the first line of the constructor. In some cases, such as if the parent class does not define a no-argument constructor, this can lead to compilation errors. Pay close attention on the exam to any class that defines a constructor with arguments and doesn't define a no-argument constructor.

Classes are initialized in a predetermined order: superclass initialization; static variables and static initializers in the order that they appear; instance variables and instance initializers in the order they appear; and finally, the constructor. All final instance variables must be assigned a value exactly once. If by the time a constructor finishes, a final instance variable is not assigned a value, then the constructor will not compile.

We reviewed overloaded, overridden, hidden, and redeclared methods and showed how they differ, especially in terms of polymorphism. A method is overloaded if it has the same name but a different signature as another accessible method. A method is overridden if it has the same signature as an inherited method, with access modifiers, exceptions, and a return type that are compatible. A static method is hidden if it has the same signature as an inherited static method. Finally, a method is redeclared if it has the same name and possibly the same signature as an uninherited method.

We also introduced the notion of hiding variables, although we strongly discourage this in practice as it often leads to confusing, difficult-to-maintain code.

Finally, this chapter introduced the concept of polymorphism, central to the Java language, and showed how objects can be accessed in a variety of forms. Make sure you understand when casts are needed for accessing objects, and be able to spot the difference between compile-time and runtime cast problems.

Exam Essentials

Be able to write code that extends other classes.   A Java class that extends another class inherits all of its public and protected methods and variables. If the class is in the same package, it also inherits all package-private members of the class. Classes that are marked final cannot be extended. Finally, all classes in Java extend java.lang.Object either directly or from a superclass.

Be able to distinguish and make use of *this, this(), super,* and *super().*   To access a current or inherited member of a class, the this reference can be used. To access an inherited member, the super reference can be used. The super reference is often used to reduce ambiguity, such as when a class reuses the name of an inherited method or variable. The calls to this() and super() are used to access constructors in the same class and parent class, respectively.

Evaluate code involving constructors.   The first line of every constructor is a call to another constructor within the class using this() or a call to a constructor of the parent class using the super() call. The compiler will insert a call to super() if no constructor call is declared. If the parent class doesn't contain a no-argument constructor, an explicit call to the parent constructor must be provided. Be able to recognize when the default constructor is provided. Remember that the order of initialization is to initialize all classes in the class hierarchy, starting with the superclass. Then, the instances are initialized, again starting with the superclass. All final variables must be assigned a value exactly once by the time the constructor is finished.

Understand the rules for method overriding.   Java allows methods to be overridden, or replaced, by a subclass if certain rules are followed: a method must have the same signature, be at least as accessible as the parent method, must not declare any new or broader exceptions, and must use covariant return types. The generic parameter types must exactly match in any of the generic method arguments or a generic return type. Methods marked final may not be overridden or hidden.

Understand the rules for hiding methods and variables.   When a static method is overridden in a subclass, it is referred to as method hiding. Likewise, variable hiding is when an inherited variable name is reused in a subclass. In both situations, the original method or variable still exists and is accessible depending on where it is accessed and the reference type used. For method hiding, the use of static in the method declaration must be the same between the parent and child class. Finally, variable and method hiding should generally be avoided since it leads to confusing and difficult-to-follow code.

Recognize the difference between method overriding and method overloading.   Both method overloading and overriding involve creating a new method with the same name as an existing method. When the method signature is the same, it is referred to as method overriding and must follow a specific set of override rules to compile. When the method signature is different, with the method taking different inputs, it is referred to as method overloading, and none of the override rules are required. Method overriding is important to polymorphism because it replaces all calls to the method, even those made in a superclass.

Understand polymorphism. An object may take on a variety of forms, referred to as polymorphism. The object is viewed as existing in memory in one concrete form but is accessible in many forms through reference variables. Changing the reference type of an object may grant access to new members, but the members always exist in memory.

Recognize valid reference casting. An instance can be automatically cast to a superclass or interface reference without an explicit cast. Alternatively, an explicit cast is required if the reference is being narrowed to a subclass of the object. The Java compiler doesn't permit casting to unrelated class types. Be able to discern between compiler-time casting errors and those that will not occur until runtime and that throw a `ClassCastException`.

Review Questions

1. Which code can be inserted to have the code print 2?

    ```java
    public class BirdSeed {
       private int numberBags;
       boolean call;

       public BirdSeed() {
          // LINE 1
          call = false;
          // LINE 2
       }

       public BirdSeed(int numberBags) {
          this.numberBags = numberBags;
       }

       public static void main(String[] args) {
          BirdSeed seed = new BirdSeed();
          System.out.print(seed.numberBags);
       } }
    ```

    A. Replace line 1 with `BirdSeed(2);`
    B. Replace line 2 with `BirdSeed(2);`
    C. Replace line 1 with `new BirdSeed(2);`
    D. Replace line 2 with `new BirdSeed(2);`
    E. Replace line 1 with `this(2);`
    F. Replace line 2 with `this(2);`
    G. The code prints 2 without any changes.

2. Which of the following statements about methods are true? (Choose all that apply.)
    A. Overloaded methods must have the same signature.
    B. Overridden methods must have the same signature.
    C. Hidden methods must have the same signature.
    D. Overloaded methods must have the same return type.
    E. Overridden methods must have the same return type.
    F. Hidden methods must have the same return type.

3. What is the output of the following program?

```
1:   class Mammal {
2:       private void sneeze() {}
3:       public Mammal(int age) {
4:           System.out.print("Mammal");
5:       } }
6:   public class Platypus extends Mammal {
7:       int sneeze() { return 1; }
8:       public Platypus() {
9:           System.out.print("Platypus");
10:      }
11:      public static void main(String[] args) {
12:          new Mammal(5);
13:      } }
```

A. Platypus

B. Mammal

C. PlatypusMammal

D. MammalPlatypus

E. The code will compile if line 7 is changed.

F. The code will compile if line 9 is changed.

4. Which of the following complete the constructor so that this code prints out 50? (Choose all that apply.)

```
class Speedster {
    int numSpots;
}
public class Cheetah extends Speedster {
    int numSpots;

    public Cheetah(int numSpots) {
        // INSERT CODE HERE
    }

    public static void main(String[] args) {
        Speedster s = new Cheetah(50);
        System.out.print(s.numSpots);
    }
}
```

A. numSpots = numSpots;

B. numSpots = this.numSpots;

C. `this.numSpots = numSpots;`

D. `numSpots = super.numSpots;`

E. `super.numSpots = numSpots;`

F. The code does not compile, regardless of the code inserted into the constructor.

G. None of the above

5. What is the output of the following code?

```
1:  class Arthropod {
2:      protected void printName(long input) {
3:          System.out.print("Arthropod");
4:      }
5:      void printName(int input) {
6:          System.out.print("Spooky");
7:      } }
8:  public class Spider extends Arthropod {
9:      protected void printName(int input) {
10:         System.out.print("Spider");
11:     }
12:     public static void main(String[] args) {
13:         Arthropod a = new Spider();
14:         a.printName((short)4);
15:         a.printName(4);
16:         a.printName(5L);
17:     } }
```

A. SpiderSpiderArthropod

B. SpiderSpiderSpider

C. SpiderSpookyArthropod

D. SpookySpiderArthropod

E. The code will not compile because of line 5.

F. The code will not compile because of line 9.

G. None of the above

6. Which of the following statements about overridden methods are true? (Choose all that apply.)

A. An overridden method must contain method parameters that are the same or covariant with the method parameters in the inherited method.

B. An overridden method may declare a new exception, provided it is not checked.

C. An overridden method must be more accessible than the method in the parent class.

D. An overridden method may declare a broader checked exception than the method in the parent class.

E. If an inherited method returns void, then the overridden version of the method must return void.

F. None of the above

7. Which of the following pairs, when inserted into the blanks, allow the code to compile? (Choose all that apply.)

```
1:  public class Howler {
2:      public Howler(long shadow) {
3:              _____;
4:      }
5:      private Howler(int moon) {
6:          super();
7:      }
8:  }
9:  class Wolf extends Howler {
10:     protected Wolf(String stars) {
11:         super(2L);
12:     }
13:     public Wolf() {
14:             _____;
15:     }
16: }
```

A. this(3) at line 3, this("") at line 14

B. this() at line 3, super(1) at line 14

C. this((short)1) at line 3, this(null) at line 14

D. super() at line 3, super() at line 14

E. this(2L) at line 3, super((short)2) at line 14

F. this(5) at line 3, super(null) at line 14

G. Remove lines 3 and 14.

8. What is the result of the following?

```
1:  public class PolarBear {
2:      StringBuilder value = new StringBuilder("t");
3:      { value.append("a"); }
4:      { value.append("c"); }
5:      private PolarBear() {
6:          value.append("b");
7:      }
8:      public PolarBear(String s) {
```

```
9:          this();
10:         value.append(s);
11:      }
12:      public PolarBear(CharSequence p) {
13:         value.append(p);
14:      }
15:      public static void main(String[] args) {
16:         Object bear = new PolarBear();
17:         bear = new PolarBear("f");
18:         System.out.println(((PolarBear)bear).value);
19:      } }
```

A. tacb

B. tacf

C. tacbf

D. tcafb

E. taftacb

F. The code does not compile.

G. An exception is thrown.

9. Which of the following method signatures are valid overrides of the hairy() method in the Alpaca class? (Choose all that apply.)

```
import java.util.*;

public class Alpaca {
   protected List<String> hairy(int p) { return null; }
}
```

A. `List<String> hairy(int p) { return null; }`

B. `public List<String> hairy(int p) { return null; }`

C. `public List<CharSequence> hairy(int p) { return null; }`

D. `private List<String> hairy(int p) { return null; }`

E. `public Object hairy(int p) { return null; }`

F. `public ArrayList<String> hairy(int p) { return null; }`

G. None of the above

10. How many lines of the following program contain a compilation error?

```
1:  public class Rodent {
2:      public Rodent(var x) {}
3:      protected static Integer chew() throws Exception {
4:          System.out.println("Rodent is chewing");
```

```
5:          return 1;
6:      }
7:  }
8:  class Beaver extends Rodent {
9:      public Number chew() throws RuntimeException {
10:         System.out.println("Beaver is chewing on wood");
11:         return 2;
12:     } }
```

A. None

B. 1

C. 2

D. 3

E. 4

F. 5

11. Which of the following statements about polymorphism are true? (Choose all that apply.)

A. An object may be cast to a subtype without an explicit cast.

B. If the type of a method argument is an interface, then a reference variable that implements the interface may be passed to the method.

C. A method that takes a parameter with type java.lang.Object can be passed any variable.

D. All cast exceptions can be detected at compile-time.

E. By defining a final instance method in the superclass, you guarantee that the specific method will be called in the parent class at runtime.

F. Polymorphism applies only to classes, not interfaces.

12. Which of the following statements can be inserted in the blank so that the code will compile successfully? (Choose all that apply.)

```
public class Snake {}
public class Cobra extends Snake {}
public class GardenSnake extends Cobra {}
public class SnakeHandler {
    private Snake snake;
    public void setSnake(Snake snake) { this.snake = snake; }
    public static void main(String[] args) {
        new SnakeHandler().setSnake(_____);
    }
}
```

A. new Cobra()

B. new Snake()

    C. `new Object()`

    D. `new String("Snake")`

    E. `new GardenSnake()`

    F. `null`

    G. None of the above. The class does not compile, regardless of the value inserted in the blank.

13. Which of these classes compile and will include a default constructor created by the compiler? (Choose all that apply.)

    A. `public class Bird {}`

    B.
```
public class Bird {
    public bird() {}
}
```

    C.
```
public class Bird {
    public bird(String name) {}
}
```

    D.
```
public class Bird {
    public Bird() {}
}
```

    E.
```
public class Bird {
    Bird(String name) {}
}
```

    F.
```
public class Bird {
    private Bird(int age) {}
}
```

    G.
```
public class Bird {
    public Bird bird() {return null;}
}
```

14. Which of the following statements about inheritance are correct? (Choose all that apply.)

    A. A class can directly extend any number of classes.

    B. A class can implement any number of interfaces.

    C. All variables inherit `java.lang.Object`.

    D. If class A is extended by B, then B is a superclass of A.

    E. If class C implements interface D, then C is subtype of D.

    F. Multiple inheritance is the property of a class to have multiple direct superclasses.

15. What is the result of the following?

```
1: class Arachnid {
2:     static StringBuilder sb = new StringBuilder();
3:     { sb.append("c"); }
```

```
4:      static
5:      { sb.append("u"); }
6:      { sb.append("r"); }
7:  }
8:  public class Scorpion extends Arachnid {
9:      static
10:     { sb.append("q"); }
11:     { sb.append("m"); }
12:     public static void main(String[] args) {
13:         System.out.print(Scorpion.sb + " ");
14:         System.out.print(Scorpion.sb + " ");
15:         new Arachnid();
16:         new Scorpion();
17:         System.out.print(Scorpion.sb);
18:     } }
```

A. qu qu qumrcrc

B. u u ucrcrm

C. uq uq uqmcrcr

D. uq uq uqcrcrm

E. qu qu qumcrcr

F. qu qu qucrcrm

G. The code does not compile.

16. Which of the following methods are valid overrides of the friendly() method in the Llama class? (Choose all that apply.)

```
import java.util.*;

public class Llama {
    void friendly(List<String> laugh, Iterable<Short> s) {}
}
```

A. void friendly(List<CharSequence> laugh, Iterable<Short> s) {}

B. void friendly(List<String> laugh, Iterable<Short> s) {}

C. void friendly(ArrayList<String> laugh, Iterable<Short> s) {}

D. void friendly(List<String> laugh, Iterable<Integer> s) {}

E. void friendly(ArrayList<CharSequence> laugh, Object s) {}

F. void friendly(ArrayList<String> laugh, Iterable... s) {}

G. None of the above

17. Which of the following statements about inheritance and variables are true? (Choose all that apply.)

A. Instance variables can be overridden in a subclass.

B. If an instance variable is declared with the same name as an inherited variable, then the type of the variable must be covariant.

C. If an instance variable is declared with the same name as an inherited variable, then the access modifier must be at least as accessible as the variable in the parent class.

D. If a variable is declared with the same name as an inherited `static` variable, then it must also be marked `static`.

E. The variable in the child class may not throw a checked exception that is new or broader than the class of any exception thrown in the parent class variable.

F. None of the above

18. Which of the following are true? (Choose all that apply.)

A. `this()` can be called from anywhere in a constructor.

B. `this()` can be called from anywhere in an instance method.

C. `this.variableName` can be called from any instance method in the class.

D. `this.variableName` can be called from any `static` method in the class.

E. You can call the default constructor written by the compiler using `this()`.

F. You can access a `private` constructor with the `main()` method in the same class.

19. Which statements about the following classes are correct? (Choose all that apply.)

```
1:  public class Mammal {
2:      private void eat() {}
3:      protected static void drink() {}
4:      public Integer dance(String p) { return null; }
5:  }
6:  class Primate extends Mammal {
7:      public void eat(String p) {}
8:  }
9:  class Monkey extends Primate {
10:     public static void drink() throws RuntimeException {}
11:     public Number dance(CharSequence p) { return null; }
12:     public int eat(String p) {}
13: }
```

A. The `eat()` method in `Mammal` is correctly overridden on line 7.

B. The `eat()` method in `Mammal` is correctly overloaded on line 7.

    C.   The drink() method in Mammal is correctly hidden on line 10.

    D.   The drink() method in Mammal is correctly overridden on line 10.

    E.   The dance() method in Mammal is correctly overridden on line 11.

    F.   The dance() method in Mammal is correctly overloaded on line 11.

    G.   The eat() method in Primate is correctly hidden on line 12.

    H.   The eat() method in Primate is correctly overloaded on line 12.

20. What is the output of the following code?

```
1:  class Reptile {
2:      {System.out.print("A");}
3:      public Reptile(int hatch) {}
4:      void layEggs() {
5:          System.out.print("Reptile");
6:      } }
7:  public class Lizard extends Reptile {
8:      static {System.out.print("B");}
9:      public Lizard(int hatch) {}
10:     public final void layEggs() {
11:         System.out.print("Lizard");
12:     }
13:     public static void main(String[] args) {
14:         Reptile reptile = new Lizard(1);
15:         reptile.layEggs();
16:     } }
```

    A.   AALizard

    B.   BALizard

    C.   BLizardA

    D.   ALizard

    E.   The code will not compile because of line 10.

    F.   None of the above

21. Which statement about the following program is correct?

```
1:  class Bird {
2:      int feathers = 0;
3:      Bird(int x) { this.feathers = x; }
4:      Bird fly() {
5:          return new Bird(1);
```

```
6:      } }
7:  class Parrot extends Bird {
8:      protected Parrot(int y) { super(y); }
9:      protected Parrot fly() {
10:         return new Parrot(2);
11:     } }
12: public class Macaw extends Parrot {
13:     public Macaw(int z) { super(z); }
14:     public Macaw fly() {
15:         return new Macaw(3);
16:     }
17:     public static void main(String... sing) {
18:         Bird p = new Macaw(4);
19:         System.out.print(((Parrot)p.fly()).feathers);
20:     } }
```

A. One line contains a compiler error.

B. Two lines contain compiler errors.

C. Three lines contain compiler errors.

D. The code compiles but throws a ClassCastException at runtime.

E. The program compiles and prints 3.

F. The program compiles and prints 0.

22. What does the following program print?

```
1:  class Person {
2:      static String name;
3:      void setName(String q) { name = q; } }
4:  public class Child extends Person {
5:      static String name;
6:      void setName(String w) { name = w; }
7:      public static void main(String[] p) {
8:          final Child m = new Child();
9:          final Person t = m;
10:         m.name = "Elysia";
11:         t.name = "Sophia";
12:         m.setName("Webby");
13:         t.setName("Olivia");
14:         System.out.println(m.name + " " + t.name);
15:     } }
```

> **A.** Elysia Sophia
>
> **B.** Webby Olivia
>
> **C.** Olivia Olivia
>
> **D.** Olivia Sophia
>
> **E.** The code does not compile.
>
> **F.** None of the above

23. What is the output of the following program?

```
1:  class Canine {
2:      public Canine(boolean t) { logger.append("a"); }
3:      public Canine() { logger.append("q"); }
4:
5:      private StringBuilder logger = new StringBuilder();
6:      protected void print(String v) { logger.append(v); }
7:      protected String view() { return logger.toString(); }
8:  }
9:
10: class Fox extends Canine {
11:     public Fox(long x) { print("p"); }
12:     public Fox(String name) {
13:         this(2);
14:         print("z");
15:     }
16: }
17:
18: public class Fennec extends Fox {
19:     public Fennec(int e) {
20:         super("tails");
21:         print("j");
22:     }
23:     public Fennec(short f) {
24:         super("eevee");
25:         print("m");
26:     }
27:
28:     public static void main(String... unused) {
29:         System.out.println(new Fennec(1).view());
30:     } }
```

A. qpz

B. qpzj

C. jzpa

D. apj

E. apjm

F. The code does not compile.

G. None of the above

24. Which statements about polymorphism and method inheritance are correct? (Choose all that apply.)

A. It cannot be determined until runtime which overridden method will be executed in a parent class.

B. It cannot be determined until runtime which hidden method will be executed in a parent class.

C. Marking a method `static` prevents it from being overridden or hidden.

D. Marking a method `final` prevents it from being overridden or hidden.

E. The reference type of the variable determines which overridden method will be called at runtime.

F. The reference type of the variable determines which hidden method will be called at runtime.

25. What is printed by the following program?

```
1:  class Antelope {
2:      public Antelope(int p) {
3:          System.out.print("4");
4:      }
5:      { System.out.print("2"); }
6:      static { System.out.print("1"); }
7:  }
8:  public class Gazelle extends Antelope {
9:      public Gazelle(int p) {
10:         super(6);
11:         System.out.print("3");
12:     }
13:     public static void main(String hopping[]) {
14:         new Gazelle(0);
15:     }
16:     static { System.out.print("8"); }
17:     { System.out.print("9"); }
18: }
```

A. 182640

B. 182943

C. 182493

D. 421389

E. The code does not compile.

F. The output cannot be determined until runtime.

26. How many lines of the following program contain a compilation error?

```
1:  class Primate {
2:      protected int age = 2;
3:      { age = 1; }
4:      public Primate() {
5:          this().age = 3;
6:      }
7:  }
8:  public class Orangutan {
9:      protected int age = 4;
10:     { age = 5; }
11:     public Orangutan() {
12:         this().age = 6;
13:     }
14:     public static void main(String[] bananas) {
15:         final Primate x = (Primate)new Orangutan();
16:         System.out.println(x.age);
17:     }
18: }
```

A. None, and the program prints 1 at runtime.

B. None, and the program prints 3 at runtime.

C. None, but it causes a ClassCastException at runtime.

D. 1

E. 2

F. 3

G. 4

Chapter

9

Advanced Class Design

OCP EXAM OBJECTIVES COVERED IN THIS CHAPTER:

✓ **Reusing Implementations Through Inheritance**

  ▪ Create and extend abstract classes

✓ **Programming Abstractly Through Interfaces**

  ▪ Create and implement interfaces

  ▪ Distinguish class inheritance from interface inheritance including abstract classes

In Chapter 8, "Class Design," we showed you how to create classes utilizing inheritance and polymorphism. In this chapter, we will continue our discussion of class design starting with abstract classes. By creating abstract class definitions, you're defining a platform that other developers can extend and build on top of. We'll then move on to interfaces and show how to use them to design a standard set of methods across classes with varying implementations. Finally, we'll conclude this chapter with a brief presentation of inner classes.

Creating Abstract Classes

We start our discussion of advanced class design with abstract classes. As you will see, abstract classes have important uses in defining a framework that other developers can use.

Introducing Abstract Classes

In Chapter 8, you learned that a subclass can override an inherited method defined in a parent class. Overriding a method potentially changes the behavior of a method in the parent class. For example, take a look at the following Bird class and its Stork subclass:

```
class Bird {
    public String getName() { return null; }
    public void printName() {
        System.out.print(getName());
    }
}

public class Stork extends Bird {
    public String getName() { return "Stork!"; }
    public static void main(String[] args) {
        new Stork().printName();
    }
}
```

This program prints Stork! at runtime. Notice that the getName() method is overridden in the subclass. Even though the implementation of printName() is defined in the Bird class, the fact that getName() is overridden in the subclass means it is replaced everywhere, even in the parent class.

Let's take this one step further. Suppose you want to define a Bird class that other developers can extend and use, but you want the developers to specify the particular type of Bird. Also, rather than having the Bird version of getName() return null (or throw an exception), you want to ensure every class that extends Bird is required to provide its own overridden version of the getName() method.

Enter abstract classes. An *abstract class* is a class that cannot be instantiated and may contain abstract methods. An *abstract method* is a method that does not define an implementation when it is declared. Both abstract classes and abstract methods are denoted with the abstract modifier. Compare our previous implementation with this new one using an abstract Bird class:

```java
abstract class Bird {
    public abstract String getName();
    public void printName() {
        System.out.print(getName());
    }
}

public class Stork extends Bird {
    public String getName() { return "Stork!"; }
    public static void main(String[] args) {
        new Stork().printName();
    }
}
```

What's different? First, the Bird class is marked abstract. Next, the getName() method in Bird is also marked abstract. Finally, the implementation of getName(), including the braces ({}), have been replaced with a single semicolon (;).

What about the Stork class? It's exactly the same as before. While it may look the same, though, the rules around how the class must be implemented have changed. In particular, the Stork class *must* now override the abstract getName() method. For example, the following implementation does not compile because Stork does not override the required abstract getName() method:

```java
public class Stork extends Bird {}  // DOES NOT COMPILE
```

While these differences may seem small, imagine the Bird and Stork class are each written by different people. By one person marking getName() as abstract in the Bird class, they are sending a message to the other developer writing the Stork class: "Hey, to use this class, you need to write a getName() method!"

An abstract class is most commonly used when you want another class to inherit properties of a particular class, but you want the subclass to fill in some of the implementation details. In our example, the author of the Bird class wrote the printName() method but did not know what it was going to do at runtime, since the getName() implementation had yet to be provided.

Override vs. Implement

Oftentimes, when an abstract method is overridden in a subclass, it is referred to as implementing the method. It is described this way because the subclass is providing an implementation for a method that does not yet have one. While we tend to use the terms *implement* and *override* interchangeably for abstract methods, the term *override* is more accurate.

When overriding an abstract method, all of the rules you learned about overriding methods in Chapter 8 are applicable. For example, you can override an abstract method with a covariant return type. Likewise, you can declare new unchecked exceptions but not checked exceptions in the overridden method. Furthermore, you can override an abstract method in one class and then override it again in a subclass of that class.

The method override rules apply whether the abstract method is declared in an abstract class or, as we shall see later in this chapter, an interface. We will continue to use override and implement interchangeably in this chapter, as this is common in software development. Just remember that providing an implementation for an abstract method is considered a method override and all of the associated rules for overriding methods apply.

Earlier, we said that an abstract class is one that cannot be instantiated. This means that if you attempt to instantiate it, the compiler will report an exception, as in this example:

```
abstract class Alligator {
    public static void main(String... food) {
        var a = new Alligator();  // DOES NOT COMPILE
    }
}
```

An abstract class can be initialized, but only as part of the instantiation of a nonabstract subclass.

Defining Abstract Methods

As you saw in the previous example, an abstract class may include nonabstract methods, in this case with the printName() method. In fact, an abstract class can include all of the same members as a nonabstract class, including variables, static and instance methods, and inner classes. As you will see in the next section, abstract classes can also include constructors.

One of the most important features of an abstract class is that it is not actually required to include any abstract methods. For example, the following code compiles even though it doesn't define any abstract methods:

```
public abstract class Llama {
    public void chew() {}
}
```

Although an abstract class doesn't have to declare any abstract methods, an abstract method can only be defined in an abstract class (or an interface, as you will see shortly). For example, the following code won't compile because the class is not marked abstract:

```
public class Egret {  // DOES NOT COMPILE
   public abstract void peck();
}
```

The exam creators like to include invalid class declarations like the Egret class, which mixes nonabstract classes with abstract methods. If you see a class that contains an abstract method, make sure the class is marked abstract.

Like the final modifier, the abstract modifier can be placed before or after the access modifier in class and method declarations, as shown in this Tiger class:

```
abstract public class Tiger {
   abstract public int claw();
}
```

There are some restrictions on the placement of the abstract modifier. The abstract modifier cannot be placed after the class keyword in a class declaration, nor after the return type in a method declaration. The following Jackal and howl() declarations do not compile for these reasons:

```
public class abstract Jackal {  // DOES NOT COMPILE
   public int abstract howl();  // DOES NOT COMPILE
}
```

 It is not possible to define an abstract method that has a body, or default implementation. You can still define a method with a body—you just can't mark it as abstract. As long as you do not mark the method as final, the subclass has the option to override an inherited method.

Constructors in Abstract Classes

Even though abstract classes cannot be instantiated, they are still initialized through constructors by their subclasses. For example, does the following program compile?

```
abstract class Bear {
   abstract CharSequence chew();
   public Bear() {
      System.out.println(chew());  // Does this compile?
   }
}

public class Panda extends Bear {
   String chew() { return "yummy!"; }
```

```
public static void main(String[] args) {
    new Panda();
}
}
```

Using the constructor rules you learned in Chapter 8, the compiler inserts a default no-argument constructor into the Panda class, which first calls super() in the Bear class. The Bear constructor is only called when the abstract class is being initialized through a subclass; therefore, there is an implementation of chew() at the time the constructor is called. This code compiles and prints yummy! at runtime.

For the exam, remember that abstract classes are initialized with constructors in the same way as nonabstract classes. For example, if an abstract class does not provide a constructor, the compiler will automatically insert a default no-argument constructor.

The primary difference between a constructor in an abstract class and a nonabstract class is that a constructor in abstract class can be called only when it is being initialized by a nonabstract subclass. This makes sense, as abstract classes cannot be instantiated.

Invalid Abstract Method Declarations

The exam writers are also fond of questions with methods marked as abstract for which an implementation is also defined. For example, can you see why each of the following methods does not compile?

```
public abstract class Turtle {
    public abstract long eat()       // DOES NOT COMPILE
    public abstract void swim() {};  // DOES NOT COMPILE
    public abstract int getAge() {   // DOES NOT COMPILE
        return 10;
    }
    public void sleep;               // DOES NOT COMPILE
    public void goInShell();         // DOES NOT COMPILE
}
```

The first method, eat(), does not compile because it is marked abstract but does not end with as semicolon (;). The next two methods, swim() and getAge(), do not compile because they are marked abstract, but they provide an implementation block enclosed in braces ({}). For the exam, remember that an abstract method declaration must end in a semicolon without any braces. The next method, sleep, does not compile because it is missing parentheses, (), for method arguments. The last method, goInShell(), does not compile because it is not marked abstract and therefore must provide a body enclosed in braces.

Make sure you understand why each of the previous methods does not compile and that you can spot errors like these on the exam. If you come across a question on the exam in which a class or method is marked abstract, make sure the class is properly implemented before attempting to solve the problem.

Invalid Modifiers

In Chapter 7, "Methods and Encapsulation," you learned about various modifiers for methods and classes. In this section, we review the abstract modifier and which modifiers it is not compatible with.

abstract and *final* Modifiers

What would happen if you marked a class or method both abstract and final? If you mark something abstract, you are intending for someone else to extend or implement it. But, if you mark something final, you are preventing anyone from extending or implementing it. These concepts are in direct conflict with each other.

Due to this incompatibility, Java does not permit a class or method to be marked both abstract and final. For example, the following code snippet will not compile:

```
public abstract final class Tortoise {  // DOES NOT COMPILE
    public abstract final void walk();   // DOES NOT COMPILE
}
```

In this example, neither the class or method declarations will compile because they are marked both abstract and final. The exam doesn't tend to use final modifiers on classes or methods often, so if you see them, make sure they aren't used with the abstract modifier.

abstract and *private* Modifiers

A method cannot be marked as both abstract and private. This rule makes sense if you think about it. How would you define a subclass that implements a required method if the method is not inherited by the subclass? The answer is you can't, which is why the compiler will complain if you try to do the following:

```
public abstract class Whale {
    private abstract void sing();  // DOES NOT COMPILE
}

public class HumpbackWhale extends Whale {
    private void sing() {
        System.out.println("Humpback whale is singing");
    }
}
```

In this example, the abstract method sing() defined in the parent class Whale is not visible to the subclass HumpbackWhale. Even though HumpbackWhale does provide an implementation, it is not considered an override of the abstract method since the abstract method is not inherited. The compiler recognizes this in the parent class and reports an error as soon as private and abstract are applied to the same method.

While it is not possible to declare a method abstract and private, it is possible (albeit redundant) to declare a method final and private.

If we changed the access modifier from `private` to `protected` in the parent class `Whale`, would the code compile? Let's take a look:

```
public abstract class Whale {
    protected abstract void sing();
}

public class HumpbackWhale extends Whale {
    private void sing() {  // DOES NOT COMPILE
        System.out.println("Humpback whale is singing");
    }
}
```

In this modified example, the code will still not compile, but for a completely different reason. If you remember the rules for overriding a method, the subclass cannot reduce the visibility of the parent method, `sing()`. Because the method is declared `protected` in the parent class, it must be marked as `protected` or `public` in the child class. Even with abstract methods, the rules for overriding methods must be followed.

abstract and *static* Modifiers

As you saw in Chapter 8, a `static` method cannot be overridden. It is defined as belonging to the class, not an instance of the class. If a `static` method cannot be overridden, then it follows that it also cannot be marked abstract since it can never be implemented. For example, the following class does not compile:

```
abstract class Hippopotamus {
    abstract static void swim();  // DOES NOT COMPILE
}
```

For the exam, make sure you know which modifiers can and cannot be used with one another, especially for abstract classes and interfaces.

Creating a Concrete Class

An abstract class becomes usable when it is extended by a concrete subclass. A *concrete class* is a nonabstract class. The first concrete subclass that extends an abstract class is required to implement all inherited abstract methods. This includes implementing any inherited abstract methods from inherited interfaces, as we will see later in this chapter.

When you see a concrete class extending an abstract class on the exam, check to make sure that it implements all of the required abstract methods. Can you see why the following `Walrus` class does not compile?

```
public abstract class Animal {
    public abstract String getName();
}

public class Walrus extends Animal { // DOES NOT COMPILE
}
```

In this example, we see that `Animal` is marked as `abstract` and `Walrus` is not, making `Walrus` a concrete subclass of `Animal`. Since `Walrus` is the first concrete subclass, it must implement all inherited abstract methods—`getName()` in this example. Because it doesn't, the compiler reports an error with the declaration of `Walrus`.

We highlight the *first* concrete subclass for a reason. An abstract class can extend a non-abstract class, and vice versa. Any time a concrete class is extending an abstract class, it must implement all of the methods that are inherited as abstract. Let's illustrate this with a set of inherited classes:

```
abstract class Mammal {
    abstract void showHorn();
    abstract void eatLeaf();
}

abstract class Rhino extends Mammal {
    void showHorn() {}
}

public class BlackRhino extends Rhino {
    void eatLeaf() {}
}
```

In this example, the `BlackRhino` class is the first concrete subclass, while the `Mammal` and `Rhino` classes are abstract. The `BlackRhino` class inherits the `eatLeaf()` method as abstract and is therefore required to provide an implementation, which it does.

What about the `showHorn()` method? Since the parent class, `Rhino`, provides an implementation of `showHorn()`, the method is inherited in the `BlackRhino` as a nonabstract method. For this reason, the `BlackRhino` class is permitted but not required to override the `showHorn()` method. The three classes in this example are correctly defined and compile.

What if we changed the `Rhino` declaration to remove the abstract modifier?

```
class Rhino extends Mammal {  // DOES NOT COMPILE
    void showHorn() {}
}
```

By changing `Rhino` to a concrete class, it becomes the first nonabstract class to extend the abstract `Mammal` class. Therefore, it must provide an implementation of both the `showHorn()` and `eatLeaf()` methods. Since it only provides one of these methods, the modified `Rhino` declaration does not compile.

Let's try one more example. The following concrete class `Lion` inherits two abstract methods, `getName()` and `roar()`:

```
public abstract class Animal {
    abstract String getName();
```

```
}

public abstract class BigCat extends Animal {
   protected abstract void roar();
}

public class Lion extends BigCat {
   public String getName() {
      return "Lion";
   }
   public void roar() {
      System.out.println("The Lion lets out a loud ROAR!");
   }
}
```

In this sample code, BigCat extends Animal but is marked as abstract; therefore, it is not required to provide an implementation for the getName() method. The class Lion is not marked as abstract, and as the first concrete subclass, it must implement all of the inherited abstract methods not defined in a parent class. All three of these classes compile successfully.

Reviewing Abstract Class Rules

For the exam, you should know the following rules about abstract classes and abstract methods. While it may seem like a lot to remember, most of these rules are pretty straightforward. For example, marking a class or method abstract and final makes it unusable. Be sure you can spot contradictions such as these if you come across them on the exam.

Abstract Class Definition Rules

1. Abstract classes cannot be instantiated.

2. All top-level types, including abstract classes, cannot be marked protected or private.

3. Abstract classes cannot be marked final.

4. Abstract classes may include zero or more abstract and nonabstract methods.

5. An abstract class that extends another abstract class inherits all of its abstract methods.

6. The first concrete class that extends an abstract class must provide an implementation for all of the inherited abstract methods.

7. Abstract class constructors follow the same rules for initialization as regular constructors, except they can be called only as part of the initialization of a subclass.

These rules for abstract methods apply regardless of whether the abstract method is defined in an abstract class or interface.

Abstract Method Definition Rules

1. Abstract methods can be defined only in abstract classes or interfaces.

2. Abstract methods cannot be declared private or final.

3. Abstract methods must not provide a method body/implementation in the abstract class in which they are declared.

4. Implementing an abstract method in a subclass follows the same rules for overriding a method, including covariant return types, exception declarations, etc.

Implementing Interfaces

Although Java doesn't allow multiple inheritance of state, it does allow a class to implement any number of interfaces. An *interface* is an abstract data type are that declares a list of abstract methods that any class implementing the interface must provide. An interface can also include constant variables. Both abstract methods and constant variables included with an interface are implicitly assumed to be public.

Interfaces and Nonabstract Methods

For the 1Z0-815 exam, you only need to know about two members for interfaces: abstract methods and constant variables. With Java 8, interfaces were updated to include static and default methods. A default method is one in which the interface method has a body and is not marked abstract. It was added for backward compatibility, allowing an older class to use a new version of an interface that contains a new method, without having to modify the existing class.

In Java 9, interfaces were updated to support private and private static methods. Both of these types were added for code reusability within an interface declaration and cannot be called outside the interface definition.

When you study for the 1Z0-816 exam, you will need to know about other kinds of interface members. For the 1Z0-815 exam, you only need to know about abstract methods and constant variables.

Defining an Interface

In Java, an interface is defined with the interface keyword, analogous to the class keyword used when defining a class. Refer to Figure 9.1 for a proper interface declaration.

FIGURE 9.1 Defining an interface

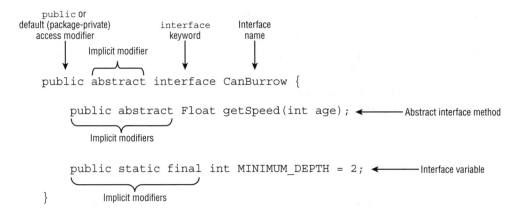

In Figure 9.1, our interface declaration includes a constant variable and an abstract method. Interface variables are referred to as constants because they are assumed to be public, static, and final. They are initialized with a constant value when they are declared. Since they are public and static, they can be used outside the interface declaration without requiring an instance of the interface. Figure 9.1 also includes an abstract method that, like an interface variable, is assumed to be public.

 For brevity, we sometimes say "an instance of an interface" to mean an instance of a class that implements the interface.

What does it mean for a variable or method to be assumed to be something? One aspect of an interface declaration that differs from an abstract class is that it contains implicit modifiers. An *implicit modifier* is a modifier that the compiler automatically adds to a class, interface, method, or variable declaration. For example, an interface is always considered to be abstract, even if it is not marked so. We'll cover rules and examples for implicit modifiers in more detail later in the chapter.

Let's start with an example. Imagine we have an interface WalksOnTwoLegs, defined as follows:

```
public abstract interface WalksOnTwoLegs {}
```

It compiles because interfaces are not required to define any methods. The abstract modifier in this example is optional for interfaces, with the compiler inserting it if it is not provided. Now, consider the following two examples, which do not compile:

```
public class Biped {
  public static void main(String[] args) {
    var e = new WalksOnTwoLegs();        // DOES NOT COMPILE
  }
```

```
}

public final interface WalksOnEightLegs {}  // DOES NOT COMPILE
```

The first example doesn't compile, as WalksOnTwoLegs is an interface and cannot be instantiated. The second example, WalksOnEightLegs, doesn't compile because interfaces cannot be marked as final for the same reason that abstract classes cannot be marked as final. In other words, marking an interface final implies no class could ever implement it.

How do you use an interface? Let's say we have an interface Climb, defined as follows:

```
interface Climb {
    Number getSpeed(int age);
}
```

Next, we have a concrete class FieldMouse that invokes the Climb interface by using the implements keyword in its class declaration, as shown in Figure 9.2.

FIGURE 9.2   Implementing an interface

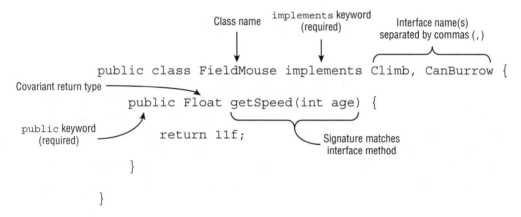

The FieldMouse class declares that it implements the Climb interface and includes an overridden version of getSpeed() inherited from the Climb interface. The method signature of getSpeed() matches exactly, and the return type is covariant. The access modifier of the interface method is assumed to be public in Climb, although the concrete class FieldMouse must explicitly declare it.

As shown in Figure 9.2, a class can implement multiple interfaces, each separated by a comma (,). If any of the interfaces define abstract methods, then the concrete class is required to override them. In this case, FieldMouse also implements the CanBurrow interface that we saw in Figure 9.1. In this manner, the class overrides two abstract methods at the same time with one method declaration. You'll learn more about duplicate and compatible interface methods shortly.

Like a class, an interface can extend another interface using the extends keyword.

```
interface Nocturnal {}

public interface HasBigEyes extends Nocturnal {}
```

Unlike a class, which can extend only one class, an interface can extend multiple interfaces.

```
interface Nocturnal {
    public int hunt();
}

interface CanFly {
    public void flap();
}

interface HasBigEyes extends Nocturnal, CanFly {}

public class Owl implements Nocturnal, CanFly {
    public int hunt() { return 5; }
    public void flap() { System.out.println("Flap!"); }
}
```

In this example, the Owl class implements the HasBigEyes interface and must implement the hunt() and flap() methods. Extending two interfaces is permitted because interfaces are not initialized as part of a class hierarchy. Unlike abstract classes, they do not contain constructors and are not part of instance initialization. Interfaces simply define a set of rules that a class implementing them must follow. They also include various static members, including constants that do not require an instance of the class to use.

Many of the rules for class declarations also apply to interfaces including the following:

- A Java file may have at most one public top-level class or interface, and it must match the name of the file.

- A top-level class or interface can only be declared with public or package-private access.

It may help to think of an interface as a specialized abstract class, as many of the rules carry over. Just remember that an interface does not follow the same rules for single inheritance and instance initialization with constructors, as a class does.

What About Enums?

In this section, we described how a Java class can have at most one public top-level element, a class or interface. This public top-level element could also be an enumeration, or *enum* for short. An enum is a specialized type that defines a set of fixed values. It is declared with the enum keyword. The following demonstrates a simple example of an enum for Color:

```
public enum Color {
    RED, YELOW, BLUE, GREEN, ORANGE, PURPLE
}
```

Like classes and interfaces, enums can have more complex formations including methods, `private` constructors, and instance variables.

Luckily for you, enums are out of scope for the 1Z0-815 exam. Like some of the more advanced interface members we described earlier, you will need to study enums when preparing for the 1Z0-816 exam.

Inserting Implicit Modifiers

As mentioned earlier, an implicit modifier is one that the compiler will automatically insert. It's reminiscent of the compiler inserting a default no-argument constructor if you do not define a constructor, which you learned about in Chapter 8. You can choose to insert these implicit modifiers yourself or let the compiler insert them for you.

The following list includes the implicit modifiers for interfaces that you need to know for the exam:

- Interfaces are assumed to be `abstract`.
- Interface variables are assumed to be `public`, `static`, and `final`.
- Interface methods without a body are assumed to be `abstract` and `public`.

For example, the following two interface definitions are equivalent, as the compiler will convert them both to the second declaration:

```
public interface Soar {
    int MAX_HEIGHT = 10;
    final static boolean UNDERWATER = true;
    void fly(int speed);
    abstract void takeoff();
    public abstract double dive();
}
public abstract interface Soar {
    public static final int MAX_HEIGHT = 10;
    public final static boolean UNDERWATER = true;
    public abstract void fly(int speed);
    public abstract void takeoff();
    public abstract double dive();
}
```

In this example, we've marked in bold the implicit modifiers that the compiler automatically inserts. First, the abstract keyword is added to the interface declaration. Next, the public, static, and final keywords are added to the interface variables if they do not exist. Finally, each abstract method is prepended with the abstract and public keywords if they do not contain them already.

Conflicting Modifiers

What happens if a developer marks a method or variable with a modifier that conflicts with an implicit modifier? For example, if an abstract method is assumed to be public, then can it be explicitly marked protected or private?

```
public interface Dance {
    private int count = 4;   // DOES NOT COMPILE
    protected void step();   // DOES NOT COMPILE
}
```

Neither of these interface member declarations compiles, as the compiler will apply the public modifier to both, resulting in a conflict.

While issues with private and protected access modifiers in interfaces are easy to spot, what about the package-private access? For example, what is the access level of the following two elements volume and start()?

```
public interface Sing {
    float volume = 10;
    abstract void start();
}
```

If you said public, then you are correct! When working with class members, omitting the access modifier indicates default (package-private) access. When working with interface members, though, the lack of access modifier always indicates public access.

Let's try another one. Which line or lines of this top-level interface declaration do not compile?

```
1: private final interface Crawl {
2:     String distance;
3:     private int MAXIMUM_DEPTH = 100;
4:     protected abstract boolean UNDERWATER = false;
5:     private void dig(int depth);
6:     protected abstract double depth();
7:     public final void surface(); }
```

Every single line of this example, including the interface declaration, does not compile! Line 1 does not compile for two reasons. First, it is marked as final, which cannot be applied to an interface since it conflicts with the implicit abstract keyword. Next, it is marked as private, which conflicts with the public or package-private access for top-level interfaces.

Line 2 does not compile because the distance variable is not initialized. Remember that interface variables are assumed to be static final constants and initialized when they are declared. Lines 3 and 4 do not compile because interface variables are also assumed to be public, and the access modifiers on these lines conflict with this. Line 4 also does not compile because variables cannot be marked abstract.

Next, lines 5 and 6 do not compile because all interface abstract methods are assumed to be public and marking them as private or protected is not permitted. Finally, the last line doesn't compile because the method is marked as final, and since interface methods without a body are assumed to be abstract, the compiler throws an exception for using both abstract and final keywords on a method.

Study these examples with conflicting modifiers carefully and make sure you know why they fail to compile. On the exam, you are likely to get at least one question in which an interface includes a member that contains an invalid modifier.

Differences between Interfaces and Abstract Classes

Even though abstract classes and interfaces are both considered abstract types, only interfaces make use of implicit modifiers. This means that an abstract class and interface with similar declarations may have very different properties. For example, how do the play() methods differ in the following two definitions?

```
abstract class Husky {
    abstract void play();
}

interface Poodle {
    void play();
}
```

Both of these method definitions are considered abstract. That said, the Husky class will not compile if the play() method is not marked abstract, whereas the method in the Poodle interface will compile with or without the abstract modifier.

What about the access level of the play() method? Even though neither has an access modifier, they do not have the same access level. The play() method in Husky class is considered default (package-private), whereas the method in the Poodle interface is assumed to be public. This is especially important when you create classes that inherit these definitions. For example, can you spot anything wrong with the following class definitions that use our abstract types?

```
class Webby extends Husky {
    void play() {}
}
class Georgette implements Poodle {
    void play() {}
}
```

The Webby class compiles, but the Georgette class does not. Even though the two method implementations are identical, the method in the Georgette class breaks the rules of method overriding. From the Poodle interface, the inherited abstract method is assumed to be public. The definition of play() in the Georgette class therefore reduces the visibility of a method from public to package-private, resulting in a compiler error. The following is the correct implementation of the Georgette class:

```
class Georgette implements Poodle {
    public void play() {}
}
```

Inheriting an Interface

An interface can be inherited in one of three ways.

- An interface can extend another interface.
- A class can implement an interface.
- A class can extend another class whose ancestor implements an interface.

When an interface is inherited, all of the abstract methods are inherited. Like we saw with abstract classes, if the type inheriting the interface is also abstract, such as an interface or abstract class, it is not required to implement the interface methods. On the other hand, the first concrete subclass that inherits the interface must implement all of the inherited abstract methods.

We illustrate this principle in Figure 9.3. How many abstract methods does the concrete Swan class inherit?

FIGURE 9.3 Interface Inheritance

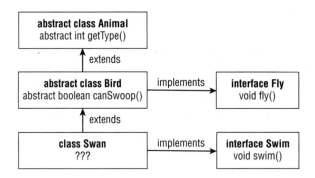

The Swan class inherits four methods: the public fly() and swim() methods, along with the package-private getType() and canSwoop() methods.

Let's take a look at another example involving an abstract class that implements an interface:

```
public interface HasTail {
    public int getTailLength();
}
public interface HasWhiskers {
    public int getNumberOfWhiskers();
}
public abstract class HarborSeal implements HasTail, HasWhiskers {
}
public class CommonSeal extends HarborSeal {  // DOES NOT COMPILE
}
```

The HarborSeal class is not required to implement any of the abstract methods it inherits from the HasTail and HasWhiskers because it is marked abstract. The concrete class CommonSeal, which extends HarborSeal, is required to implement all inherited abstract methods. In this example, CommonSeal doesn't provide an implementation for the inherited abstract interface methods, so CommonSeal doesn't compile.

Mixing Class and Interface Keywords

The exam creators are fond of questions that mix class and interface terminology. Although a class can implement an interface, a class cannot extend an interface. Likewise, while an interface can extend another interface, an interface cannot implement another interface. The following examples illustrate these principles:

```
public interface CanRun {}
public class Cheetah extends CanRun {}   // DOES NOT COMPILE

public class Hyena {}
public interface HasFur extends Hyena {} // DOES NOT COMPILE
```

The first example shows a class trying to extend an interface that doesn't compile. The second example shows an interface trying to extend a class, which also doesn't compile. Be wary of examples on the exam that mix class and interface definitions. The following is the only valid syntax for relating classes and interfaces in their declarations:

```
class1 extends class2

interface1 extends interface2, interface3, ...

class1 implements interface2, interface3, ...
```

Duplicate Interface Method Declarations

Since Java allows for multiple inheritance via interfaces, you might be wondering what will happen if you define a class that inherits from two interfaces that contain the same abstract method.

```
public interface Herbivore {
    public void eatPlants();
}

public interface Omnivore {
    public void eatPlants();
    public void eatMeat();
}
```

In this scenario, the signatures for the two interface methods eatPlants() are duplicates. As they have identical method declarations, they are also considered *compatible*. By compatibility, we mean that the compiler can resolve the differences between the two declarations without finding any conflicts. You can define a class that fulfills both interfaces simultaneously.

```
public class Bear implements Herbivore, Omnivore {
    public void eatMeat() {
        System.out.println("Eating meat");
    }
    public void eatPlants() {
        System.out.println("Eating plants");
    }
}
```

As we said earlier, interfaces simply define a set of rules that a class implementing them must follow. If two abstract interface methods have identical behaviors—or in this case the same method declaration—you just need to be able to create a single method that overrides both inherited abstract methods at the same time.

What if the duplicate methods have different signatures? If the method name is the same but the input parameters are different, there is no conflict because this is considered a method overload. We demonstrate this principle in the following example:

```
public interface Herbivore {
    public int eatPlants(int quantity);
}

public interface Omnivore {
    public void eatPlants();
}

public class Bear implements Herbivore, Omnivore {
```

```
    public int eatPlants(int quantity) {
        System.out.println("Eating plants: "+quantity);
        return quantity;
    }
    public void eatPlants() {
        System.out.println("Eating plants");
    }
}
```

In this example, we see that the class that implements both interfaces must provide implementations of both versions of eatPlants(), since they are considered separate methods.

What if the duplicate methods have the same signature but different return types? In that case, you need to review the rules for overriding methods. Let's try an example:

```
interface Dances {
    String swingArms();
}
interface EatsFish {
    CharSequence swingArms();
}

public class Penguin implements Dances, EatsFish {
    public String swingArms() {
        return "swing!";
    }
}
```

In this example, the Penguin class compiles. The Dances version of the swingArms() method is trivially overridden in the Penguin class, as the declaration in Dances and Penguin have the same method declarations. The EatsFish version of swingArms() is also overridden as String and CharSequence are covariant return types.

Let's take a look at a sample where the return types are not covariant:

```
interface Dances {
    int countMoves();
}
interface EatsFish {
    boolean countMoves();
}

public class Penguin implements Dances, EatsFish { // DOES NOT COMPILE
    ...
}
```

Since it is not possible to define a version of countMoves() that returns both int and boolean, there is no implementation of the Penguin that will allow this declaration to compile. It is the equivalent of trying to define two methods in the same class with the same signature and different return types.

The compiler would also throw an exception if you define an abstract class or interface that inherits from two conflicting abstract types, as shown here:

```java
interface LongEars {
   int softSkin();
}
interface LongNose {
   void softSkin();
}

interface Donkey extends LongEars, LongNose {}  // DOES NOT COMPILE

abstract class Aardvark implements LongEars, LongNose {}
                                          // DOES NOT COMPILE
```

All of the types in this example are abstract, with none being concrete. Despite the fact they are all abstract, the compiler detects that Donkey and Aardvark contain incompatible methods and prevents them from compiling.

Polymorphism and Interfaces

In Chapter 8, we introduced polymorphism and showed how an object in Java can take on many forms through references. While many of the same rules apply, the fact that a class can inherit multiple interfaces limits some of the checks the compiler can perform.

Abstract Reference Types

When working with abstract types, you may prefer to work with the abstract reference types, rather than the concrete class. This is especially common when defining method parameters. Consider the following implementation:

```java
import java.util.*;
public class Zoo {
   public void sortAndPrintZooAnimals(List<String> animals) {
      Collections.sort(animals);
      for(String a : animals) {
         System.out.println(a);
      }
   }
}
```

This class defines a method that sorts and prints animals in alphabetical order. At no point is this class interested in what the actual underlying object for animals is. It might be an ArrayList, which you have seen before, but it may also be a LinkedList or a Vector (neither of which you need to know for the exam).

Casting Interfaces

Let's say you have an abstract reference type variable, which has been instantiated by a concrete subclass. If you need access to a method that is only declared in the concrete subclass, then you will need to cast the interface reference to that type, assuming the cast is supported at runtime. That brings us back to a rule we discussed in Chapter 8, namely, that the compiler does not allow casts to unrelated types. For example, the following is not permitted as the compiler detects that the String and Long class cannot be related:

```
String lion = "Bert";
Long tiger = (Long)lion;
```

With interfaces, there are limitations to what the compiler can validate. For example, does the following program compile?

```
1: interface Canine {}
2: class Dog implements Canine {}
3: class Wolf implements Canine {}
4:
5: public class BadCasts {
6:     public static void main(String[] args) {
7:         Canine canine = new Wolf();
8:         Canine badDog = (Dog)canine;
9:     } }
```

In this program, a Wolf object is created and then assigned to a Canine reference type on line 7. Because of polymorphism, Java cannot be sure which specific class type the canine instance on line 8 is. Therefore, it allows the invalid cast to the Dog reference type, even though Dog and Wolf are not related. The code compiles but throws a ClassCastException at runtime.

This limitation aside, the compiler can enforce one rule around interface casting. The compiler does not allow a cast from an interface reference to an object reference if the object type does not implement the interface. For example, the following change to line 8 causes the program to fail to compile:

```
8:         Object badDog = (String)canine;  // DOES NOT COMPILE
```

Since String does implement Canine, the compiler recognizes that this cast is not possible.

Interfaces and the *instanceof* Operator

In Chapter 3, "Operators," we showed that the compiler will report an error if you attempt to use the `instanceof` operator with two unrelated classes, as follows:

```
Number tickets = 4;
if(tickets instanceof String) {}  // DOES NOT COMPILE
```

With interfaces, the compiler has limited ability to enforce this rule because even though a reference type may not implement an interface, one of its subclasses could. For example, the following does compile:

```
Number tickets = 5;
if(tickets instanceof List) {}
```

Even though `Number` does not inherit `List`, it's possible the `tickets` variable may be a reference to a subclass of `Number` that does inherit `List`. As an example, the `tickets` variable could be assigned to an instance of the following `MyNumber` class (assuming all inherited methods were implemented):

```
public class MyNumber extends Number implements List
```

That said, the compiler can check for unrelated interfaces if the reference is a class that is marked `final`.

```
Integer tickets = 6;
if(tickets instanceof List) {}  // DOES NOT COMPILE
```

The compiler rejects this code because the `Integer` class is marked `final` and does not inherit `List`. Therefore, it is not possible to create a subclass of `Integer` that inherits the `List` interface.

Reviewing Interface Rules

We summarize the interface rules in this part of the chapter in the following list. If you compare the list to our list of rules for an abstract class definition, the first four rules are similar.

Interface Definition Rules

1. Interfaces cannot be instantiated.
2. All top-level types, including interfaces, cannot be marked `protected` or `private`.
3. Interfaces are assumed to be abstract and cannot be marked `final`.
4. Interfaces may include zero or more abstract methods.
5. An interface can extend any number of interfaces.
6. An interface reference may be cast to any reference that inherits the interface, although this may produce an exception at runtime if the classes aren't related.

7. The compiler will only report an unrelated type error for an `instanceof` operation with an interface on the right side if the reference on the left side is a `final` class that does not inherit the interface.

8. An interface method with a body must be marked `default`, `private`, `static`, or `private static` (covered when studying for the 1Z0-816 exam).

The following are the five rules for abstract methods defined in interfaces.

Abstract Interface Method Rules

1. Abstract methods can be defined only in abstract classes or interfaces.

2. Abstract methods cannot be declared `private` or `final`.

3. Abstract methods must not provide a method body/implementation in the abstract class in which is it declared.

4. Implementing an abstract method in a subclass follows the same rules for overriding a method, including covariant return types, exception declarations, etc.

5. Interface methods without a body are assumed to be `abstract` and `public`.

Notice anything? The first four rules for abstract methods, whether they be defined in abstract classes or interfaces, are exactly the same! The only new rule you need to learn for interfaces is the last one.

Finally, there are two rules to remember for interface variables.

Interface Variables Rules

1. Interface variables are assumed to be `public`, `static`, and `final`.

2. Because interface variables are marked `final`, they must be initialized with a value when they are declared.

It may be helpful to think of an interface as a specialized kind of abstract class, since it shares many of the same properties and rules as an abstract class. The primary differences between the two are that interfaces include implicit modifiers, do not contain constructors, do not participate in the instance initialization process, and support multiple inheritance.

 Real World Scenario

Using an Interface vs. Implementing an Interface

An interface provides a way for one individual to develop code that uses another individual's code, without having access to the other individual's underlying implementation. Interfaces can facilitate rapid application development by enabling development teams to create applications in parallel, rather than being directly dependent on each other.

For example, two teams can work together to develop a one-page standard interface at the start of a project. One team then develops code that *uses* the interface, while the other team develops code that *implements* the interface. The development teams can then combine their implementations toward the end of the project, and as long as both teams developed with the same interface, they will be compatible. Of course, testing will still be required to make sure that the class implementing the interface behaves as expected.

Introducing Inner Classes

We conclude this chapter with a brief discussion of inner classes. For the 1Z0-815 exam, you only need to know the basics of inner classes. In particular, you should know the difference between a top-level class and an inner class, permitted access modifiers for an inner class, and how to define a member inner class.

> For simplicity, we will often refer to inner or nested interfaces as *inner classes*, as the rules described in this chapter for inner classes apply to both class and interface types.

Defining a Member Inner Class

A *member inner class* is a class defined at the member level of a class (the same level as the methods, instance variables, and constructors). It is the opposite of a top-level class, in that it cannot be declared unless it is inside another class.

Developers often define a member inner class inside another class if the relationship between the two classes is very close. For example, a Zoo sells tickets for its patrons; therefore, it may want to manage the lifecycle of the Ticket object.

> For the 1Z0-816 exam, there are four types of nested classes you will need to know about: member inner classes, local classes, anonymous classes, and static nested classes. You'll also need to know more detail about member inner classes. For this chapter, we limit our discussion to just the basics of member inner classes, as this is all you need to know on the 1Z0-815 exam.

The following is an example of an outer class Zoo with an inner class Ticket:

```
public class Zoo {
    public class Ticket {}
}
```

We can expand this to include an interface.

```
public class Zoo {
   private interface Paper {}
   public class Ticket implements Paper {}
}
```

While top-level classes and interfaces can only be set with `public` or package-private access, member inner classes do not have the same restriction. A member inner class can be declared with all of the same access modifiers as a class member, such as `public`, protected, default (package-private), or `private`.

A member inner class can contain many of the same methods and variables as a top-level class. Some members are disallowed in member inner classes, such as `static` members, although you don't need to know that for the 1Z0-815 exam. Let's update our example with some instance members.

```
public class Zoo {
   private interface Paper {
      public String getId();
   }
   public class Ticket implements Paper {
      private String serialNumber;
      public String getId() { return serialNumber;}
   }
}
```

Our `Zoo` and `Ticket` examples are starting to become more interesting. In the next section, we will show you how to use them.

Using a Member Inner Class

One of the ways a member inner class can be used is by calling it in the outer class. Continuing with our previous example, let's define a method in `Zoo` that makes use of the member inner class with a new `sellTicket()` method.

```
public class Zoo {
   private interface Paper {
      public String getId();
   }
   public class Ticket implements Paper {
      private String serialNumber;
      public String getId() { return serialNumber; }
   }
   public Ticket sellTicket(String serialNumber) {
```

```
        var t = new Ticket();
        t.serialNumber = serialNumber;
        return t;
    }
}
```

The advantage of using a member inner class in this example is that the Zoo class completely manages the lifecycle of the Ticket class.

Let's add an entry point to this example.

```
public class Zoo {
    ...
    public static void main(String... unused) {
        var z = new Zoo();
        var t = z.sellTicket("12345");
        System.out.println(t.getId()+" Ticket sold!");
    }
}
```

This compiles and prints 12345 Ticket sold! at runtime.

For the 1Z0-815 exam, this is the extent of what you need to know about inner classes. As discussed, when you study for the 1Z0-816 exam, there is a lot more you will need to know.

Summary

In this chapter, we presented advanced topics in class design, starting with abstract classes. An abstract class is just like a regular class except that it cannot be instantiated and may contain abstract methods. An abstract class can extend a nonabstract class, and vice versa. Abstract classes can be used to define a framework that other developers write subclasses against.

An abstract method is one that does not include a body when it is declared. An abstract method may be placed inside an abstract class or interface. Next, an abstract method can be overridden with another abstract declaration or a concrete implementation, provided the rules for overriding methods are followed. The first concrete class must implement all of the inherited abstract methods, whether they are inherited from an abstract class or interface.

An interface is a special type of abstract structure that primarily contains abstract methods and constant variables. Interfaces include implicit modifiers, which are modifiers that the compiler will automatically apply to the interface declaration. For the 1Z0-815 exam, you should know which modifiers are assumed in interfaces and be able to spot potential conflicts. When you prepare for the 1Z0-816 exam, you will study the four additional non-abstract methods that interfaces now support. Finally, while the compiler can often prevent casting to unrelated types, it has limited ability to prevent invalid casts when working with interfaces.

We concluded this chapter with a brief presentation of member inner classes. For the exam, you should be able to recognize member inner classes and know which access modifiers are allowed. Member inner classes, along with the other types of nested classes, will be covered in much more detail when you study for the 1Z0-816 exam.

Exam Essentials

Be able to write code that creates and extends abstract classes.   In Java, classes and methods can be declared as abstract. An abstract class cannot be instantiated. An instance of an abstract class can be obtained only through a concrete subclass. Abstract classes can include any number, including zero, of abstract and nonabstract methods. Abstract methods follow all the method override rules and may be defined only within abstract classes. The first concrete subclass of an abstract class must implement all the inherited methods. Abstract classes and methods may not be marked as final.

Be able to write code that creates, extends, and implements interfaces.   Interfaces are specialized abstract types that focus on abstract methods and constant variables. An interface may extend any number of interfaces and, in doing so, inherits their abstract methods. An interface cannot extend a class, nor can a class extend an interface. A class may implement any number of interfaces.

Know the implicit modifiers that the compiler will automatically apply to an interface. All interfaces are assumed to be abstract. An interface method without a body is assumed to be public and abstract. An interface variable is assumed to be public, static, and final and initialized with a value when it is declared. Using a modifier that conflicts with one of these implicit modifiers will result in a compiler error.

Distinguish between top-level and inner classes/interfaces and know which access modifiers are allowed.   A top-level class or interface is one that is not defined within another class declaration, while an inner class or interface is one defined within another class. Inner classes can be marked public, protected, package-private, or private.

Review Questions

1. What modifiers are implicitly applied to all interface methods that do not declare a body? (Choose all that apply.)

    A. protected

    B. public

    C. static

    D. void

    E. abstract

    F. default

2. Which of the following statements can be inserted in the blank line so that the code will compile successfully? (Choose all that apply.)

    ```
    interface CanHop {}
    public class Frog implements CanHop {
        public static void main(String[] args) {
            _____ frog = new TurtleFrog();
        }
    }
    class BrazilianHornedFrog extends Frog {}
    class TurtleFrog extends Frog {}
    ```

    A. Frog

    B. TurtleFrog

    C. BrazilianHornedFrog

    D. CanHop

    E. Object

    F. Long

    G. None of the above; the code contains a compilation error.

3. Which of the following is true about a concrete class? (Choose all that apply.)

    A. A concrete class can be declared as abstract.

    B. A concrete class must implement all inherited abstract methods.

    C. A concrete class can be marked as final.

    D. If a concrete class inherits an interface from one of its superclasses, then it must declare an implementation for all methods defined in that interface.

    E. A concrete method that implements an abstract method must match the method declaration of the abstract method exactly.

4. Which statements about the following program are correct? (Choose all that apply.)

```
1:  interface HasExoskeleton {
2:      double size = 2.0f;
3:      abstract int getNumberOfSections();
4:  }
5:  abstract class Insect implements HasExoskeleton {
6:      abstract int getNumberOfLegs();
7:  }
8:  public class Beetle extends Insect {
9:      int getNumberOfLegs() { return 6; }
10:     int getNumberOfSections(int count) { return 1; }
11: }
```

A. It compiles without issue.

B. The code will produce a ClassCastException if called at runtime.

C. The code will not compile because of line 2.

D. The code will not compile because of line 5.

E. The code will not compile because of line 8.

F. The code will not compile because of line 10.

5. What modifiers are implicitly applied to all interface variables? (Choose all that apply.)

A. private

B. nonstatic

C. final

D. const

E. abstract

F. public

G. default (package-private)

6. Which statements about the following program are correct? (Choose all that apply.)

```
1: public abstract interface Herbivore {
2:     int amount = 10;
3:     public void eatGrass();
4:     public abstract int chew() { return 13; }
5: }
6:
7: abstract class IsAPlant extends Herbivore {
8:     Object eatGrass(int season) { return null; }
9: }
```

A. It compiles and runs without issue.

B. The code will not compile because of line 1.

C. The code will not compile because of line 2.

D. The code will not compile because of line 4.

E. The code will not compile because of line 7.

F. The code will not compile because line 8 contains an invalid method override.

7. Which statements about the following program are correct? (Choose all that apply.)

```
1: abstract class Nocturnal {
2:     boolean isBlind();
3: }
4: public class Owl extends Nocturnal {
5:     public boolean isBlind() { return false; }
6:     public static void main(String[] args) {
7:         var nocturnal = (Nocturnal)new Owl();
8:         System.out.println(nocturnal.isBlind());
9: } }
```

A. It compiles and prints true.

B. It compiles and prints false.

C. The code will not compile because of line 2.

D. The code will not compile because of line 5.

E. The code will not compile because of line 7.

F. The code will not compile because of line 8.

G. None of the above

8. Which statements are true about the following code? (Choose all that apply.)

```
interface Dog extends CanBark, HasVocalCords {
    abstract int chew();
}

public interface CanBark extends HasVocalCords {
    public void bark();
}

interface HasVocalCords {
    public abstract void makeSound();
}
```

A. The CanBark declaration doesn't compile.

B. A class that implements HasVocalCords must override the makeSound() method.

    C. A class that implements `CanBark` inherits both the `makeSound()` and `bark()` methods.

    D. A class that implements `Dog` must be marked `final`.

    E. The `Dog` declaration does not compile because an interface cannot extend two interfaces.

9. Which access modifiers can be applied to member inner classes? (Choose all that apply.)

    A. `static`

    B. `public`

    C. default (package-private)

    D. `final`

    E. `protected`

    F. `private`

10. Which statements are true about the following code? (Choose all that apply.)

```
5: public interface CanFly {
6:     int fly()
7:     String fly(int distance);
8: }
9: interface HasWings {
10:    abstract String fly();
11:    public abstract Object getWingSpan();
12: }
13: abstract class Falcon implements CanFly, HasWings {}
```

    A. It compiles without issue.

    B. The code will not compile because of line 5.

    C. The code will not compile because of line 6.

    D. The code will not compile because of line 7.

    E. The code will not compile because of line 9.

    F. The code will not compile because of line 10.

    G. The code will not compile because of line 13.

11. Which modifier pairs can be used together in a method declaration? (Choose all that apply.)

    A. `static` and `final`

    B. `private` and `static`

    C. `static` and `abstract`

    D. `private` and `abstract`

    E. `abstract` and `final`

    F. `private` and `final`

12. Which of the following statements about the `FruitStand` program are correct? (Choose all that apply.)

```
1:  interface Apple {}
2:  interface Orange {}
3:  class Gala implements Apple {}
4:  class Tangerine implements Orange {}
5:  final class Citrus extends Tangerine {}
6:  public class FruitStand {
7:      public static void main(String... farm) {
8:          Gala g = new Gala();
9:          Tangerine t = new Tangerine();
10:         Citrus c = new Citrus();
11:         System.out.print(t instanceof Gala);
12:         System.out.print(c instanceof Tangerine);
13:         System.out.print(g instanceof Apple);
14:         System.out.print(t instanceof Apple);
15:         System.out.print(c instanceof Apple);
16: } }
```

A. Line 11 contains a compiler error.

B. Line 12 contains a compiler error.

C. Line 13 contains a compiler error.

D. Line 14 contains a compiler error.

E. Line 15 contains a compiler error.

F. None of the above

13. What is the output of the following code?

```
1:  interface Jump {
2:      static public int MAX = 3;
3:  }
4:  public abstract class Whale implements Jump {
5:      public abstract void dive();
6:      public static void main(String[] args) {
7:          Whale whale = new Orca();
8:          whale.dive(3);
9:      }
10: }
11: class Orca extends Whale {
12:     public void dive() {
13:         System.out.println("Orca diving");
14:     }
```

```
15:     public void dive(int... depth) {
16:         System.out.println("Orca diving deeper "+MAX);
17: } }
```

A. Orca diving

B. Orca diving deeper 3

C. The code will not compile because of line 2.

D. The code will not compile because of line 4.

E. The code will not compile because of line 11.

F. The code will not compile because of line 16.

G. None of the above

14. Which statements are true for both abstract classes and interfaces? (Choose all that apply.)

A. Both can be extended using the extends keyword.

B. All methods within them are assumed to be abstract.

C. Both can contain public static final variables.

D. The compiler will insert the implicit abstract modifier automatically on methods declared without a body, if they are not marked as such.

E. Both interfaces and abstract classes can be declared with the abstract modifier.

F. Both inherit java.lang.Object.

15. What is the result of the following code?

```
1:  abstract class Bird {
2:      private final void fly() { System.out.println("Bird"); }
3:      protected Bird() { System.out.print("Wow-"); }
4:  }
5:  public class Pelican extends Bird {
6:      public Pelican() { System.out.print("Oh-"); }
7:      protected void fly() { System.out.println("Pelican"); }
8:      public static void main(String[] args) {
9:          var chirp = new Pelican();
10:         chirp.fly();
11: } }
```

A. Oh-Bird

B. Oh-Pelican

C. Wow-Oh-Bird

D. Wow-Oh-Pelican

E. The code contains a compilation error.

F. None of the above

16. Which of the following statements about this program is correct?

```
1: interface Aquatic {
2:     int getNumOfGills(int p);
3: }
4: public class ClownFish implements Aquatic {
5:     String getNumOfGills() { return "14"; }
6:     int getNumOfGills(int input) { return 15; }
7:     public static void main(String[] args) {
8:         System.out.println(new ClownFish().getNumOfGills(-1));
9: } }
```

A. It compiles and prints 14.

B. It compiles and prints 15.

C. The code will not compile because of line 4.

D. The code will not compile because of line 5.

E. The code will not compile because of line 6.

F. None of the above

17. Which statements about top-level types and member inner classes are correct? (Choose all that apply.)

A. A member inner class can be marked `final`.

B. A top-level type can be marked `protected`.

C. A member inner class cannot be marked `public` since that would make it a top-level class.

D. A top-level type must be stored in a `.java` file with a name that matches the class name.

E. If a member inner class is marked `private`, then it can be referenced only in the outer class for which it is defined.

18. What types can be inserted in the blanks on the lines marked X and Z that allow the code to compile? (Choose all that apply.)

```
interface Walk { public List move(); }
interface Run extends Walk { public ArrayList move(); }
public class Leopard {
    public _____ move() { // X
        return null;
    }
}
public class Panther implements Run {
    public _____ move() { // Z
        return null;
    }
}
```

A. Integer on the line marked X

B. ArrayList on the line marked X

C. List on the line marked Z

D. ArrayList on the line marked Z

E. None of the above, since the Run interface does not compile.

F. The code does not compile for a different reason.

19. Which statements about interfaces are correct? (Choose all that apply.)

A. A class cannot extend multiple interfaces.

B. Java enables true multiple inheritance via interfaces.

C. Interfaces cannot be declared abstract.

D. If an interface does not contain a constructor, the compiler will insert one automatically.

E. An interface can extend multiple interfaces.

F. An interface cannot be instantiated.

20. Which of the following classes and interfaces are correct and compile? (Choose all that apply.)

```
abstract class Camel {
    void travel();
}
interface EatsGrass {
    protected int chew();
}
abstract class Elephant {
    abstract private class SleepsAlot {
        abstract int sleep();
    }
}
class Eagle {
    abstract soar();
}
```

A. SleepsAlot

B. Eagle

C. Camel

D. Elephant

E. EatsGrass

F. None of the classes or interfaces compile.

Chapter

10

Exceptions

OCP EXAM OBJECTIVES COVERED IN THIS CHAPTER:

✓ **Handling Exceptions**

- Describe the advantages of Exception handling and differentiate among checked, unchecked exceptions, and Errors

- Create try-catch blocks and determine how exceptions alter program flow

- Create and invoke a method that throws an exception

Many things can go wrong in a program. Java uses exceptions to deal with some of these scenarios. This chapter focuses on how exceptions are created, how to handle them, and how to distinguish between various types of exceptions and errors.

Understanding Exceptions

A program can fail for just about any reason. Here are just a few possibilities:

- The code tries to connect to a website, but the Internet connection is down.
- You made a coding mistake and tried to access an invalid index in an array.
- One method calls another with a value that the method doesn't support.

As you can see, some of these are coding mistakes. Others are completely beyond your control. Your program can't help it if the Internet connection goes down. What it *can* do is deal with the situation.

First, we'll look at the role of exceptions. Then we'll cover the various types of exceptions, followed by an explanation of how to throw an exception in Java.

The Role of Exceptions

An *exception* is Java's way of saying, "I give up. I don't know what to do right now. You deal with it." When you write a method, you can either deal with the exception or make it the calling code's problem.

As an example, think of Java as a child who visits the zoo. The *happy path* is when nothing goes wrong. The child continues to look at the animals until the program nicely ends. Nothing went wrong, and there were no exceptions to deal with.

This child's younger sister doesn't experience the happy path. In all the excitement she trips and falls. Luckily, it isn't a bad fall. The little girl gets up and proceeds to look at more animals. She has handled the issue all by herself. Unfortunately, she falls again later in the day and starts crying. This time, she has declared she needs help by crying. The story ends well. Her daddy rubs her knee and gives her a hug. Then they go back to seeing more animals and enjoy the rest of the day.

These are the two approaches Java uses when dealing with exceptions. A method can handle the exception case itself or make it the caller's responsibility. You saw both in the trip to the zoo.

You saw an exception in Chapter 1, "Welcome to Java," with a simple Zoo example. You wrote a class that printed out the name of the zoo:

```
1: public class Zoo {
2:     public static void main(String[] args) {
3:         System.out.println(args[0]);
4:         System.out.println(args[1]);
5: } }
```

Then you tried to call it without enough arguments:

```
$ javac Zoo.java
$ java Zoo Zoo
```

On line 4, Java realized there's only one element in the array and index 1 is not allowed. Java threw up its hands in defeat and threw an exception. It didn't try to handle the exception. It just said, "I can't deal with it," and the exception was displayed:

```
Zoo
Exception in thread "main" java.lang.ArrayIndexOutOfBoundsException:
Index 1 out of bounds for length 1
    at Zoo.main(Zoo.java:4)
```

Exceptions can and do occur all the time, even in solid program code. In our example, toddlers falling are a fact of life. When you write more advanced programs, you'll need to deal with failures in accessing files, networks, and outside services. On the exam, exceptions deal largely with mistakes in programs. For example, a program might try to access an invalid position in an array. The key point to remember is that exceptions alter the program flow.

 Real World Scenario

Return Codes vs. Exceptions

Exceptions are used when "something goes wrong." However, the word *wrong* is subjective. The following code returns –1 instead of throwing an exception if no match is found:

```
public int indexOf(String[] names, String name) {
    for (int i = 0; i < names.length; i++) {
        if (names[i].equals(name)) { return i; }
    }
    return -1;
}
```

This approach is common when writing a method that does a search. For example, imagine being asked to find the name Joe in the array. It is perfectly reasonable that Joe might not appear in the array. When this happens, a special value is returned. An exception should be reserved for exceptional conditions like names being null.

In general, try to avoid return codes. Return codes are commonly used in searches, so programmers are expecting them. In other methods, you will take your callers by surprise by returning a special value. An exception forces the program to deal with the problem or end with the exception if left unhandled, whereas a return code could be accidentally ignored and cause problems later in the program. Even worse, a return value could be confused with real data. In the context of a school, does -1 mean an error or the number of students removed from a class? An exception is like shouting, "Deal with me!" and avoids possible ambiguity.

Understanding Exception Types

As we've explained, an exception is an event that alters program flow. Java has a Throwable superclass for all objects that represent these events. Not all of them have the word *exception* in their class name, which can be confusing. Figure 10.1 shows the key subclasses of Throwable.

FIGURE 10.1 Categories of exception

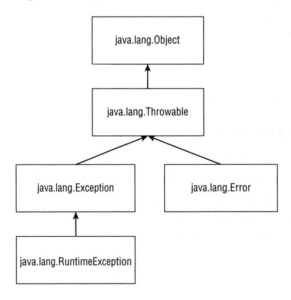

Error means something went so horribly wrong that your program should not attempt to recover from it. For example, the disk drive "disappeared" or the program ran out of memory. These are abnormal conditions that you aren't likely to encounter and cannot recover from.

For the exam, the only thing you need to know about Throwable is that it's the parent class of all exceptions, including the Error class. While you can handle Throwable and Error exceptions, it is not recommended you do so in your application code. In this chapter, when we refer to exceptions, we generally mean any class that inherits Throwable, although we are almost always working with the Exception class or subclasses of it.

Checked Exceptions

A *checked exception* is an exception that must be declared or handled by the application code where it is thrown. In Java, checked exceptions all inherit Exception but not RuntimeException. Checked exceptions tend to be more anticipated—for example, trying to read a file that doesn't exist.

> Checked exceptions also include any class that inherits Throwable, but not Error or RuntimeException. For example, a class that directly extends Throwable would be a checked exception. For the exam, though, you just need to know about checked exceptions that extend Exception.

Checked exceptions? What are we checking? Java has a rule called the handle or declare rule. The *handle or declare rule* means that all checked exceptions that could be thrown within a method are either wrapped in compatible try and catch blocks or declared in the method signature.

Because checked exceptions tend to be anticipated, Java enforces the rule that the programmer must do something to show the exception was thought about. Maybe it was handled in the method. Or maybe the method declares that it can't handle the exception and someone else should.

> While only checked exceptions must be handled or declared in Java, unchecked exceptions (which we will present in the next section) may also be handled or declared. The distinction is that checked exceptions must be handled or declared, while unchecked exceptions can be optionally handled or declared.

Let's take a look at an example. The following fall() method declares that it might throw an IOException, which is a checked exception:

```
void fall(int distance) throws IOException {
    if(distance > 10) {
        throw new IOException();
    }
}
```

Notice that you're using two different keywords here. The throw keyword tells Java that you want to throw an Exception, while the throws keyword simply declares that the method might throw an Exception. It also might not. You will see the throws keyword again later in the chapter.

Now that you know how to declare an exception, how do you instead handle it? The following alternate version of the fall() method handles the exception:

```java
void fall(int distance) {
   try {
      if(distance > 10) {
         throw new IOException();
      }
   } catch (Exception e) {
      e.printStackTrace();
   }
}
```

Notice that the catch statement uses Exception, not IOException. Since IOException is a subclass of Exception, the catch block is allowed to catch it. We'll cover try and catch blocks in more detail later in this chapter.

Unchecked Exceptions

An *unchecked exception* is any exception that does not need to be declared or handled by the application code where it is thrown. Unchecked exceptions are often referred to as runtime exceptions, although in Java, unchecked exceptions include any class that inherits RuntimeException or Error.

A *runtime exception* is defined as the RuntimeException class and its subclasses. Runtime exceptions tend to be unexpected but not necessarily fatal. For example, accessing an invalid array index is unexpected. Even though they do inherit the Exception class, they are not checked exceptions.

Runtime vs. at the Time the Program Is Run

A runtime (unchecked) exception is a specific type of exception. All exceptions occur at the time that the program is run. (The alternative is compile time, which would be a compiler error.) People don't refer to them as "run time" exceptions because that would be too easy to confuse with runtime! When you see *runtime*, it means unchecked.

An unchecked exception can often occur on nearly any line of code, as it is not required to be handled or declared. For example, a NullPointerException can be thrown in the body of the following method if the input reference is null:

```java
void fall(String input) {
   System.out.println(input.toLowerCase());
}
```

We work with objects in Java so frequently, a `NullPointerException` can happen almost anywhere. If you had to declare unchecked exceptions everywhere, every single method would have that clutter! The code will compile if you declare an unchecked exception. However, it is redundant.

Checked vs. Unchecked (Runtime) Exceptions

In the past, developers used checked exceptions more often than they do now. According to Oracle, they are intended for issues a programmer "might reasonably be expected to recover from." Then developers started writing code where a chain of methods kept declaring the same exception and nobody actually handled it. Some libraries started using unchecked exceptions for issues a programmer might reasonably be expected to recover from. Many programmers can hold a debate with you on which approach is better. For the exam, you need to know the rules for how checked versus unchecked exceptions function. You don't have to decide philosophically whether an exception should be checked or unchecked.

Throwing an Exception

Any Java code can throw an exception; this includes code you write. The exam is limited to exceptions that someone else has created. Most likely, they will be exceptions that are provided with Java. You might encounter an exception that was made up for the exam. This is fine. The question will make it obvious that these are exceptions by having the class name end with `Exception`. For example, `MyMadeUpException` is clearly an exception.

On the exam, you will see two types of code that result in an exception. The first is code that's wrong. Here's an example:

```java
String[] animals = new String[0];
System.out.println(animals[0]);
```

This code throws an `ArrayIndexOutOfBoundsException` since the array has no elements. That means questions about exceptions can be hidden in questions that appear to be about something else.

 On the exam, many questions have a choice about not compiling and about throwing an exception. Pay special attention to code that calls a method on a `null` reference or that references an invalid array or `List` index. If you spot this, you know the correct answer is that the code throws an exception at runtime.

The second way for code to result in an exception is to explicitly request Java to throw one. Java lets you write statements like these:

```
throw new Exception();
throw new Exception("Ow! I fell.");
throw new RuntimeException();
throw new RuntimeException("Ow! I fell.");
```

The throw keyword tells Java you want some other part of the code to deal with the exception. This is the same as the young girl crying for her daddy. Someone else needs to figure out what to do about the exception.

---

throw vs. throws

Anytime you see throw or throws on the exam, make sure the correct one is being used. The throw keyword is used as a statement inside a code block to throw a new exception or rethrow an existing exception, while the throws keyword is used only at the end of a method declaration to indicate what exceptions it supports. On the exam, you might start reading a long class definition only to realize the entire thing does not compile due to the wrong keyword being used.

When creating an exception, you can usually pass a String parameter with a message, or you can pass no parameters and use the defaults. We say *usually* because this is a convention. Someone could create an exception class that does not have a constructor that takes a message. The first two examples create a new object of type Exception and throw it. The last two show that the code looks the same regardless of which type of exception you throw.

Additionally, you should know that an Exception is an Object. This means you can store in a variable, and this is legal:

```
Exception e = new RuntimeException();
throw e;
```

The code instantiates an exception on one line and then throws on the next. The exception can come from anywhere, even passed into a method. As long as it is a valid exception, it can be thrown.

The exam might also try to trick you. Do you see why this code doesn't compile?

```
throw RuntimeException();   // DOES NOT COMPILE
```

If your answer is that there is a missing keyword, you're absolutely right. The exception is never instantiated with the new keyword.

Let's take a look at another place the exam might try to trick you. Can you see why the following does not compile?

```
3: try {
4:     throw new RuntimeException();
5:     throw new ArrayIndexOutOfBoundsException();  // DOES NOT COMPILE
6: } catch (Exception e) {
7: }
```

Since line 4 throws an exception, line 5 can never be reached during runtime. The compiler recognizes this and reports an unreachable code error.

The types of exceptions are important. Be sure to closely study everything in Table 10.1. Remember that a `Throwable` is either an `Exception` or an `Error`. You should not catch `Throwable` directly in your code.

TABLE 10.1   Types of exceptions and errors

Type	How to recognize	Okay for program to catch?	Is program required to handle or declare?
Runtime exception	Subclass of `RuntimeException`	Yes	No
Checked exception	Subclass of `Exception` but not subclass of `RuntimeException`	Yes	Yes
Error	Subclass of `Error`	No	No

Recognizing Exception Classes

You need to recognize three groups of exception classes for the exam: `RuntimeException`, checked `Exception`, and `Error`. We'll look at common examples of each type. For the exam, you'll need to recognize which type of an exception it is and whether it's thrown by the Java virtual machine (JVM) or a programmer. So that you can recognize them, we'll show you some code examples for those exceptions. For some exceptions, you also need to know which are inherited from one another.

RuntimeException Classes

`RuntimeException` and its subclasses are unchecked exceptions that don't have to be handled or declared. They can be thrown by the programmer or by the JVM. Common `RuntimeException` classes include the following:

`ArithmeticException`   Thrown when code attempts to divide by zero

`ArrayIndexOutOfBoundsException`   Thrown when code uses an illegal index to access an array

`ClassCastException`   Thrown when an attempt is made to cast an object to a class of which it is not an instance

`NullPointerException`   Thrown when there is a `null` reference where an object is required

`IllegalArgumentException`   Thrown by the programmer to indicate that a method has been passed an illegal or inappropriate argument

NumberFormatException   Subclass of IllegalArgumentException thrown when an attempt is made to convert a string to a numeric type but the string doesn't have an appropriate format

ArithmeticException

Trying to divide an int by zero gives an undefined result. When this occurs, the JVM will throw an ArithmeticException:

```
int answer = 11 / 0;
```

Running this code results in the following output:

```
Exception in thread "main" java.lang.ArithmeticException: / by zero
```

Java doesn't spell out the word *divide*. That's okay, though, because we know that / is the division operator and that Java is trying to tell you division by zero occurred.

The thread "main" is telling you the code was called directly or indirectly from a program with a main method. On the exam, this is all the output you will see. Next comes the name of the exception, followed by extra information (if any) that goes with the exception.

ArrayIndexOutOfBoundsException

You know by now that array indexes start with 0 and go up to 1 less than the length of the array—which means this code will throw an ArrayIndexOutOfBoundsException:

```
int[] countsOfMoose = new int[3];
System.out.println(countsOfMoose[-1]);
```

This is a problem because there's no such thing as a negative array index. Running this code yields the following output:

```
Exception in thread "main" java.lang.ArrayIndexOutOfBoundsException:
Index -1 out of bounds for length 3
```

At least Java tells us what index was invalid. Can you see what's wrong with this one?

```
int total = 0;
int[] countsOfMoose = new int[3];
for (int i = 0; i <= countsOfMoose.length; i++)
   total += countsOfMoose[i];
```

The problem is that the for loop should have < instead of <=. On the final iteration of the loop, Java tries to call countsOfMoose[3], which is invalid. The array includes only three elements, making 2 the largest possible index. The output looks like this:

```
Exception in thread "main" java.lang.ArrayIndexOutOfBoundsException:
Index 3 out of bounds for length 3
```

ClassCastException

Java tries to protect you from impossible casts. This code doesn't compile because `Integer` is not a subclass of `String`:

```
String type = "moose";
Integer number = (Integer) type;  // DOES NOT COMPILE
```

More complicated code thwarts Java's attempts to protect you. When the cast fails at runtime, Java will throw a `ClassCastException`:

```
String type = "moose";
Object obj = type;
Integer number = (Integer) obj;
```

The compiler sees a cast from `Object` to `Integer`. This could be okay. The compiler doesn't realize there's a `String` in that `Object`. When the code runs, it yields the following output:

```
Exception in thread "main" java.lang.ClassCastException:
java.base/java.lang.String
cannot be cast to java.lang.base/java.lang.Integer
```

Java tells you both types that were involved in the problem, making it apparent what's wrong.

NullPointerException

Instance variables and methods must be called on a non-`null` reference. If the reference is `null`, the JVM will throw a `NullPointerException`. It's usually subtle, such as in the following example, which checks whether you remember instance variable references default to `null`:

```
String name;
public void printLength() {
    System.out.println(name.length());
}
```

Running this code results in this output:

```
Exception in thread "main" java.lang.NullPointerException
```

IllegalArgumentException

`IllegalArgumentException` is a way for your program to protect itself. You first saw the following setter method in the Swan class in Chapter 7, "Methods and Encapsulation."

```
6: public void setNumberEggs(int numberEggs) { // setter
7:     if (numberEggs >= 0) // guard condition
8:         this.numberEggs = numberEggs;
9: }
```

This code works, but you don't really want to ignore the caller's request when they tell you a Swan has -2 eggs. You want to tell the caller that something is wrong—preferably in an obvious way that the caller can't ignore so that the programmer will fix the problem. Exceptions are an efficient way to do this. Seeing the code end with an exception is a great reminder that something is wrong:

```java
public void setNumberEggs(int numberEggs) {
   if (numberEggs < 0)
      throw new IllegalArgumentException(
         "# eggs must not be negative");
   this.numberEggs = numberEggs;
}
```

The program throws an exception when it's not happy with the parameter values. The output looks like this:

```
Exception in thread "main"
java.lang.IllegalArgumentException: # eggs must not be negative
```

Clearly this is a problem that must be fixed if the programmer wants the program to do anything useful.

NumberFormatException

Java provides methods to convert strings to numbers. When these are passed an invalid value, they throw a NumberFormatException. The idea is similar to IllegalArgumentException. Since this is a common problem, Java gives it a separate class. In fact, NumberFormatException is a subclass of IllegalArgumentException. Here's an example of trying to convert something non-numeric into an int:

```java
Integer.parseInt("abc");
```

The output looks like this:

```
Exception in thread "main"
java.lang.NumberFormatException: For input string: "abc"
```

For the exam, you need to know that NumberFormatException is a subclass of IllegalArgumentException. We'll cover more about why that is important later in the chapter.

Checked *Exception* Classes

Checked exceptions have Exception in their hierarchy but not RuntimeException. They must be handled or declared. Common checked exceptions include the following:

IOException   Thrown programmatically when there's a problem reading or writing a file

FileNotFoundException   Subclass of IOException thrown programmatically when code tries to reference a file that does not exist

For the exam, you need to know that these are both checked exceptions. You also need to know that `FileNotFoundException` is a subclass of `IOException`. You'll see shortly why that matters.

Error Classes

Errors are unchecked exceptions that extend the `Error` class. They are thrown by the JVM and should not be handled or declared. Errors are rare, but you might see these:

ExceptionInInitializerError   Thrown when a static initializer throws an exception and doesn't handle it

StackOverflowError   Thrown when a method calls itself too many times (This is called *infinite recursion* because the method typically calls itself without end.)

NoClassDefFoundError   Thrown when a class that the code uses is available at compile time but not runtime

ExceptionInInitializerError

Java runs `static` initializers the first time a class is used. If one of the `static` initializers throws an exception, Java can't start using the class. It declares defeat by throwing an `ExceptionInInitializerError`. This code throws an `ArrayIndexOutOfBounds` in a `static` initializer:

```
static {
   int[] countsOfMoose = new int[3];
   int num = countsOfMoose[-1];
}
public static void main(String... args) { }
```

This code yields information about the error and the underlying exception:

```
Exception in thread "main" java.lang.ExceptionInInitializerError
Caused by: java.lang.ArrayIndexOutOfBoundsException: -1 out of bounds for length 3
```

When executed, you get an `ExceptionInInitializerError` because the error happened in a `static` initializer. That information alone wouldn't be particularly useful in fixing the problem. Therefore, Java also tells you the original cause of the problem: the `ArrayIndexOutOfBoundsException` that you need to fix.

The `ExceptionInInitializerError` is an error because Java failed to load the whole class. This failure prevents Java from continuing.

StackOverflowError

When Java calls methods, it puts parameters and local variables on the stack. After doing this a very large number of times, the stack runs out of room and overflows. This is called a `StackOverflowError`. Most of the time, this error occurs when a method calls itself.

```
public static void doNotCodeThis(int num) {
    doNotCodeThis(1);
}
```

The output contains this line:

```
Exception in thread "main" java.lang.StackOverflowError
```

Since the method calls itself, it will never end. Eventually, Java runs out of room on the stack and throws the error. This is called infinite recursion. It is better than an infinite loop because at least Java will catch it and throw the error. With an infinite loop, Java just uses all your CPU until you can kill the program.

NoClassDefFoundError

A `NoClassDefFoundError` occurs when Java can't find the class at runtime. Generally, this means a library available when the code was compiled is not available when the code is executed.

Handling Exceptions

What do you do when you encounter an exception? How do you handle or recover from the exception? In this section, we will show the various statements in Java that support handling exceptions and ensuring certain code, like closing a resource, is always executed.

Using *try* and *catch* Statements

Now that you know what exceptions are, let's explore how to handle them. Java uses a `try` statement to separate the logic that might throw an exception from the logic to handle that exception. Figure 10.2 shows the syntax of a *try statement*.

FIGURE 10.2   The syntax of a try statement

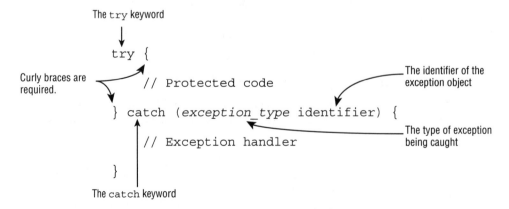

The code in the try block is run normally. If any of the statements throws an exception that can be caught by the exception type listed in the catch block, the try block stops running and execution goes to the catch statement. If none of the statements in the try block throws an exception that can be caught, the *catch clause* is not run.

You probably noticed the words *block* and *clause* used interchangeably. The exam does this as well, so get used to it. Both are correct. *Block* is correct because there are braces present. *Clause* is correct because they are part of a try statement.

There aren't a ton of syntax rules here. The curly braces are required for the try and catch blocks.

In our example, the little girl gets up by herself the first time she falls. Here's what this looks like:

```
3:  void explore() {
4:      try {
5:          fall();
6:          System.out.println("never get here");
7:      } catch (RuntimeException e) {
8:          getUp();
9:      }
10:     seeAnimals();
11: }
12: void fall() {  throw new RuntimeException(); }
```

First, line 5 calls the fall() method. Line 12 throws an exception. This means Java jumps straight to the catch block, skipping line 6. The girl gets up on line 8. Now the try statement is over, and execution proceeds normally with line 10.

Now let's look at some invalid try statements that the exam might try to trick you with. Do you see what's wrong with this one?

```
try  // DOES NOT COMPILE
    fall();
catch (Exception e)
    System.out.println("get up");
```

The problem is that the braces {} are missing. It needs to look like this:

```
try {
    fall();
} catch (Exception e) {
    System.out.println("get up");
}
```

The try statements are like methods in that the curly braces are required even if there is only one statement inside the code blocks, while if statements and loops are special and allow you to omit the curly braces.

What about this one?

```
try { // DOES NOT COMPILE
    fall();
}
```

This code doesn't compile because the try block doesn't have anything after it. Remember, the point of a try statement is for something to happen if an exception is thrown. Without another clause, the try statement is lonely. As you will see shortly, there is a special type of try statement that includes an implicit finally block, although the syntax for this is quite different from this example.

Chaining *catch* Blocks

So far, you have been catching only one type of exception. Now let's see what happens when different types of exceptions can be thrown from the same try/catch block.

For the exam, you won't be asked to create your own exception, but you may be given exception classes and need to understand how they function. Here's how to tackle them. First, you must be able to recognize if the exception is a checked or an unchecked exception. Second, you need to determine whether any of the exceptions are subclasses of the others.

```
class AnimalsOutForAWalk extends RuntimeException { }
class ExhibitClosed extends RuntimeException { }
class ExhibitClosedForLunch extends ExhibitClosed { }
```

In this example, there are three custom exceptions. All are unchecked exceptions because they directly or indirectly extend RuntimeException. Now we chain both types of exceptions with two catch blocks and handle them by printing out the appropriate message:

```
public void visitPorcupine() {
    try {
        seeAnimal();
    } catch (AnimalsOutForAWalk e) { // first catch block
        System.out.print("try back later");
    } catch (ExhibitClosed e) { // second catch block
        System.out.print("not today");
    }
}
```

There are three possibilities for when this code is run. If seeAnimal() doesn't throw an exception, nothing is printed out. If the animal is out for a walk, only the first catch block runs. If the exhibit is closed, only the second catch block runs. It is not possible for both catch blocks to be executed when chained together like this.

A rule exists for the order of the catch blocks. Java looks at them in the order they appear. If it is impossible for one of the catch blocks to be executed, a compiler error about unreachable code occurs. For example, this happens when a superclass catch block appears before a subclass catch block. Remember, we warned you to pay attention to any subclass exceptions.

In the porcupine example, the order of the catch blocks could be reversed because the exceptions don't inherit from each other. And yes, we have seen a porcupine be taken for a walk on a leash.

The following example shows exception types that do inherit from each other:

```
public void visitMonkeys() {
   try {
      seeAnimal();
   } catch (ExhibitClosedForLunch e) {  // subclass exception
      System.out.print("try back later");
   } catch (ExhibitClosed e) {  // superclass exception
      System.out.print("not today");
   }
}
```

If the more specific ExhibitClosedForLunch exception is thrown, the first catch block runs. If not, Java checks whether the superclass ExhibitClosed exception is thrown and catches it. This time, the order of the catch blocks does matter. The reverse does not work.

```
public void visitMonkeys() {
   try {
      seeAnimal();
   } catch (ExhibitClosed e) {
      System.out.print("not today");
   } catch (ExhibitClosedForLunch e) {  // DOES NOT COMPILE
      System.out.print("try back later");
   }
}
```

This time, if the more specific ExhibitClosedForLunch exception is thrown, the catch block for ExhibitClosed runs—which means there is no way for the second catch block to ever run. Java correctly tells you there is an unreachable catch block.

Let's try this one more time. Do you see why this code doesn't compile?

```
public void visitSnakes() {
   try {
   } catch (IllegalArgumentException e) {
   } catch (NumberFormatException e) {  // DOES NOT COMPILE
   }
}
```

Remember we said earlier you needed to know that `NumberFormatException` is a subclass of `IllegalArgumentException`? This example is the reason why. Since `NumberFormatException` is a subclass, it will always be caught by the first catch block, making the second catch block unreachable code that does not compile. Likewise, for the exam you need to know that `FileNotFoundException` is subclass of `IOException` and cannot be used in a similar manner.

To review multiple catch blocks, remember that at most one catch block will run, and it will be the first catch block that can handle it. Also, remember that an exception defined by the catch statement is only in scope for that catch block. For example, the following causes a compiler error since it tries to use the exception class outside the block for which it was defined:

```
public void visitManatees() {
    try {
    } catch (NumberFormatException e1) {
        System.out.println(e1);
    } catch (IllegalArgumentException e2) {
        System.out.println(e1);  // DOES NOT COMPILE
    }
}
```

Applying a Multi-catch Block

Oftentimes, we want the result of an exception being thrown to be the same, regardless of which particular exception is thrown. For example, take a look at this method:

```
public static void main(String args[]) {
    try {
        System.out.println(Integer.parseInt(args[1]));
    } catch (ArrayIndexOutOfBoundsException e) {
        System.out.println("Missing or invalid input");
    } catch (NumberFormatException e) {
        System.out.println("Missing or invalid input");
    }
}
```

Notice that we have the same `println()` statement for two different catch blocks. How can you reduce the duplicate code? One way is to have the related exception classes all inherit the same interface or extend the same class. For example, you can have a single catch block that just catches `Exception`. This will catch everything and anything. Another way is to move the `println()` statements into a separate method and have every related catch block call that method.

While these solutions are valid, Java provides another structure to handle this more gracefully called a *multi-catch* block. A multi-catch block allows multiple exception types to be caught by the same catch block. Let's rewrite the previous example using a multi-catch block:

```
public static void main(String[] args) {
   try {
      System.out.println(Integer.parseInt(args[1]));
   } catch (ArrayIndexOutOfBoundsException | NumberFormatException e) {
      System.out.println("Missing or invalid input");
   }
}
```

This is much better. There's no duplicate code, the common logic is all in one place, and the logic is exactly where you would expect to find it. If you wanted, you could still have a second catch block for Exception in case you want to handle other types of exceptions differently.

Figure 10.3 shows the syntax of multi-catch. It's like a regular catch clause, except two or more exception types are specified separated by a pipe. The pipe (|) is also used as the "or" operator, making it easy to remember that you can use either/or of the exception types. Notice how there is only one variable name in the catch clause. Java is saying that the variable named e can be of type Exception1 or Exception2.

FIGURE 10.3   The syntax of a multi-catch block

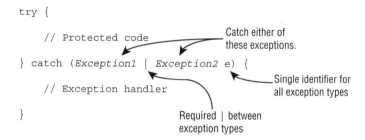

The exam might try to trick you with invalid syntax. Remember that the exceptions can be listed in any order within the catch clause. However, the variable name must appear only once and at the end. Do you see why these are valid or invalid?

```
catch(Exception1 e | Exception2 e | Exception3 e) // DOES NOT COMPILE

catch(Exception1 e1 | Exception2 e2 | Exception3 e3) // DOES NOT COMPILE

catch(Exception1 | Exception2 | Exception3 e)
```

The first line is incorrect because the variable name appears three times. Just because it happens to be the same variable name doesn't make it okay. The second line is incorrect because the variable name again appears three times. Using different variable names doesn't make it any better. The third line does compile. It shows the correct syntax for specifying three exceptions.

Java intends multi-catch to be used for exceptions that aren't related, and it prevents you from specifying redundant types in a multi-catch. Do you see what is wrong here?

```
try {
   throw new IOException();
} catch (FileNotFoundException | IOException p) {} // DOES NOT COMPILE
```

Specifying it in the multi-catch is redundant, and the compiler gives a message such as this:

```
The exception FileNotFoundException is already caught by the alternative IOException
```

Since `FileNotFoundException` is a subclass of `IOException`, this code will not compile. A multi-catch block follows similar rules as chaining `catch` blocks together that you saw in the previous section. For example, both trigger compiler errors when they encounter unreachable code or duplicate exceptions being caught. The one difference between multi-catch blocks and chaining `catch` blocks is that order does not matter for a multi-catch block within a single `catch` expression.

Getting back to the example, the correct code is just to drop the extraneous subclass reference, as shown here:

```
try {
   throw new IOException();
} catch (IOException e) { }
```

To review multi-catch, see how many errors you can find in this `try` statement:

```
11: public void doesNotCompile() { // METHOD DOES NOT COMPILE
12:     try {
13:         mightThrow();
14:     } catch (FileNotFoundException | IllegalStateException e) {
15:     } catch (InputMismatchException e | MissingResourceException e) {
16:     } catch (FileNotFoundException | IllegalArgumentException e) {
17:     } catch (Exception e) {
18:     } catch (IOException e) {
19:     }
20: }
21: private void mightThrow() throws DateTimeParseException, IOException { }
```

This code is just swimming with errors. In fact, some errors hide others, so you might not see them all in the compiler. Once you start fixing some errors, you'll see the others. Here's what's wrong:

- Line 15 has an extra variable name. Remember that there can be only one exception variable per catch block.

- Line 16 cannot catch `FileNotFoundException` because that exception was already caught on line 14. You can't list the same exception type more than once in the same try statement, just like with "regular" catch blocks.

- Lines 17 and 18 are reversed. The more general superclasses must be caught after their subclasses. While this doesn't have anything to do with multi-catch, you'll see "regular" catch block problems mixed in with multi-catch.

Don't worry—you won't see this many problems in the same example on the exam!

Adding a *finally* Block

The try statement also lets you run code at the end with a *finally clause* regardless of whether an exception is thrown. Figure 10.4 shows the syntax of a try statement with this extra functionality.

FIGURE 10.4   The syntax of a try statement with finally

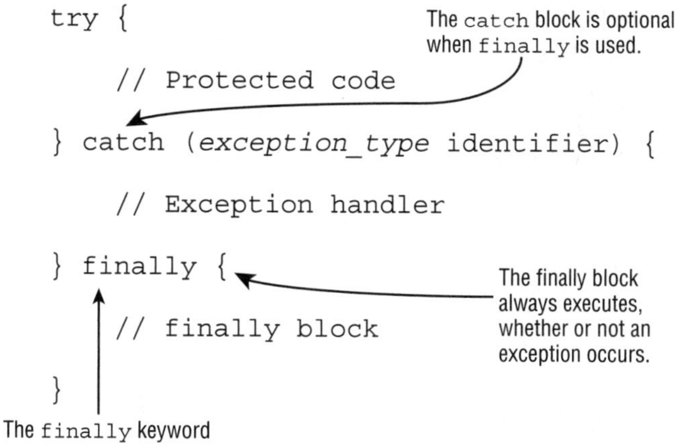

There are two paths through code with both a catch and a finally. If an exception is thrown, the finally block is run after the catch block. If no exception is thrown, the finally block is run after the try block completes.

Let's go back to our young girl example, this time with finally:

```
12: void explore() {
13:     try {
14:         seeAnimals();
15:         fall();
16:     } catch (Exception e) {
17:         getHugFromDaddy();
18:     } finally {
19:         seeMoreAnimals();
20:     }
21:     goHome();
22: }
```

The girl falls on line 15. If she gets up by herself, the code goes on to the `finally` block and runs line 19. Then the `try` statement is over, and the code proceeds on line 21. If the girl doesn't get up by herself, she throws an exception. The `catch` block runs, and she gets a hug on line 17. With that hug she is ready to see more animals on line 19. Then the `try` statement is over, and the code proceeds on line 21. Either way, the ending is the same. The `finally` block is executed, and execution continues after the `try` statement.

The exam will try to trick you with missing clauses or clauses in the wrong order. Do you see why the following do or do not compile?

```
25: try { // DOES NOT COMPILE
26:    fall();
27: } finally {
28:    System.out.println("all better");
29: } catch (Exception e) {
30:    System.out.println("get up");
31: }
32:
33: try { // DOES NOT COMPILE
34:    fall();
35: }
36:
37: try {
38:    fall();
39: } finally {
40:    System.out.println("all better");
41: }
```

The first example (lines 25–31) does not compile because the `catch` and `finally` blocks are in the wrong order. The second example (lines 33–35) does not compile because there must be a `catch` or `finally` block. The third example (lines 37–41) is just fine. The `catch` block is not required if `finally` is present.

One problem with `finally` is that any realistic uses for it are out of the scope of the exam. A `finally` block is typically used to close resources such as files or databases—neither of which is a topic on this exam. This means most of the examples you encounter on the exam with `finally` are going to look contrived. For example, you'll get asked questions such as what this code outputs:

```
public static void main(String[] unused) {
   StringBuilder sb = new StringBuilder();
   try {
      sb.append("t");
   } catch (Exception e) {
      sb.append("c");
   } finally {
      sb.append("f");
```

```
    }
    sb.append("a");
    System.out.print(sb.toString());
}
```

The answer is tfa. The try block is executed. Since no exception is thrown, Java goes straight to the finally block. Then the code after the try statement is run. We know that this is a silly example, but you can expect to see examples like this on the exam.

There is one additional rule you should know for finally blocks. If a try statement with a finally block is entered, then the finally block will always be executed, regardless of whether the code completes successfully. Take a look at the following goHome() method. Assuming an exception may or may not be thrown on line 14, what are the possible values that this method could print? Also, what would the return value be in each case?

```
12: int goHome() {
13:    try {
14:        // Optionally throw an exception here
15:        System.out.print("1");
16:        return -1;
17:    } catch (Exception e) {
18:        System.out.print("2");
19:        return -2;
20:    } finally {
21:        System.out.print("3");
22:        return -3;
23:    }
24: }
```

If an exception is not thrown on line 14, then the line 15 will be executed, printing 1. Before the method returns, though, the finally block is executed, printing 3. If an exception is thrown, then lines 15–16 will be skipped, and lines 17–19 will be executed, printing 2, followed by 3 from the finally block. While the first value printed may differ, the method always prints 3 last since it's in the finally block.

What is the return value of the goHome() method? In this case, it's always -3. Because the finally block is executed shortly before the method completes, it interrupts the return statement from inside both the try and catch blocks.

For the exam, you need to remember that a finally block will always be executed. That said, it may not complete successfully. Take a look at the following code snippet. What would happen if info was null on line 32?

```
31: } finally {
32:     info.printDetails();
33:     System.out.print("Exiting");
34:     return "zoo";
35: }
```

If info is null, then the finally block would be executed, but it would stop on line 32 and throw a NullPointerException. Lines 33–34 would not be executed. In this example, you see that while a finally block will always be executed, it may not finish.

System.exit()

There is one exception to "the finally block always be executed" rule: Java defines a method that you call as System.exit(). It takes an integer parameter that represents the error code that gets returned.

```
try {
   System.exit(0);
} finally {
   System.out.print("Never going to get here");  // Not printed
}
```

System.exit() tells Java, "Stop. End the program right now. Do not pass go. Do not collect $200." When System.exit() is called in the try or catch block, the finally block does not run.

Finally Closing Resources

Oftentimes, your application works with files, databases, and various connection objects. Commonly, these external data sources are referred to as *resources*. In many cases, you *open* a connection to the resource, whether it's over the network or within a file system. You then *read/write* the data you want. Finally, you *close* the resource to indicate you are done with it.

What happens if you don't close a resource when you are done with it? In short, a lot of bad things could happen. If you are connecting to a database, you could use up all available connections, meaning no one can talk to the database until you release your connections. Although you commonly hear about memory leaks as causing programs to fail, a *resource leak* is just as bad and occurs when a program fails to release its connections to a resource, resulting in the resource becoming inaccessible.

Writing code that simplifies closing resources is what this section is about. Let's take a look at a method that opens a file, reads the data, and closes it:

```
4:  public void readFile(String file) {
5:      FileInputStream is = null;
6:      try {
7:          is = new FileInputStream("myfile.txt");
8:          // Read file data
9:      } catch (IOException e) {
10:         e.printStackTrace();
```

```
11:      } finally {
12:         if(is != null) {
13:            try {
14:               is.close();
15:            } catch (IOException e2) {
16:               e2.printStackTrace();
17:            }
18:         }
19:      }
20: }
```

Wow, that's a long method! Why do we have two `try` and `catch` blocks? Well, the code on lines 7 and 14 both include checked `IOException` calls, so they both need to be caught in the method or rethrown by the method. Half the lines of code in this method are just closing a resource. And the more resources you have, the longer code like this becomes. For example, you may have multiple resources and they need to be closed in a particular order. You also don't want an exception from closing one resource to prevent the closing of another resource.

To solve this, Java includes the *try-with-resources* statement to automatically close all resources opened in a `try` clause. This feature is also known as *automatic resource management*, because Java automatically takes care of the closing.

 For the 1Z0-815 exam, you are not required to know any File IO, network, or database classes, although you are required to know try-with-resources. If you see a question on the exam or in this chapter that uses these types of resources, assume that part of the code compiles without issue. In other words, these questions are actually a gift, since you know the problem must be about basic Java syntax or exception handling. That said, for the 1Z0-816 exam, you will need to know numerous resources classes.

Let's take a look at our same example using a try-with-resources statement:

```
4:  public void readFile(String file) {
5:     try (FileInputStream is = new FileInputStream("myfile.txt")) {
6:        // Read file data
7:     } catch (IOException e) {
8:        e.printStackTrace();
9:     }
10: }
```

Functionally, they are both quite similar, but our new version has half as many lines. More importantly, though, by using a try-with-resources statement, we guarantee that as soon as a connection passes out of scope, Java will attempt to close it within the same method.

In the following sections, we will look at the try-with-resources syntax and how to indicate a resource can be automatically closed.

Implicit *finally* Blocks

Behind the scenes, the compiler replaces a try-with-resources block with a try and finally block. We refer to this "hidden" finally block as an implicit finally block since it is created and used by the compiler automatically. You can still create a programmer-defined finally block when using a try-with-resources statement; just be aware that the implicit one will be called first.

Basics of Try-with-Resources

Figure 10.5 shows what a try-with-resources statement looks like. Notice that one or more resources can be opened in the try clause. When there are multiple resources opened, they are closed in the *reverse* order from which they were created. Also, notice that parentheses are used to list those resources, and semicolons are used to separate the declarations. This works just like declaring multiple indexes in a for loop.

FIGURE 10.5   The syntax of a basic try-with-resources

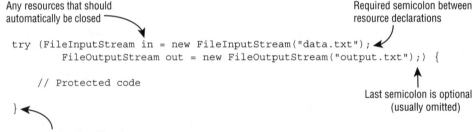

What happened to the catch block in Figure 10.5? Well, it turns out a catch block is optional with a try-with-resources statement. For example, we can rewrite the previous readFile() example so that the method rethrows the exception to make it even shorter:

```
4: public void readFile(String file) throws IOException {
5:     try (FileInputStream is = new FileInputStream("myfile.txt")) {
6:         // Read file data
7:     }
8: }
```

Earlier in the chapter, you learned that a try statement must have one or more catch blocks or a finally block. This is still true. The finally clause exists implicitly. You just don't have to type it.

Remember that only a try-with-resources statement is permitted to omit both the catch and finally blocks. A traditional try statement must have either or both. You can easily distinguish between the two by the presence of parentheses, (), after the try keyword.

Figure 10.6 shows that a try-with-resources statement is still allowed to have catch and/or finally blocks. In fact, if the code within the try block throws a checked exception not declared by the method in which it is defined or handled by another try/catch block, then it will need to be handled by the catch block. Also, the catch and finally blocks are run in addition to the implicit one that closes the resources. For the exam, you need to know that the implicit finally block runs *before* any programmer-coded ones.

FIGURE 10.6 The syntax of try-with-resources including catch/finally

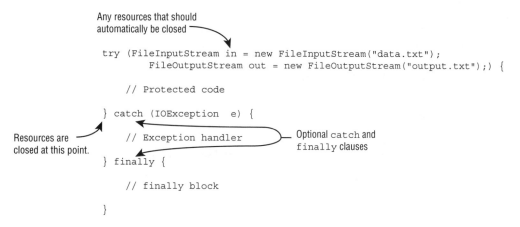

To make sure that you've wrapped your head around the differences, you should be able to fill in Table 10.2 and Table 10.3 with whichever combinations of catch and finally blocks are legal configurations.

TABLE 10.2 Legal vs. illegal configurations with a traditional try statement

	0 finally blocks	1 finally block	2 or more finally blocks
0 catch blocks	Not legal	Legal	Not legal
1 or more catch blocks	Legal	Legal	Not legal

TABLE 10.3 Legal vs. illegal configurations with a try-with-resources statement

	0 finally blocks	**1 finally block**	**2 or more finally blocks**
0 catch blocks	Legal	Legal	Not legal
1 or more catch blocks	Legal	Legal	Not legal

You can see that for both of these try statements, two or more programmer-defined finally blocks are not allowed. Remember that the implicit finally block defined by the compiler is not counted here.

AutoCloseable

You can't just put any random class in a try-with-resources statement. Java requires classes used in a try-with-resources implement the AutoCloseable interface, which includes a void close() method. You'll learn more about resources that implement this method when you study for the 1Z0-816 exam.

Declaring Resources

While try-with-resources does support declaring multiple variables, each variable must be declared in a separate statement. For example, the following do not compile:

```
try (MyFileClass is = new MyFileClass(1),  // DOES NOT COMPILE
     os = new MyFileClass(2)) {
}


try (MyFileClass ab = new MyFileClass(1),  // DOES NOT COMPILE
     MyFileClass cd = new MyFileClass(2)) {
}
```

A try-with-resources statement does not support multiple variable declarations. The first example does not compile because it is missing the data type and it uses a comma (,) instead of a semicolon (;). The second example does not compile because it also uses a comma (,) instead of a semicolon (;). Each resource must include the data type and be separated by a semicolon (;).

You can declare a resource using var as the data type in a try-with-resources statement, since resources are local variables.

```
try (var f = new BufferedInputStream(new FileInputStream("it.txt"))) {
   // Process file
}
```

Declaring resources is a common situation where using var is quite helpful, as it shortens the already long line of code.

Scope of Try-with-Resources

The resources created in the try clause are in scope only within the try block. This is another way to remember that the implicit finally runs before any catch/finally blocks that you code yourself. The implicit close has run already, and the resource is no longer available. Do you see why lines 6 and 8 don't compile in this example?

```
3: try (Scanner s = new Scanner(System.in)) {
4:     s.nextLine();
5: } catch(Exception e) {
6:     s.nextInt(); // DOES NOT COMPILE
7: } finally {
8:     s.nextInt(); // DOES NOT COMPILE
9: }
```

The problem is that Scanner has gone out of scope at the end of the try clause. Lines 6 and 8 do not have access to it. This is actually a nice feature. You can't accidentally use an object that has been closed. In a traditional try statement, the variable has to be declared before the try statement so that both the try and finally blocks can access it, which has the unpleasant side effect of making the variable in scope for the rest of the method, just inviting you to call it by accident.

Following Order of Operation

You've learned two new rules for the order in which code runs in a try-with-resources statement:

- Resources are closed after the try clause ends and before any catch/finally clauses.
- Resources are closed in the reverse order from which they were created.

Let's review these principles with a more complex example. First, we define a custom class that you can use with a try-with-resources statement, as it implements AutoCloseable.

```
public class MyFileClass implements AutoCloseable {
    private final int num;
    public MyFileClass(int num) { this.num = num; }
    public void close() {
        System.out.println("Closing: " + num);
    }
}
```

This is a pretty simple class that prints the number, set by the constructor, when a resource is closed. Based on these rules, can you figure out what this method prints?

```java
public static void main(String... xyz) {
    try (MyFileClass a1 = new MyFileClass(1);
            MyFileClass a2 = new MyFileClass(2)) {
        throw new RuntimeException();
    } catch (Exception e) {
        System.out.println("ex");
    } finally {
        System.out.println("finally");
    }
}
```

Since the resources are closed in the reverse order from which they were opened, we have `Closing: 2` and then `Closing: 1`. After that, the `catch` block and `finally` block are run—just as they are in a regular `try` statement. The output is as follows:

```
Closing: 2
Closing: 1
ex
finally
```

For the exam, make sure you understand why the method prints the statements in this order. Remember, the resources are closed in the reverse order from which they are declared, and the implicit `finally` is executed before the programmer-defined `finally`.

 Real World Scenario

Try-with-Resources Guarantees

Does a try-with-resources statement guarantee a resource will be closed? Although this is beyond the scope of the exam, the short answer is "no." The try-with-resources statement guarantees only the `close()` method will be called. If the `close()` method encounters an exception of its own or the method is implemented poorly, a resource leak can still occur. For the exam, you just need to know try-with-resources is guaranteed to call the `close()` method on the resource.

Throwing Additional Exceptions

A `catch` or `finally` block can have any valid Java code in it—including another `try` statement. What happens when an exception is thrown inside of a `catch` or `finally` block?

To answer this, let's take a look at a concrete example:

```
16: public static void main(String[] a) {
17:     FileReader reader = null;
18:     try {
19:         reader = read();
20:     } catch (IOException e) {
21:         try {
22:             if (reader != null)  reader.close();
23:         } catch (IOException inner) {
24:         }
25:     }
26: }
27: private static FileReader read() throws IOException {
28:     // CODE GOES HERE
29: }
```

The easiest case is if line 28 doesn't throw an exception. Then the entire catch block on lines 20–25 is skipped. Next, consider if line 28 throws a NullPointerException. That isn't an IOException, so the catch block on lines 20–25 will still be skipped, resulting in the main() method terminating early.

If line 28 does throw an IOException, the catch block on lines 20–25 gets run. Line 22 tries to close the reader. If that goes well, the code completes, and the main() method ends normally. If the close() method does throw an exception, Java looks for more catch blocks. This exception is caught on line 23. Regardless, the exception on line 28 is handled. A different exception might be thrown, but the one from line 28 is done.

Most of the examples you see with exception handling on the exam are abstract. They use letters or numbers to make sure you understand the flow. This one shows that only the last exception to be thrown matters:

```
26: try {
27:     throw new RuntimeException();
28: } catch (RuntimeException e) {
29:     throw new RuntimeException();
30: } finally {
31:     throw new Exception();
32: }
```

Line 27 throws an exception, which is caught on line 28. The catch block then throws an exception on line 29. If there were no finally block, the exception from line 29 would be thrown. However, the finally block runs after the catch block. Since the finally block throws an exception of its own on line 31, this one gets thrown. The exception from the catch block gets forgotten about. This is why you often see another try/catch inside a finally block—to make sure it doesn't mask the exception from the catch block.

Next we are going to show you one of the hardest examples you can be asked related to exceptions. What do you think this method returns? Go slowly. It's tricky.

```java
30: public String exceptions() {
31:     StringBuilder result = new StringBuilder();
32:     String v = null;
33:     try {
34:         try {
35:             result.append("before_");
36:             v.length();
37:             result.append("after_");
38:         } catch (NullPointerException e) {
39:             result.append("catch_");
40:             throw new RuntimeException();
41:         } finally {
42:             result.append("finally_");
43:             throw new Exception();
44:         }
45:     } catch (Exception e) {
46:         result.append("done");
47:     }
48:     return result.toString();
49: }
```

The correct answer is before_catch_finally_done. First on line 35, "before_" is added. Line 36 throws a NullPointerException. Line 37 is skipped as Java goes straight to the catch block. Line 38 does catch the exception, and "catch_" is added on line 39. Then line 40 throws a RuntimeException. The finally block runs after the catch regardless of whether an exception is thrown; it adds "finally_" to result. At this point, we have completed the inner try statement that ran on lines 34–44. The outer catch block then sees an exception was thrown and catches it on line 45; it adds "done" to result.

Did you get that right? If so, you are well on your way to acing this part of the exam. If not, we recommend reading this section again before moving on.

Calling Methods That Throw Exceptions

When you're calling a method that throws an exception, the rules are the same as within a method. Do you see why the following doesn't compile?

```java
class NoMoreCarrotsException extends Exception {}
public class Bunny {
    public static void main(String[] args) {
        eatCarrot(); // DOES NOT COMPILE
```

```
    }
    private static void eatCarrot() throws NoMoreCarrotsException {
    }
}
```

The problem is that `NoMoreCarrotsException` is a checked exception. Checked exceptions must be handled or declared. The code would compile if you changed the `main()` method to either of these:

```
public static void main(String[] args)
        throws NoMoreCarrotsException { // declare exception
    eatCarrot();
}


public static void main(String[] args) {
    try {
        eatCarrot();
    } catch (NoMoreCarrotsException e ) { // handle exception
        System.out.print("sad rabbit");
    }
}
```

You might have noticed that `eatCarrot()` didn't actually throw an exception; it just declared that it could. This is enough for the compiler to require the caller to handle or declare the exception.

The compiler is still on the lookout for unreachable code. Declaring an unused exception isn't considered unreachable code. It gives the method the option to change the implementation to throw that exception in the future. Do you see the issue here?

```
public void bad() {
    try {
        eatCarrot();
    } catch (NoMoreCarrotsException e ) { // DOES NOT COMPILE
        System.out.print("sad rabbit");
    }
}

public void good() throws NoMoreCarrotsException {
    eatCarrot();
}

private void eatCarrot() { }
```

Java knows that eatCarrot() can't throw a checked exception—which means there's no way for the catch block in bad() to be reached. In comparison, good() is free to declare other exceptions.

 When you see a checked exception declared inside a catch block on the exam, check and make sure the code in the associated try block is capable of throwing the exception or a subclass of the exception. If not, the code is unreachable and does not compile. Remember that this rule does not extend to unchecked exceptions or exceptions declared in a method signature.

Declaring and Overriding Methods with Exceptions

Now that you have a deeper understanding of exceptions, let's look at overriding methods with exceptions in the method declaration. When a class overrides a method from a superclass or implements a method from an interface, it's not allowed to add new checked exceptions to the method signature. For example, this code isn't allowed:

```java
class CanNotHopException extends Exception { }
class Hopper {
   public void hop() { }
}
class Bunny extends Hopper {
   public void hop() throws CanNotHopException { } // DOES NOT COMPILE
}
```

Java knows hop() isn't allowed to throw any checked exceptions because the hop() method in the superclass Hopper doesn't declare any. Imagine what would happen if the subclasses versions of the method could add checked exceptions—you could write code that calls Hopper's hop() method and not handle any exceptions. Then if Bunny were used in its place, the code wouldn't know to handle or declare CanNotHopException.

An overridden method in a subclass is allowed to declare fewer exceptions than the superclass or interface. This is legal because callers are already handling them.

```java
class Hopper {
   public void hop() throws CanNotHopException { }
}
class Bunny extends Hopper {
   public void hop()  { }
}
```

An overridden method not declaring one of the exceptions thrown by the parent method is similar to the method declaring it throws an exception that it never actually throws. This is perfectly legal.

Similarly, a class is allowed to declare a subclass of an exception type. The idea is the same. The superclass or interface has already taken care of a broader type. Here's an example:

```
class Hopper {
   public void hop() throws Exception { }
}
class Bunny extends Hopper {
   public void hop() throws CanNotHopException { }
}
```

Bunny could declare that it throws Exception directly, or it could declare that it throws a more specific type of Exception. It could even declare that it throws nothing at all.

This rule applies only to checked exceptions. The following code is legal because it has an unchecked exception in the subclass's version:

```
class Hopper {
   public void hop() { }
}
class Bunny extends Hopper {
   public void hop() throws IllegalStateException { }
}
```

The reason that it's okay to declare new unchecked exceptions in a subclass method is that the declaration is redundant. Methods are free to throw any unchecked exceptions they want without mentioning them in the method declaration.

Printing an Exception

There are three ways to print an exception. You can let Java print it out, print just the message, or print where the stack trace comes from. This example shows all three approaches:

```
5:  public static void main(String[] args) {
6:      try {
7:          hop();
8:      } catch (Exception e) {
9:          System.out.println(e);
10:         System.out.println(e.getMessage());
11:         e.printStackTrace();
12:     }
13: }
14: private static void hop() {
15:     throw new RuntimeException("cannot hop");
16: }
```

This code results in the following output:

```
java.lang.RuntimeException: cannot hop
cannot hop
java.lang.RuntimeException: cannot hop
    at Handling.hop(Handling.java:15)
    at Handling.main(Handling.java:7)
```

The first line shows what Java prints out by default: the exception type and message. The second line shows just the message. The rest shows a stack trace.

The stack trace is usually the most helpful one because it is a picture in time the moment the exception is thrown. It shows the hierarchy of method calls that were made to reach the line that threw the exception. On the exam, you will mostly see the first approach. This is because the exam often shows code snippets.

The stack trace shows all the methods on the stack. Figure 10.7 shows what the stack looks like for this code. Every time you call a method, Java adds it to the stack until it completes. When an exception is thrown, it goes through the stack until it finds a method that can handle it or it runs out of stack.

FIGURE 10.7 A method stack

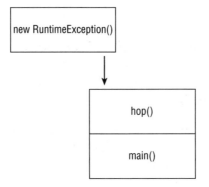

Real World Scenario

Why Swallowing Exceptions Is Bad

Because checked exceptions require you to handle or declare them, there is a temptation to catch them so they "go away." But doing so can cause problems. In the following code, there's a problem reading the file:

```
public static void main(String... p) {
    String textInFile = null;
    try {
        textInFile = readInFile();
```

```
    } catch (IOException e) {
        // ignore exception
    }
    // imagine many lines of code here
    System.out.println(textInFile.replace(" ", ""));
}
private static String readInFile() throws IOException {
    throw new IOException();
}
```

The code results in a NullPointerException. Java doesn't tell you anything about the original IOException because it was handled. Granted, it was handled poorly, but it was handled.

When writing this book, we tend to swallow exceptions because many of our examples are artificial in nature. However, when you're writing your own code, you should print out a stack trace or at least a message when catching an exception. Also, consider whether continuing is the best course of action. In our example, the program can't do anything after it fails to read in the file. It might as well have just thrown the IOException.

Summary

An exception indicates something unexpected happened. A method can handle an exception by catching it or declaring it for the caller to deal with. Many exceptions are thrown by Java libraries. You can throw your own exceptions with code such as throw new Exception().

All exceptions inherit Throwable. Subclasses of Error are exceptions that a programmer should not attempt to handle. Classes that inherit RuntimeException and Error are runtime (unchecked) exceptions. Classes that inherit Exception, but not RuntimeException, are checked exceptions. Java requires checked exceptions to be handled with a catch block or declared with the throws keyword.

A try statement must include at least one catch block or a finally block. A multi-catch block is one that catches multiple unrelated exceptions in a single catch block. If a try statement has multiple catch blocks chained together, at most one catch block can run. Java looks for an exception that can be caught by each catch block in the order they appear, and the first match is run. Then execution continues after the try statement. If both catch and finally throw an exception, the one from finally gets thrown.

A try-with-resources block is used to ensure a resource like a database or a file is closed properly after it is created. A try-with-resources statement does not require a catch or finally block but may optionally include them. The implicit finally block is executed before any programmer-defined catch or finally blocks.

RuntimeException classes you should know for the exam include the following:

- `ArithmeticException`
- `ArrayIndexOutOfBoundsException`
- `ClassCastException`
- `IllegalArgumentException`
- `NullPointerException`
- `NumberFormatException`

`IllegalArgumentException` is typically thrown by the programmer, whereas the others are typically thrown by the standard Java library.

Checked Exception classes you should know for the exam include the following:

- `IOException`
- `FileNotFoundException`

Error classes you should know for the exam include the following:

- `ExceptionInInitializerError`
- `StackOverflowError`
- `NoClassDefFoundError`

For the exam, remember that `NumberFormatException` is a subclass of `IllegalArgumentException`, and `FileNotFoundException` is a subclass of `IOException`.

When a method overrides a method in a superclass or interface, it is not allowed to add checked exceptions. It is allowed to declare fewer exceptions or declare a subclass of a declared exception. Methods declare exceptions with the keyword `throws`.

Exam Essentials

Understand the various types of exceptions.   All exceptions are subclasses of `java.lang.Throwable`. Subclasses of `java.lang.Error` should never be caught. Only subclasses of `java.lang.Exception` should be handled in application code.

Differentiate between checked and unchecked exceptions.   Unchecked exceptions do not need to be caught or handled and are subclasses of `java.lang.RuntimeException` and `java.lang.Error`. All other subclasses of `java.lang.Exception` are checked exceptions and must be handled or declared.

Understand the flow of a `try` statement.   A try statement must have a catch or a finally block. Multiple catch blocks can be chained together, provided no superclass exception type appears in an earlier catch block than its subclass. A multi-catch expression may be used to handle multiple exceptions in the same catch block, provided one exception is not a subclass of another. The finally block runs last regardless of whether an exception is thrown.

Be able to follow the order of a try-with-resources statement.   A try-with-resources statement is a special type of `try` block in which one or more resources are declared and automatically closed in the reverse order of which they are declared. It can be used with or without a `catch` or `finally` block, with the implicit `finally` block always executed first.

Identify whether an exception is thrown by the programmer or the JVM. `IllegalArgumentException` and `NumberFormatException` are commonly thrown by the programmer. Most of the other unchecked exceptions are typically thrown by the JVM or built-in Java libraries.

Write methods that declare exceptions.   The `throws` keyword is used in a method declaration to indicate an exception might be thrown. When overriding a method, the method is allowed to throw fewer or narrower checked exceptions than the original version.

Recognize when to use throw versus throws.   The `throw` keyword is used when you actually want to throw an exception—for example, `throw new RuntimeException()`. The `throws` keyword is used in a method declaration.

Review Questions

1. Which of the following statements are true? (Choose all that apply.)

   A. Exceptions of type `RuntimeException` are unchecked.

   B. Exceptions of type `RuntimeException` are checked.

   C. You can declare unchecked exceptions.

   D. You can declare checked exceptions.

   E. You can handle only `Exception` subclasses.

   F. All exceptions are subclasses of `Throwable`.

2. Which of the following pairs fill in the blanks to make this code compile? (Choose all that apply.)

   ```
   6: public void ohNo(ArithmeticException ae) _____ Exception {
   7:    if(ae==null) _____ Exception();
   8:    else _____ ae;
   9: }
   ```

   A. On line 6, fill in `throw`

   B. On line 6, fill in `throws`

   C. On line 7, fill in `throw`

   D. On line 7, fill in `throw new`

   E. On line 8, fill in `throw`

   F. On line 8, fill in `throw new`

   G. None of the above

3. What is printed by the following? (Choose all that apply.)

   ```
   1:  public class Mouse {
   2:     public String name;
   3:     public void findCheese() {
   4:        System.out.print("1");
   5:        try {
   6:           System.out.print("2");
   7:           name.toString();
   8:           System.out.print("3");
   9:        } catch (NullPointerException e | ClassCastException e) {
   10:          System.out.print("4");
   11:          throw e;
   12:       }
   13:       System.out.print("5");
   14:    }
   ```

```
15:    public static void main(String... tom) {
16:       Mouse jerry = new Mouse();
17:       jerry.findCheese();
18:    } }
```

A. 1

B. 2

C. 3

D. 4

E. 5

F. The stack trace for a `NullPointerException`

G. None of the above

4. Which of the following statements about `finally` blocks are true? (Choose all that apply.)

A. A `finally` block is never required with a regular `try` statement.

B. A `finally` block is required when there are no `catch` blocks in a regular `try` statement.

C. A `finally` block is required when the program code doesn't terminate on its own.

D. A `finally` block is never required with a try-with-resources statement.

E. A `finally` block is required when there are no `catch` blocks in a try-with-resources statement.

F. A `finally` block is required in order to make sure all resources are closed in a try-with-resources statement.

G. A `finally` block is executed before the resources declared in a try-with-resources statement are closed.

5. Which exception will the following method throw?

```
3: public static void main(String[] other) {
4:    Object obj = Integer.valueOf(3);
5:    String str = (String) obj;
6:    obj = null;
7:    System.out.println(obj.equals(null));
8: }
```

A. `ArrayIndexOutOfBoundsException`

B. `IllegalArgumentException`

C. `ClassCastException`

D. `NumberFormatException`

E. `NullPointerException`

F. None of the above

6. What does the following method print?

```
11: public void tryAgain(String s) {
12:    try(FileReader r = null, p = new FileReader("")) {
13:       System.out.print("X");
14:       throw new IllegalArgumentException();
15:    } catch (Exception s) {
16:       System.out.print("A");
17:       throw new FileNotFoundException();
18:    } finally {
19:       System.out.print("O");
20:    }
21: }
```

A. XAO

B. XOA

C. One line of this method contains a compiler error.

D. Two lines of this method contain compiler errors.

E. Three lines of this method contain compiler errors.

F. The code compiles, but a `NullPointerException` is thrown at runtime.

G. None of the above

7. What will happen if you add the following statement to a working `main()` method?

```
System.out.print(4 / 0);
```

A. It will not compile.

B. It will not run.

C. It will run and throw an `ArithmeticException`.

D. It will run and throw an `IllegalArgumentException`.

E. None of the above

8. What is printed by the following program?

```
1:  public class DoSomething {
2:     public void go() {
3:        System.out.print("A");
4:        try {
5:           stop();
6:        } catch (ArithmeticException e) {
7:           System.out.print("B");
8:        } finally {
9:           System.out.print("C");
10:       }
11:       System.out.print("D");
12:    }
13:    public void stop() {
```

```
14:        System.out.print("E");
15:        Object x = null;
16:        x.toString();
17:        System.out.print("F");
18:    }
19:    public static void main(String n[]) {
20:        new DoSomething().go();
21:    }
22: }
```

A. AE

B. AEBCD

C. AEC

D. AECD

E. AE followed by a stack trace

F. AEBCD followed by a stack trace

G. AEC followed by a stack trace

H. A stack trace with no other output

9. What is the output of the following snippet, assuming a and b are both 0?

```
3:  try {
4:      System.out.print(a / b);
5:  } catch (RuntimeException e) {
6:      System.out.print(-1);
7:  } catch (ArithmeticException e) {
8:      System.out.print(0);
9:  } finally {
10:     System.out.print("done");
11: }
```

A. -1

B. 0

C. done-1

D. done0

E. The code does not compile.

F. An uncaught exception is thrown.

G. None of the above

10. What is the output of the following program?

```
1:  public class Laptop {
2:      public void start() {
3:          try {
4:              System.out.print("Starting up_");
```

```
5:            throw new Exception();
6:         } catch (Exception e) {
7:            System.out.print("Problem_");
8:            System.exit(0);
9:         } finally {
10:           System.out.print("Shutting down");
11:        }
12:     }
13:     public static void main(String[] w) {
14:        new Laptop().start();
15:     } }
```

A. Starting up_

B. Starting up_Problem_

C. Starting up_Problem_Shutting down

D. Starting up_Shutting down

E. The code does not compile.

F. An uncaught exception is thrown.

11. What is the output of the following program?

```
1:  public class Dog {
2:      public String name;
3:      public void runAway() {
4:         System.out.print("1");
5:         try {
6:            System.out.print("2");
7:            int x = Integer.parseInt(name);
8:            System.out.print("3");
9:         } catch (NumberFormatException e) {
10:           System.out.print("4");
11:        }
12:     }
13:     public static void main(String... args) {
14:        Dog webby = new Dog();
15:        webby.name = "Webby";
16:        webby.runAway();
17:        System.out.print("5");
18:     } }
```

A. 1234

B. 1235

C. 124

D. 1245

E. The code does not compile.

F. An uncaught exception is thrown.

G. None of the above

12. What is the output of the following program?

```
1:  public class Cat {
2:      public String name;
3:      public void knockStuffOver() {
4:          System.out.print("1");
5:          try {
6:              System.out.print("2");
7:              int x = Integer.parseInt(name);
8:              System.out.print("3");
9:          } catch (NullPointerException e) {
10:             System.out.print("4");
11:         }
12:         System.out.print("5");
13:     }
14:     public static void main(String args[]) {
15:         Cat loki = new Cat();
16:         loki.name = "Loki";
17:         loki.knockStuffOver();
18:         System.out.print("6");
19:     } }
```

A. The output is 12, followed by a stack trace for a NumberFormatException.

B. The output is 124, followed by a stack trace for a NumberFormatException.

C. The output is 12456.

D. The output is 1256, followed by a stack trace for a NumberFormatException.

E. The code does not compile.

F. An uncaught exception is thrown.

G. None of the above

13. Which of the following statements are true? (Choose all that apply.)

A. You can declare a method with Exception as the return type.

B. You can declare a method with RuntimeException as the return type.

C. You can declare any subclass of Error in the throws part of a method declaration.

D. You can declare any subclass of Exception in the throws part of a method declaration.

E. You can declare any subclass of Object in the throws part of a method declaration.

F. You can declare any subclass of RuntimeException in the throws part of a method declaration.

14. Which of the following can be inserted on line 8 to make this code compile? (Choose all that apply.)

```
7: public void whatHappensNext() throws IOException {
8:    // INSERT CODE HERE
9: }
```

A. System.out.println("it's ok");

B. throw new Exception();

C. throw new IllegalArgumentException();

D. throw new java.io.IOException();

E. throw new RuntimeException();

F. None of the above

15. What is printed by the following program? (Choose all that apply.)

```
1:  public class Help {
2:      public void callSuperhero() {
3:          try (String raspberry = new String("Olivia")) {
4:              System.out.print("Q");
5:          } catch (Error e) {
6:              System.out.print("X");
7:          } finally {
8:              System.out.print("M");
9:          }
10:     }
11:     public static void main(String[] args) {
12:         new Help().callSuperhero();
13:         System.out.print("S");
14:     } }
```

A. SQM

B. QXMS

C. QSM

D. QMS

E. A stack trace

F. The code does not compile because NumberFormatException is not declared or caught.

G. None of the above

16. Which of the following do not need to be handled or declared? (Choose all that apply.)

A. ArrayIndexOutOfBoundsException

B. IllegalArgumentException

C. IOException

D. `Error`

E. `NumberFormatException`

F. Any exception that extends `RuntimeException`

G. Any exception that extends `Exception`

17. Which lines can fill in the blank to make the following code compile? (Choose all that apply.)

```
void rollOut() throws ClassCastException {}

  public void transform(String c) {
    try {
      rollOut();
    } catch (IllegalArgumentException | _____) {
    }
  }
```

A. `IOException a`

B. `Error b`

C. `NullPointerException c`

D. `RuntimeException d`

E. `NumberFormatException e`

F. `ClassCastException f`

G. None of the above. The code contains a compiler error regardless of what is inserted into the blank.

18. Which scenario is the best use of an exception?

A. An element is not found when searching a list.

B. An unexpected parameter is passed into a method.

C. The computer caught fire.

D. You want to loop through a list.

E. You don't know how to code a method.

19. Which of the following can be inserted into `Lion` to make this code compile? (Choose all that apply.)

```
class HasSoreThroatException extends Exception {}
class TiredException extends RuntimeException {}
interface Roar {
    void roar() throws HasSoreThroatException;
}
class Lion implements Roar {
    // INSERT CODE HERE
}
```

A. `public void roar() {}`

B. `public int roar() throws RuntimeException {}`

C. `public void roar() throws Exception {}`

D. `public void roar() throws HasSoreThroatException {}`

E. `public void roar() throws IllegalArgumentException {}`

F. `public void roar() throws TiredException {}`

20. Which of the following are true? (Choose all that apply.)

A. Checked exceptions are allowed, but not required, to be handled or declared.

B. Checked exceptions are required to be handled or declared.

C. Errors are allowed, but not required, to be handled or declared.

D. Errors are required to be handled or declared.

E. Unchecked exceptions are allowed, but not required, to be handled or declared.

F. Unchecked exceptions are required to be handled or declared.

21. Which of the following pairs fill in the blanks to make this code compile? (Choose all that apply.)

```
6: public void ohNo(IOException ie) _____ Exception {
7:        _____ FileNotFoundException();
8:        _____ ie;
9: }
```

A. On line 6, fill in `throw`

B. On line 6, fill in `throws`

C. On line 7, fill in `throw`

D. On line 7, fill in `throw new`

E. On line 8, fill in `throw`

F. On line 8, fill in `throw new`

G. None of the above

22. Which of the following can be inserted in the blank to make the code compile? (Choose all that apply.)

```
public void dontFail() {
    try {
        System.out.println("work real hard");
    } catch (_____ e) {
    } catch (RuntimeException e) {}
}
```

A. `var`

B. `Exception`

C. `IOException`

D. `IllegalArgumentException`

E. `RuntimeException`

F. `StackOverflowError`

G. None of the above

23. What does the output of the following method contain? (Choose all that apply.)

```
12: public static void main(String[] args) {
13:     System.out.print("a");
14:     try {
15:         System.out.print("b");
16:         throw new IllegalArgumentException();
17:     } catch (IllegalArgumentException e) {
18:         System.out.print("c");
19:         throw new RuntimeException("1");
20:     } catch (RuntimeException e) {
21:         System.out.print("d");
22:         throw new RuntimeException("2");
23:     } finally {
24:         System.out.print("e");
25:         throw new RuntimeException("3");
26:     }
27: }
```

A. abce

B. abde

C. An exception with the message set to "1"

D. An exception with the message set to "2"

E. An exception with the message set to "3"

F. Nothing; the code does not compile.

24. What does the following class output?

```
1: public class MoreHelp {
2:     class Sidekick implements AutoCloseable {
3:         protected String n;
4:         public Sidekick(String n) { this.n = n; }
5:         public void close() { System.out.print("L"); }
6:     }
7:     public void requiresAssistance() {
8:         try (Sidekick is = new Sidekick("Adeline")) {
9:             System.out.print("O");
10:         } finally {
```

```
11:            System.out.print("K");
12:        }
13:    }
14:    public static void main(String... league) {
15:        new MoreHelp().requiresAssistance();
16:        System.out.print("I");
17:    } }
```

A. LOKI

B. OKLI

C. OLKI

D. OKIL

E. The output cannot be determined until runtime.

F. Nothing; the code does not compile.

G. None of the above

25. What does the following code snippet return, assuming a and b are both 1?

```
13: try {
14:     return a / b;
15: } catch (ClassCastException e) {
16:     return 10;
17: } catch (RuntimeException e) {
18:     return 20;
19: } finally {
20:     return 30;
21: }
```

A. 1

B. 10

C. 20

D. 30

E. The code does not compile.

F. An uncaught exception is thrown.

G. None of the above

Chapter

11

Modules

OCP EXAM OBJECTIVES COVERED IN THIS CHAPTER:

✓ **Understanding Modules**

- ▪ Describe the Modular JDK
- ▪ Declare modules and enable access between modules
- ▪ Describe how a modular project is compiled and run

Since Java 9, packages can be grouped into modules. In this chapter, we will explain the purpose of modules and how to build your own. We will also show how to run them and how to discover existing modules. This book only covers the basics of modules that you need to know for the 1Z0-815 exam.

We've made the code in this chapter available online. Since it can be tedious to create the directory structure, this will save you some time. Additionally, the commands need to be exactly right, so we've included those online so you can copy and paste them and compare them with what you typed. Both are available in the resources section of the online test bank and in our GitHub repo linked to from:

```
http://www.selikoff.net/ocp11-1
```

Introducing Modules

When writing code for the exam, you generally see small classes. After all, exam questions have to fit on a single screen! When you work on real programs, they are much bigger. A real project will consist of hundreds or thousands of classes grouped into packages. These packages are grouped into *Java archive (JAR)* files. A JAR is a zip file with some extra information, and the extension is .jar.

In addition to code written by your team, most applications also use code written by others. *Open source* is software with the code supplied and is often free to use. Java has a vibrant open-source software (OSS) community, and those libraries are also supplied as JAR files. For example, there are libraries to read files, connect to a database, and much more.

Some open source projects even depend on functionality in other open source projects. For example, Spring is a commonly used framework, and JUnit is a commonly used testing library. To use either, you need to make sure you had compatible versions of all the relevant JARs available at runtime. This complex chain of dependencies and minimum versions is often referred to by the community as *JAR hell*. Hell is an excellent way of describing the wrong version of a class being loaded or even a ClassNotFoundException at runtime.

The *Java Platform Module System* (JPMS) was introduced in Java 9 to group code at a higher level and tries to solve the problems that Java has been plagued with since the beginning. The main purpose of a module is to provide groups of related packages to offer a particular set of functionality to developers. It's like a JAR file except a developer chooses which packages are accessible outside the module. Let's look at what modules are and what problems they are designed to solve.

The Java Platform Module System includes the following:

- A format for module JAR files
- Partitioning of the JDK into modules
- Additional command-line options for Java tools

Exploring a Module

In Chapter 1, "Welcome to Java," we had a small Zoo application. It had only one class and just printed out one thing. Now imagine we had a whole staff of programmers and were automating the operations of the zoo. There are many things that need to be coded including the interactions with the animals, visitors, the public website, and outreach.

A *module* is a group of one or more packages plus a special file called module-info .java. Figure 11.1 lists just a few of the modules a zoo might need. We decided to focus on the animal interactions in our example. The full zoo could easily have a dozen modules. In Figure 11.1, notice that there are arrows between many of the modules. These represent *dependencies* where one module relies on code in another. The staff needs to feed the animals to keep their jobs. The line from zoo.staff to zoo.animal.feeding shows the former depends on the latter.

FIGURE 11.1   Design of a modular system

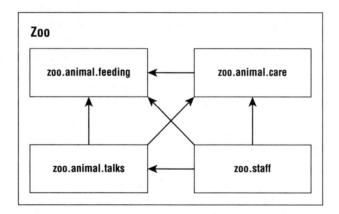

Now let's drill down into one of these modules. Figure 11.2 shows what is inside the zoo.animals.talks module. There are three packages with two classes each. (It's a small zoo.) There is also a strange file called module-info.java. This file is required to be inside all modules. We will explain this in more detail later in the chapter.

FIGURE 11.2   Looking inside a module

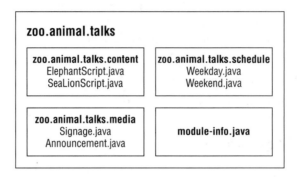

Benefits of Modules

Modules look like another layer of things you need to know in order to program. While using modules is optional, it is important to understand the problems they are designed to solve. Besides, knowing why modules are useful is required for the exam!

Better Access Control

In Chapter 7, "Methods and Encapsulation," you saw the traditional four levels of access control available in Java 8: private, package-private, protected, and public access. These levels of access control allowed you to restrict access to a certain class or package. You could even allow access to subclasses without exposing them to the world.

However, what if we wrote some complex logic that we wanted to restrict to just some packages? For example, we would like the packages in the zoo.animal.talks module to just be available to the packages in the zoo.staff module without making them available to any other code. Our traditional access modifiers cannot handle this scenario.

Developers would resort to hacks like naming a package zoo.animal.internal. That didn't work, though, because other developers could still call the "internal" code. There was a class named sun.misc.Unsafe, and it got used in places. And that class had Unsafe in the name. Clearly, relying on naming conventions was insufficient at preventing developers from calling it in the past.

Modules solve this problem by acting as a fifth level of access control. They can expose packages within the modular JAR to specific other packages. This stronger form of encapsulation really does create internal packages. You'll see how to code it when we talk about the module-info.java file later in this chapter.

Clearer Dependency Management

It is common for libraries to depend on other libraries. For example, the JUnit 4 testing library depends on the Hamcrest library for matching logic. Developers would have to find this out by reading the documentation or files in the project itself.

If you forgot to include Hamcrest in your classpath, your code would run fine until you used a Hamcrest class. Then it would blow up at runtime with a message about not finding a required class. (We did mention JAR hell, right?)

In a fully modular environment, each of the open source projects would specify their dependencies in the module-info.java file. When launching the program, Java would complain that Hamcrest isn't in the module path and you'd know right away.

Custom Java Builds

The Java Development Kit (JDK) is larger than 150 MB. Even the Java Runtime Environment (JRE) was pretty big when it was available as a separate download. In the past, Java attempted to solve this with a *compact profile*. The three compact profiles provided a subset of the built-in Java classes so there would be a smaller package for mobile and embedded devices.

However, the compact profiles lacked flexibility. Many packages were included that developers were unlikely to use, such as Java Native Interface (JNI), which is for working with OS-specific programs. At the same time, using other packages like Image I/O required the full JRE.

The Java Platform Module System allows developers to specify what modules they actually need. This makes it possible to create a smaller runtime image that is customized to what the application needs and nothing more. Users can run that image without having Java installed at all.

A tool called jlink is used to create this runtime image. Luckily, you only need to know that custom smaller runtimes are possible. How to create them is out of scope for the exam.

In addition to the smaller scale package, this approach improves security. If you don't use AWT and a security vulnerability is reported for AWT, applications that packaged a runtime image without AWT aren't affected.

Improved Performance

Since Java now knows which modules are required, it only needs to look at those at class loading time. This improves startup time for big programs and requires less memory to run.

While these benefits may not seem significant for the small programs we've been writing, they are far more important for big applications. A web application can easily take a minute to start. Additionally, for some financial applications, every millisecond of performance is important.

Unique Package Enforcement

Another manifestation of JAR hell is when the same package is in two JARs. There are a number of causes of this problem including renaming JARs, clever developers using a package name that is already taken, and having two versions of the same JAR on the classpath.

The Java Platform Module System prevents this scenario. A package is only allowed to be supplied by one module. No more unpleasant surprises about a package at runtime.

🌐 **Real World Scenario**

Modules for Existing Code

While there are many benefits of using modules, there is also significant work for an existing large application to switch over. In particular, it is common for applications to be on old open source libraries that do not have module support. The bill for all that technical debt comes due when making the switch to modules.

While not all open source projects have switched over, more than 4000 have. There's a list of all Java modules on GitHub at https://github.com/sormuras/modules/blob/master/README.md.

The 1Z0-816 exam covers some strategies for migrating existing applications to modules. For now, just beware that the 1Z0-815 exam covers just the simplest use cases for modules.

Creating and Running a Modular Program

In this section, we will create, build, and run the zoo.animal.feeding module. We chose this one to start with because all the other modules depend on it. Figure 11.3 shows the design of this module. In addition to the module-info.java file, it has one package with one class inside.

FIGURE 11.3 Contents of zoo.animal.feeding

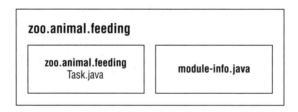

In the next sections, we will create, compile, run, and package the zoo.animal.feeding module.

Creating the Files

First we have a really simple class that prints one line in a `main()` method. We know, that's not much of an implementation. All those programmers we hired can fill it in with business logic. In this book, we will focus on what you need to know for the exam. So, let's create a simple class.

```
package zoo.animal.feeding;

public class Task {
   public static void main(String... args) {
      System.out.println("All fed!");
   }
}
```

Next comes the `module-info.java` file. This is the simplest possible one.

```
module zoo.animal.feeding {
}
```

There are a few key differences between a `module-info` file and a regular Java class:

- The `module-info` file must be in the root directory of your module. Regular Java classes should be in packages.

- The `module-info` file must use the keyword `module` instead of `class`, `interface`, or `enum`.

- The module name follows the naming rules for package names. It often includes periods (`.`) in its name. Regular class and package names are not allowed to have dashes (-). Module names follow the same rule.

That's a lot of rules for the simplest possible file. There will be many more rules when we flesh out this file later in the chapter.

Can a *module-info.java* File Be Empty?

Yes. As a bit of trivia, it was legal to compile any empty file with a `.java` extension even before modules. The compiler sees there isn't a `class` in there and exits without creating a `.class` file.

The next step is to make sure the files are in the right directory structure. Figure 11.4 shows the expected directory structure.

FIGURE 11.4   Module `zoo.animal.feeding` directory structure

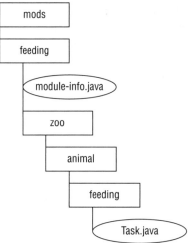

In particular, `feeding` is the module directory, and the `module-info` file is directly under it. Just as with a regular JAR file, we also have the `zoo.animal.feeding` package with one subfolder per portion of the name. The `Task` class is in the appropriate subfolder for its package.

Also, note that we created a directory called `mods` at the same level as the module. We will use it for storing the module artifacts a little later in the chapter. This directory can be named anything, but `mods` is a common name. If you are following along with the online code example, note that the `mods` directory is not included, because it is empty.

Compiling Our First Module

Before we can run modular code, we need to compile it. Other than the `module-path` option, this code should look familiar from Chapter 1:

```
javac --module-path mods
   -d feeding
   feeding/zoo/animal/feeding/*.java
   feeding/module-info.java
```

When you're entering commands at the command line, they should be typed all on one line. We use line breaks in the book to make the commands easier to read and study. If you wanted to use multiple lines at the command prompt, the approach varies by operating system. Linux uses a backslash (\) as the line break.

As a review, the -d option specifies the directory to place the class files in. The end of the command is a list of the .java files to compile. You can list the files individually or use a wildcard for all .java files in a subdirectory.

The new part is the module-path. This option indicates the location of any custom module files. In this example, module-path could have been omitted since there are no dependencies. You can think of module-path as replacing the classpath option when you are working on a modular program.

What Happened to the Classpath?

In the past, you would reference JAR files using the classpath option. It had three possible forms: -cp, -class-path, and -classpath. You can still use these options in Java 11. In fact, it is common to do so when writing nonmodular programs.

Just like classpath, you can use an abbreviation in the command. The syntax --module-path and -p are equivalent. That means we could have written many other commands in place of the previous command. The following four commands show the -p option:

```
javac -p mods
    -d feeding
    feeding/zoo/animal/feeding/*.java
    feeding/*.java
```

```
javac -p mods
    -d feeding
    feeding/zoo/animal/feeding/*.java
    feeding/module-info.java
```

```
javac -p mods
    -d feeding
    feeding/zoo/animal/feeding/Task.java
    feeding/module-info.java
```

```
javac -p mods
    -d feeding
    feeding/zoo/animal/feeding/Task.java
    feeding/*.java
```

While you can use whichever you like best, be sure that you can recognize all valid forms for the exam. Table 11.1 lists the options you need to know well when compiling modules. There are many more options you can pass to the javac command, but these are the ones you can expect to be tested on.

TABLE 11.1 Options you need to know for using modules with javac

Use for	Abbreviation	Long form
Directory for class files	-d \<dir\>	n/a
Module path	-p \<path\>	--module-path \<path\>

 Real World Scenario

Building Modules

Even before modules, it was rare to run javac and java commands manually on a real project. They get long and complicated very quickly. Most developers use a build tool such as Maven or Gradle. These build tools suggest directories to place the class files like target/classes.

With modules, there is even more typing to run these commands by hand. After all, with modules, you are using more directories by definition. This means that it is likely the only time you need to know the syntax of these commands is when you take the exam. The concepts themselves are useful regardless.

Do be sure to memorize the module command syntax. You will be tested on it on the exam. We will be sure to give you lots of practice questions on the syntax to reinforce it.

Running Our First Module

Before we package our module, we should make sure it works by running it. To do that, we need to learn the full syntax. Suppose there is a module named book.module. Inside that module is a package named com.sybex, which has a class named OCP with a main() method. Figure 11.5 shows the syntax for running a module. Pay special attention to the book.module/com.sybex.OCP part. It is important to remember that you specify the module name followed by a slash (/) followed by the fully qualified class name.

FIGURE 11.5 Running a module using java

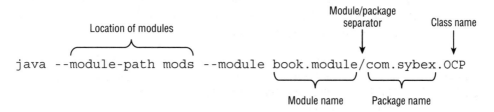

Now that we've seen the syntax, we can write the command to run the Task class in the zoo.animal.feeding package. In the following example, the package name and module name are the same. It is common for the module name to match either the full package name or the beginning of it.

```
java --module-path feeding
  --module zoo.animal.feeding/zoo.animal.feeding.Task
```

Since you already saw that --module-path uses the short form of -p, we bet you won't be surprised to learn there is a short form of --module as well. The short option is -m. That means the following command is equivalent:

```
java -p feeding
  -m zoo.animal.feeding/zoo.animal.feeding.Task
```

In these examples, we used feeding as the module path because that's where we compiled the code. This will change once we package the module and run that.

Table 11.2 lists the options you need to know for the java command.

TABLE 11.2 Options you need to know for using modules with java

Use for	Abbreviation	Long form
Module name	-m <name>	--module <name>
Module path	-p <path>	--module-path <path>

Packaging Our First Module

A module isn't much use if we can run it only in the folder it was created in. Our next step is to package it. Be sure to create a mods directory before running this command:

```
jar -cvf mods/zoo.animal.feeding.jar -C feeding/ .
```

There's nothing module-specific here. In fact, you might remember seeing this command in Chapter 1. We are packaging everything under the feeding directory and storing it in a JAR file named zoo.animal.feeding.jar under the mods folder. This represents how the module JAR will look to other code that wants to use it.

It is possible to version your module using the --module-version option. This isn't on the exam but is good to do when you are ready to share your module with others.

Now let's run the program again, but this time using the mods directory instead of the loose classes:

```
java -p mods
  -m zoo.animal.feeding/zoo.animal.feeding.Task
```

You might notice that this command looks identical to the one in the previous section except for the directory. In the previous example, it was feeding. In this one, it is the module path of mods. Since the module path is used, a module JAR is being run.

Figure 11.6 shows what the directory structure looks like now that we've compiled and packaged the code.

FIGURE 11.6   Module zoo.animal.feeding directory structure with class and jar files

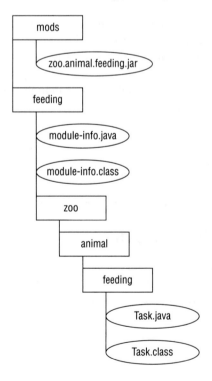

Updating Our Example for Multiple Modules

Now that our zoo.animal.feeding module is solid, we can start thinking about our other modules. As you can see in Figure 11.7, all three of the other modules in our system depend on the zoo.animal.feeding module.

FIGURE 11.7 Modules depending on zoo.animal.feeding

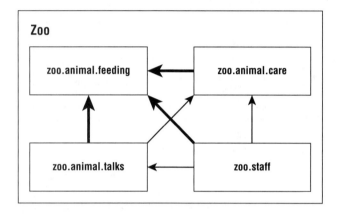

Updating the Feeding Module

Since we will be having our other modules call code in the zoo.animal.feeding package, we need to declare this intent in the module-info file.

The exports keyword is used to indicate that a module intends for those packages to be used by Java code outside the module. As you might expect, without an exports keyword, the module is only available to be run from the command line on its own. In the following example, we export one package:

```
module zoo.animal.feeding {
    exports zoo.animal.feeding;
}
```

Recompiling and repackaging the module will update the module-info inside our zoo.animals.feeding.jar file. These are the same javac and jar commands you ran previously.

```
javac -p mods
   -d feeding
   feeding/zoo/animal/feeding/*.java
   feeding/module-info.java

jar -cvf mods/zoo.animal.feeding.jar -C feeding/ .
```

Creating a Care Module

Next, let's create the zoo.animal.care module. This time, we are going to have two packages. The zoo.animal.care.medical package will have the classes and methods that are intended for use by other modules. The zoo.animal.care.details package is only going to be used by this module. It will not be exported from the module. Think of it as healthcare privacy for the animals.

Figure 11.8 shows the contents of this module. Remember that all modules must have a module-info file.

FIGURE 11.8   Contents of zoo.animal.care

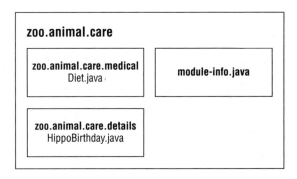

The module contains two basic packages and classes in addition to the module-info.java file:

```
// HippoBirthday.java
package zoo.animal.care.details;
import zoo.animal.feeding.*;
public class HippoBirthday {
   private Task task;
}

// Diet.java
package zoo.animal.care.medical;
public class Diet { }
```

This time the module-info.java file specifies three things.

```
1: module zoo.animal.care {
2:    exports zoo.animal.care.medical;
3:    requires zoo.animal.feeding;
4: }
```

Line 1 specifies the name of the module. Line 2 lists the package we are exporting so it can be used by other modules. So far, this is similar to the zoo.animal.feeding module.

On line 3, we see a new keyword. The requires statement specifies that a module is needed. The zoo.animal.care module depends on the zoo.animal.feeding module.

Next we need to figure out the directory structure. We will create two packages. The first is zoo.animal.care.details and contains one class named HippoBirthday. The second is zoo.animal.care.medical and contains one class named Diet. Try to draw the directory structure on paper or create it on your computer. If you are trying to run these examples without using the online code, just create classes without variables or methods for everything except the module-info.java files.

Figure 11.9 shows the directory structure of this module. Note that module-info.java is in the root of the module. The two packages are underneath it.

FIGURE 11.9   Module zoo.animal.care directory structure

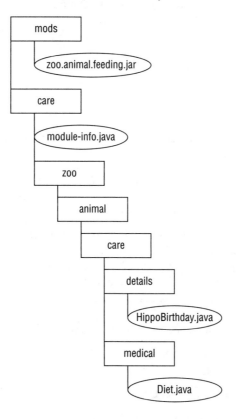

You might have noticed that the packages begin with the same prefix as the module name. This is intentional. You can think of it as if the module name "claims" the matching package and all subpackages.

To review, we now compile and package the module:

```
javac -p mods
   -d care
   care/zoo/animal/care/details/*.java
   care/zoo/animal/care/medical/*.java
   care/module-info.java
```

We compile both packages and the `module-info` file. In the real world, you'll use a build tool rather than doing this by hand. For the exam, you just list all the packages and/or files you want to compile.

Order Matters!

Note that order matters when compiling a module. Suppose we list the `module-info` file first when trying to compile:

```
javac -p mods
   -d care
   care/module-info.java
   care/zoo/animal/care/details/*.java
   care/zoo/animal/care/medical/*.java
```

The compiler complains that it doesn't know anything about the package `zoo.animal.care.medical`.

```
care/module-info.java:3: error: package is empty or does not exist:
zoo.animal.care.medical
exports zoo.animal.care.medical;
```

A package must have at least one class in it in order to be exported. Since we haven't yet compiled `zoo.animal.care.medical.Diet`, the compiler acts as if it doesn't exist. If you get this error message, you can reorder the `javac` statement. Alternatively, you can compile the packages in a separate `javac` command, before compiling the `module-info` file.

Now that we have compiled code, it's time to create the module JAR:

```
jar -cvf mods/zoo.animal.care.jar -C care/ .
```

Creating the Talks Module

So far, we've used only one exports and requires statement in a module. Now you'll learn how to handle exporting multiple packages or requiring multiple modules. In Figure 11.10, observe that the zoo.animal.talks module depends on two modules: zoo.animal.feeding and `zoo.animal.care`. This means that there must be two `requires` statements in the `module-info.java` file.

FIGURE 11.10   Dependencies for `zoo.animal.talks`

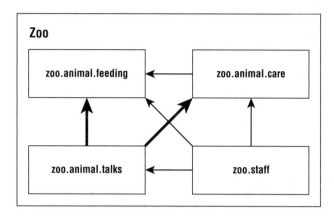

Figure 11.11 shows the contents of this module. We are going to export all three packages in this module.

FIGURE 11.11   Contents of `zoo.animal.talks`

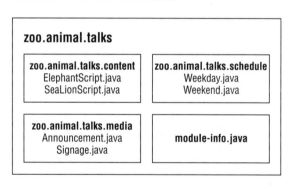

First let's look at the `module-info.java` file for `zoo.animal.talks`:

```
1: module zoo.animal.talks {
2:     exports zoo.animal.talks.content;
3:     exports zoo.animal.talks.media;
4:     exports zoo.animal.talks.schedule;
5:
6:     requires zoo.animal.feeding;
7:     requires zoo.animal.care;
8: }
```

Line 1 shows the module name. Lines 2–4 allow other modules to reference all three packages. Lines 6–7 specify the two modules that this module depends on.

Then we have the six classes, as shown here:

```
// ElephantScript.java
package zoo.animal.talks.content;
public class ElephantScript { }


// SeaLionScript.java
package zoo.animal.talks.content;
public class SeaLionScript { }


// Announcement.java
package zoo.animal.talks.media;
public class Announcement {
   public static void main(String[] args) {
      System.out.println("We will be having talks");
   }
}


// Signage.java
package zoo.animal.talks.media;
public class Signage { }


// Weekday.java
package zoo.animal.talks.schedule;
public class Weekday { }


// Weekend.java
package zoo.animal.talks.schedule;
public class Weekend {}
```

If you are still following along on your computer, create empty classes in the packages. The following are the commands to compile and build the module:

```
javac -p mods
   -d talks
   talks/zoo/animal/talks/content/*.java
   talks/zoo/animal/talks/media/*.java
   talks/zoo/animal/talks/schedule/*.java
   talks/module-info.java


jar -cvf mods/zoo.animal.talks.jar -C talks/ .
```

Creating the Staff Module

Our final module is zoo.staff. Figure 11.12 shows there is only one package inside. We will not be exposing this package outside the module.

FIGURE 11.12   Contents of zoo.staff

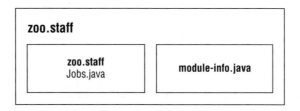

Based on this information, do you know what should go in the module-info?

```
module zoo.staff {
    requires zoo.animal.feeding;
    requires zoo.animal.care;
    requires zoo.animal.talks;
}
```

There are three arrows in Figure 11.13 pointing from zoo.staff to other modules. These represent the three modules that are required. Since no packages are to be exposed from zoo.staff, there are no exports statements.

FIGURE 11.13   Dependencies for zoo.staff

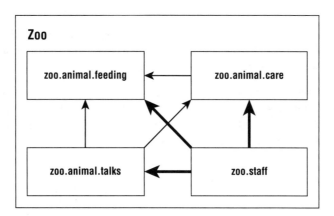

In this module, we have a single class in file Jobs.java:

```
package zoo.staff;
public class Jobs { }
```

For those of you following along on your computer, create an empty class in the package. The following are the commands to compile and build the module:

```
javac -p mods
   -d staff
   staff/zoo/staff/*.java
   staff/module-info.java

jar -cvf mods/zoo.staff.jar -C staff/ .
```

Diving into the *module-info* File

Now that we've successfully created modules, we can learn more about the `module-info` file. In these sections, we will look at exports, requires, provides, uses, and opens. Now would be a good time to mention that these keywords can appear in any order in the `module-info` file.

Real World Scenario

Are *exports* and *requires* Keywords?

In Chapter 2, "Java Building Blocks," we provided a list of keywords. However, exports wasn't on that list. Nor was module or requires or any of the other special words in a module-info file.

Java is a bit sneaky here. These "keywords" are only keywords inside a module-info .java file. In other files, like classes and interfaces, you are free to name your variable exports. These special keywords are called directives.

Backward compatibility is really important to the Java language designers so they don't want to risk preventing existing code from compiling just to introduce new global keywords. However, the module file type is new. Since there are no legacy module files, it is safe to introduce new keywords in that context.

exports

We've already seen how exports *packageName* exports a package to other modules. It's also possible to export a package to a specific module. Suppose the zoo decides that only staff members should have access to the talks. We could update the module declaration as follows:

```
module zoo.animal.talks {
    exports zoo.animal.talks.content to zoo.animal.staff;
    exports zoo.animal.talks.media;
    exports zoo.animal.talks.schedule;

    requires zoo.animal.feeding;
    requires zoo.animal.care;
}
```

From the zoo.animal.staff module, nothing has changed. However, no other modules would be allowed to access that package.

You might have noticed that none of our other modules requires zoo.animal.talks in the first place. However, we don't know what other modules will exist in the future. It is important to consider future use when designing modules. Since we want only the one module to have access, we only allow access for that module.

Exported Types

We've been talking about exporting a package. But what does that mean exactly? All public classes, interfaces, and enums are exported. Further, any public and protected fields and methods in those files are visible.

Fields and methods that are private are not visible because they are not accessible outside the class. Similarly, package-private fields and methods are not visible because they are not accessible outside the package.

The exports keyword essentially gives us more levels of access control. Table 11.3 lists the full access control options.

TABLE 11.3 Access control with modules

Level	Within module code	Outside module
private	Available only within class	No access
default (package-private)	Available only within package	No access
protected	Available only within package or to subclasses	Accessible to subclasses only if package is exported
public	Available to all classes	Accessible only if package is exported

requires transitive

As you saw earlier in this chapter, requires *moduleName* specifies that the current module depends on *moduleName*. There's also a requires transitive *moduleName*, which means that any module that requires this module will also depend on *moduleName*.

Well, that was a mouthful. Let's look at an example. Figure 11.14 shows the modules with dashed lines for the redundant relationships and solid lines for relationships specified in the module-info. This shows how the module relationships would look if we were to only use transitive dependencies.

FIGURE 11.14   Transitive dependency version of our modules

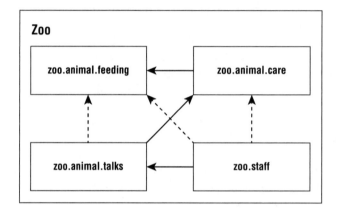

For example, zoo.animals.talks depends on zoo.animals.care, which depends on zoo.animals.feeding. That means the arrow between zoo.animals.talks and zoo.animals.feeding no longer appears in Figure 11.14.

Now let's look at the four module-info files. The first module remains unchanged. We are exporting one package to any packages that use the module.

```
module zoo.animal.feeding {
    exports zoo.animal.feeding;
}
```

The zoo.animal.care module is the first opportunity to improve things. Rather than forcing all remaining modules to explicitly specify zoo.animal.feeding, the code uses requires transitive.

```
module zoo.animal.care {
    exports zoo.animal.care.medical;
    requires transitive zoo.animal.feeding;
}
```

In the zoo.animal.talks module, we make a similar change and don't force other modules to specify zoo.animal.care. We also no longer need to specify zoo.animal.feeding, so that line is commented out.

```
module zoo.animal.talks {
    exports zoo.animal.talks.content to zoo.animal.staff;
    exports zoo.animal.talks.media;
    exports zoo.animal.talks.schedule;

    // no longer needed requires zoo.animal.feeding;
    // no longer needed requires zoo.animal.care;
    requires transitive zoo.animal.care;
}
```

Finally, in the zoo.staff module, we can get rid of two requires statements.

```
module zoo.staff {
    // no longer needed requires zoo.animal.feeding;
    // no longer needed requires zoo.animal.care;
    requires zoo.animal.talks;
}
```

The more modules you have, the more benefits of requires transitive compound. It is also more convenient for the caller. If you were trying to work with this zoo, you could just require zoo.staff and have the remaining dependencies automatically inferred.

Effects of *requires transitive*

Given our newly updated module-info files and using Figure 11.14, what is the effect of applying the transitive modifier to the requires statement in our zoo.animal.care module? Applying the transitive modifiers has the following effect:

- Module zoo.animal.talks can optionally declare it requires the zoo.animal.feeding module, but it is not required.
- Module zoo.animal.care cannot be compiled or executed without access to the zoo.animal.feeding module.
- Module zoo.animal.talks cannot be compiled or executed without access to the zoo.animal.feeding module.

These rules hold even if the zoo.animal.care and zoo.animal.talks modules do not explicitly reference any packages in the zoo.animal.feeding module. On the other hand, without the transitive modifier in our module-info file of zoo.animal.care, the other modules would have to explicitly use requires in order to reference any packages in the zoo.animal.feeding module.

Duplicate *requires* Statements

One place the exam might try to trick you is mixing requires and requires transitive together. Can you think of a reason this code doesn't compile?

```
module bad.module {
    requires zoo.animal.talks;
    requires transitive zoo.animal.talks;
}
```

Java doesn't allow you to repeat the same module in a requires clause. It is redundant and most like an error in coding. Keep in mind that requires transitive is like requires plus some extra behavior.

provides, uses, and *opens*

For the remaining three keywords (provides, uses, and opens), you only need to be aware they exist rather than understanding them in detail for the 1Z0-815 exam.

The provides keyword specifies that a class provides an implementation of a service. The topic of services is covered on the 1Z0-816 exam, so for now, you can just think of a service as a fancy interface. To use it, you supply the API and class name that implements the API:

```
provides zoo.staff.ZooApi with zoo.staff.ZooImpl
```

The uses keyword specifies that a module is relying on a service. To code it, you supply the API you want to call:

```
uses zoo.staff.ZooApi
```

Java allows callers to inspect and call code at runtime with a technique called *reflection*. This is a powerful approach that allows calling code that might not be available at compile time. It can even be used to subvert access control! Don't worry—you don't need to know how to write code using reflection for the exam.

Since reflection can be dangerous, the module system requires developers to explicitly allow reflection in the module-info if they want calling modules to be allowed to use it. Here are two examples:

```
opens zoo.animal.talks.schedule;
opens zoo.animal.talks.media to zoo.staff;
```

The first example allows any module using this one to use reflection. The second example only gives that privilege to the zoo.staff package.

Discovering Modules

So far, we've been working with modules that we wrote. Since Java 9, the classes built into the JDK were modularized as well. In this section, we will show you how to use commands to learn about modules.

You do not need to know the output of the commands in this section. You do, however, need to know the syntax of the commands and what they do. We include the output where it facilitates remembering what is going on. But you don't need to memorize that (which frees up more space in your head to memorize command-line options).

The *java* Command

The java command has three module-related options. One describes a module, another lists the available modules, and the third shows the module resolution logic.

 It is also possible to add modules, exports, and more at the command line. But please don't. It's confusing and hard to maintain. Note these flags are available on java, but not all commands.

Describing a Module

Suppose you are given the zoo.animal.feeding module JAR file and want to know about its module structure. You could "unjar" it and open the module-info file. This would show you that the module exports one package and doesn't require any modules.

```
module zoo.animal.feeding {
    exports zoo.animal.feeding;
}
```

However, there is an easier way. The java command now has an option to describe a module. The following two commands are equivalent:

```
java -p mods
   -d zoo.animal.feeding
```

```
java -p mods
   --describe-module zoo.animal.feeding
```

Each prints information about the module. For example, it might print this:

```
zoo.animal.feeding file:///absolutePath/mods/zoo.animal.feeding.jar
exports zoo.animal.feeding
requires java.base mandated
```

The first line is the module we asked about: zoo.animal.feeding. The second line starts information about the module. In our case, it is the same package exports statement we had in the module-info file.

On the third line, we see requires java.base mandated. Now wait a minute. The module-info file very clearly does not specify any modules that zoo.animal.feeding has as dependencies.

The java.base module is special. It is automatically added as a dependency to all modules. This module has frequently used packages like java.util. That's what the mandated is about. You get java.base whether you asked for it or not.

In classes, the java.lang package is automatically imported whether you type it or not. The java.base module works the same way. It is automatically available to all other modules.

More About Describing Modules

You only need to know how to run --describe-module for the exam. However, you might encounter some surprises when experimenting with this feature, so we describe them in a bit more detail here.

As a reminder, the following are the contents of module-info in zoo.animal.care:

```
module zoo.animal.care {
    exports zoo.animal.care.medical to zoo.staff;
    requires transitive zoo.animal.feeding;
}
```

Now we have the command to describe the module and the output.

```
java -p mods -d zoo.animal.care
```

```
zoo.animal.care file:///absolutePath/mods/zoo.animal.care.jar
requires zoo.animal.feeding transitive
requires java.base mandated
qualified exports zoo.animal.care.medical to zoo.staff
contains zoo.animal.care.details
```

The first line of the output is the absolute path of the module file. The two requires lines should look familiar as well. The first is in the module-info, and the other is added to all modules. Next comes something new. The qualified exports is the full name of exporting to a specific module.

Finally, the contains means that there is a package in the module that is not exported at all. This is true. Our module has two packages, and one is available only to code inside the module.

Listing Available Modules

In addition to describing modules, you can use the java command to list the modules that are available. The simplest form lists the modules that are part of the JDK:

```
java --list-modules
```

When we ran it, the output went on for 70 lines and looked like this:

```
java.base@11.0.2
java.compiler@11.0.2
java.datatransfer@11.0.2
```

This is a listing of all the modules that come with Java and their version numbers. You can tell that we were using Java 11.0.2 when testing this example.

More interestingly, you can use this command with custom code. Let's try again with the directory containing our zoo modules.

```
java -p mods --list-modules
```

How many lines do you expect to be in the output this time? There are 74 lines now: the 70 built-in modules plus the four in our zoo system. The custom lines look like this:

```
zoo.animal.care file:///absolutePath/mods/zoo.animal.care.jar
zoo.animal.feeding file:///absolutePath/mods/zoo.animal.feeding.jar
zoo.animal.talks file:///absolutePath/mods/zoo.animal.talks.jar
zoo.staff file:///absolutePath/mods/zoo.staff.jar
```

Since these are custom modules, we get a location on the file system. If the project had a module version number, it would have both the version number and the file system path.

 Note that --list-modules exits as soon as it prints the observable modules. It does not run the program.

Showing Module Resolution

In case listing the modules didn't give you enough output, you can also use the --show-module-resolution option. You can think of it as a way of debugging modules. It spits out a lot of output when the program starts up. Then it runs the program.

```
java --show-module-resolution
    -p feeding
    -m zoo.animal.feeding/zoo.animal.feeding.Task
```

Luckily you don't need to understand this output. That said, having seen it will make it easier to remember. Here's a snippet of the output:

```
root zoo.animal.feeding file:///absolutePath/feeding/
java.base binds java.desktop jrt:/java.desktop
java.base binds jdk.jartool jrt:/jdk.jartool
...
jdk.security.auth requires java.naming jrt:/java.naming
jdk.security.auth requires java.security.jgss jrt:/java.security.jgss
...
All fed!
```

It starts out by listing the root module. That's the one we are running: zoo.animal .feeding. Then it lists many lines of packages included by the mandatory java.base module. After a while, it lists modules that have dependencies. Finally, it outputs the result of the program All fed!. The total output of this command is 66 lines.

The *jar* Command

Like the java command, the jar command can describe a module. Both of these commands are equivalent:

```
jar -f mods/zoo.animal.feeding.jar -d
jar --file mods/zoo.animal.feeding.jar --describe-module
```

The output is slightly different from when we used the java command to describe the module. With jar, it outputs the following:

```
zoo.animal.feeding jar:file:///absolutePath/mods/zoo.animal.feeding.jar
/!module-info.class
exports zoo.animal.feeding
requires java.base mandated
```

The JAR version includes the module-info in the filename, which is not a particularly significant difference in the scheme of things. You don't need to know this difference. You do need to know that both commands can describe a module.

The *jdeps* Command

The jdeps command gives you information about dependencies within a module. Unlike describing a module, it looks at the code in addition to the module-info file. This tells you what dependencies are actually used rather than simply declared.

Let's start with a simple example and ask for a summary of the dependencies in zoo.animal.feeding. Both of these commands give the same output:

```
jdeps -s mods/zoo.animal.feeding.jar

jdeps -summary mods/zoo.animal.feeding.jar
```

Notice that there is one dash (-) before -summary rather than two. Regardless, the output tells you that there is only one package and it depends on the built-in java.base module.

```
zoo.animal.feeding -> java.base
```

Alternatively, you can call jdeps without the summary option and get the long form:

```
jdeps mods/zoo.animal.feeding.jar
[file:///absolutePath/mods/zoo.animal.feeding.jar]
   requires mandated java.base (@11.0.2)
zoo.animal.feeding -> java.base
   zoo.animal.feeding         -> java.io
      java.base
   zoo.animal.feeding         -> java.lang
      java.base
```

The first part of the output shows the module filename and path. The second part lists the required java.base dependency and version number. This has the high-level summary that matches the previous example.

Finally, the last four lines of the output list the specific packages within the java.base modules that are used by zoo.animal.feeding.

Now, let's look at a more complicated example. This time, we pick a module that depends on zoo.animal.feeding. We need to specify the module path so jdeps knows where to find information about the dependent module. We didn't need to do that before because all dependent modules were built into the JDK.

Following convention, these two commands are equivalent:

```
jdeps -s
   --module-path mods
   mods/zoo.animal.care.jar

jdeps -summary
   --module-path mods
   mods/zoo.animal.care.jar
```

There is not a short form of --module-path in the jdeps command. The output is only two lines:

```
zoo.animal.care -> java.base
zoo.animal.care -> zoo.animal.feeding
```

We can see that the zoo.animal.care module depends on our custom zoo.animal.feeding module along with the built-in java.base.

In case you were worried the output was too short, we can run it in full mode:

```
jdeps --module-path mods
   mods/zoo.animal.care.jar
```

This time we get lots of output:

```
zoo.animal.care
  [file:///absolutePath/mods/zoo.animal.care.jar]
    requires mandated java.base (@11.0.2)
    requires transitive zoo.animal.feeding
  zoo.animal.care -> java.base
  zoo.animal.care -> zoo.animal.feeding
    zoo.animal.care.details      -> java.lang
      java.base
    zoo.animal.care.details      -> zoo.animal.feeding
      zoo.animal.feeding
    zoo.animal.care.medical      -> java.lang
      java.base
```

As before, there are three sections. The first section is the filename and required dependencies. The second section is the summary showing the two module dependencies with an arrow. The last six lines show the package-level dependencies.

The *jmod* Command

The final command you need to know for the exam is jmod. You might think a JMOD file is a Java module file. Not quite. Oracle recommends using JAR files for most modules. JMOD files are recommended only when you have native libraries or something that can't go inside a JAR file. This is unlikely to affect you in the real world.

The most important thing to remember is that jmod is only for working with the JMOD files. Conveniently, you don't have to memorize the syntax for jmod. Table 11.4 lists the common modes.

TABLE 11.4   Modes using jmod

Operation	Description
create	Creates a JMOD file.
extract	Extracts all files from the JMOD. Works like unzipping.
describe	Prints the module details such as requires.
list	Lists all files in the JMOD file.
hash	Shows a long string that goes with the file

Reviewing Command-Line Options

Congratulations on reaching the last section of the book. This section is a number of tables that cover what you need to know about running command-line options for the 1Z0-815 exam.

Table 11.5 shows the command lines you should expect to encounter on the exam.

TABLE 11.5 Comparing command-line operations

Description	Syntax
Compile nonmodular code	**javac -cp** *classpath* -d *directory classesToCompile*
	javac --class-path *classpath* -d *directory classesToCompile*
	javac -classpath *classpath* -d *directory classesToCompile*
Run nonmodular code	**java -cp** *classpath package.className*
	java -classpath *classpath package.className*
	java --class-path *classpath package.className*
Compile a module	**javac -p** *moduleFolderName* -d *directory classesToCompileIncludingModuleInfo*
	javac --module-path *moduleFolderName* -d directory *classesToCompileIncludingModuleInfo*
Run a module	**java -p** *moduleFolderName* **-m** *moduleName/package.className*
	java --module-path *moduleFolderName* **--module** *moduleName/package.className*
Describe a module	**java -p** *moduleFolderName* **-d** *moduleName*
	java --module-path *moduleFolderName* **--describe-module** *moduleName*
	jar --file *jarName* **--describe-module**
	jar -f *jarName* **-d**
List available modules	**java --module-path** *moduleFolderName* **--list-modules**
	java -p *moduleFolderName* **--list-modules**
	java --list-modules
View dependencies	**jdeps -summary --module-path** *moduleFolderName jarName*
	jdeps -s --module-path *moduleFolderName jarName*
Show module resolution	**java --show-module-resolution -p** *moduleFolderName* **-d** *moduleName*
	java --show-module-resolution --module-path *moduleFolderName* **--describe-module** *moduleName*

Since there are so many commands you need to know, we've made a number of tables to review the available options that you need to know for the exam. There are many more options in the documentation. For example, there is a --module option on javac that limits compilation to that module. Luckily, you don't need to know those.

Table 11.6 shows the options for javac, Table 11.7 shows the options for java, Table 11.8 shows the options for jar, and Table 11.9 shows the options for jdeps.

TABLE 11.6 Options you need to know for the exam: javac

Option	Description
-cp <classpath> -classpath <classpath> --class-path <classpath>	Location of JARs in a nonmodular program
-d <dir>	Directory to place generated class files
-p <path> --module-path <path>	Location of JARs in a modular program

TABLE 11.7 Options you need to know for the exam: java

Option	Description
-p <path> --module-path <path>	Location of JARs in a modular program
-m <name> --module <name>	Module name to run
-d --describe-module	Describes the details of a module
--list-modules	Lists observable modules without running a program
--show-module-resolution	Shows modules when running program

TABLE 11.8   Options you need to know for the exam: jar

Option	Description
-c --create	Create a new JAR file
-v --verbose	Prints details when working with JAR files
-f --file	JAR filename
-C	Directory containing files to be used to create the JAR
-d --describe-module	Describes the details of a module

TABLE 11.9   Options you need to know for the exam: jdeps

Option	Description
--module-path <path>	Location of JARs in a modular program
-s -summary	Summarizes output

Summary

The Java Platform Module System organizes code at a higher level than packages. Each module contains one or more packages and a module-info file. Advantages of the JPMS include better access control, clearer dependency management, custom runtime images, improved performance, and unique package enforcement.

The process of compiling and running modules uses the --module-path, also known as -p. Running a module uses the --module option, also known as -m. The class to run is specified in the format moduleName/className.

The module-info file supports a number of keywords. The exports keyword specifies that a package should be accessible outside the module. It can optionally restrict that export to a specific package. The requires keyword is used when a module depends on code in another module. Additionally, requires transitive can be used when all modules that require one module should always require another. The provides and uses keywords are used when sharing and consuming an API. Finally, the opens keyword is used for allowing access via reflection.

Both the java and jar commands can be used to describe the contents of a module. The java command can additionally list available modules and show module resolution. The jdeps command prints information about packages used in addition to module-level information. Finally, the jmod command is used when dealing with files that don't meet the requirements for a JAR.

Exam Essentials

Identify benefits of the Java Platform Module System.   Be able to identify benefits of the JPMS from a list such as access control, dependency management, custom runtime images, performance, and unique package enforcement. Also be able to differentiate benefits of the JPMS from benefits of Java as a whole. For example, garbage collection is not a benefit of the JPMS.

Use command-line syntax with modules.   Use the command-line options for javac, java, and jar. In particular, understand the module (-m) and module path (-p) options.

Create basic module-info files.   Place the module-info.java file in the root directory of the module. Know how to code using exports to expose a package and how to export to a specific module. Also, know how to code using requires and requires transitive to declare a dependency on a package or to share that dependency with any modules using the current module.

Identify advanced module-info keywords.   The provides keyword is used when exposing an API. The uses keyword is for consuming an API. The opens keyword is for allowing the use of reflection.

Display information about modules.   The java command can describe a module, list available modules, or show the module resolution. The jar command can describe a module similar to how the java command does. The jdeps command prints details about a module and packages. The jmod command provides various modes for working with JMOD files rather than JAR files.

Review Questions

1. Which of the following is an advantage of the Java Platform Module System?

    A. A central repository of all modules

    B. Encapsulating packages

    C. Encapsulating objects

    D. No defined types

    E. Platform independence

2. Which statement is true of the following module?

    ```
    zoo.staff
    |---zoo
        |-- staff
          |-- Vet.java
    ```

    A. The directory structure shown is a valid module.

    B. The directory structure would be a valid module if `module.java` were added directly underneath `zoo.staff`.

    C. The directory structure would be a valid module if `module.java` were added directly underneath `zoo`.

    D. The directory structure would be a valid module if `module-info.java` were added directly underneath `zoo.staff`.

    E. The directory structure would be a valid module if `module-info.java` were added directly underneath `zoo`.

    F. None of these changes would make this directory structure a valid module.

3. Suppose module puppy depends on module dog and module dog depends on module animal. Fill in the blank so that code in module dog can access the `animal.behavior` package in module animal.

    ```
    module animal {
        _____ animal.behavior;
    }
    ```

    A. `export`

    B. `exports`

    C. `require`

    D. `requires`

    E. `require transitive`

    F. `requires transitive`

    G. None of the above

4. Fill in the blanks so this command to run the program is correct:

   ```
   java
   _____ zoo.animal.talks/zoo/animal/talks/Peacocks
   _____ modules
   ```

   A. -d and -m

   B. -d and -p

   C. -m and -d

   D. -m and -p

   E. -p and -d

   F. -p and -m

   G. None of the above

5. Which of the following statements are true in a `module-info.java` file? (Choose all that apply.)

   A. The opens keyword allows the use of reflection.

   B. The opens keyword declares an API is called.

   C. The use keyword allows the use of reflection.

   D. The use keyword declares an API is called.

   E. The uses keyword allows the use of reflection.

   F. The uses keyword declares an API is called.

   G. The file can be empty (zero bytes).

6. What is true of a module containing a file named `module-info.java` with the following contents? (Choose all that apply.)

   ```
   module com.food.supplier {}
   ```

   A. All packages inside the module are automatically exported.

   B. No packages inside the module are automatically exported.

   C. A main method inside the module can be run.

   D. A main method inside the module cannot be run since the class is not exposed.

   E. The `module-info.java` file contains a compiler error.

   F. The `module-info.java` filename is incorrect.

7. Suppose module puppy depends on module dog and module dog depends on module animal. Which two lines allow module puppy to access the `animal.behavior` package in module animal? (Choose two.)

   ```
   module animal {
       exports animal.behavior to dog;
   }
   module dog {
       _____ animal;   // line S
   }
   ```

```
module puppy {
    _____ dog;      // line T
}
```

A. require on line S

B. require on line T

C. requires on line S

D. requires on line T

E. require transitive on line S

F. require transitive on line T

G. requires transitive on line S

H. requires transitive on line T

8. Which commands take a --module-path parameter? (Choose all that apply.)

A. javac

B. java

C. jar

D. jdeps

E. jmod

F. None of the above

9. Which of the following are legal commands to run a modular program? (Choose all that apply.)

A. java -p x -m x/x

B. java -p x-x -m x/x

C. java -p x -m x-x/x

D. java -p x -m x/x-x

E. java -p x -m x.x

F. java -p x.x -m x.x

G. None of the above

10. Which would best fill in the blank to complete the following code?

```
module _____ {
    exports com.unicorn.horn;
    exports com.unicorn.magic;
}
```

A. com

B. com.unicorn

C. com.unicorn.horn

D. com.unicorn.magic

   E. The code does not compile.

   F. The code compiles, but none of these would be a good choice.

11. Which are valid modes for the jmod command? (Choose all that apply.)

   A. add

   B. create

   C. delete

   D. describe

   E. extract

   F. list

   G. show

12. Suppose you have the commands javac, java, and jar. How many of them support a --show-module-resolution option?

   A. 0

   B. 1

   C. 2

   D. 3

13. Which are true statements about the following module? (Choose all that apply.)

```
class dragon {
    exports com.dragon.fire;
    exports com.dragon.scales to castle;
}
```

   A. All modules can reference the com.dragon.fire package.

   B. All modules can reference the com.dragon.scales package.

   C. Only the castle module can reference the com.dragon.fire package.

   D. Only the castle module can reference the com.dragon.scales package.

   E. None of the above

14. Which would you expect to see when describing any module?

   A. requires java.base mandated

   B. requires java.core mandated

   C. requires java.lang mandated

   D. requires mandated java.base

   E. requires mandated java.core

   F. requires mandated java.lang

   G. None of the above

15. Which of the following statements are correct? (Choose all that apply.)

   A. The jar command allows adding exports as command-line options.

   B. The java command allows adding exports as command-line options.

   C. The jdeps command allows adding exports as command-line options.

   D. Adding an export at the command line is discouraged.

   E. Adding an export at the command line is recommended.

16. Which are valid calls to list a summary of the dependencies? (Choose all that apply.)

   A. jdeps flea.jar

   B. jdeps -s flea.jar

   C. jdeps -summary flea.jar

   D. jdeps --summary flea.jar

   E. None of the above

17. Which is the first line to contain a compiler error?

```
1: module snake {
2:     exports com.snake.tail;
3:     exports com.snake.fangs to bird;
4:     requires skin;
5:     requires transitive skin;
6: }
```

   A. Line 1.

   B. Line 2.

   C. Line 3.

   D. Line 4.

   E. Line 5.

   F. The code does not contain any compiler errors.

18. Which of the following would be a legal module name? (Choose all that apply.)

   A. com.book

   B. com-book

   C. com.book$

   D. com-book$

   E. 4com.book

   F. 4com-book

19. What can be created using the Java Platform Module System that could not be created without it? (Choose all that apply.)

    A. JAR file

    B. JMOD file

    C. Smaller runtime images for distribution

    D. Operating system specific bytecode

    E. TAR file

    F. None of the above

20. Which of the following options does not have a one-character shortcut in any of the commands studied in this chapter? (Choose all that apply.)

    A. `describe-module`

    B. `list-modules`

    C. `module`

    D. `module-path`

    E. `show-module-resolution`

    F. `summary`

21. Which of the following are legal commands to run a modular program where n is the package name and c is the class name? (Choose all that apply.)

    A. `java –module-path x -m n.c`

    B. `java --module-path x -p n.c`

    C. `java --module-path x -m n/c`

    D. `java --module-path x -p n/c`

    E. `java --module-path x -m n c`

    F. `java --module-path x -p n c`

    G. None of the above

Appendix

Answers to Review Questions

Chapter 1: Welcome to Java

1. B, E. C++ has operator overloading and pointers. Java made a point of not having either. Java does have references to objects, but these are pointing to an object that can move around in memory. Option B is correct because Java is platform independent. Option E is correct because Java is object-oriented. While it does support some parts of functional programming, these occur within a class.

2. C, D. Java puts source code in `.java` files and bytecode in `.class` files. It does not use a `.bytecode` file. When running a Java program, you pass just the name of the class without the `.class` extension.

3. C, D. This example is using the single-file source-code launcher. It compiles in memory rather than creating a `.class` file, making option A incorrect. To use this launcher, programs can only reference classes built into the JDK. Therefore, option B is incorrect, and options C and D are correct.

4. C, D. The Tank class is there to throw you off since it isn't used by `AquariumVisitor`. Option C is correct because it imports `Jelly` by class name. Option D is correct because it imports all the classes in the `jellies` package, which includes `Jelly`. Option A is incorrect because it only imports classes in the `aquarium` package—Tank in this case—and not those in lower-level packages. Option B is incorrect because you cannot use wildcards anywhere other than the end of an `import` statement. Option E is incorrect because you cannot `import` parts of a class with a regular `import` statement. Option F is incorrect because options C and D do make the code compile.

5. A, C, D, E. Eclipse is an integrated development environment (IDE). It is not included in the Java Development Kit (JDK), making option B incorrect. The JDK comes with a number of command-line tools including a compiler, packager, and documentation, making options A, D, and E correct. The JDK also includes the Java Virtual Machine (JVM), making option C correct.

6. E. The first two imports can be removed because `java.lang` is automatically imported. The following two imports can be removed because Tank and Water are in the same package, making the correct option E. If Tank and Water were in different packages, exactly one of these two imports could be removed. In that case, the answer would be option D.

7. A, B, C. Option A is correct because it imports all the classes in the `aquarium` package including `aquarium.Water`. Options B and C are correct because they import Water by class name. Since importing by class name takes precedence over wildcards, these compile. Option D is incorrect because Java doesn't know which of the two wildcard Water classes to use. Option E is incorrect because you cannot specify the same class name in two imports.

8. A, B. The wildcard is configured for files ending in `.java`, making options E and F incorrect. Additionally, wildcards aren't recursive, making options C and D incorrect. Therefore, options A and B are correct.

9. B. Option B is correct because arrays start counting from zero and strings with spaces must be in quotes. Option A is incorrect because it outputs Blue. C is incorrect because it outputs Jay. Option D is incorrect because it outputs Sparrow. Options E and F are incorrect because they output `java.lang.ClassNotFoundException: BirdDisplay .class`.

10. E. Option E is the canonical `main()` method signature. You need to memorize it. Option A is incorrect because the `main()` method must be public. Options B and F are incorrect because the `main()` method must have a `void` return type. Option C is incorrect because the `main()` method must be static. Option D is incorrect because the `main()` method must be named `main`.

11. C, D. While we wish it were possible to guarantee bug-free code, this is not something a language can ensure, making option A incorrect. Deprecation is an indication that other code should be preferred. It doesn't preclude or require eventual removal, making option B incorrect. Option E is incorrect because backward compatibility is a design goal, not sideways compatibility. Options C and D are correct.

12. C, E. When compiling with `javac`, you can specify a classpath with `-cp` or a directory with `-d`, making options C and E correct. Since the options are case sensitive, option D is incorrect. The other options are not valid on the `javac` command.

13. C. When running a program using `java`, you specify the classpath with `-cp`, making option C correct. Options D and F are incorrect because `-d` and `-p` are used for modules. Options A and B are not valid options on the `java` command.

14. A, B, C, E. When creating a `jar` file, you use the options `-cf` or `-cvf`, making options A and E correct. The `jar` command allows the use of the classpath, making option C correct. It also allows the specification of a directory using `-C`, making option B correct. Options D and F are incorrect because `-d` and `-p` are used for modules.

15. E. The `main()` method isn't `static`. It is a method that happens to be named `main()`, but it's not an application entry point. When the program is run, it gives the error. If the method were `static`, the answer would be option D. Arrays are zero-based, so the loop ignores the first element and throws an exception when accessing the element after the last one.

16. D. The package name represents any folders underneath the current path, which is named `.A` in this case. Option C is incorrect because package names are case sensitive, just like variable names and other identifiers.

17. A, E. Bunny is a class, which can be seen from the declaration: `public class Bunny`. The variable bun is a reference to an object. The method `main()` is the standard entry point to a program. Option G is incorrect because the parameter type matters, not the parameter name.

18. C, D, E. The `package` and `import` statements are both optional. If both are present, the order must be `package`, then `import`, and then `class`. Option A is incorrect because `class` is before `package` and `import`. Option B is incorrect because `import` is before `package`. Option F is incorrect because `class` is before `package`.

19. B, C. Eclipse is an integrated development environment (IDE). It is available from the Eclipse Foundation, not from Oracle, making option C one of the answers. The other answer is option B because the Java Development Kit (JDK) is what you download to get started. The Java Runtime Environment (JRE) was an option for older versions of Java, but it's no longer a download option for Java 11.

20. A, B, E. Unfortunately, this is something you have to memorize. The code with the hyphenated word class-path uses two dashes in front, making option E correct and option D incorrect. The reverse is true for the unhyphenated classpath, making option B correct and option C incorrect. Finally, the short form is option A.

Chapter 2: Java Building Blocks

1. B, E, G. Option A is invalid because a single underscore is no longer allowed as an identifier as of Java 9. Option B is valid because you can use an underscore within identifiers, and a dollar sign ($) is also a valid character. Option C is not a valid identifier because true is a Java reserved word. Option D is not valid because a period (.) is not allowed in identifiers. Option E is valid because Java is case sensitive. Since Public is not a reserved word, it is allowed as an identifier, whereas public would not be allowed. Option F is not valid because the first character is not a letter, dollar sign ($), or underscore (_). Finally, option G is valid as identifiers can contain underscores (_) and numbers, provided the number does not start the identifier.

2. D, F, G. The code compiles and runs without issue, so options A and B are incorrect. A boolean field initializes to false, making option D correct with Empty = false being printed. Object references initialize to null, not the empty String, so option F is correct with Brand = null being printed. Finally, the default value of floating-point numbers is 0.0. Although float values can be declared with an f suffix, they are not printed with an f suffix. For these reasons, option G is correct and Code = 0.0 is printed.

3. B, D, E, H. A var cannot be initialized with a null value without a type, but it can be assigned a null value if the underlying type is not a primitive. For these reasons, option H is correct, but options A and C are incorrect. Options B and D are correct as the underlying types are String and Object, respectively. Option E is correct, as this is a valid numeric expression. You might know that dividing by zero produces a runtime exception, but the question was only about whether the code compiled. Finally, options F and G are incorrect as var cannot be used in a multiple-variable assignment.

4. A, B, D, E. Line 4 does not compile because the L suffix makes the literal value a long, which cannot be stored inside a short directly, making option A correct. Line 5 does not compile because int is an integral type, but 2.0 is a double literal value, making option B correct. Line 6 compiles without issue. Lines 7 and 8 do not compile because numPets and numGrains are both primitives, and you can call methods only on reference types, not primitive values, making options D and E correct, respectively. Finally, line 9 compiles because there is a length() method defined on String.

5. A, D. The class does not compile, so options E, F, G, and H are incorrect. You might notice things like loops and increment/decrement operators in this problem, which we will cover in the next two chapters, but understanding them is not required to answer this question. The first compiler error is on line 3. The variable temp is declared as a float, but the assigned value is 50.0, which is a double without the F/f postfix. Since a double doesn't fit inside a float, line 3 does not compile. Next, depth is declared inside the for loop and only has scope inside this loop. Therefore, reading the value on line 10 triggers a compiler error. Note that the variable Depth on line 2 is never used. Java is case sensitive, so Depth and depth are distinct variables. For these reasons, options A and D are the correct answers.

6. C, E. Option C is correct because float and double primitives default to 0.0, which also makes option A incorrect. Option E is correct because all nonprimitive values default to null, which makes option F incorrect. Option D is incorrect because int primitives default to 0. Option B is incorrect because char defaults to the NUL character, '\u0000'. You don't need to know this value for the exam, but you should know the default value is not null since it is a primitive.

7. G. Option G is correct because local variables do not get assigned default values. The code fails to compile if a local variable is used when not being explicitly initialized. If this question were about instance variables, options B, D, and E would be correct. A boolean primitive defaults to false, and a float primitive defaults to 0.0f.

8. B, E. Option B is correct because boolean primitives default to false. Option E is correct because long values default to 0L.

9. C, E, F. In Java, there are no guarantees when garbage collection will run. The JVM is free to ignore calls to System.gc(). For this reason, options A, B, and D are incorrect. Option C is correct, as the purpose of garbage collection is to reclaim used memory. Option E is also correct that an object may never be garbage collected, such as if the program ends before garbage collection runs. Option F is correct and is the primary means by which garbage collection algorithms determine whether an object is eligible for garbage collection. Finally, option G is incorrect as marking a variable final means it is constant within its own scope. For example, a local variable marked final will be eligible for garbage collection after the method ends, assuming there are no other references to the object that exist outside the method.

10. C. The class does compiles without issue, so options E, F, and G are incorrect. The key thing to notice is line 4 does not define a constructor, but instead a method named PoliceBox(), since it has a return type of void. This method is never executed during the program run, and color and age get assigned the default values null and 0L, respectively. Lines 11 and 12 change the values for an object associated with p, but then on line 13 the p variable is changed to point to the object associated with q, which still has the default values. For this reason, the program prints Q1=null, Q2=0, P1=null, and P2=0, making option C the only correct answer.

11. A, D, E. From Chapter 1, a main() method must have a valid identifier of type String... or String[]. For this reason, option G can be eliminated immediately. Option A is correct because var is not a reserved word in Java and may be used as an identifier. Option B is incorrect as a period (.) may not be used in an identifier. Option C is also incorrect as an identifier may include digits but not start with one. Options D and E are correct as an underscore (_) and dollar sign ($) may appear anywhere in an identifier. Finally, option F is incorrect, as a var may not be used as a method argument.

12. A, E, F. An underscore (_) can be placed in any numeric literal, so long as it is not at the beginning, the end, or next to a decimal point (.). Underscores can even be placed next to each other. For these reasons, options A, E, and F are correct. Options B and D are incorrect, as the underscore (_) is next to a decimal point (.). Options C and G are incorrect, because an underscore (_) cannot be placed at the beginning or end of the literal.

13. B, D, H. The Rabbit object from line 3 has two references to it: one and three. The references are set to null on lines 6 and 8, respectively. Option B is correct because this makes the object eligible for garbage collection after line 8. Line 7 sets the reference four to null, since that is the value of one, which means it has no effect on garbage collection. The Rabbit object from line 4 has only a single reference to it: two. Option D is correct because this single reference becomes null on line 9. The Rabbit object declared on line 10 becomes eligible for garbage collection at the end of the method on line 12, making option H correct. Calling System.gc() has no effect on eligibility for garbage collection.

14. B, C, F. A var cannot be used for a constructor or method parameter or for an instance or class variable, making option A incorrect and option C correct. The type of var is known at compile-time and the type cannot be changed at runtime, although its value can change at runtime. For these reasons, options B and F are correct, and option E is incorrect. Option D is incorrect, as var is not permitted in multiple-variable declarations. Finally, option G is incorrect, as var is not a reserved word in Java.

15. C, F, G. First off, 0b is the prefix for a binary value, and 0x is the prefix for a hexadecimal value. These values can be assigned to many primitive types, including int and double, making options C and F correct. Option A is incorrect because naming the variable Amount will cause the System.out.print(amount) call on the next line to not compile. Option B is incorrect because 9L is a long value. If the type was changed to long amount = 9L, then it would compile. Option D is incorrect because 1_2.0 is a double value. If the type was changed to double amount = 1_2.0, then it would compile. Options E and H are incorrect because the underscore (_) appears next to the decimal point (.), which is not allowed. Finally, option G is correct and the underscore and assignment usage is valid.

16. A, C, D. The code contains three compilation errors, so options E, F, G, and H are incorrect. Line 2 does not compile, as this is incorrect syntax for declaring multiple variables, making option A correct. The data type is declared only once and shared among all variables in a multiple variable declaration. Line 3 compiles without issue, as it declares a local variable inside an instance initializer that is never used. Line 4 does not compile because Java, unlike some other programming languages, does not support setting default method parameter values, making option C correct. Finally, line 7 does not compile because fins is in scope and accessible only inside the instance initializer on line 3, making option D correct.

17. A, E, F, G. The question is primarily about variable scope. A variable defined in a statement such as a loop or initializer block is accessible only inside that statement. For this reason, options A and E are correct. Option B is incorrect because variables can be defined inside initializer blocks. Option C is incorrect, as a constructor argument is accessible only in the constructor itself, not for the life of the instance of the class. Constructors and instance methods can access any instance variable, even ones defined after their declaration, making option D incorrect and options F and G correct.

18. F, G. The code does not compile, so options A, B, C, and D are all incorrect. The first compilation error occurs on line 5. Since char is an unsigned data type, it cannot be assigned a negative value, making option F correct. The second compilation error is on line 9, since mouse is used without being initialized, making option G correct. You could fix this by initializing a value on line 4, but the compiler reports the error where the variable is used, not where it is declared.

19. F. To solve this problem, you need to trace the braces {} and see when variables go in and out of scope. You are not required to understand the various data structures in the question, as this will be covered in the next few chapters. We start with hairs, which goes in and out of scope on line 2, as it is declared in an instance initializer, so it is not in scope on line 14. The three variables—water, air, twoHumps, declared on lines 3 and 4—are instance variables, so all three are in scope in all instance methods of the class, including spit() and on line 14. The distance method parameter is in scope for the life of the spit() method, making it the fourth value in scope on line 14. The path variable is in scope on line 6 and stays in scope until the end of the method on line 16, making it the fifth variable in scope on line 14. The teeth variable is in scope on line 7 and immediately goes out of scope on line 7 since the statement ends. The two variables age and i defined on lines 9 and 10, respectively, both stay in scope until the end of the while loop on line 15, bringing the total variables in scope to seven on line 14. Finally, Private is in scope on 12 but out of scope after the for loop ends on line 13. Since the total in-scope variables is seven, option F is the correct answer.

20. D. The class compiles and runs without issue, so options F and G are incorrect. We start with the main() method, which prints 7- on line 11. Next, a new Salmon instance is created on line 11. This calls the two instance initializers on lines 3 and 4 to be executed in order. The default value of an instance variable of type int is 0, so 0- is printed next and count is assigned a value of 1. Next, the constructor is called. This assigns a value of 4 to count and prints 2-. Finally, line 12 prints 4-, since that is the value of count. Putting it altogether, we have 7-0-2-4-, making option D the correct answer.

21. A, D, F. The class compiles and runs without issue, so option H is incorrect. The program creates two Bear objects, one on line 9 and one on line 10. The first Bear object is accessible until line 13 via the brownBear reference variable. The second Bear object is passed to the first object's roar() method on line 11, meaning it is accessible via both the polarBear reference and the brownBear.pandaBear reference. After line 12, the object is still accessible via brownBear.pandaBear. After line 13, though, it is no longer accessible since brownBear is no longer accessible. In other words, both objects become eligible for garbage collection after line 13, making options A and D correct. Finally, garbage collection is never guaranteed to run or not run, since the JVM decides this for you. For this reason, option F is correct, and options E and G are incorrect. The class contains a finalize() method, although this does not contribute to the answer. For the exam, you may see finalize() in a question, but since it's deprecated as of Java 9, you will not be tested on it.

22. H. None of these declarations is a valid instance variable declaration, as var cannot be used with instance variables, only local variables. For this reason, option H is the only correct answer. If the question were changed to be about local variable declarations, though, then the correct answers would be options C, D, and E. An identifier must start with a letter, $, or _, so options F and G would be incorrect. As of Java 9, a single underscore is not allowed as an identifier, so option A would be incorrect. Options A and G would also be incorrect because their numeric expressions use underscores incorrectly. An underscore cannot appear at the end of literal value, nor next to a decimal point (.). Finally, null is a reserved word, but var is not, so option B would be incorrect, and option E would be correct.

Chapter 3: Operators

1. A, D, G. Option A is the equality operator and can be used on primitives and object references. Options B and C are both arithmetic operators and cannot be applied to a boolean value. Option D is the logical complement operator and is used exclusively with boolean values. Option E is the modulus operator, which can be used only with numeric primitives. Option F is a relational operator that compares the values of two numbers. Finally, option G is correct, as you can cast a boolean variable since boolean is a type.

2. A, B, D. The expression apples + oranges is automatically promoted to int, so int and data types that can be promoted automatically from int will work. Options A, B, and D are such data types. Option C will not work because boolean is not a numeric data type. Options E and F will not work without an explicit cast to a smaller data type.

3. B, C, D, F. The code will not compile as is, so option A is not correct. The value 2 * ear is automatically promoted to long and cannot be automatically stored in hearing, which is in an int value. Options B, C, and D solve this problem by reducing the long value to int. Option E does not solve the problem and actually makes it worse by attempting to place the value in a smaller data type. Option F solves the problem by increasing the data type of the assignment so that long is allowed.

4. B. The code compiles and runs without issue, so option E is not correct. This example is tricky because of the second assignment operator embedded in line 5. The expression (wolf=false) assigns the value false to wolf and returns false for the entire expression. Since teeth does not equal 10, the left side returns true; therefore, the exclusive or (^) of the entire expression assigned to canine is true. The output reflects these assignments, with no change to teeth, so option B is the only correct answer.

5. A, C. Options A and C show operators in increasing or the same order of precedence. Options B and E are in decreasing or the same order of precedence. Options D, F, and G are in neither increasing or decreasing order of precedence. In option D, the assignment operator (=) is between two unary operators, with the multiplication operator (*) incorrectly having the highest order or precedence. In option F, the logical complement operator (!) has the highest order of precedence, so it should be last. In option G, the assignment operators have the lowest order of precedence, not the highest, so the last two operators should be first.

6.   F. The code does not compile because line 3 contains a compilation error. The cast (int) is applied to fruit, not the expression fruit+vegetables. Since the cast operator has a higher operator precedence than the addition operator, it is applied to fruit, but the expression is promoted to a float, due to vegetables being float. The result cannot be returned as long in the addCandy() method without a cast. For this reason, option F is correct. If parentheses were added around fruit+vegetables, then the output would be 3-5-6, and option B would be correct. Remember that casting floating point numbers to integral values results in truncation, not rounding.

7.   D. In the first boolean expression, vis is 2 and ph is 7, so this expression evaluates to true & (true || false), which reduces to true. The second boolean expression uses the short-circuit operator, and since (vis > 2) is false, the right side is not evaluated, leaving ph at 7. In the last assignment, ph is 7, and the pre-decrement operator is applied first, reducing the expression to 7 <= 6 and resulting in an assignment of false. For these reasons, option D is the correct answer.

8.   A. The code compiles and runs without issue, so option E is incorrect. Line 7 does not produce a compilation error since the compound operator applies casting automatically. Line 5 increments pig by 1, but it returns the original value of 4 since it is using the post-increment operator. The pig variable is then assigned this value, and the increment operation is discarded. Line 7 just reduces the value of goat by 1, resulting in an output of 4 - 1 and making option A the correct answer.

9.   A, D, E. The code compiles without issue, so option G is incorrect. In the first expression, a > 2 is false, so b is incremented to 5 but since the post-increment operator is used, 4 is printed, making option D correct. The --c was not applied, because only one right side of the ternary expression was evaluated. In the second expression, a!=c is false since c was never modified. Since b is 5 due to the previous line and the post-increment operator is used, b++ returns 5. The result is then assigned to b using the assignment operator, overriding the incremented value for b and printing 5, making option E correct. In the last expression, parentheses are not required but lack of parentheses can make ternary expressions difficult to read. From the previous lines, a is 2, b is 5, and c is 2. We can rewrite this expression with parentheses as (2 > 5 ? (5 < 2 ? 5 : 2) : 1). The second ternary expression is never evaluated since 2 > 5 is false, and the expression returns 1, making option A correct.

10.   G. The code does not compile due to an error on the second line. Even though both height and weight are cast to byte, the multiplication operator automatically promotes them to int, resulting in an attempt to store an int in a short variable. For this reason, the code does not compile, and option G is the only correct answer. This line contains the only compilation error. If the code were corrected to add parentheses around the entire expression and cast it to a byte or short, then the program would print 3, 6, and 2 in that order.

11.   D. First off, the * and % have the same operator precedence, so the expression is evaluated from left to right unless parentheses are present. The first expression evaluates to 8 % 3, which leaves a remainder of 2. The second expression is just evaluated left to right since * and % have the same operator precedence, and it reduces to 6 % 3, which is 0. The last expression reduces to 5 * 1, which is 5. Therefore, the output on line 6 is 2-0-5, making option D the correct answer.

12. D. The *pre-* prefix indicates the operation is applied first, and the new value is returned, while the *post-* prefix indicates the original value is returned prior to the operation. Next, increment increases the value, while decrement decreases the value. For these reasons, option D is the correct answer.

13. F. The first expression is evaluated from left to right since the operator precedence of & and ^ is the same, letting us reduce it to `false` ^ sunday, which is true, because sunday is `true`. In the second expression, we apply the negation operator, (`!`), first, reducing the expression to sunday `&&` `true`, which evaluates to `true`. In the last expression, both variables are `true` so they reduce to `!(true && true)`, which further reduces to `!true`, aka `false`. For these reasons, option F is the correct answer.

14. B, E, G. The return value of an assignment operation in the expression is the same as the value of the newly assigned variable. For this reason, option A is incorrect, and option E is correct. Option B is correct, and the equality (==) and inequality (!=) operators can both be used with objects. Option C is incorrect, as boolean and numeric types are not comparable with each other. For example, you can't say `true` == 3 without a compilation error. Option D is incorrect, as only the short-circuit operator (&&) may cause only the left side of the expression to be evaluated. The (|) operator will cause both sides to be evaluated. Option F is incorrect, as Java does not accept numbers for boolean values. Finally, option G is correct, as you need to use the negation operator (-) to flip or negate numeric values, not the logical complement operator (!).

15. D. The ternary operator is the only operator that takes three values, making option D the only correct choice. Options A, B, C, E, and G are all binary operators. While they can be strung together in longer expressions, each operation uses only two values at a time. Option F is a unary operator and takes only one value.

16. B. The first line contains a compilation error. The value 3 is cast to `long`. The 1 `*` 2 value is evaluated as `int` but promoted to `long` when added to the 3. Trying to store a `long` value in an `int` variable triggers a compiler error. The other lines do not contain any compilation errors, as they store smaller values in larger or same-size data types, with the third and fourth lines using casting to do so.

17. C, F. The starting values of `ticketsTaken` and `ticketsSold` are 1 and 3, respectively. After the first compound assignment, `ticketsTaken` is incremented to 2. The `ticketsSold` value is increased from 3 to 5; since the post-increment operator was used the value of `ticketsTaken++` returns 1. On the next line, `ticketsTaken` is doubled to 4. On the final line, `ticketsSold` is increased by 1 to 6. The final values of the variables are 4 and 6, for `ticketsTaken` and `ticketsSold`, respectively, making options C and F the correct answers. Note the last line does not trigger a compilation error as the compound operator automatically casts the right-hand operand.

18. C. Only parentheses, ( ), can be used to change the order of operation in an expression. The other operators, such as [ ], < >, and { }, cannot be used as parentheses in Java.

19. B, F. The code compiles and runs successfully, so options G and H are incorrect. On line 5, the pre-increment operator is executed first, so start is incremented to 8, and the new value is returned as the right side of the expression. The value of end is computed by adding 8 to the original value of 4, leaving a new value of 12 for end, and making option F a correct answer. On line 6, we are incrementing one past the maximum byte value. Due to overflow, this will result in a negative number, making option B the correct answer. Even if you didn't know the maximum value of byte, you should have known the code compiles and runs and looked for the answer for start with a negative number.

20. A, D, E. Unary operators have the highest order of precedence, making option A correct. The negation operator (-) is used only for numeric values, while the logical complement operator (!) is used exclusively for boolean values. For these reasons, option B is incorrect, and option E is correct. Finally, the pre-increment/pre-decrement operators return the new value of the variable, while the post-increment/post-decrement operators return the original variable. For these reasons, option C is incorrect, and option D is correct.

Chapter 4: Making Decisions

1. A, B, C, E, F, G. A switch statement supports the primitives int, byte, short, and char, along with their associated wrapper classes Integer, Byte, Short, and Character, respectively, making options B, C, and F correct. It also supports enum and String, making options A and E correct. Finally, switch supports var if the type can be resolved to a supported switch data type, making option G correct. Options D and H are incorrect as long, float, double, and their associated wrapped classes Long, Float, and Double, respectively, are not supported in switch statements.

2. B. The code compiles and runs without issue, so options D, E, and F are incorrect. Even though the two consecutive else statements on lines 7 and 8 look a little odd, they are associated with separate if statements on lines 5 and 6, respectively. The value of humidity on line 4 is equal to -4 + 12, which is 8. The first if statement evaluates to true on line 5, so line 6 is executed and its associated else statement on line 8 is not. The if statement on line 6 evaluates to false, causing the else statement on line 7 to activate. The result is the code prints Just Right, making option B the correct answer.

3. E. The second for-each loop contains a continue followed by a print() statement. Because the continue is not conditional and always included as part of the body of the for-each loop, the print() statement is not reachable. For this reason, the print() statement does not compile. As this is the only compilation error, option E is correct. The other lines of code compile without issue. In particular, because the data type for the elements of myFavoriteNumbers is Integer, they can be easily unboxed to int or referenced as Object. For this reason, the lines containing the for-each expressions each compile.

4. C, E. A for-each loop can be executed on any Collections object that implements `java.lang.Iterable`, such as `List` or `Set`, but not all Collections classes, such as `Map`, so option A is incorrect. The body of a do/while loop is executed one or more times, while the body of a `while` loop is executed zero or more times, making option E correct and option B incorrect. The conditional expression of `for` loops is evaluated at the start of the loop execution, meaning the `for` loop may execute zero or more times, making option C correct. Option D is incorrect, as a `default` statement is not required in a `switch` statement. If no `case` statements match and there is no `default` statement, then the application will exit the `switch` statement without executing any branches. Finally, each `if` statement has at most one matching `else` statement, making option F incorrect. You can chain multiple `if` and `else` statements together, but each `else` statement requires a new `if` statement.

5. B, D. Option A is incorrect because on the first iteration it attempts to access `weather[weather.length]` of the nonempty array, which causes an `ArrayIndexOutOfBoundsException` to be thrown. Option B is correct and will print the elements in order. It is only a slight modification of a common `for` loop, with `i<weather.length` replaced with an equivalent `i<=weather.length-1`. Option C is incorrect because the snippet creates a compilation problem in the body of the `for` loop, as `i` is undefined in `weather[i]`. For this to work, the body of the for-each loop would have to be updated as well. Option D is also correct and is a common way to print the elements of an array in reverse order. Option E does not compile and is therefore incorrect. You can declare multiple elements in a `for` loop, but the data type must be listed only once, such as in `for(int i=0, j=3; ...)`. Finally, option F is incorrect because the first element of the array is skipped. The loop update operation is optional, so that part compiles, but the increment is applied as part of the conditional check for the loop. Since the conditional expression is checked before the loop is executed the first time, the first value of `i` used inside the body of the loop will be 1.

6. B, C, E. The code contains a nested loop and a conditional expression that is executed if the sum of `col` + `row` is an even number, else `count` is incremented. Note that options E and F are equivalent to options B and D, respectively, since unlabeled statements apply to the most inner loop. Studying the loops, the first time the condition is true is in the second iteration of the inner loop, when `row` is 1 and `col` is 1. Option A is incorrect, because this causes the loop to exit immediately with `count` only being set to 1. Options B, C, and E follow the same pathway. First, `count` is incremented to 1 on the first inner loop, and then the inner loop is exited. On the next iteration of the outer loop, `row` is 2 and `col` is 0, so execution exits the inner loop immediately. On the third iteration of the outer loop, `row` is 3 and `col` is 0, so `count` is incremented to 2. In the next iteration of the inner loop, the sum is even, so we exit, and our program is complete, making options B, C, and E each correct. Options D and F are both incorrect, as they cause the outer loops to execute multiple times, with `count` having a value of 5 when done. You don't need to trace through all the iterations; just stop when the value of `count` exceeds 2.

7. E. This code contains numerous compilation errors, making options A and H incorrect. All of the compilation errors are contained within the `switch` statement. The `default` statement is fine and does not cause any issues. The first `case` statement does not compile, as `continue` cannot be used inside a `switch` statement. The second `case` statement also does not compile. While the `thursday` variable is marked `final`, it is not a compile-time constant required for a switch statement, as any int value can be passed in at runtime. The third case statement is valid and does compile, as break is compatible with switch statements. The fourth case statement does not compile. Even though Sunday is effectively final, it is not a compile-time constant. If it were explicitly marked final, then this case statement would compile. Finally, the last case statement does not compile because DayOfWeek.MONDAY is not an int value. While switch statements do support enum values, each case statement must have the same data type as the switch variable otherDay, which is int. Since exactly four lines do not compile, option E is the correct answer.

8. C. Prior to the first iteration, sing = 8, squawk = 2, and notes = 0. After the iteration of the first loop, sing is updated to 7, squawk to 4, and notes to the sum of the new values for sing + squawk, 7 + 4 = 11. After the iteration of the second loop, sing is updated to 6, squawk to 6, and notes to the sum of itself, plus the new values for sing + squawk, 11 + 6 + 6 = 23. On the third iteration of the loop, sing > squawk evaluates to false, as 6 > 6 is false. The loop ends and the most recent value of sing, 23, is output, so the correct answer is option C.

9. G. This example may look complicated, but the code does not compile. Line 8 is missing the required parentheses around the boolean conditional expression. Since the code does not compile and it is not because of line 6, option G is the correct answer. If line 8 was corrected with parentheses, then the loop would be executed twice, and the output would be 11.

10. B, D, F. The code does compile, making option G incorrect. In the first for-each loop, the right side of the for-each loop has a type of int[], so each element penguin has a type of int, making option B correct. In the second for-each loop, ostrich has a type of Character[], so emu has a data type of Character, making option D correct. In the last for-each loop, parrots has a data type of List. Since no generic type is used, the default type is a List of Object values, and macaw will have a data type of Object, making option F correct.

11. F. The code does not compile, although not for the reason specified in option E. The second case statement contains invalid syntax. Each case statement must have the keyword case—in other words, you cannot chain them with a colon (:) as shown in case 'B' : 'C' :. For this reason, option F is the correct answer. If this line were fixed to add the keyword case before 'C', then the rest of the code would have compiled and printed great good at runtime.

12. A, B, D. To print items in the wolf array in reverse order, the code needs to start with wolf[wolf.length-1] and end with wolf[0]. Option A accomplishes this and is the first correct answer, albeit not using any of for loop structures, and ends when the index is 0. Option B is also correct and is one of the most common ways a reverse loop is written. The termination condition is often m>=0 or m>-1, and both are correct. Options C and F each cause an ArrayIndexOutOfBoundsException at runtime since both read from wolf[wolf.length] first, with an index that is passed the length of the 0-based array wolf. The form of option C would be successful if the value was changed to wolf[wolf.length-z-1]. Option D is also correct, as the j is extraneous and can be ignored in this example. Finally, option E is incorrect and produces an infinite loop at runtime, as w is repeatedly set to r-1, in this case 4, on every loop iteration. Since the update statement has no effect after the first iteration, the condition is never met, and the loop never terminates.

13. B, E. The code compiles without issue and prints three distinct numbers at runtime, so options G and H are incorrect. The first loop executes a total of five times, with the loop ending when participants has a value of 10. For this reason, option E is correct. In the second loop, animals already starts out not less than or equal to 1, but since it is a do/while loop, it executes at least once. In this manner, animals takes on a value of 3 and the loop terminates, making option B correct. Finally, the last loop executes a total of two times, with performers starting with -1, going to 1 at the end of the first loop, and then ending with a value of 3 after the second loop, which breaks the loop. This makes option B a correct answer twice over.

14. E. The variable snake is declared within the body of the do/while statement, so it is out of scope on line 7. For this reason, option E is the correct answer. If snake were declared before line 3 with a value of 1, then the output would have been 1 2 3 4 5 -5.0, and option G would have been the correct answer choice.

15. A, E. The most important thing to notice when reading this code is that the innermost loop is an infinite loop without a statement to branch out of it, since there is no loop termination condition. Therefore, you are looking for solutions that skip the innermost loop entirely or ones that exit that loop. Option A is correct, as break L2 on line 8 causes the second inner loop to exit every time it is entered, skipping the innermost loop entirely. For option B, the first continue on line 8 causes the execution to skip the innermost loop on the first iteration of the second loop, but not the second iteration of the second loop. The innermost loop is executed, and with continue on line 12, it produces an infinite loop at runtime, making option B incorrect. Option C is incorrect because it contains a compiler error. The label L3 is not visible outside its loop. Option D is incorrect, as it is equivalent to option B since unlabeled break and continue apply to the nearest loop and therefore produce an infinite loop at runtime. Like option A, the continue L2 on line 8 allows the innermost loop to be executed the second time the second loop is called. The continue L2 on line 12 exits the infinite loop, though, causing control to return to the second loop. Since the first and second loops terminate, the code terminates, and option E is a correct answer.

16. E. The code compiles without issue, making options F and G incorrect. Since Java 10, var is supported in both switch and while loops, provided the type can be determined by the compiler. In addition, the variable one is allowed in a case statement because it is a final local variable, making it a compile-time constant. The value of tailFeathers is 3, which matches the second case statement, making 5 the first output. The while loop is executed twice, with the pre-increment operator (--) modifying the value of tailFeathers from 3 to 2, and then to 1 on the second loop. For this reason, the final output is 5 2 1, making option E the correct answer.

17. F. Line 19 starts with an else statement, but there is no preceding if statement that it matches. For this reason, line 19 does not compile, making option F the correct answer. If the else keyword was removed from line 19, then the code snippet would print Success.

18. A, D, E. The right side of a for-each statement must be a primitive array or any class that implements java.lang.Iterable, which includes the Collection interface, although not all Collections Framework classes. For these reasons, options A, D, and E are correct. Option B is incorrect as Map does not implement Collection nor Iterable, since it is not a list of items, but a mapping of items to other items. Option C and F are incorrect as well. While you may consider them to be a list of characters, strictly speaking they are not considered Iterable in Java, since they do not implement Iterable. That said, you can

iterate over them using a traditional `for` loop and member methods, such as `charAt()` and `length()`.

19. D. The code does compile without issue, so option F is incorrect. The `viola` variable created on line 8 is never used and can be ignored. If it had been used as the `case` value on line 15, it would have caused a compilation error since it is not marked `final`. Since `"violin"` and `"VIOLIN"` are not an exact match, the `default` branch of the `switch` statement is executed at runtime. This execution path increments `p` a total of three times, bringing the final value of `p` to 2 and making option D the correct answer.

20. F. The code snippet does not contain any compilation errors, so options D and E are incorrect. There is a problem with this code snippet, though. While it may seem complicated, the key is to notice that the variable `r` is updated outside of the `do/while` loop. This is allowed from a compilation standpoint, since it is defined before the loop, but it means the innermost loop never breaks the termination condition `r <= 1`. At runtime, this will produce an infinite loop the first time the innermost loop is entered, making option F the correct answer.

Chapter 5: Core Java APIs

1. F. Line 5 does not compile. This question is checking to see whether you are paying attention to the types. `numFish` is an `int`, and 1 is an `int`. Therefore, we use numeric addition and get 5. The problem is that we can't store an `int` in a `String` variable. Supposing line 5 said `String anotherFish = numFish + 1 + "";`. In that case, the answer would be option A and option C. The variable defined on line 5 would be the string `"5"`, and both output statements would use concatenation.

2. A, C, D. The code compiles fine. Line 3 points to the `String` in the string pool. Line 4 calls the `String` constructor explicitly and is therefore a different object than `s`. Lines 5 checks for object equality, which is true, and so prints `one`. Line 6 uses object reference equality, which is not true since we have different objects.

Line 7 calls `intern()`, which returns the value from the string pool and is therefore the same reference as `s`. Line 8 also compares references but is true since both references point to the object from the string pool. Finally, line 9 is a trick. The string `Hello` is already in the string pool, so calling `intern()` does not change anything. The reference `t` is a different object, so the result is still `false`.

3. A, C, F. The code does compile, making option G incorrect. In the first for-each loop, `gorillas` has a type of `List<String>`, so each element `koko` has a type of `String`, making option A correct. In the second for-each loop, you might think that the diamond operator `<>` cannot be used with `var` without a compilation error, but it absolutely can. This result is `monkeys` having a type of `ArrayList<Object>` with `albert` having a data type of `Object`, making option C correct. While `var` might indicate an ambiguous data type, there is no such thing as an undefined data type in Java, so option D is incorrect.

In the last for-each loop, `chimpanzee` has a data type of `List`. Since the left side does not define a generic type, the compiler will treat this as `List<Object>`, and `ham` will have a data type of Object, making option F correct. Even though the elements of chimpanzees might be Integer as defined, ham would require an explicit cast to call an Integer method, such as ham.intValue().

4.   B. This example uses method chaining. After the call to append(), sb contains "aaa". That result is passed to the first insert() call, which inserts at index 1. At this point sb contains abbaa. That result is passed to the final insert(), which inserts at index 4, resulting in abbaccca.

5.   G. The question is trying to distract you into paying attention to logical equality versus object reference equality. The exam creators are hoping you will miss the fact that line 18 does not compile. Java does not allow you to compare String and StringBuilder using ==.

6.   B. A String is immutable. Calling concat() returns a new String but does not change the original. A StringBuilder is mutable. Calling append() adds characters to the existing character sequence along with returning a reference to the same object.

7.   A, B, F. Remember that indexes are zero-based, which means that index 4 corresponds to 5 and option A is correct. For option B, the replace() method starts the replacement at index 2 and ends before index 4. This means two characters are replaced, and charAt(3) is called on the intermediate value of 1265. The character at index 3 is 5, making option B correct. Option C is similar, making the intermediate value 126 and returning 6.

Option D results in an exception since there is no character at index 5. Option E is incorrect. It does not compile because the parentheses for the length() method are missing. Finally, option F's replace results in the intermediate value 145. The character at index 2 is 5, so option F is correct.

8.   A, D, E. substring() has two forms. The first takes the index to start with and the index to stop immediately before. The second takes just the index to start with and goes to the end of the String. Remember that indexes are zero-based. The first call starts at index 1 and ends with index 2 since it needs to stop before index 3. The second call starts at index 7 and ends in the same place, resulting in an empty String. This prints out a blank line. The final call starts at index 7 and goes to the end of the String.

9.   C, F. This question is tricky because it has two parts. The first is trying to see if you know that String objects are immutable. Line 17 returns "PURR", but the result is ignored and not stored in s1. Line 18 returns "purr" since there is no whitespace present, but the result is again ignored. Line 19 returns "ur" because it starts with index 1 and ends before index 3 using zero-based indexes. The result is ignored again. Finally, on line 20 something happens. We concatenate three new characters to s1 and now have a String of length 7, making option C correct.

For the second part, a += 2 expands to a = a + 2. A String concatenated with any other type gives a String. Lines 22, 23, and 24 all append to a, giving a result of "2cfalse". The if statement on line 27 returns true because the values of the two String objects are the same using object equality. The if statement on line 26 returns false because the two String objects are not the same in memory. One comes directly from the string pool, and the other comes from building using String operations.

10. A, G. The substring() method includes the starting index but not the ending index. When called with 1 and 2, it returns a single character String, making option A correct and option E incorrect. Calling substring() with 2 as both parameters is legal. It returns an empty String, making options B and F incorrect. Java does not allow the indexes to be specified in reverse order. Option G is correct because it throws a StringIndexOutOfBoundsException. Finally, option H is incorrect because it returns an empty String.

11. A. First, we delete the characters at index 2 until the character one before index 8. At this point, 0189 is in numbers. The following line uses method chaining. It appends a dash to the end of the characters sequence, resulting in 0189-, and then inserts a plus sign at index 2, resulting in 01+89-.

12. F. This is a trick question. The first line does not compile because you cannot assign a String to a StringBuilder. If that line were StringBuilder b = new StringBuilder("rumble"), the code would compile and print rum4. Watch out for this sort of trick on the exam. You could easily spend a minute working out the character positions for no reason at all.

13. A, C. The reverse() method is the easiest way of reversing the characters in a StringBuilder; therefore, option A is correct. In option B, substring() returns a String, which is not stored anywhere. Option C uses method chaining. First, it creates the value "JavavaJ$". Then, it removes the first three characters, resulting in "avaJ$". Finally, it removes the last character, resulting in "avaJ". Option D throws an exception because you cannot delete the character after the last index. Remember that deleteCharAt() uses indexes that are zero-based, and length() counts starting with 1.

14. C, E, F. Option C uses the variable name as if it were a type, which is clearly illegal. Options E and F don't specify any size. Although it is legal to leave out the size for later dimensions of a multidimensional array, the first one is required. Option A declares a legal 2D array. Option B declares a legal 3D array. Option D declares a legal 2D array. Remember that it is normal to see on the exam types you might not have learned. You aren't expected to know anything about them.

15. A, H. Arrays define a property called length. It is not a method, so parentheses are not allowed, making option A correct. The ArrayList class defines a method called size(), making option H the other correct answer.

16. A, F, G. An array is not able to change size, making option A correct and option B incorrect. Neither is immutable, making options C and D incorrect. The elements can change in value. An array does not override equals(), so it uses object equality, making option E incorrect. ArrayList does override equals() and defines it as the same elements in the same order, making option F correct.

The compiler does not know when an index is out of bounds and thus can't give you a compiler error, making option G correct. The code will throw an exception at runtime, though, making option H the final incorrect answer.

17. F. The code does not compile because list is instantiated using generics. Only String objects can be added to list, and 7 is an int.

18. C. The put() method is used on a Map rather than a List or Set, making options A and D incorrect. The replace() method does not exist on either of these interfaces. Finally, the set method is valid on a List rather than a Set because a List has an index. Therefore, option C is correct.

19. A, F. The code compiles and runs fine. However, an array must be sorted for binarySearch() to return a meaningful result. Option F is correct because line 14 prints a number, but the behavior is undefined. Line 8 creates a list backed by a fixed-size array of 4. Line 10 sorts it. Line 12 converts it back to an array. The brackets aren't in the traditional place, but they are still legal. Line 13 prints the first element, which is now –1, making option A the other correct answer.

20. B, C, E. Remember to watch return types on math operations. One of the tricks is option B on line 24. The round() method returns an int when called with a float. However, we are calling it with a double so it returns a long. The other trick is option C on line 25. The random() method returns a double. Converting from an array to an ArrayList uses Arrays.asList(names). There is no asList() method on an array instance, and option E is correct.

21. D. After sorting, hex contains [30, 3A, 8, FF]. Remember that numbers sort before letters, and strings sort alphabetically. This makes 30 come before 8. A binary search correctly finds 8 at index 2 and 3A at index 1. It cannot find 4F but notices it should be at index 2. The rule when an item isn't found is to negate that index and subtract 1. Therefore, we get –2–1, which is –3.

22. A, B, D. Lines 5 and 7 use autoboxing to convert an int to an Integer. Line 6 does not because valueOf() returns an Integer. Line 8 does not because null is not an int. The code does compile. However, when the for loop tries to unbox null into an int, it fails and throws a NullPointerException.

23. B. The first if statement is false because the variables do not point to the same object. The second if statement is true because ArrayList implements equality to mean the same elements in the same order.

24. D, E. The first line of code in the method creates a fixed size List backed by an array. This means option D is correct, making options B and F incorrect. The second line of code in the method creates an immutable list, which means no changes are allowed. Therefore, option E is correct, making options A and C incorrect.

25. A, B, D. The compare() method returns a positive integer when the arrays are different and s1 is larger. This is the case for option A since the element at index 1 comes first alphabetically. It is not the case for option C because the s4 is longer or option E because the arrays are the same.

    The mismatch() method returns a positive integer when the arrays are different in a position index 1 or greater. This is the case for option B since the difference is at index 1. It is not the case for option D because the s3 is shorter than the s4 or option F because there is no difference.

Chapter 6: Lambdas and Functional Interfaces

1. **A.** This code is correct. Line 8 creates a lambda expression that checks whether the age is less than 5. Since there is only one parameter and it does not specify a type, the parentheses around the type parameter are optional. Lines 11 and 13 use the `Predicate` interface, which declares a `test()` method.

2. **C.** The interface takes two `int` parameters. The code on line 7 attempts to use them as if one is a `String`. It is tricky to use types in a lambda when they are implicitly specified. Remember to check the interface for the real type.

3. **A, D, F.** The `removeIf()` method expects a `Predicate`, which takes a parameter list of one parameter using the specified type. Options B and C are incorrect because they do not use the `return` keyword. This keyword is required to be inside the braces of a lambda body. Option E is incorrect because it is missing the parentheses around the parameter list. This is only optional for a single parameter with an inferred type.

4. **A, F.** Option B is incorrect because it does not use the `return` keyword. Options C, D, and E are incorrect because the variable e is already in use from the lambda and cannot be redefined. Additionally, option C is missing the `return` keyword, and option E is missing the semicolon.

5. **B, D.** `Predicate<String>` takes a parameter list of one parameter using the specified type. Options A and F are incorrect because they specify the wrong number of parameters. Option C is incorrect because parentheses are required around the parameter list when the type is specified. Option E is incorrect because the name used in the parameter list does not match the name used in the body.

6. **E.** While there appears to have been a variable name shortage when this code was written, it does compile. Lambda variables and method names are allowed to be the same. The x lambda parameter is scoped to within each lambda, so it is allowed to be reused. The type is inferred by the method it calls. The first lambda maps x to a `String` and the second to a `Boolean`. Therefore, option E is correct.

7. **A, B, E, F.** The `forEach()` method with one lambda parameter works with a `List` or a `Set`. Therefore, options A and B are correct. Additionally, options E and F return a `Set` and can be used as well. Options D and G refer to methods that do not exist. Option C is tricky because a `Map` does have a `forEach()` method. However, it uses two lambda parameters rather than one.

8. **A, C, F.** Option A is correct because a `Supplier` returns a value while a `Consumer` takes one and acts on it. Option C is correct because a `Comparator` returns a negative number, zero, or a positive number depending on the values passed. A `Predicate` always returns a `boolean`. It does have a method named `test()`, making option F correct.

9. **A, B, C.** Since the scope of start and c is within the lambda, the variables can be declared after it without issue, making options A, B, and C correct. Option D is incorrect because

setting end prevents it from being effectively final. Lambdas are only allowed to reference effectively final variables.

10. C. Since the new `ArrayList<>(set)` constructor makes a copy of `set`, there are two elements in each of `set` and `list`. The `forEach()` methods print each element on a separate line. Therefore, four lines are printed, and option C is the answer.

11. A. The code correctly sorts in descending order. Since uppercase normally sorts before lowercase, the order is reversed here, and option A is correct.

12. C, D, E. The first line takes no parameters, making it a `Supplier`. Option E is correct because Java can autobox from a primitive `double` to a `Double` object. Option F is incorrect because it is a `float` rather than a `double`.

The second line takes one parameter and returns a `boolean`, making it a `Predicate`. Since the lambda parameter is unused, any generic type is acceptable, and options C and D are both correct.

13. E. Lambdas are only allowed to reference effectively final variables. You can tell the variable `j` is effectively final because adding a `final` keyword before it wouldn't introduce a compile error. Each time the `else` statement is executed, the variable is redeclared and goes out of scope. Therefore, it is not re-assigned. Similarly, `length` is effectively final. There are no compile errors, and option E is correct.

14. C. Lambdas are not allowed to redeclare local variables, making options A and B incorrect. Option D is incorrect because setting end prevents it from being effectively final. Lambdas are only allowed to reference effectively final variables. Option C is tricky because it does compile but throws an exception at runtime. Since the question only asks about compilation, option C is correct.

15. C. `Set` is not an ordered `Collection`. Since it does not have a `sort()` method, the code does not compile, making option C correct.

16. A, D. Method parameters and local variables are effectively final if they aren't changed after initialization. Options A and D meet this criterion.

17. C. Line 8 uses braces around the body. This means the `return` keyword and semicolon are required.

18. D. Lambda parameters are not allowed to use the same name as another variable in the same scope. The variable names s and x are taken from the object declarations and therefore not available to be used inside the lambda.

19. A, C. This interface specifies two `String` parameters. We can provide the parameter list with or without parameter types. However, it needs to be consistent, making option B incorrect. Options D, E, and F are incorrect because they do not use the arrow operator.

20. A, C. `Predicate<String>` takes a parameter list of one parameter using the specified type. Options E and F are incorrect because it specifies the wrong type. Options B and D are incorrect because they use the wrong syntax for the arrow operator.

Chapter 7: Methods and Encapsulation

1. **B, C.** The keyword void is a return type. Only the access modifier or optional specifiers are allowed before the return type. Option C is correct, creating a method with private access. Option B is also correct, creating a method with default access and the optional specifier final. Since default access does not require a modifier, we get to jump right to final. Option A is incorrect because default access omits the access modifier rather than specifying default. Option D is incorrect because Java is case sensitive. It would have been correct if public were the choice. Option E is incorrect because the method already has a void return type. Option F is incorrect because labels are not allowed for methods.

2. **A, D.** Options A and D are correct because the optional specifiers are allowed in any order. Options B and C are incorrect because they each have two return types. Options E and F are incorrect because the return type is before the optional specifier and access modifier, respectively.

3. **A, C, D.** Options A and C are correct because a void method is optionally allowed to have a return statement as long as it doesn't try to return a value. Option B does not compile because null requires a reference object as the return type. Since int is primitive, it is not a reference object. Option D is correct because it returns an int value. Option E does not compile because it tries to return a double when the return type is int. Since a double cannot be assigned to an int, it cannot be returned as one either. Option F does not compile because no value is actually returned.

4. **A, B, F.** Options A and B are correct because the single varargs parameter is the last parameter declared. Option F is correct because it doesn't use any varargs parameters. Option C is incorrect because the varargs parameter is not last. Option D is incorrect because two varargs parameters are not allowed in the same method. Option E is incorrect because the ... for a varargs must be after the type, not before it.

5. **D, F.** Option D passes the initial parameter plus two more to turn into a varargs array of size 2. Option F passes the initial parameter plus an array of size 2. Option A does not compile because it does not pass the initial parameter. Option E does not compile because it does not declare an array properly. It should be new boolean[] {true, true}. Option B creates a varargs array of size 0, and option C creates a varargs array of size 1.

6. **D.** Option D is correct. This is the common implementation for encapsulation by setting all fields to be private and all methods to be public. Option A is incorrect because protected access allows everything that package-private access allows and additionally allows subclasses access. Option B is incorrect because the class is public. This means that other classes can see the class. However, they cannot call any of the methods or read any of the fields. It is essentially a useless class. Option C is incorrect because package-private access applies to the whole package. Option E is incorrect because Java has no such wildcard access capability.

7. **B, C, D, F.** The two classes are in different packages, which means private access and default (package-private) access will not compile. This causes compile errors in lines 5, 6, and 7, making options B, C, and D correct answers. Additionally, protected access will not compile since School does not inherit from Classroom. This causes the compiler error on line 9, making option F a correct answer as well.

8. A, B, E. Encapsulation allows using methods to get and set instance variables so other classes are not directly using them, making options A and B correct. Instance variables must be private for this to work, making option E correct and option D incorrect. While there are common naming conventions, they are not required, making option C incorrect.

9. B, D, F. Option A is incorrect because the methods differ only in return type. Option C is tricky. It is incorrect because var is not a valid return type. Remember that var can be used only for local variables. Option E is incorrect because the method signature is identical once the generic types are erased. Options B and D are correct because they represent interface and superclass relationships. Option F is correct because the arrays are of different types.

10. B. Rope runs line 3, setting LENGTH to 5, and then immediately after runs the static initializer, which sets it to 10. Line 5 in the Chimp class calls the static method normally and prints swing and a space. Line 6 also calls the static method. Java allows calling a static method through an instance variable although it is not recommended. Line 7 uses the static import on line 2 to reference LENGTH.

11. B, E. Line 10 does not compile because static methods are not allowed to call instance methods. Even though we are calling play() as if it were an instance method and an instance exists, Java knows play() is really a static method and treats it as such. If line 10 is removed, the code works. It does not throw a NullPointerException on line 17 because play() is a static method. Java looks at the type of the reference for rope2 and translates the call to Rope.play().

12. D. There are two details to notice in this code. First, note that RopeSwing has an instance initializer and not a static initializer. Since RopeSwing is never constructed, the instance initializer does not run. The other detail is that length is static. Changes from one object update this common static variable.

13. E. If a variable is static final, it must be set exactly once, and it must be in the declaration line or in a static initialization block. Line 4 doesn't compile because bench is not set in either of these locations. Line 15 doesn't compile because final variables are not allowed to be set after that point. Line 11 doesn't compile because name is set twice: once in the declaration and again in the static block. Line 12 doesn't compile because rightRope is set twice as well. Both are in static initialization blocks.

14. B. The two valid ways to do this are import static java.util.Collections.*; and import static java.util.Collections.sort;. Option A is incorrect because you can do a static import only on static members. Classes such as Collections require a regular import. Option C is nonsense as method parameters have no business in an import. Options D, E, and F try to trick you into reversing the syntax of import static.

15. E. The argument on line 17 is a short. It can be promoted to an int, so print() on line 5 is invoked. The argument on line 18 is a boolean. It can be autoboxed to a Boolean, so print() on line 11 is invoked. The argument on line 19 is a double. It can be autoboxed to a Double, so print() on line 11 is invoked. Therefore, the output is int-Object-Object-, and the correct answer is option E.

16. B. Since Java is pass-by-value and the variable on line 8 never gets reassigned, it stays as 9. In the method square, x starts as 9. The y value becomes 81, and then x gets set to –1. Line 9 does set result to 81. However, we are printing out value and that is still 9.

17. **B, D, E.** Since Java is pass-by-value, assigning a new object to a does not change the caller. Calling append() does affect the caller because both the method parameter and the caller have a reference to the same object. Finally, returning a value does pass the reference to the caller for assignment to s3.

18. **B, C, E.** The variable value1 is a final instance variable. It can be set only once: in the variable declaration, an instance initializer, or a constructor. Option A does not compile because the final variable was already set in the declaration. The variable value2 is a static variable. Both instance and static initializers are able to access static variables, making options B and E correct. The variable value3 is an instance variable. Options D and F do not compile because a static initializer does not have access to instance variables.

19. **A, E.** The 100 parameter is an int and so calls the matching int method. When this method is removed, Java looks for the next most specific constructor. Java prefers autoboxing to varargs, so it chooses the Integer constructor. The 100L parameter is a long. Since it can't be converted into a smaller type, it is autoboxed into a Long, and then the method for Object is called.

20. **A, C, F.** Option B is incorrect because var cannot be a method parameter. It must be a local variable or lambda parameter. Option D is incorrect because the method declarations are identical. Option E is tricky. The variable long is illegal because *long* is a reserved word. Options A, C, and F are correct because they represent different types.

21. **A, B, C.** Instance variables must include the private access modifier, making option D incorrect. While it is common for methods to be public, this is not required. Options A, B, and C are all correct, although some are more useful than others. Since the class can be written to be encapsulated, options E and F are incorrect.

Chapter 8: Class Design

1. **E.** Options A and B will not compile because constructors cannot be called without new. Options C and D will compile but will create a new object rather than setting the fields in this one. The result is the program will print 0, not 2, at runtime. Calling an overloaded constructor, using this(), or a parent constructor, using super(), is only allowed on the first line of the constructor, making option E correct and option F incorrect. Finally, option G is incorrect because the program prints 0 without any changes, not 2.

2. **B, C.** Overloaded methods have the method name but a different signature (the method parameters differ), making option A incorrect. Overridden instance methods and hidden static methods must have the same signature (the name and method parameters must match), making options B and C correct. Overloaded methods can have different return types, while overridden and hidden methods can have covariant return types. None of these methods are required to use the same return type, making options D, E, and F incorrect.

3. **F.** The code will not compile as is, because the parent class Mammal does not define a no-argument constructor. For this reason, the first line of a Platypus constructor should be an explicit call to super(int), making option F the correct answer. Option E is incorrect,

as line 7 compiles without issue. The sneeze() method in the Mammal class is marked private, meaning it is not inherited and therefore is not overridden in the Platypus class. For this reason, the sneeze() method in the Platypus class is free to define the same method with any return type.

4. E. The code compiles, making option F incorrect. An instance variable with the same name as an inherited instance variable is hidden, not overridden. This means that both variables exist, and the one that is used depends on the location and reference type. Because the main() method uses a reference type of Speedster to access the numSpots variable, the variable in the Speedster class, not the Cheetah class, must be set to 50. Option A is incorrect, as it reassigns the method parameter to itself. Option B is incorrect, as it assigns the method parameter the value of the instance variable in Cheetah, which is 0. Option C is incorrect, as it assigns the value to the instance variable in Cheetah, not Speedster. Option D is incorrect, as it assigns the method parameter the value of the instance variable in Speedster, which is 0. Options A, B, C, and D all print 0 at runtime. Option E is the only correct answer, as it assigns the instance variable numSpots in the Speedster class a value of 50. The numSpots variable in the Speedster class is then correctly referenced in the main() method, printing 50 at runtime.

5. A. The code compiles and runs without issue, so options E and F are incorrect. The Arthropod class defines two overloaded versions of the printName() method. The printName() method that takes an int value on line 5 is correctly overridden in the Spider class on line 9. Remember, an overridden method can have a broader access modifier, and protected access is broader than package-private access. Because of polymorphism, the overridden method replaces the method on all calls, even if an Arthropod reference variable is used, as is done in the main() method. For these reasons, the overridden method is called on lines 15 and 16, printing Spider twice. Note that the short value is automatically cast to the larger type of int, which then uses the overridden method. Line 17 calls the overloaded method in the Arthropod class, as the long value 5L does not match the overridden method, resulting in Arthropod being printed. Therefore, option A is the correct answer.

6. B, E. The signature must match exactly, making option A incorrect. There is no such thing as a covariant signature. An overridden method must not declare any new checked exceptions or a checked exception that is broader than the inherited method. For this reason, option B is correct, and option D is incorrect. Option C is incorrect because an overridden method may have the same access modifier as the version in the parent class. Finally, overridden methods must have covariant return types, and only void is covariant with void, making option E correct.

7. A, C. Option A is correct, as this(3) calls the constructor declared on line 5, while this("") calls the constructor declared on line 10. Option B does not compile, as inserting this() at line 3 results in a compiler error, since there is no matching constructor. Option C is correct, as short can be implicitly cast to int, resulting in this((short)1) calling the constructor declared on line 5. In addition, this(null) calls the String constructor declared on line 10. Option D does not compile because inserting super() on line 14 results in an invalid constructor call. The Howler class does not contain a no-argument constructor. Option E is also incorrect. Inserting this(2L) at line 3 results in a recursive constructor definition. The compiler detects this and reports an error. Option F is incorrect, as using super(null) on line 14 does not match any parent constructors. If an explicit cast

was used, such as super((Integer)null), then the code would have compiled but would throw an exception at runtime during unboxing. Finally, option G is incorrect because the superclass Howler does not contain a no-argument constructor. Therefore, the constructor declared on line 13 will not compile without an explicit call to an overloaded or parent constructor.

8. C. The code compiles and runs without issue, making options F and G incorrect. Line 16 initializes a PolarBear instance and assigns it to the bear reference. The variable declaration and instance initializers are run first, setting value to tac. The constructor declared on line 5 is called, resulting in value being set to tacb. Remember, a static main() method can access private constructors declared in the same class. Line 17 creates another PolarBear instance, replacing the bear reference declared on line 16. First, value is initialized to tac as before. Line 17 calls the constructor declared on line 8, since String is the narrowest match of a String literal. This constructor then calls the overloaded constructor declared on line 5, resulting in value being updated to tacb. Control returns to the previous constructor, with line 10 updating value to tacbf, and making option C the correct answer. Note that if the constructor declared on line 8 did not exist, then the constructor on line 12 would match. Finally, the bear reference is properly cast to PolarBear on line 18, making the value parameter accessible.

9. B, F. A valid override of a method with generic arguments must have a return type that is covariant, with matching generic type parameters. Option B is correct, as it is just restating the original return type. Option F is also correct, as ArrayList is a subtype of List. The rest of the method declarations do not compile. Options A and D are invalid because the access levels, package-private and private, are more restrictive than the inherited access modifier, protected. Option C is incorrect because while CharSquence is a subtype of String, the generic type parameters must match exactly. Finally, option E is incorrect as Object is a supertype of List and therefore not covariant.

10. D. The code doesn't compile, so option A is incorrect. The first compilation error is on line 2, as var cannot be used as a constructor argument type. The second compilation error is on line 8. Since Rodent declares at least one constructor and it is not a no-argument constructor, Beaver must declare a constructor with an explicit call to a super() constructor. Line 9 contains two compilation errors. First, the return types are not covariant since Number is a supertype, not a subtype, of Integer. Second, the inherited method is static, but the overridden method is not, making this an invalid override. The code contains four compilation errors, although they are limited to three lines, making option D the correct answer.

11. B, C, E. An object may be cast to a supertype without an explicit cast but requires an explicit cast to be cast to a subtype, making option A incorrect. Option B is correct, as an interface method argument may take any reference type that implements the interface. Option C is also correct, as a method that accepts java.lang.Object can accept any variable since all objects inherit java.lang.Object. This also includes primitives, which can be autoboxed to their wrapper classes. Some cast exceptions can be detected as errors at compile-time, but others can only be detected at runtime, so option D is incorrect. Due to the nature of polymorphism, a final instance method cannot be overridden in a subclass, so calls in the parent class will not be replaced, making option E correct. Finally, polymorphism applies to classes and interfaces alike, making option F incorrect.

12. A, B, E, F. The code compiles if the correct type is inserted in the blank, so option G is incorrect. The setSnake() method requires an instance of Snake or any subtype of Snake. The Cobra class is a subclass of Snake, so it is a subtype. The GardenSnake class is a subclass of Cobra, which, in turn, is a subclass of Snake, also making GardenSnake a subtype of Snake. For these reasons, options A, B, and E are correct. Option C is incorrect because Object is a supertype of Snake, not a subtype, as all instances inherit Object. Option D is incorrect as String is an unrelated class and does not inherit Snake. Finally, a null value can always be passed as an object value, regardless of type, so option F is correct.

13. A, G. The compiler will insert a default no-argument constructor if the class compiles and does not define any constructors. Options A and G fulfill this requirement, making them the correct answers. The bird() declaration in option G is a method declaration, not a constructor. Options B and C do not compile. Since the constructor name does not match the class name, the compiler treats these as methods with missing return types. Options D, E, and F all compile, but since they declare at least one constructor, the compiler does not supply one.

14. B, E, F. A class can only directly extend a single class, making option A incorrect. A class can implement any number of interfaces, though, making option B correct. Option C is incorrect because primitive types do not inherit java.lang.Object. If a class extends another class, then it is a subclass, not a superclass, making option D incorrect. A class that implements an interface is a subtype of that interface, making option E correct. Finally, option F is correct as it is an accurate description of multiple inheritance, which is not permitted in Java.

15. D. The code compiles, so option G is incorrect. Based on order of initialization, the static components are initialized first, starting with the Arachnid class, since it is the parent of the Scorpion class, which initializes the StringBuilder to u. The static initializer in Scorpion then updates sb to contain uq, which is printed twice by lines 13 and 14 along with spaces separating the values. Next, an instance of Arachnid is initialized on line 15. There are two instance initializers in Arachnid, and they run in order, appending cr to the StringBuilder, resulting in a value of uqcr. An instance of Scorpion is then initialized on line 16. The instance initializers in the superclass Arachnid run first, appending cr again and updating the value of sb to uqcrcr. Finally, the instance initializer in Scorpion runs and appends m. The program completes with the final value printed being uq uq uqcrcrm, making option D the correct answer.

16. B. A valid override of a method with generic arguments must have the same signature with the same generic types. For this reason, only option B is correct. Because of type erasure, the generic type parameter will be removed when the code is compiled. Therefore, the compiler requires that the types match. Options A and D do not compile for this reason. Options C, E, and F do compile, but since the generic class changed, they are overloads, not overrides. Remember, covariant types only apply to return values of overridden methods, not method parameters.

17. F. Options A–E are incorrect statements about inheritance and variables, making option F the correct answer. Option A is incorrect because variables can only be hidden, not overridden via inheritance. This means that they are still accessible in the parent class and do not replace the variable everywhere, as overriding does. Options B, C, and E are also incorrect as they more closely match rules for overriding methods. Also, option E is invalid as variables do not throw exceptions. Finally, option D is incorrect as this is a rule for hiding `static` methods.

18. C, F. Calling an overloaded constructor with `this()` may be used only as the first line of a constructor, making options A and B incorrect. Accessing `this.variableName` can be performed from any instance method, constructor, or instance initializer, but not from a `static` method or `static` initializer. For this reason, option C is correct, and option D is incorrect. Option E is tricky. The default constructor is written by the compiler only if no user-defined constructors were provided. And `this()` can only be called from a constructor in the same class. Since there can be no user-defined constructors in the class if a default constructor was created, it is impossible for option E to be true. Since the `main()` method is in the same class, it can call `private` methods in the class, making option F correct.

19. C, F. The `eat()` method is `private` in the `Mammal` class. Since it is not inherited in the `Primate` class, it is neither overridden nor overloaded, making options A and B incorrect. The `drink()` method in `Mammal` is correctly hidden in the `Monkey` class, as the signature is the same, making option C correct and option D incorrect. The version in the `Monkey` class throws a new exception, but it is unchecked; therefore, it is allowed. The `dance()` method in `Mammal` is correctly overloaded in the `Monkey` class because the signatures are not the same, making option E incorrect and option F correct. For methods to be overridden, the signatures must match exactly. Finally, line 12 is an invalid override and does not compile, as `int` is not covariant with `void`, making options G and H both incorrect.

20. F. The `Reptile` class defines a constructor, but it is not a no-argument constructor. Therefore, the `Lizard` constructor must explicitly call `super()`, passing in an `int` value. For this reason, line 9 does not compile, and option F is the correct answer. If the `Lizard` class were corrected to call the appropriate `super()` constructor, then the program would print BALizard at runtime, with the `static` initializer running first, followed by the instance initializer, and finally the method call using the overridden method.

21. E. The program compiles and runs without issue, making options A through D incorrect. The `fly()` method is correctly overridden in each subclass since the signature is the same, the access modifier is less restrictive, and the return types are covariant. For covariance, `Macaw` is a subtype of `Parrot`, which is a subtype of `Bird`, so overridden return types are valid. Likewise, the constructors are all implemented properly, with explicit calls to the parent constructors as needed. Line 19 calls the overridden version of `fly()` defined in the `Macaw` class, as overriding replaces the method regardless of the reference type. This results in `feathers` being assigned a value of 3. The `Macaw` object is then cast to `Parrot`, which is allowed because `Macaw` inherits `Parrot`. The `feathers` variable is visible since it is defined in the `Bird` class, and line 19 prints 3, making option E the correct answer.

22. D. The code compiles and runs without issue, making option E incorrect. The `Child` class overrides the `setName()` method and hides the `static` name variable defined in the inherited `Person` class. Since variables are only hidden, not overridden, there are two distinct name variables accessible, depending on the location and reference type. Line 8 creates a `Child` instance, which is implicitly cast to a `Person` reference type on line 9. Line 10 uses the `Child` reference type, updating `Child.name` to Elysia. Line 11 uses the `Person` reference type, updating `Person.name` to Sophia. Lines 12 and 13 both call the overridden `setName()` instance method declared on line 6. This sets `Child.name` to Webby on line 12 and then to Olivia on line 13. The final values of `Child.name` and `Person.name` are Olivia and Sophia, respectively, making option D the correct answer.

23. B. The program compiles, making option F incorrect. The constructors are called from the child class upward, but since each line of a constructor is a call to another constructor, via this() or super(), they are ultimately executed in top-down manner. On line 29, the main() method calls the Fennec() constructor declared on line 19. Remember, integer literals in Java are considered int by default. This constructor calls the Fox() constructor defined on line 12, which in turn calls the overloaded Fox() constructor declared on line 11. Since the constructor on line 11 does not explicitly call a parent constructor, the compiler inserts a call to the no-argument super() constructor, which exists on line 3 of the Canine class. Since Canine does not extend any classes, the compiler will also insert a call to the no-argument super() constructor defined in java.lang.Object, although this has little impact on the output. Line 3 is then executed, adding q to the output, and the compiler chain is unwound. Line 11 then executes, adding p, followed by line 14, adding z. Finally, line 21 is executed, and j is added, resulting in a final value for logger of qpzj, and making option B correct. For the exam, remember to follow constructors from the lowest level upward to determine the correct pathway, but then execute them from the top down using the established order.

24. A, D, F. Polymorphism is the property of an object to take on many forms. Part of polymorphism is that methods are replaced through overriding wherever they are called, regardless of whether they're in a parent or child class. For this reason, option A is correct, and option E incorrect. With hidden static methods, Java relies on the location and reference type to determine which method is called, making option B incorrect and F correct. Finally, making a method final, not static, prevents it from being overridden, making option D correct and option C incorrect.

25. C. The code compiles and runs without issue, making options E and F incorrect. First, the class is initialized, starting with the superclass Antelope and then the subclass Gazelle. This involves invoking the static variable declarations and static initializers. The program first prints 1, followed by 8. Then, we follow the constructor pathway from the object created on line 14 upward, initializing each class instance using a top-down approach. Within each class, the instance initializers are run, followed by the referenced constructors. The Antelope instance is initialized, printing 24, followed by the Gazelle instance, printing 93. The final output is 182493, making option C the correct answer.

26. F. The code does not compile, so options A through C are incorrect. Both lines 5 and 12 do not compile, as this() is used instead of this. Remember, this() refers to calling a constructor, whereas this is a reference to the current instance. Next, the compiler does not allow casting to an unrelated class type. Since Orangutan is not a subclass of Primate, the cast on line 15 is invalid, and the code does not compile. Due to these three lines containing compilation errors, option F is the correct answer. Note that if Orangutan was made a subclass of Primate and the this() references were changed to this, then the code would compile and print 3 at runtime.

Chapter 9: Advanced Class Design

1. B, E. A method that does not declare a body is by definition abstract, making option E correct. All abstract interface methods are assumed to be public, making option B correct. Interface methods cannot be marked protected, so option A is incorrect. Interface methods can be marked `static` or `default`, although if they are, they must provide a body, making options C and F incorrect. Finally, `void` is a return type, not a modifier, so option D is incorrect.

2. A, B, D, E. The code compiles without issue, so option G is incorrect. The blank can be filled with any class or interface that is a supertype of `TurtleFrog`. Option A is the direct superclass of `TurtleFrog`, and option B is the same class, so both are correct. `BrazilianHornedFrog` is not a superclass of `TurtleFrog`, so option C is incorrect. `TurtleFrog` inherits the `CanHop` interface, so option D is correct. All classes inherit `Object`, so option E is also correct. Finally, `Long` is an unrelated class that is not a superclass of `TurtleFrog` and is therefore incorrect.

3. B, C. Concrete classes are, by definition, not `abstract`, so option A is incorrect. A concrete class must implement all inherited abstract methods, so option B is correct. Concrete classes can be optionally marked `final`, so option C is correct. Option D is incorrect; a superclass may have already implemented an inherited interface method. The concrete class only needs to implement the inherited abstract methods. Finally, a method in a concrete class that implements an inherited abstract method overrides the method. While the method signature must match, the method declaration does not need to match, such as using a covariant return type or changing the throws declaration. For these reasons, option E is incorrect.

4. E. First, the declarations of `HasExoskeleton` and `Insect` are correct and do not contain any errors, making options C and D incorrect. The concrete class `Beetle` extends `Insect` and inherits two abstract methods, `getNumberOfSections()` and `getNumberOfLegs()`. The `Beetle` class includes an overloaded version of `getNumberOfSections()` that takes an `int` value. The method declaration is valid, making option F incorrect, although it does not satisfy the abstract method requirement. For this reason, only one of the two abstract methods is properly overridden. The `Beetle` class therefore does not compile, and option E is correct. Since the code fails to compile, options A and B are incorrect.

5. C, F. All interface variables are implicitly assumed to be `public`, `static`, and `final`, making options C and F correct. Option A and G, `private` and default (package-private), are incorrect since they conflict with the implicit `public` access modifier. Options B and D are incorrect, as nonstatic and `const` are not modifiers. Finally, option E is incorrect because a variable cannot be marked `abstract`.

6. D, E. Lines 1 and 2 are declared correctly, with the implicit modifier `abstract` being applied to the interface and the implicit modifiers `public`, `static`, and `final` being applied to the interface variable, making options B and C incorrect. Option D is correct, as an abstract method cannot include a body. Option E is also correct because the wrong keyword is used. A class implements an interface; it does extend it. Option F is incorrect as the implementation of `eatGrass()` in `IsAPlant` does not have the same signature; therefore, it is an overload, not an override.

7. C. The code does not compile because the `isBlind()` method in `Nocturnal` is not marked `abstract` and does not contain a method body. The rest of the lines compile without issue, making option C the only correct answer. If the `abstract` modifier was added to line 2, then the code would compile and print `false` at runtime, making option B the correct answer.

8.   C. The code compiles without issue, so option A is incorrect. Option B is incorrect, as an abstract class could implement HasVocalCords without the need to override the makeSound() method. Option C is correct; a class that implements CanBark automatically inherits its abstract methods, in this case makeSound() and bark(). Option D is incorrect, as a concrete class that implements Dog may be optionally marked final. Finally, an interface can extend multiple interfaces, so option E is incorrect.

9.   B, C, E, F. Member inner classes, including both classes and interfaces, can be marked with any of the four access modifiers: public, protected, default (package-private), or private. For this reason, options B, C, E, and F are correct. Options A and D are incorrect as static and final are not access modifiers.

10. C, G. The implicitly abstract interface method on line 6 does not compile because it is missing a semicolon (;), making option C correct. Line 7 compiles, as it provides an overloaded version of the fly() method. Lines 5, 9, and 10 do not contain any compilation errors, making options A, E, and F incorrect. Line 13 does not compile because the two inherited fly() methods, declared on line 6 and 10, conflict with each other. The compiler recognizes that it is impossible to create a class that overrides fly() to return both String and int, since they are not covariant return types, and therefore blocks the Falcon class from compiling. For this reason, option G is correct.

11. A, B, F. The final modifier can be used with private and static, making options A and F correct. Marking a private method final is redundant but allowed. A private method may also be marked static, making option B correct. Options C, D, and E are incorrect because methods marked static, private, or final cannot be overridden; therefore, they cannot be marked abstract.

12. A, E. Line 11 does not compile because a Tangerine and Gala are unrelated types, which the compiler can enforce for classes, making option A correct. Line 12 is valid since Citrus extends Tangerine and would print true at runtime if the rest of the class compiled. Likewise, Gala implements Apple, so line 13 would also print true at runtime if the rest of the code compiled.

Line 14 does compile, even though Apple and Tangerine are unrelated types. While the compiler can enforce unrelated type rules for classes, it has limited ability to do so for interfaces, since there may be a subclass of Tangerine that implements the Apple interface. Therefore, this line would print false if the rest of the code compiled.

Line 15 does not compile. Since Citrus is marked final, the compiler knows that there cannot be a subclass of Citrus that implements Apple, so it can enforce the unrelated type rule. For this reason, option E is correct.

13. G. The interface and classes are structured correctly, but the body of the main() method contains a compiler error. The Orca object is implicitly cast to a Whale reference on line 7. This is permitted because Orca is a subclass of Whale. By performing the cast, the whale reference on line 8 does not have access to the dive(int... depth) method. For this reason, line 8 does not compile. Since this is the only compilation error, option G is the correct answer. If the reference type of whale was changed to Orca, then the main() would compile and print Orca diving deeper 3 at runtime, making option B the correct answer. Note that line 16 compiles because the interface variable MAX is inherited as part of the class structure.

14. A, C, E. A class may extend another class, and an interface may extend another interface, making option A correct. Option B is incorrect. An abstract class can contain concrete instance and `static` methods. Interfaces can also contain nonabstract methods, although knowing this is not required for the 1Z0-815 exam. Option C is correct, as both can contain `static` constants. Option D is incorrect. The compiler only inserts implicit modifiers for interfaces. For abstract classes, the `abstract` keyword must be used on any method that does not define a body. An abstract class must be declared with the `abstract` keyword, while the `abstract` keyword is optional for interfaces. Since both can be declared with the `abstract` keyword, option E is correct. Finally, interfaces do not extend `java.lang.Object`. If they did, then Java would support true multiple inheritance, with multiple possible parent constructors being called as part of initialization. Therefore, option F is incorrect.

15. D. The code compiles without issue. The question is making sure you know that superclass constructors are called in the same manner in abstract classes as they are in nonabstract classes. Line 9 calls the constructor on line 6. The compiler automatically inserts `super()` as the first line of the constructor defined on line 6. The program then calls the constructor on line 3 and prints `Wow-`. Control then returns to line 6, and `Oh-` is printed. Finally, the method call on line 10 uses the version of `fly()` in the `Pelican` class, since it is marked `private` and the reference type of `var` is resolved as `Pelican`. The final output is `Wow-Oh-Pelican`, making option D the correct answer. Remember that `private` methods cannot be overridden. If the reference type of `chirp` was `Bird`, then the code would not compile as it would not be accessible outside the class.

16. E. The inherited interface method `getNumOfGills(int)` is implicitly `public`; therefore, it must be declared `public` in any concrete class that implements the interface. Since the method uses the default (package-private) modifier in the `ClownFish` class, line 6 does not compile, making option E the correct answer. If the method declaration was corrected to include `public` on line 6, then the program would compile and print `15` at runtime, and option B would be the correct answer.

17. A, E. An inner class can be marked `abstract` or `final`, just like a regular class, making option A correct. A top-level type, such as a class, interface, or enum, can only be marked `public` or default (package-private), making option B incorrect. Option C is incorrect, as a member inner class can be marked `public`, and this would not make it a top-level class. A `.java` file may contain multiple top-level classes, making option D incorrect. The precise rule is that there is at most one `public` top-level type, and that type is used in the filename. Finally, option E is correct. When a member inner class is marked `private`, it behaves like any other `private` members and can be referenced only in the class in which it is defined.

18. A, B, D. The Run interface correctly overrides the inherited method `move()` from the `Walk` interface using a covariant return type. Options A and B are both correct. Notice that the `Leopard` class does not implement or inherit either interface, so the return type of `move()` can be any valid reference type that is compatible with the body returning `null`. Because the `Panther` class inherits both interfaces, it must override a version of `move()` that is covariant with both interfaces. Option C is incorrect, as `List` is not a subtype of `ArrayList`, and using it here conflicts with the Run interface declaration. Option D is correct, as `ArrayList` is compatible with both `List` and `ArrayList` return types. Since the code is capable of compiling, options E and F are incorrect.

19. A, E, F. A class cannot extend any interface, as a class can only extend other classes and interfaces can only extend other interfaces, making option A correct. Java enables only limited multiple inheritance with interfaces, making option B incorrect. True multiple inheritance would be if a class could extend multiple classes directly. Option C is incorrect, as interfaces are implicitly marked abstract. Option D is also incorrect, as interfaces do not contain constructors and do not participate in object initialization. Option E is correct, an interface can extend multiple interfaces. Option F is also correct, as abstract types cannot be instantiated.

20. A, D. The implementation of Elephant and its member inner class SleepsAlot are valid, making options A and D correct. Option B is incorrect, as Eagle must be marked abstract to contain an abstract method. Option C is also incorrect. Since the travel() method does not declare a body, it must be marked abstract in an abstract class. Finally, option E is incorrect, as interface methods are implicitly public. Marking them protected results in a compiler error.

Chapter 10: Exceptions

1. A, C, D, F. Runtime exceptions are unchecked, making option A correct and option B incorrect. Both runtime and checked exceptions can be declared, although only checked exceptions must be handled or declared, making options C and D correct. Legally, you can handle java.lang.Error subclasses, which are not subclasses of Exception, but it's not a good idea, so option E is incorrect. Finally, it is true that all exceptions are subclasses of Throwable, making option F correct.

2. B, D, E. In a method declaration, the keyword throws is used, making option B correct and option A incorrect. To actually throw an exception, the keyword throw is used. The new keyword must be used if the exception is being created. The new keyword is not used when throwing an existing exception. For these reasons, options D and E are correct, while options C and F are incorrect. Since the code compiles with options B, D, and E, option G is incorrect.

3. G. When using a multi-catch block, only one variable can be declared. For this reason, line 9 does not compile and option G correct.

4. B, D. A regular try statement is required to have a catch clause and/or finally clause. If a regular try statement does not have any catch clauses, then it must have a finally block, making option B correct and option A incorrect. Alternatively, a try-with-resources block is not required to have a catch or finally block, making option D correct and option E incorrect. Option C is incorrect, as there is no requirement a program must terminate. Option F is also incorrect. A try-with-resources statement automatically closes all declared resources. While additional resources can be created or declared in a try-with-resources statement, none are required to be closed by a finally block. Option G is also incorrect. The implicit or hidden finally block created by the JVM when a try-with-resources statement is declared is executed first, followed by any programmer-defined finally block.

5. C. Line 5 tries to cast an Integer to a String. Since String does not extend Integer, this is not allowed, and a ClassCastException is thrown, making option C correct. If line 5 were removed, then the code would instead produce a `NullPointerException` on line 7. Since the program stops after line 5, though, line 7 is never reached.

6. E. The code does not compile, so options A, B, and F are incorrect. The first compiler error is on line 12. Each resource in a try-with-resources statement must have its own data type and be separated by a semicolon (;). The fact that one of the references is declared `null` does not prevent compilation. Line 15 does not compile because the variable s is already declared in the method. Line 17 also does not compile. The `FileNotFoundException`, which inherits from `IOException` and `Exception`, is a checked exception, so it must be handled in a `try/catch` block or declared by the method. Because these three lines of code do not compile, option E is the correct answer. Line 14 does compile; since it is an unchecked exception, it does not need to be caught, although in this case it is caught by the `catch` block on line 15.

7. C. The compiler tests the operation for a valid type but not a valid result, so the code will still compile and run. At runtime, evaluation of the parameter takes place before passing it to the `print()` method, so an `ArithmeticException` object is raised, and option C is correct.

8. G. The `main()` method invokes `go()`, and A is printed on line 3. The `stop()` method is invoked, and E is printed on line 14. Line 16 throws a `NullPointerException`, so `stop()` immediately ends, and line 17 doesn't execute. The exception isn't caught in `go()`, so the `go()` method ends as well, but not before its `finally` block executes and C is printed on line 9. Because `main()` doesn't catch the exception, the stack trace displays, and no further output occurs. For these reasons, AEC is printed followed by a stack trace for a `NullPointerException`, making option G correct.

9. E. The order of `catch` blocks is important because they're checked in the order they appear after the `try` block. Because `ArithmeticException` is a child class of `RuntimeException`, the `catch` block on line 7 is unreachable (if an `ArithmeticException` is thrown in the `try` block, it will be caught on line 5). Line 7 generates a compiler error because it is unreachable code, making option E correct.

10. B. The `main()` method invokes `start` on a new `Laptop` object. Line 4 prints `Starting up_`, and then line 5 throws an `Exception`. Line 6 catches the exception. Line 7 then prints `Problem_`, and line 8 calls `System.exit(0)`, which terminates the JVM. The `finally` block does not execute because the JVM is no longer running. For these reasons, option B is correct.

11. D. The `runAway()` method is invoked within `main()` on a new `Dog` object. Line 4 prints 1. The `try` block executes, and 2 is printed. Line 7 throws a `NumberFormatException`, so line 8 doesn't execute. The exception is caught on line 9, and line 10 prints 4. Because the exception is handled, execution resumes normally. The `runAway()` method runs to completion, and line 17 executes, printing 5. That's the end of the program, so the output is 1245, and option D is correct.

12. A. The `knockStuffOver()` method is invoked on a new `Cat` object. Line 4 prints 1. The `try` block is entered, and line 6 prints 2. Line 7 throws a `NumberFormatException`. It isn't caught, so `knockStuffOver()` ends. The `main()` method doesn't catch the exception either, so the program terminates, and the stack trace for the `NumberFormatException` is printed. For these reasons, option A is correct.

13. A, B, C, D, F. Any Java type, including Exception and RuntimeException, can be declared as the return type. However, this will simply return the object rather than throw an exception. For this reason, options A and B are correct. Classes listed in the throws part of a method declaration must extend java.lang.Throwable. This includes Error, Exception, and RuntimeException, making options C, D, and F correct. Arbitrary classes such as String can't be declared in a throws clause, making option E incorrect.

14. A, C, D, E. A method that declares an exception isn't required to throw one, making option A correct. Unchecked exceptions can be thrown in any method, making options C and E correct. Option D matches the exception type declared, so it's also correct. Option B is incorrect because a broader exception is not allowed.

15. G. The class does not compile because String does not implement AutoCloseable, making option G the only correct answer.

16. A, B, D, E, F. Any class that extends RuntimeException or Error, including the classes themselves, is an unchecked exception, making options D and F correct. The classes ArrayIndexOutOfBoundsException, IllegalArgumentException, and NumberFormatException all extend RuntimeException, making them unchecked exceptions and options A, B, and E correct. (Sorry, you have to memorize them.) Classes that extend Exception but not RuntimeException are checked exceptions, making options C and G incorrect.

17. B, F. The try block is not capable of throwing an IOException. For this reason, declaring it in the catch block is considered unreachable code, making option A incorrect. Options B and F are correct, as both are unchecked exceptions that do not extend or inherit from IllegalArgumentException. Remember, it is not a good idea to catch Error in practice, although because it is possible, it may come up on the exam. Option C is incorrect, but not because of the data type. The variable c is declared already in the method declaration, so it cannot be used again as a local variable in the catch block. If the variable name was changed, option C would be correct. Option D is incorrect because the IllegalArgumentException inherits from RuntimeException, making the first declaration unnecessary. Similarly, option E is incorrect because NumberFormatException inherits from IllegalArgumentException, making the second declaration unnecessary. Since options B and F are correct, option G is incorrect.

18. B. An IllegalArgumentException is used when an unexpected parameter is passed into a method. Option A is incorrect because returning null or -1 is a common return value for searching for data. Option D is incorrect because a for loop is typically used for this scenario. Option E is incorrect because you should find out how to code the method and not leave it for the unsuspecting programmer who calls your method. Option C is incorrect because you should run!

19. A, D, E, F. An overridden method is allowed to throw no exceptions at all, making option A correct. It is also allowed to throw new unchecked exceptions, making options E and F correct. Option D is also correct since it matches the signature in the interface. Option B is incorrect because it has the wrong return type for the method signature. Option C is incorrect because an overridden method cannot throw new or broader checked exceptions.

20. B, C, E. Checked exceptions are required to be handled or declared, making option B correct. Unchecked exceptions include both runtime exceptions and errors, both of which may be handled or declared but are not required to be making options C and E correct. Note that handling or declaring `Error` is a bad practice.

21. G. The code does not compile, regardless of what is inserted into the blanks. You cannot add a statement after a line that throws an exception. For this reason, line 8 is unreachable after the exception is thrown on line 7, making option G correct.

22. D, F. A var is not allowed in a `catch` block since it doesn't indicate the exception being caught, making option A incorrect. With multiple `catch` blocks, the exceptions must be ordered from more specific to broader, or be in an unrelated inheritance tree. For these reasons, options D and F are correct, respectively. Alternatively, if a broad exception is listed before a specific exception or the same exception is listed twice, it becomes unreachable. For these reasons, options B and E are incorrect, respectively. Finally, option C is incorrect because the method called inside the `try` block doesn't declare an `IOException` to be thrown. The compiler realizes that `IOException` would be an unreachable `catch` block.

23. A, E. The code begins normally and prints a on line 13, followed by b on line 15. On line 16, it throws an exception that's caught on line 17. Remember, only the most specific matching `catch` is run. Line 18 prints c, and then line 19 throws another exception. Regardless, the `finally` block runs, printing e. Since the `finally` block also throws an exception, that's the one printed.

24. C. The code compiles and runs without issue, so options E and F are incorrect. Since `Sidekick` correctly implements `AutoCloseable`, it can be used in a try-with-resources statement. The first value printed is O on line 9. For this question, you need to remember that a try-with-resources statement executes the resource's `close()` method before a programmer-defined `finally` block. For this reason, L is printed on line 5. Next, the `finally` block is expected, and K is printed. The `requiresAssistance()` method ends, and the `main()` method prints I on line 16. The combined output is OLKI, making option C the correct answer.

25. D. The code compiles without issue since `ClassCastException` is a subclass of `RuntimeException` and it is properly listed first, so option E is incorrect. Line 14 executes dividing 1 by itself, resulting in a value of 1. Since no exception is thrown, options B and C are incorrect. The value returned is on track to be 1, but the `finally` block interrupts the flow, causing the method to return 30 instead and making option D correct. Remember, barring use of `System.exit()`, a `finally` block is always executed if the `try` statement is entered, even if no exception is thrown or a `return` statement is used.

Chapter 11: Modules

1. B. Option B is correct since modules allow you to specify which packages can be called by external code. Options C and E are incorrect because they are provided by Java without the module system. Option A is incorrect because there is not a central repository of modules. Option D is incorrect because Java defines types.

2. D. Modules are required to have a `module-info.java` file at the root directory of the module. Option D matches this requirement.

3. B. Options A, C, and E are incorrect because they refer to keywords that don't exist. The `exports` keyword is used when allowing a package to be called by code outside of the module, making option B the correct answer. Notice that options D and F are incorrect because `requires` uses module names and not package names.

4. G. The `-m` or `--module` option is used to specify the module and class name. The `-p` or `-module-path` option is used to specify the location of the modules. Option D would be correct if the rest of the command were correct. However, running a program requires specifying the package name with periods (`.`) instead of slashes. Since the command is incorrect, option G is correct.

5. A, F, G. Options C and D are incorrect because there is no `use` keyword. Options A and F are correct because `opens` is for reflection and `uses` declares an API that consumes a service. Option G is also correct as the file can be completely empty. This is just something you have to memorize.

6. B, C. Packages inside a module are not exported by default, making option B correct and option A incorrect. Exporting is necessary for other code to use the packages; it is not necessary to call the `main()` method at the command line, making option C correct and option D incorrect. The `module-info.java` file has the correct name and compiles, making options E and F incorrect.

7. D, G. Options A, B, E, and F are incorrect because they refer to keywords that don't exist. The `requires transitive` keyword is used when specifying a module to be used by the requesting module and any other modules that use the requesting module. Therefore, dog needs to specify the transitive relationship, and option G is correct. The module puppy just needs to `require dog`, and it gets the transitive dependencies, making option D correct.

8. A, B, D. Options A and B are correct because the `-p` (`--module-path`) option can be passed when compiling or running a program. Option D is also correct because `jdeps` can use the `--module-path` option when listing dependency information.

9. A, B. The `-p` specifies the module path. This is just a directory, so all of the options have a legal module path. The `-m` specifies the module, which has two parts separated by a slash. Options E and F are incorrect since there is no slash. The first part is the module name. It is separated by periods (`.`) rather than dashes (`-`), making option C incorrect. The second part is the package and class name, again separated by periods. The package and class names must be legal Java identifiers. Dashes (`-`) are not allowed, ruling out option D. This leaves options A and B as the correct answers.

10. **B.** A module claims the packages underneath it. Therefore, options C and D are not good module names. Either would exclude the other package name. Options A and B both meet the criteria of being a higher-level package. However, option A would claim many other packages including `com.sybex`. This is not a good choice, making option B the correct answer.

11. **B, D, E, F.** This is another question you just have to memorize. The `jmod` command has five modes you need to be able to list: `create`, `extract`, `describe`, `list`, and `hash`. The hash operation is not an answer choice. The other four are making options B, D, E, and F correct.

12. **B.** The `java` command uses this option to print information when the program loads. You might think `jar` does the same thing since it runs a program too. Alas, this parameter does not exist on `jar`.

13. **E.** There is a trick here. A module definition uses the keyword `module` rather than `class`. Since the code does not compile, option E is correct. If the code did compile, options A and D would be correct.

14. **A.** When running `java` with the `-d` option, all the required modules are listed. Additionally, the `java.base` module is listed since it is included automatically. The line ends with `mandated`, making option A correct. The `java.lang` is a trick since that is a package that is imported by default in a class rather than a module.

15. **B, D.** The `java` command has an `--add-exports` option that allows exporting a package at runtime. However, it is not encouraged to use it, making options B and D the answer.

16. **B, C.** Option A will run, but it will print details rather than a summary. Options B and C are both valid options for the `jdeps` command. Remember that `-summary` uses a single dash (-).

17. **E.** The module name is valid as are the `exports` statements. Lines 4 and 5 are tricky because each is valid independently. However, the same module name is not allowed to be used in two `requires` statements. The second one fails to compile on line 5, making option E the answer.

18. **A, C.** Module names look a lot like package names. Each segment is separated by a period (.) and uses characters valid in Java identifiers. Since identifiers are not allowed to begin with numbers, options E and F are incorrect. Dashes (-) are not allowed either, ruling out options B and D. That leaves options A and C as the correct answers.

19. **B, C.** Option A is incorrect because JAR files have always been available regardless of the JPMS. Option D is incorrect because bytecode runs on the JVM and is not operating system specific by definition. While it is possible to run the `tar` command, this has nothing to do with Java, making option E incorrect. Option B is one of the correct answers as the `jmod` command creates a JMOD file. Option C is the other correct answer because specifying dependencies is one of the benefits of the JPMS.

20. B, E. Option A is incorrect because `describe-module` has the d equivalent. Option C is incorrect because `module` has the m equivalent. Option D is incorrect because `module-path` has the p equivalent. Option F is incorrect because `summary` has the s equivalent. Options B and E are the correct answers because they do not have equivalents.

21. C. The `-p` option is a shorter form of `--module-path`. Since the same option cannot be specified twice, options B, D, and F are incorrect. The `--module-path` option is an alternate form of `-p`. The module name and class name are separated with a slash, making option C the answer.

Index

W–Z

Online Test Bank

Register to gain one year of FREE access to the online interactive test bank to help you study for your OCP Java SE 11 Programmer I certification—included with your purchase of this book! All of the chapter review questions and the practice tests in this book are included in the online test bank so you can practice in a timed and graded setting.

Register and Access the Online Test Bank

To register your book and get access to the online test bank, follow these steps:

1. Go to bit.ly/SybexTest (this address is case sensitive)!
2. Select your book from the list.
3. Complete the required registration information, including answering the security verification to prove book ownership. You will be emailed a pin code.
4. Follow the directions in the email or go to www.wiley.com/go/sybextestprep.
5. Find your book on that page and click the "Register or Login" link with it. Then enter the pin code you received and click the "Activate PIN" button.
6. On the Create an Account or Login page, enter your username and password, and click Login or, if you don't have an account already, create a new account.
7. At this point, you should be in the test bank site with your new test bank listed at the top of the page. If you do not see it there, please refresh the page or log out and log back in.